FRENCH B MOVIES

NEW DIRECTIONS IN NATIONAL CINEMAS
Robert Rushing, editor

FRENCH B MOVIES

Suburban Spaces, Universalism, and the Challenge of Hollywood

DAVID PETTERSEN

INDIANA UNIVERSITY PRESS

This book is a publication of

Indiana University Press
Office of Scholarly Publishing
Herman B Wells Library 350
1320 East 10th Street
Bloomington, Indiana 47405 USA

iupress.org

© 2023 by David A. Pettersen

All rights reserved
No part of this book may be reproduced or utilized in any form or by any means, electronic or mechanical, including photocopying and recording, or by any information storage and retrieval system, without permission in writing from the publisher. The paper used in this publication meets the minimum requirements of the American National Standard for Information Sciences—Permanence of Paper for Printed Library Materials, ANSI Z39.48-1992.

Manufactured in the United States of America

First printing 2023

Cataloging information is available from the Library of Congress.

ISBN 978-0-253-06488-2 (hdbk.)
ISBN 978-0-253-06489-9 (pbk.)
ISBN 978-0-253-06490-5 (web PDF)

*For my parents,
Brian and Barbara*

CONTENTS

Acknowledgments ix

Note on Film Titles and French-Language Citations xiii

Introduction 1
1. Suburban Cinema between Art and Genre 39
2. Luc Besson's EuropaCorp and Parkour in the Suburbs 89
3. Suburban Gangsters: Screen Violence and the Banlieues 126
4. Suburbanoia and French Banlieue Horror Films 166
5. Omar Sy: Black Superstardom in Contemporary France 204
6. Beyond the Art/Genre Divide: Céline Sciamma's *Girlhood* 241

   Conclusion: Genre, Inclusive Casting, and the Suburbs in the Age of SVoD 275

Bibliography 287

Index 315

ACKNOWLEDGMENTS

THE GENESIS OF THIS BOOK was my second trip to France on a high school exchange program in the summer of 1995. We spent a week in Paris, and somehow I learned that the movie *La Haine* had just come out in theaters and that everyone was talking about it. I snuck out of the hotel where we were staying (apologies, chaperones) and went to see the film. My French was not yet good enough to understand the film's use of suburban vernacular, but its power still came through. I went out the next night and saw it again. While I wouldn't begin working on this book until many years later, *La Haine* taught me to pay attention to different kinds of French cinema and to how French films employ Hollywood genre traditions. The second beginning for this project was when I was teaching at Davidson College, where I advised Blake Evitt's senior thesis on parkour in the late 2000s. Blake shared with me his personal library of parkour documentaries and films, including the cult hit *District B13*. I had already been researching French genre films, but *District B13* reminded me so strongly of *La Haine* that I began to collect French genre films set in the banlieues and to think about how genre and the suburbs were related.

Working on a project for over a decade means that I have acquired a lot of debts, and I will do my best to acknowledge them here. My colleagues and students in the Department of French and Italian and in the Film and Media Studies Program at the University of Pittsburgh have contributed invaluable insights through our many conversations over the years. First, thank you to all my students and advisees. I have learned so much from all of you. I especially want to thank those students in the spring 2012 graduate seminar I taught in which I first tried out some of the emerging ideas for this book. That was a special seminar, and I think of you all often. I'm especially grateful to my colleagues Mark Lynn Anderson, Jim Coleman, Lorraine Denman, Charles Exley, Chloé Hogg, Lina Insana, Alberto Iozzia, Giuseppina Mecchia, Kaliane Ung, John Walsh, Brett Wells, and the late Jane Feuer. Having completed this book during the COVID-19 pandemic, I miss our many informal conversations even more acutely. I'm grateful to the Kenneth P. Dietrich School of Arts and Sciences and the European Studies Center at the University of Pittsburgh for travel and research support during the writing of this book. Many thanks to Jonathan Arac and the University of Pittsburgh's Humanities Center for the support of a faculty research fellowship at a crucial juncture. Thank you to Jeanette Jouili and Adam Lowenstein for discussing the book's introduction in the public workshop during that fellowship semester. I appreciate Mark Best, Adam Hart, and Neepa Majumdar's careful readings of chapters 1 and 3 during our summer writing group just before the pandemic began. Finally, a special thank-you to Randall Halle and Todd Reeser for their constant encouragement and advice over the years I have spent writing this book.

I also want to express my gratitude to the many colleagues and coconspirators in the field who invited me to be on panels and to give talks and who generally encouraged me to keep working on this this project: Martin Barnier, Lia Brozgal, Sébastien David, Audrey Evrard, Maggie Flinn, Rémi Fontanel, Michael Gott, Mary Harrod, Elizabeth Hodges, Josh Lund, Charlie Michael, Raphaëlle Moine, Dan Morgan, Phil Powrie, and Luc Vancheri. Thank you to series editor Rob Rushing and the editorial team at Indiana University Press, Allison Chaplin and Sophia Hebert, for supporting this book and shepherding it through the publication process. Special thanks to Jhonphilipp Yonan for drawing such amazing art for the front and back covers and to Morgan Genevieve Blue for creating such a wonderful index. And finally, thank you to the press's two anonymous readers for their generous and careful reading of the manuscript.

Part of chapter 1 first appeared in *Cincinnati Romance Review*, part of chapter 2 first appeared in *Cinema Journal* (now *Journal of Cinema and Media Studies*), and part of chapter 5 first appeared in *Modern & Contemporary France*. I am grateful to the editors of those journals for permission to reuse the material from those articles in revised form here.

On a personal note, I want to thank my wife, Stacey Triplette, for her constant love and support throughout the time it took me to write this book. She always thought the book was a good idea, even though she didn't always want to see the films I was watching. With great patience, she listened to my many ideas about the book at the dinner table, and once again, she read every word of the manuscript and offered invaluable copy editing. If my commas are in the right place, it's largely thanks to her. I'm grateful to have two wonderful sisters, Holly and Tracy Pettersen, who supported the human being behind the computer throughout the writing process. We all live in different parts of the country, but we met regularly for sibling weekends that were a welcome break from writing. Finally, a very special thank-you to my parents, Brian and Barbara Pettersen. They always gave me space to discover what I wanted to do, and they have supported me unquestioningly throughout my life, despite the many twists and turns it has taken. Above all, they sensed my love of French early on and found ways to send me to France at a young age. For that and many other things besides, I am very grateful. I love you both so much, and this book is for you.

NOTE ON FILM TITLES AND FRENCH-LANGUAGE CITATIONS

I USE THE ENGLISH-LANGUAGE TITLES of French films throughout this book for readability except when certain films are best known in English by their original French titles (*La Haine* or *Intouchables*) or when the English-language translation is inaccurate (*Baise-moi*). On first mention of a French film in each chapter, I give the original French-language title in parentheses along with the release year. When selecting the English-language titles for French films, I chose the ones that international distributors used for release in English-language markets or the ones by which the films are best known in English-language scholarship.

This book focuses on French cinema of the past three decades, and consequently it references contemporary scholarship, newspaper and magazine articles, and cinephile blogs written in French that have not been translated into English. When I quote from these kinds of sources, I cite the French original but give only my translation of the quotation. However, I will occasionally include words or phrases from the French original in parentheses alongside the translation when the language choices are relevant for my analysis. For scholarly sources originally written in French that have been translated into English, I worked from the French originals while writing, but I only cite and quote from the published English translation unless I indicate otherwise.

FRENCH B MOVIES

INTRODUCTION

JACQUES AUDIARD'S 2015 FILM *DHEEPAN* tells the story of three Tamil refugees who end up living in one of France's impoverished, multicultural suburban neighborhoods, called *banlieues*. The family of refugees is in fact fake: father, mother, and daughter are not related. Rather, they have acquired the passports of a real family who was killed. They work hard and seek to fit into the texture of everyday French society. He takes on the position of building caretaker, she becomes a personal care assistant for a neighbor, and the daughter attends the local school. However, their new life is upended when the local drug gang begins to fight with rivals, turning their neighborhood into a war zone. When his "wife's" life is threatened, the main character, a former Tamil Tiger, takes up arms and brutally executes most of the gang to save her. While the eruption of violence is not entirely unexpected, its excess comes as something of a surprise, as if the film were not quite sure what its genre was.

In fact, stylistic dissonances define *Dheepan*: much of the film unfolds in Tamil, a language that Audiard, most of his French audience, and the French characters in the film do not speak. The film alternates between slice-of-life sequences shot in a loosely ethnographic style and intense images of gang activity that conclude in spectacular violence. These are not the only two styles in the film; Audiard references the gangster film, the vigilante film, the school film, the Western, the documentary, the romantic comedy, and the family comedy. *Dheepan* is also, strangely, a French banlieue film, part of a corpus of films in France stretching at least as far back as Mathieu Kassovitz's *La Haine* (1995), when the genre was first described in journalistic and academic venues.

Critics and audiences often take banlieue films to be social documents about France's suburbs, and despite *Dheepan*'s use of spectacle, the film assumes something of this role in the way that it draws attention to the underappreciated Tamil migratory flows to France that followed decades of civil war in Sri Lanka. North African and sub-Saharan African immigrants from former colonies and their descendants, now full French citizens, often dominate public attention in debates about multiculturalism in France. And yet, a consequential Tamil immigrant community has established itself in the region around Paris over the past three decades (Goreau-Ponceaud 2011). The film's over-the-top violence and its ending—the family flees to the United Kingdom—make it hard to know how to read its ideology. Is it progressive? Is it reactionary? Does it simply reproduce stereotypes about the banlieues as spaces of criminality? Do the other genres the film invokes challenge or, to use Mireille Rosello's term (1998, 10–20), *decline* these stereotypes in the overlapping sense of refusing them and changing their forms? And how might we situate the film and its director? A recognized auteur with a significant body of work, Audiard won the Palme d'Or in 2015 at Cannes for *Dheepan*, yet he is often criticized as not sufficiently French because of his reliance on the codes of genre filmmaking.

The main contention of this book is that a film like *Dheepan*, and the knot of thorny issues about identity and belonging that it raises, are not aberrations that will soon be forgotten. Rather, *Dheepan* is part of a growing category of films that deploy the language of genre to challenge notions of what art and culture mean in France. This category comprises a diverse set of filmmakers and films made in a variety of production contexts. Some of the filmmakers are from the banlieues, while others are not; some are Maghrebi, some are Black, and some are white; and some are men and others are women. The films range from expensive (for Europe) blockbusters to those produced on a shoestring budget, sometimes with state funding. The category includes well-known directors and producers such as Luc Besson and Audiard and lesser-known filmmakers like Xavier Gens and the Kourtrajmé collective. I playfully refer to this corpus as *French B movies* because what unites these figures is that they all seek to use Hollywood genre conventions to mediate the questions of identity, belonging, and exclusion posed by the French banlieues.

Indeed, one of the reasons why these films have not received sufficient attention is that they confound the categories that scholars usually employ with respect to French and minority cinemas. This is not to say that realist films about the banlieues do not exist or that there are not suburban or minority auteurs who deserve to be considered as such. There are, and they tend to receive the most extensive consideration in the secondary literature. But what should we make of these wild exercises in genre filmmaking that run the gambit from mainstream buddy comedy to extreme forms of body horror? The central argument of this book is that these films use the language and iconography of Hollywood genres to examine questions of multiculturalism, migration, colonial memory, postcolonial identity, and globalization in contemporary France. They do this by dismantling the opposition between a nationally specific cinema of art and auteurs and a transnationally oriented cinema interested in spectacle and entertainment. The reappraisal of cultural values around genre we find in *Dheepan* and other films like it creates a space through which other cultures and histories might claim a place in the French mainstream. However, this gesture is, as Audiard's film amply illustrates, unpredictable and equivocal. Ultimately, I contend that the turn to genre as a way to engage with debates about France's multiculture represents a challenge to French universalism, a set of deeply held cultural beliefs that are as much artistic as they are political.[1]

B PICTURES, BLOCKBUSTERS, AND BANLIEUES

The *B* in the book's title plays on three distinct meanings. The first sense of *B* references the Hollywood B-picture genres—that is, the cheap, low-prestige movies that filled out the double features of the 1940s and 1950s. The term *genre* sometimes functions as a neutral word marking the type of a film, but it can also positively or negatively mark distinctions of taste. When the notion of genre indicates quality or taste preference, it often depends on a hierarchy between high, properly artistic forms of cinema and cheap, popular forms of filmed entertainment. For many in France, genres are very much associated with Hollywood, such that when contemporary French directors use them, critics and French moviegoers alike often view the films as being in poor taste, of bad quality, or simply not French.

The reception of *Dheepan* in France's most storied film magazine, the *Cahiers du cinéma*, exemplifies these tensions. In his review of Audiard's film, editor Stéphane Delorme lambasted contemporary French cinema for its turn to genre. Adapting the ideas of French philosopher Jacques Rancière, Delorme compared the politics of French genre films to the police baton used to subdue suspects. In Delorme's view, genres trade in stereotypes, rather than knowledge. Furthermore, a filmmaker's choice to employ genre conventions betrays a preference for the imagination, rather than reality. In terms of aesthetics, Delorme argues that genre films contain no artistic value because the filmmaker simply copies conventions. What is more, these conventions, in his view, can only reproduce a reactionary worldview because, again in terms of Rancière, a properly political film should offer a reconfiguration of the world through the creative work of the artist.

For Delorme, there is nothing wrong with French directors working in genres, so long as they know their place: "If Audiard were just a minor B-picture director whose films were produced by Besson, no one would be surprised, but come on, we're dealing with a supposedly 'great French auteur'" (2015, 6). Here we can see the stakes of this rant: a French genre cinema with pretensions to quality calls into question the very identity of French cinema. In this reading, bad French genre pictures would only be acceptable in the cinematic ghetto that France's major producer of transnational blockbusters, Besson, created at his mini-major studio, EuropaCorp. Genre, for Delorme, is the antithesis of a true artistic, social, and political French cinema.

Antipathy to genre runs deep in the DNA of French cinema, and Raphaëlle Moine explains that French cinema throughout its history has not generally thought of itself in terms of genres (2015, 2–3). Outside of a few broad categories like comedy, drama, or the crime film (*film policier*), it is challenging to organize French cinema around genres because the corpuses are not large and regular enough to be considered genres in the traditional sense of having an industrial basis, something taken for granted with Hollywood genres. Furthermore, French genre films do not always have enough in common in terms of style, iconography, narrative, or means of production to organize them into a standardized category. Even if we understand genres in the more contemporary sense as an effect of discourse around films, be it fan, critical, or promotional discourse, working on these films remains difficult because auteurism structures so much of French critical discourse, even in the case of genre films at home and from abroad.

When genre is broached, it is often subservient to the category of the auteur. In part, this is the afterlife of the *Cahiers du cinéma* directors of the French New Wave who championed Hollywood genre directors like Alfred Hitchcock or John Ford in their magazine's pages. When it came time for them to make genre films—for example, Jean-Luc Godard's gangster film *Breathless* (*A Bout de souffle*, 1960) or science fiction film *Alphaville* (1965) or François Truffaut's gangster film *Shoot the Piano Player* (*Tirez sur le pianiste*, 1960)— the result is much less about the recognizable pleasures of genre conventions and more about an exercise in artistic expressivity and modernist reflexivity. The pleasure of genre conventions in such films is analogous to the pleasures of cinephilia: it is the satisfaction of recognizing intertextual citations and being a part of the community that can recognize such citations. This has become a standard account of the pleasures of genre filmmaking in the age of postmodernism and pastiche, as seen in the reception of filmmakers like Quentin Tarantino (Cho 2015, 45–46). There, irony and a sense of play prevent

Tarantino's use of genre conventions from seeming oppressive. Part of what disturbs viewers about many of the French genre films considered in this book is that they very often play genres literally, for which critics accuse them of being amateurish.

Many of the French genre films considered here are not necessarily the best exemplars of their genre(s), and many of the films mix different genres within a single film. For some critics in France, this is proof that French directors should not even try to work in genres, especially Hollywood-inspired ones. Yet in the absence of industrial conditions that permit French genre films like these to iterate, it is, I argue, worth looking at those that do exist, especially the ones that use the language of genre to reimagine the banlieues. In essence, I will show throughout this book that these filmmakers and films use the language of genre explicitly to reexamine what it means to be French within France's tradition of universalism.

The second sense of B is the blockbuster. As the Hollywood blockbusters that followed *Jaws* (1975) or *Star Wars* (1977) began to claim a dominant position at the French domestic box office in the 1980s, French film producers and government policy makers created quotas and public funding mechanisms to protect the French national film industry from American competition. Blockbusters came to symbolize the antithesis of the artistic qualities that made French cinema distinctive, to the point that when contemporary French directors produce entertainment-oriented blockbuster films, they are often accused of not being sufficiently French or of further solidifying Hollywood's dominance at the French box office.

Charlie Michael has written the most sustained history of French blockbusters as a cultural and industrial phenomenon in the French film industry, and he registers the ambivalence of scholars and commentators who do not always recognize the economic changes that are behind the rise of French blockbusters since the 1980s. Michael notes that the blockbuster is often understood as an exclusively Hollywood phenomenon; however, in his view, it is more properly understood as "a concept de-linked from nationality or place-ness, designating a type of filmmaking that arose over the past four decades to exceed national specificities by design, often doing so through ties to corporate business culture, formulaic and 'universalist' themes and digitized special effects" (2019, 17, 13). Accusing French blockbusters of being too American or Hollywood is thus part of a cultural politics that seeks to distance such films from a properly French cinema. This book builds on Michael's work by remaining receptive to the Frenchness of such films and by attending to the industrial contexts from which they emerge.

Despite the anti-blockbuster sentiment that can be found in critical discourse surrounding French cinema, regulatory institutions in France have in fact created the conditions for Gallic blockbusters to flourish. Paradoxically, these industrial changes occurred simultaneously with France's vigorous resistance to the United States' attempts to have cultural objects declared goods like any other so that they are not subject to protection under free trade agreements. The central motivating factor behind France's protectionist efforts since World War II has been the fear of cultural standardization—or, in other words, a fear of American mass culture. One French scholar in the late 1960s likened Hollywood cinema to the Catholic missionaries that followed colonial conquerors (quoted in Buchsbaum 2017, 52). Despite this sentiment, the financial success of blockbusters actually funds French film production through taxes on the sale of movie tickets. These taxes help fund selective and automatic forms of aid, and since a producer must be French or European to draw on them, Hollywood producers cannot benefit from the success of their own films (Buchsbaum 2017, 159, 40–41).

What we might call the artistic anticommercialism of the French cinema changed during the years when Jack Lang was minister of culture in the 1980s and 1990s. These were the same years when other forms of mass culture, such as French rap and hip hop, came to be recognized as legitimate forms of art deserving of state funding. Lang acknowledged that French cinema was not connecting with popular audiences, and he succeeded in convincing people that film was an art form that depended on money. In his view, protecting cinema required crafting laws that dealt with the economic structures of the industry (Buchsbaum 2017, 24, 53). Jean-François Court's 1987 report on the French film industry recommended that producers and regulators conceive of the system in three scales of production: small auteurist films without commercial ambitions, medium "modest" or "healthy entertainment" films for the domestic market, and big films that seek to compete on the export market (quoted in Buchsbaum 2017, 35). When industry representatives speak of diversity in the context of the French film industry, they are partly talking about production scales. Michael explains that blockbuster films in this last category tend to take one of three production strategies: shedding cultural specificity and the French language to perform in global markets, focusing on the European regional market through coproductions, and keeping the French language and cultural specificity, but crafting a flexible film that can be understood differently in various release contexts (Michael 2015, 215–220).

In 1989, Lang announced that the French government would fund ten to fifteen super-productions a year to compete with Hollywood. While the films produced did not perform as expected, Michael shows that this initiative nevertheless had long-ranging implications for the whole industry, as it led to the deregulation of the audiovisual industry, especially television, in a way that enabled the vertical integration of media companies. Furthermore, it created new rules that allowed for big productions to be funded through tax-sheltered private organizations. Besson's EuropaCorp studio is a direct outcome of these new structures. Ultimately, Michael argues that films of the kind Lang envisioned still exist, even if there is no longer a concerted government effort to produce them. Moreover, according to Michael, the vertical integration among French studios and media companies starves the middle- and small-budget productions because of its concentration of power and funding, in effect channeling resources toward bigger productions (2015, 223–225, 231, 251).

Despite these arguments for diversity in the sense of production scale, several commentators and industry representatives still view small auteurist films as the guarantors of French cinema's national identity. Jonathan Buchsbaum cites a report from Pascale Ferran arguing for supporting more *films du milieu*, or middle-scale films that fall somewhere between small auteurist films that do not care about box office performance and French blockbusters. Interestingly, in Ferran's view, French blockbusters are dangerous because they channel audiences to the multiplexes, which drives them away from smaller French productions and toward Hollywood cinema (2017, 53, 226). The distrust of French blockbusters is thus as much about exhibition as it as about production.

French genre films about the banlieues exist at all three production scales, but they imply a different mode of film production and filmmaking, one that again challenges the heritage of auteurist filmmaking inherited from the New Wave. Genre filmmaking does not align well with the improvised nature of small-budget auteurist filmmaking because it necessarily depends on moments of spectacle, be they fountains of blood, car chases, or musical numbers. Such sequences require advance planning and storyboarding, the antithesis of creative discovery on set. They also require collaboration at all moments of the filmmaking process (preproduction, production, and postproduction). Sometimes this means cooperating with makeup effects artists, stunt coordinators, and choreographers. At other times, it means working with co-screenwriters in advance of shooting. In fact, an aspect of genre filmmaking that challenges the auteurist model is the written screenplay, something both Audiard and Rachid Bouchareb note.[2] In a way, this focus on the screenplay in genre filmmaking can, for some, be viewed as a return to the dreaded Tradition of Quality or "cinéma de papa" that Truffaut decried in his famous 1954 polemic as too focused on literary writing, adaptation, and collaboration to be properly artistic (Truffaut 2009).

It is crucial to remember that French government funding for low-budget or small-budget films does not automatically translate to support for French genre films. In the case of horror, for example, French directors have explained that even modest horror films require budgets on the scale of one to two million euros to have credible effects, which takes them out of the small-budget scale (Sayanoff and Schulmann 2009). What is more, selective aid based on screenplay proposals requires jury approval for genre films, which often reproduces the cultural consensus that French genre films are not worth making.[3] Presenting further difficulties, automatic aid based on previous finished films means that for genre films to be made, producers with an existing track record must become interested in them. On the other side of the scale, French blockbusters with ambitions for international distribution continue to provoke anxiety, especially when they eliminate French cultural specificity and language to target global audiences (Michael 2015, 215–220). Creativity and artistic singularity are valorized much more than the repetition required for genres to take root, which produces the common scenario that French genre filmmakers do not remain within a single genre, but often move between them. They also tend to brand themselves in interviews as auteurs, rather than as directors with an interest in genre.

The third sense of *B* is the banlieues themselves as a space, a subset of French citizens, and a cinematic genre. For many, the word *banlieue* evokes images of mass housing blocks in an interwar modernist style, concrete courtyards that give way to the French countryside, and groups of young people hanging out in the streets with little to do. However, it does not denote a clear and unequivocal set of spaces or geographic realities. The word *banlieue* refers as much to imagined relationships to space and cultural difference as it does to real neighborhoods and historical processes. While it may be difficult to appreciate now, the built environment of what would come to be known as the banlieues was once part of a utopic social vision, one that represented an instance of French universalism. The *grands ensembles*, or mass apartment blocks sometimes referred to as HLMs (habitation à loyer modéré, low-income rent-controlled housing) in French, and the *villes nouvelles*, or new towns, were two elements in the construction of the post–World War II French welfare state, one of the primary institutional expressions of French universalism in the twentieth century. They emerged in France after the war as a response to economic growth, immigration from the country's soon-to-be-former colonies, and an acute housing shortage.[4] French sociologists, architects, city planners, and politicians at the time shared the belief that urban planning could engineer new harmonious social structures (Vieillard-Baron 2001, 270).

The postwar enthusiasm for social reengineering did not benefit everyone equally, and factory workers from France's colonies were mercilessly exploited in deplorable living conditions. Contrary to the image of contemporary banlieues as working-class and culturally diverse neighborhoods, Kenny Cupers reminds us that the original grands ensembles were predominantly meant to house white middle-class nuclear families whose breadwinners worked in white-collar jobs. In fact, French urban and housing policy neglected the poor until the late 1960s, leaving construction and factory workers, many of immigrant origin, to live in *bidonvilles*, or shantytowns, outside the major French cities or in shacks adjacent to their construction jobs (2014, 51). We might say that these shantytowns are France's true proto-banlieue spaces, if we understand that term as a marker of social marginalization and cultural exclusion.

It was not until the 1960s, when upwardly mobile middle-class families began to move out of the grands ensembles and into single-family dwellings (*pavillons*), that the grands ensembles began to house predominantly the working poor, repatriated *pieds noirs* or French settlers in Algeria after the Evian accords, young families, senior citizens, guest workers, and immigrants (Cupers 2014, 275). As Cupers has shown, middle-class families also moved because the quality of construction for housing blocks was highly variable, and many buildings quickly fell into disrepair, making them less desirable (2014, 271–275). Paul Silverstein argues that the social housing with a focus on "integration" that came to define many of these suburban areas in France is a continuation of the colonial-era civilizing mission. Further, he suggests that the spatial forms of segregation in contemporary French metropolises reproduce colonial-era divisions between indigenous neighborhoods and the city of the colonizers (2004, 97, 120).

The term *banlieues* thus points to a significant disjuncture between real spaces and the images and associations through which individuals relate to them. The origin of the term is not, as it might seem, in the word *banished* (*banni*)—that is, the place where the banished go. Rather, *banlieue* descends from a medieval term for the locations (*lieue*) outside the city proper where the lord's *ban* still applies in terms of taxes, laws, and military protection. Hervé Vieillard-Baron explains that the word maintained this juridical sense until the nineteenth century, when, at the time of the Restoration and the July monarchy, it began to mean the way an industrializing country sought to divide space socially. Like the opposition between Paris and the provinces, which also emerged around the same time, the word *banlieue* came to carry negative connotations of class division and rejected spaces. These negative charges would only increase as the banlieues became the dumping ground for the waste products of industrial capitalism and a location for factories that were too dirty to locate in the city proper (Vieillard-Baron 2008, 10, 25).

Given the term's polysemy, urban geographers are especially suspicious of it, and they often prefer other proximate terms that have the advantage of being more precise, such as *quartier* (neighborhood), *cité* (project), or *zone*. Thierry Paquot chooses to maintain the term *banlieue*, but he speaks of it as a plural singular, a set of spaces that is imagined as singular yet is quite varied in reality (2008). In my own usage, I prefer to refer to the banlieues in the plural to mark the term's polysemy and heterogeneity. In the popular imagination, the banlieues often evoke images of working-class and especially multicultural immigrant neighborhoods, and not always in a negative sense. *Banlieue* can refer just as much to an assumed youth subcultural identity as to a geographic space of origin. For disaffected young people across the Hexagon, adopting the identity markers and behaviors of banlieue youth can be a way of venting frustrations and affirming an identity. What is more, if one goes by government designations of "quartiers sensibles" or "zones urbaines sensibles," some of these "sensitive" neighborhoods can actually be found in rural small towns and city centers, such as the Belleville neighborhood of Paris, in addition to the suburbs proper (Vieillard-Baron 2001, 129). Even if these formerly working-class neighborhoods within cities, the *quartiers populaires*, are gentrifying, pushing their urban poor out, they often represent the urban poor in the public imagination. It is for this reason that I will consider some films set in culturally diverse working-class Paris neighborhoods like the Goutte d'Or alongside films that take place in the suburban peripheries; the film scholar is not as beholden to real geography as the urban geographer or policy maker. The French suburbs represent many conflicting things, from urban ghettos and lawless wastelands to vibrant hubs of cultural hybridity, entrepreneurship, and creativity. For detractors and advocates alike, the banlieues have come to symbolize France's multicultural present and future.

THE FRENCH BANLIEUES AT THE CINEMA

Throughout the twentieth and twenty-first centuries, the banlieues have existed primarily as a media phenomenon for those who do not live there. The banlieues exist across a range of forms and media that include the novel (Louis-Ferdinand Céline's 1932 *Voyage au bout de la nuit*, or *Journey to the End of Night*, is among the earliest), photojournalism, television, and film. Cupers argues that media have shaped public perceptions of and policy regarding the banlieues in ways both positive and negative from their very beginning in the 1940s up until the present (2014, 317). In terms of cultural representations, Annie Fourcaut notes that all manner of negative stereotypes came to be associated with these peri-urban spaces and the "dangerous working classes" that lived there (2008, 125). As French television stations competed for viewers in the age of privatization during the 1980s, they increasingly turned to sensationalistic images of protest and violence that would repeatedly occur in the suburbs of Lyon and Paris during the 1980s and 1990s (Sedel 2009, 36–40).

Despite the importance of television, cinema is arguably the dominant media form to have visualized the banlieues for French and international audiences. Both Vieillard-Baron (Vieillard-Baron 2008, 33) and film historian Jean-Pierre Jeancolas (quoted in Moinereau 1994) suggest that it was cinema that truly showed the banlieues to French viewers. Their observations align with Rick Altman's account of how film genres can create "constellated communities" whose "members cohere only through repeated acts of imagination" (1999, 161). From the Belle Époque to the present, films about the banlieues anchored many of France's spectacular images of youth. For example, Jacques Becker immortalized the Apaches, those romantic turn-of-the-twentieth-century gangsters, in his 1952 film *Casque d'or*. Marcel Carné's *Wasteland* (*Terrain vague*, 1960) represented suburban youth in James Dean–like leather jackets. Today's banlieue films dress their young characters like hip-hop stars in fashionable sneakers, track pants, and hoodies.

The banlieues gave rise to a distinct cinematic genre in the 1990s with recognizable settings, characters, and narratives, including a young, multiracial cast of characters, the clothing and gestural styles of hip hop, the iconography of mass housing and concrete courtyards, scenes of conflict with police, and trips to the city center by train. Yet, in many discussions of banlieue cinema as a genre, space emerges as the defining feature, and the genre is often compared to the Western because of a similar importance of space in its definition (Fourcaut 2000, 113; Konstantarakos 1999, 160, 169).[5] In her analysis of banlieue cinema, Carole Milleliri maps out different periods and shifts in how the genre was conceptualized. In the 1990s, it was understood as a variant of auteur cinema about specific kinds of suburban spaces. In the 2000s, critics noted a shift from the hypermasculinist universe of the 1990s to one increasingly open to women or one that problematized gender relations in the banlieues. The 2000s also witnessed a shift from negative and fatalistic narratives to cautiously hopeful and optimistic ones in which emancipation might be possible without leaving the banlieues. Critics framed the genre as *métissé*, or a mixed form of cinema, though by *mixed*, critics tended to mean racial identity, which they framed through the lens of North African heritage and not sub-Saharan African heritage (Milleliri 2011). Carrie Tarr and Will Higbee establish a direct filiation between the so-called cinema *beur*, or Franco-Arab cinema of the 1980s, and the banlieue cinema genre as it emerged in the 1990s. Both Tarr and Higbee focus primarily on French Maghrebi filmmakers and characters (2005, 13; 2013). However, this narrow framing risks missing the multiethnic and multiracial set of characters that one regularly finds in films about the banlieues.

Despite the importance of space for banlieue films, post-2000 films about the banlieues are increasingly set outside the suburbs. Sometimes the connection is young characters who are from the banlieues but are involved in narratives elsewhere in the city. At other times, the language of Hollywood genres distorts the narrative conventions of banlieue cinema or the realistic images of the banlieues to the point of misrecognition. Milleliri notes that films not situated in the banlieues tend not to be categorized as banlieue films. Furthermore, she explains that critics tend to believe that banlieue films are or should be social documents (2011). In a related vein, Julia Dobson argues that spectators who assume banlieue films reveal a documentary reality employ a logic of "double determinism" in which "pre-established perception of the nature of the banlieue leads to the privileging of particular characteristics to form a self-fulfilling genericity" (2017, 35). Popular or mainstream films that filter the banlieues through the language of Hollywood genres are relegated to what Milleliri calls "the periphery of the genre," if they are included at all (2011). Higbee is more attentive than Tarr to such mainstream popular films. He argues that mainstream filmmaking is an important site of struggle for visibility and agency for minority communities, though he limits his consideration to Maghrebi filmmakers and actors (2013, 59–60). Milleliri at least suggests that it would be worth thinking about the references to American films as something more than intertextual winks, especially because ordinary viewers also notice these connections (2011). Yet there is much more work to be done, especially in terms of the production models for genre filmmaking in France (Milleliri 2012).

One of the central claims of this book is that an analysis of Franco-American genre mixing in popular films about the banlieues reveals how the imaginative resources of different genres can at times help combat the invisibility of racial and cultural difference in French public discourse. This could be the rise and fall of the marginalized immigrant in Hollywood gangster narratives or the ways horror cinema exposes the monstrosity and violence that lie beneath polite society. In this book, I show how a body of French popular films uses Hollywood genres to challenge France's culture of universalism and change public misperceptions of the banlieues and its residents in ways that are complementary to, but distinct from, other banlieue films that take a sociological, documentary, or militant approach to the subject.

American references and the use of Hollywood genres distort the traditional codes of banlieue cinema as a genre, and this can have several consequences for how we must think about these films. First, one of the central claims of this book is that the banlieues in cinema are predominantly an imaginary category. To say this is not to disappear the very real spaces of urban poverty and social neglect of the individual cités and quartiers that are often amalgamated into the more general category of banlieues. Rather, it is to recognize that cinematic images of the banlieue are shot through with stereotypes and stock narratives that occlude as much as they reveal about these spaces. It is also to recognize that by freeing the banlieues from the grip of referentiality, especially as they are represented in cinema, we can better see how popular genre films about the banlieues might constitute a ground of struggle through which stereotypes could be reframed. Rather than solely measuring images against reality, we must measure them against other images. In this book, I seek to ask what images these French B movies iterate and how they do so.

Second, we need to consider how the production of French B movies interacts or does not interact with the real spaces of the banlieues. For me, it does not make sense to ask how realistic a horror film, a science fiction film, or a comedy is with respect to the banlieues. It does make sense, however, to ask about how the making of these films and their embeddedness in the institutional structures of the French film industry from production to reception might have real effects on those living in the banlieues. This could involve work opportunities for suburban youth, national and international visibility on the festival circuit, or access to funding. Many accounts of the politics of production have focused on oppositional forms of cinema that seek to make films off the grid, completely independently. Part of my argument here is that mainstream structures can also be progressive, especially in an institutional context in which the government is so active in regulating and funding the industry. Of course, government intervention and cultural policy can become a way to restructure the industry in terms of neoliberal capitalism or a neo-colonial relationship to art and culture. My task will be to assess the potentials and pitfalls of different production strategies through a consideration of individual films and filmmakers as they negotiate both the material conditions of making films in France and the imaginary worlds of film genres.

The *real* in this book about banlieue cinema is thus as much the real of the films themselves as process as it is the worlds they represent. This orientation will allow me to avoid a common tendency in scholarly work on banlieue cinema, which is to adjudicate the extent to which an individual film or filmmaker accurately and progressively represents the banlieues. While this kind of work is helpful, it often misses how an individual film, however messy and ambivalent it might be, could contain stylistic features or production strategies that are worth examining. To this end, I will neither assume that all films about the banlieues are unproblematically "social documents" nor seek to arbitrate definitively the extent to which individual films represent the banlieues accurately. To my mind, this question risks obscuring what makes post-2000 popular genre films about the banlieues so important in the cultural landscape of contemporary France—their use of images and the imaginary.

Third, the visual iconography of the banlieues functions as an interface between local and transnational cinematic contexts. In his history of architecture in the banlieues, Cupers notes that "mass housing developments are often pervasively global and yet nationally specific, never quite unique nor completely alike" (2014, xiv). I suggest that this characterization also applies to the French suburbs as they are visualized in cinema. Furthermore, it speaks to how the banlieues, in their emphasis on urban poverty and cultural mixing, are simultaneously specific and general; that is, they can serve as an interface for French cinema to be translated and adapted to different international release contexts *and* as a medium through which to translate and adapt international genre conventions to France. Genre films about the banlieues are themselves indicative of this tension between very specific national, colonial, and postcolonial histories and also similar to marginalized spaces with which other developed and developing countries are dealing. In this understanding, banlieue films are not just symptomatic of a French malaise regarding globalization; they are also an important mode of cultural production in which French cinema is being reimagined for the realities of globalization and the transnational flows of film financing and distribution.

Fourth, the ways in which popular genre films about the banlieues call into question banlieue cinema as a genre do not indicate that it is time to leave the category behind. Rather, I suggest that it is time to admit that banlieue cinema has always been a mixed genre, not just in the sense of its mixing of multiethnic and multiracial characters, but in the sense of mixing multiple cinematic genres and cultures, including French, American, and the many cultures of immigration and migration that make up contemporary France. Jason Mittell, in his work on genre in the context of American television, has argued that genre mixing is a better way to conceptualize multi-genre programs than hybridity, because the latter implies "a single act of combination to create a static hybrid." He favors "genre mixing," as it is "more indicative of an ongoing process of generic combination and interplay, not rooted in biological notions of taxonomic purity" (2013, 154), and Jennifer Yee makes a similar point about the dangers of hybridity for thinking about cultural mixing (2003, 423). Mittell argues for thinking about genre mixing across multiple sites beyond just the text, extending it to questions of context, industry, and audience (2013, 157). The notion of mixing, as opposed to hybridity, also lets us think about these popular genre films in terms of another key component of French suburban culture: French hip hop. France boasts the largest hip-hop and rap scene outside the United States (Higgins 2009, 107–108), and hip-hop music is often funded by the French Ministry of Culture, positioning it somewhat uncomfortably as a recognized and subsidized form of opposition culture.

Given hip hop's origins in street culture, it should come as no surprise that the visual, sonic, gestural, and sartorial vocabularies of hip hop also inflect genre films about the banlieues. What interests me here is not so much the cultures surrounding French hip hop, but how the creative modes at the heart of hip hop's musical forms mirror those at play in French genre films about the banlieues. Richard Schur argues that hip hop as a form of music and performance art is based on sampling, the flow and rupture of rhythms created through layering, parody, and irony (2009, 43). Sampling and layering are modes of creative recontextualization that comment on preexisting source materials without destroying the pleasures of listening to a song or dancing to a beat. In his view, this creative practice also requires a mastery of sociohistorical context in terms of how samples are used and transformed through irony (Schur 2009, 46). The mixing of genres in the films I study in this book operates in an analogous manner. These films reveal more generally how Hollywood genre traditions are explicitly politicized when they are appropriated abroad. Appreciating the sociohistorical contexts of how genres are mixed in France requires an understanding of France's historical sense of universalism, how popular French genre films might challenge and rearticulate it, and how this challenge is significantly mediated by American understandings of race and ethnicity.

WHO'S AFRAID OF UNIVERSALISM?

When the French team won the 2018 World Cup, South African comedian Trevor Noah celebrated on the *Daily Show* on July 17 by chanting that Africa had won the World Cup, a reference to the diverse cultural backgrounds of the players on the French team.[6] This comment so incensed the French ambassador to the United States, Gérard Araud, that he wrote a letter to Noah in which he explained that the majority of the team's players were born and educated in France and were full French citizens. Araud's letter encapsulates the French logic of color-blind universalism and is worth quoting at some length:

> The rich and various backgrounds of these players is a reflection of France's diversity. France is indeed a cosmopolitan country, but every citizen is part of the French identity and together they belong to the nation of France. Unlike in the United States of America, France does not refer to its citizens based on their race, religion, or origin. To us, there is no hyphenated identity, roots are an individual reality. By calling them an African team, it seems you are denying their Frenchness. This, even in jest, legitimizes the ideology which claims whiteness as the only definition of being French. (French Embassy US 2018)

Noah, in a backstage segment of the show the following day, read parts of the letter and offered his response, suggesting that the phrase "France's diversity" is a euphemistic way of saying "France's colonialism" and expressing his surprise that, according to French perceptions, the World Cup team members could not be both African and French (Guyonnet 2018). While it is possible to see the debate in terms of the differences between a white French politician and a biracial South African comedian, it is important to note that other French athletes of African and Caribbean descent shared Araud's perspective and took to Twitter to express in harsh words their outrage at how Noah was trying to deny their Frenchness. Both sides make valid points, and this public scandal throws into relief the deep investments of France and the United States in color-blind universalism on one side and a pluralism that is aware of race and ethnicity on the other. Noah's comments and his audience's laughs reveal an Anglo-American sense of bewilderment at the ongoing relevance of universalism in France. Nevertheless, the concept is essential for understanding French politics, society, and culture, especially the ways France thinks about cultural difference.

The term *universalism* in France refers to a wide range of beliefs, practices, and institutions. It indicates a model of human subjectivity, a mode of democratic politics, and a sense of national and cultural identity. It refers to the Enlightenment-era conception of truth as defined by human reason, empirical observation, and the consensus of science as opposed to superstition, received opinions, and religion. Translated into the realm of politics, this notion of rational human faculties led to classical conceptions of abstract citizenship and liberal democracy, especially the idea of universal human rights. While most democratic countries share at least a theoretical investment in human rights, France is unique in that its political tradition holds that rights can only be attributed to generic individuals, independent of all particularisms (Samuels 2016, 3; Scott 2005, 16–17). This notion of citizenship differs from that held by the United Kingdom or the United States, for example, which do not require citizens to abstract themselves when conducting the work of politics and which recognize group affiliations to a greater degree than France.

As much as the French republican tradition would like to believe that universalism exists outside time and space, it very much has a history, one that helps explain its contradictions, especially in terms of religion and secularism. The sense that a rationalist and democratic model of life has a universalist vocation descends paradoxically from the evangelizing mission of the Catholic Church, and the meaning of *katholikos* in Greek is *universal* (Schor 2001, 43–44). During the Wars of Religion in the sixteenth century, France promoted cultural homogeneity, and thus universalism, when Louis the XIV revoked the Edict of Nantes, officially ending France's tolerance of Protestants in French public life (Moulier Boutang 2005, 92). Even when France's Jews became citizens of the new nation during the 1790s, they were included as individuals, not as a community, and their religious practices were considered a personal matter relegated to the private sphere (Scott 2005, 15–16). Despite the 1905 legislation of official secularism, or what the French call *laïcité*, the expectation of cultural homogeneity that is the legacy of French Catholicism endures.[7] As Maurice Samuels explains, unlike the American sense of separation of church and state that "allows a certain religiosity to pervade the public sphere," laïcité in the French context "implies freedom *from* religion as much as freedom *of* religion" (2016, 3). It would be difficult to overstate the importance of laïcité for contemporary France. Thomas Kirzbaum notes that many politicians on the left were open to a version of multiculturalism in France prior to the 1989 headscarf affair in Creil. However, when several young girls were forced to remove their hijabs after wearing them to school, the left and the right paradoxically circled the wagons in the next decade around a rigid notion of laïcité as essential to French democracy (Kirszbaum 2015, 22; Sedel 2009, 54).

Universalism is also shot through with the particular history and culture of the part of France located in Europe. Political philosopher Étienne Balibar explains that one of the contradictions of the universal is that it is always articulated from the place of a particular (2016, 76). In the French case, this includes the importance of the French language, culture, history, and art as somehow embodying the spirit of universalism (on the question of language, see Schor 2001, 44–46). The sense that the French nation embodies the universal fuels the rhetoric of exceptionalism—that is, the belief that French language, culture, history, and art are particularly excellent and should be spread throughout the world. This exceptionalism has made it difficult for France to recognize its own regional languages and cultures, to say nothing of the languages and cultures immigrants bring with them or of the increasing importance of English as a world language. As philosopher Achille Mbembe explains, France has been so convinced of its grandeur that it does not often look outside to understand itself or its world: "[Outspoken French critics of postcolonialism] do not want any ethnography of France that would pass through the Other nor any questioning of France through its interstices or its places of interlace with its innumerable elsewheres. They want to keep intact the fiction of a France that would never have to answer for its own foreignness because, having already merged what is its own [le propre] and what is universal, France has nothing to learn from the world and cannot receive its name from the outside" (2010, 178, translation mine). Mbembe also observes that many French scholars hesitate to learn English despite its importance as a global vehicle for economic and scientific exchange. I would add that anxiety about the importance of the English language likely informs France's ambivalence about Hollywood cinema and American mass culture.

The most controversial form that French universalism's abstract conception of the citizen took during the second half of the twentieth century is the official blindness to all forms of difference, save class and anatomical sexual difference, in the constitutions of the Fourth and Fifth Republics. While the "civilizing mission" during the French colonial period was also universalizing in its desire to bring French culture, language, and bureaucracy to its colonies, French colonial institutions depended on an explicit hierarchy of races, and colonial laws did not hesitate to assign different legal status to indigenous colonial subjects. The post-1945 constitutional language of blindness to racial and ethnic difference, which emerged from the idealistic belief that equality can be legislated in a top-down fashion, also stemmed from a desire to prevent a recurrence of one of the darkest moments of French racism, namely antisemitism. In the wake of World War II and the Vichy Government's active contributions to the deportation and extermination of France's Jewish population, it was unthinkable to legislate in terms of race (Blanchard and Boëtsch 2016, 51).

However, this color-blind universalism has not always helped prevent discrimination in contemporary France (Ndiaye 2009, 36–42). If anything, it has made it difficult for discrimination to be recognized as such. As Mbembe puts it, color-blind universalism amounts to a "radical indifference to difference" (2011, 93). This lack of language, conceptual frameworks, and official statistics to account for racial and ethnic difference has produced linguistic and conceptual gaps that French culture tries to fill or talk around in various ways as individuals seek to discuss questions of cultural pluralism and racial discrimination. As Dominic Thomas notes, France lacks an accepted word for multiculturalism, so the word *immigration* in French does double duty, referring both to migratory flows of human beings *and* the multicultural reality of contemporary society (2013, 7). Paradoxically, it also discursively excludes second- and third-generation children of immigrants who are full French citizens but are nevertheless commonly referred to as *issu de l'immigration* (from an immigrant background).

Multiculturalism is polemical in France, because there is so little consensus on what the term means and whether it is a positive or negative phenomenon. On the one hand, Alana Lentin and Gavan Titley speak about multiculture as the lived reality of many contemporary European nations, including France. By this, they simply mean the coexistence of immigrants and citizens from a diverse set of historical, cultural, and ethnic origins within the spatial confines of the nation. On the other, they prefer to think of multiculturalism as an assemblage that draws on a wide range of discourses and political imaginaries. During the 1980s, multiculturalism for some on the left gestured to the *droit à la différence* (right to difference) that supposedly anchored liberal notions of tolerance and inclusivity in a postcolonial age. However, over the course of the 1980s and 1990s, many conservative thinkers twisted multiculturalism into something far more monstrous. It became everything from demands on the part of minorities for recognition, special dispensations, and advantages to a preference for separate spaces in which to live, a kind of elective apartheid that would fragment the homogenous culture and history of the nation's dominant white community. For such thinkers, multiculturalism signaled the failure of the national community to integrate its immigrant minorities. Ultimately, multiculturalism marked the shift from race to culture on the right— and increasingly on some parts of the left—as the anchor point for racism and antidiscriminatory politics (Lentin and Titley 2011, 49–77).

Race has been thoroughly discredited as a scientific concept with any significance in biology, and the National Assembly in 2013 sought to strike the word *race* from France's penal and labor codes (Blanchard and Boëtsch 2016, 53). This has not, however, put an end to racism; it has simply forced it to find other terms and modes, and culture is one that has stepped in to fill that void. Lentin and Titley have traced the decades-long process through which racism based on phenotype has morphed into what they call *cultural racism* across European nations. While it became taboo to speak about skin color, other racialized phenomena, including behavior, religion, and culture, continue to be part of public discourse. French polemics over multiculturalism have moved racism away from the supposedly biological basis of physiognomy toward a basis in cultural tradition and lifestyle. Cultural racism enables racist discrimination without appearing racist, and it perversely disables antiracist movements, because appeals that call attention to race open themselves to charges of bringing a reactionary notion back into public debates (Lentin and Titley 2011, 49–77). While this trend in France stretches back at least to the 1980s in a figure like Alain Finkielkraut, Hughes Lagrange represents the latest iteration of this move when he argues that French sociologists and politicians must return to a notion of cultural—rather than racial or ethnic—difference in order to make sense of suburban unrest and growing inequalities (2013, 21–23). Culture allows for race and ethnicity to be discussed indirectly, and it also inhibits discussion of the economic inequalities and power asymmetries that affect marginalized communities.

Finally, I would add that the word *banlieue* itself has also filled this linguistic and conceptual void. As we saw earlier, the term is not an unequivocal reference to actual geographic spaces, yet it continues to function as a shorthand for France's working-class and immigrant neighborhoods and populations. As Vieillard-Baron explains, using the word *banlieue* is often a way of speaking about something other than space: social inequalities, deficiencies in public services, feelings of insecurity, fear of hybridity, worries about breakdowns in the social contract, and anxieties about France in an age of globalization (2001, 4, 142, 270–271; 2008, 33). In a related vein, Mame-Fatou Niang argues that "through rhetorical displacement, the impossibility of [French] republicanism to articulate alterities (especially racial ones) is translated onto urban space" (2019, 3). Such usage spatializes cultural, racial, and ethnic difference into an imagined national geography that enables the kinds of social segregation (some would say apartheid) that universalism is meant to counter. What is more, because French politics does not allow for legislation that would target individual communities along racial or ethnic lines, even to benefit them, spatial zones have perversely become one of the few ways the French government can legally legislate to redress discrimination and social inequalities (Fourcaut 2008, 123, 129; Tissot 2007; Mucchielli and Aït-Omar 2006, 6).

Given the history of French universalism and the practical and theoretical challenges it poses to thinking about difference, Anglo-American scholars are not entirely wrong to question its relevance. In the wake of political liberation movements from the 1960s to the present and their academic correlates, such as post-structuralism and French theory, many in the United States and the United Kingdom challenged how universalism was often code for white, male, heterosexual, cisgender privilege. Consequently, the notion of universalism has very little purchase in Anglo-American intellectual and political contexts, where, if it is invoked, it serves as a boogeyman designed to mark the follies of totalitarianism, fascism, or cultural homogeneity (Laclau 2007, 26). This all serves to create the impression that France, with its desire to hold onto universalism, is somehow behind the times.

And yet, this reaction, I argue, comes not from the universalist tradition itself, but from how universalism has ossified into what Samuels terms "hard-line positions" on both sides of the Atlantic that speak past each other in caricatures. On the one hand, there are hard-line thinkers in France on the right (Finkielkraut) and philosophers on the left (Alain Badiou and Rancière) who argue that universalism must necessarily ignore all forms of difference because this is the only way to maintain truth, real democracy, or an authentic politics (Finkielkraut 2015, 110–111; Badiou 2009, 11, 14; Rancière 1999, 34). On the other, there are American thinkers, such as Wendy Brown and Joan W. Scott and French philosophers like Balibar, who argue that universalism's hostility to particularism replicates colonial and neocolonial violence and seeks to put minorities at a disadvantage (Samuels 2016, 9–10; Maniglier 2016, 775–776).

If universalism has so many problems, why not simply get rid of it? Samuels suggests that the problem is not so much with the notion of universalism itself as with the hard-line versions that have come to dominate public discourse on both sides of the Atlantic. In his study of how France has theorized universalism through its Jewish community, Samuels reminds us that universalism has a history and has been imagined in other ways in France at different times. Ultimately, he wants to preserve what he considers the ideal of justice and equality at the heart of French universalism and show that there have been moments in French history when other modes of universalism were theorized or even practiced (Samuels 2016, 6, 10). Universalism functions then as a regulatory ideal, analogous to the distinction between formal and substantive equality articulated in US critical race theory (Raengo 2016, 15–17; Fredman 2016). This perspective depends on seeing universalism as an ongoing process that is never finished and that requires the work of politics to move in the direction of social justice and real equality. Balibar, in his discussion of the conflictual and violent struggle between competing universalisms within a national, regional, or global space, argues that the universal is always a *procès*, which in English means both a *process* and a *trial*. For Balibar, any universalism depends on categories of difference—what he calls an *anthropological discourse*. Rather than view this as a reason to reject universalism outright, he suggests that it is a danger to be assumed and carefully negotiated as a society deliberates about how to balance equality and liberty. In his view, the world is saturated with different universalisms struggling to speak "in the mode of the universal" (Balibar 2016, 34–38). If US models of cultural pluralism and race consciousness represent possible alternatives or at least interlocutors in this ongoing process of rearticulation, especially in the context of adapting Hollywood genres abroad, what exactly do these models represent in France?

AMERICAN UNIVERSALISMS IN THE BANLIEUES

The hard-line position on universalism in France translates into a caricatural stance regarding American experiences of race and ethnicity. America seen from France arguably represents at least four different universalisms competing in Balibar's sense, revealing much about how France imagines multiculturalism to be operating in the United States and what that might mean for France now or in the future. First, there is the sense that the United States represents the model in which all particularisms are equivalent, something that Balibar and Badiou argue simply serves the logic of global capitalism (Balibar 2016, 135; Badiou 2009, 10–11). This is the total cultural relativism seen in some accounts of multiculturalism. As several critics of this kind of universalism have pointed out, the equivalence model does little to overturn the asymmetrical power relations between particularisms in a given spatial context (Laclau 2007, 26–27; Kilani 2014, 291). If anything, it solidifies the status quo of inequality. Seeing the United States in this light evokes anxieties about the pressures and contradictions of a globalized free market economy (Balibar 2016, 135).

Second, there is the sense that recognizing racial and ethnic differences in the United States has produced a regime of de facto segregation or apartheid. For some in France, the United States represents the risks of multiculturalism. This negative universalism, which often depends on a Black-white binary, is felt most strongly around debates in France as to whether the banlieues are ghettos, not in the sense of the Jewish ghettos of European history, but in the sense of contemporary American inner cities. In a country that sees itself as color-blind and universalist, the history of segregation in the United States and the ongoing discrimination against minorities often serve to exteriorize and ultimately minimize French domestic social problems like discrimination and segregation. Using the term *ghetto* to describe the French banlieues is a way to suggest polemically that similar forms of social exclusion and violence are taking place in the Hexagon and that they are organized around racial and ethnic discrimination. In effect heated debates among French sociologists have focused on framing the problems of the banlieues in terms of class *or* race.

This is not simply a matter of conceptual precision; it is an ongoing struggle over the meanings and relevance of French universalism.

The best-known position on the class side of the debate is that of French sociologist Loïc Wacquant, who has worked on American inner cities and French banlieues. For him, equating the French banlieues to the "ghettos" or inner cities of the United States is inaccurate and is more an emotional effect of public discourse in France than an accurate assessment of the lived realities of those spaces. Wacquant's comparative analysis highlights the demographic and institutional differences between the two spaces. He admits that there are similarities, including that both spaces are minority enclaves defined by a declining population, have a high concentration of young people relative to the rest of the city, and are oppressive places that have a social stigma attached to them. However, American ghettos are spatially bigger and house a greater percentage of the urban population than the banlieues, and they are more autonomous in terms of the businesses, social services, and community organizations they offer. Whereas residents of the banlieues can and often have to leave their cités to access work, social services, and commercial areas, Wacquant argues that American ghettos are truly segregated spaces in terms of infrastructure. The French banlieues, moreover, do concentrate the urban poor, but they are ethnically, racially, and nationally diverse in terms of the backgrounds of the citizens and immigrants who live there. By contrast, American ghettos in his estimation reproduce publicly sanctioned segregation by concentrating all the people of a certain race in a single area, often regardless of social class (Wacquant 2007, 155–170).

Interestingly, Wacquant does not broach the question of the historical differences between the two kinds of urban spaces. While he signals the importance of slavery in spatial segregation in the US context, he does not deal with the question of colonial and postcolonial history or the legacy of slavery in the French context. A point of contention among sociologists, political scientists, and other public commentators about the banlieues is the relationship between discourse about race and ethnicity and France's ongoing difficulties in processing its own colonial history. For Wacquant, the ethnic, racial, and national "diversity" of banlieue neighborhoods is a clear indicator that the real issue is social class (Wacquant 2007, 202). However, it is important to remember that in the early nineteenth century, class was not a recognized aspect of the abstract citizen. Originally, it was an excluded form of particularism, much like race and ethnicity or, until more recently, anatomical sexual difference. It was only through working-class revolutions of the nineteenth century that universal male suffrage was instituted in 1848. As of the 2000 *parité* law, class and anatomical sexual differences are the only forms of particularism that have become part of the abstract conception of the French citizen (Scott 2005, 17–19). Consequently, one way to read the debates around framing the banlieues in terms of class is as a way of avoiding reconceptualizing the role of race or ethnicity in French citizenship.

On the other side of the debate, there are those who do frame the banlieues as French ghettos and argue for the importance of race and ethnicity in understanding them. One of the best-known articulations of this position comes from French sociologist Didier Lapeyronnie. He grants that while the term *ghetto* might not have been appropriate in the 1980s and 1990s because of the social and racial mixing of the neighborhoods, it does have relevance for the twenty-first century. Lapeyronnie notes that after the 2005 protests, these neighborhoods have become increasingly segregated and difficult to leave. Furthermore, they have created their own internal culture as a form of defense against the society outside them. In his view, ghettoization is not simply the result of increasing social isolation; it is also "a political, social, and cultural construction. It is the result of dissymmetrical power relations between social groups and of the capacity of dominant groups to impose their norms and values and to impose their definitions of situations and problems" (Lapeyronnie and Courtois 2008, 12–13, 16–17). For Lapyeronnie (2008, 17), economist Yann Moulier Boutang (2005, 72–73, 98), and sociologist Gérard Mauger (2006, 114–115), emphasizing class as the fundamental issue in the banlieues is a way of ignoring the afterlives of slavery and colonial history. What is more, some argue that this blindness to the importance of race and ethnicity participates in a French resistance to postcolonial modes of thought in certain quarters, which is perceived by some in France as the latest Anglo-Saxon imposition (Murphy and Forsdick 2010). This brings us to the third possible understanding of American universalism in France.

Anglo-American postcolonial and cultural studies, which drew on a group of French post-structuralist thinkers who were often marginalized in France, have not always been welcome in the country that indirectly launched them (see Cusset 2006). While it is reductive to say that postcolonial studies emerged solely in the United States or even the Anglo-American academy, it is often perceived in France as coming principally from the other side of the Atlantic along with other "bad" objects (according to some), like political correctness and affirmative action (translated as "positive discrimination" in French). Since the 2005 suburban protests and the founding of the movement Les Indigènes de la République (The Republic's Indigenous Peoples) that same year, interest in postcolonial questions has grown in France. While an increasing number of scholars are aware of the research and theories that have emerged in the Anglo-American academy over the past three decades, many scholars of the French-speaking world on both sides of the Atlantic seek to develop new models that would account for the specificities of French colonial and postcolonial history (Smouts 2010; Coquery-Vidrovitch 2010). David Murphy and Charles Forsdick note that one of the ironies of Anglo-American postcolonial studies in the 1990s and 2000s is that the field thought it was universal. In the past decade, the field has had to relativize its own assumptions and adopt a more comparatist approach (2010, 148).

The field of cultural studies, for its part, explicitly challenges the hierarchy between so-called high and low forms of culture, arguing that all are equally worthy of value and study. In a country whose elite institutions remain committed to the notion of high art, this reconceptualization of aesthetic value and academic scholarship has not always been well received.[8] I argue that one of the reasons why popular genre films about the banlieues are rarely objects of academic study in France has to do with the ways they destabilize binaries like high and low and national and transnational. We might call this third possible sense of American universalism: the universalism of difference and heterogeneity.

A fourth sense of American universalism, one that offers an alternative model for thinking about histories of immigration and multiculturalism in the United States, has to do with an emerging discourse around Latinx identities and cultures. If African Americans are the most visible and significant minority in the United States because of the history of slavery, immigrants from Latin America and their citizen descendants represent the most significant recent community to "come from" immigration, as the French would say. As Ed Morales has argued, Latinx immigrants and citizens bring a new model of cultural difference to the United States with roots in the history of Spanish colonialism and its attendant conceptions of race and racism (2018, 28–33). This model diverges from the Black-white binary that opposes white and Black Americans. While the Latinx model, as Morales describes it, does not always challenge the hegemony of whites, it has been more open to racial mixing, or *mestizaje*, among the Spanish, indigenous, and African peoples who lived together in the spaces of Central and South America over several centuries. The category of whiteness in Latinx cultures, while still problematic in terms of power relations, is much more flexible, malleable, and inclusive than whiteness as it has been traditionally understood in the United States. Mestizaje, meanwhile, does not erase the many cultures, traditions, and languages that continue to mix in Latinx identities (Morales 2018, 34–41, 56–57, 287).

The Latinx model does hold important parallels and potential for thinking about multiculture in the French context, in which histories of colonialism are extremely diverse. One of the main problems with both French universalism and certain strains of American universalism is that they enact a process of forgetting, repressing memories of colonization, conquest, and slavery. They do this in different ways—first by preventing colonial and postcolonial memories from entering national narratives in the name of unity, then by reducing memory to a Black-white binary that makes the question of race hypervisible at the same time that it obscures the history of slavery and oversimplifies the complex racial and ethnic landscapes of the United States. A flexible notion of cultural mixing arguably has potential in both contexts. The term *métissage* has a history in France, though not an unproblematic one (Yee 2003), and the French Caribbean in particular has focused much more on cultural creolization, hybridity, and mixing than other parts of France's former empire. In the Latinx context, Morales suggests that Latinx cultures anticipated and prefigured the hugely influential concept of intersectionality (2018, 14, 39, 104–105, 122). *Intersectionality* refers to how various axes of difference—for example, those based on class, race, or gender—often work together in the experiences of marginalized individuals or communities (see Hill Collins and Bilge 2020, 1–36). For French scholars who are working between French and American academic contexts, either in academic positions in France or in the United States, but are in dialogue with intellectual trends in the United States, intersectionality is a potentially fruitful way to adapt Anglo-American postcolonial studies to French-speaking contexts (see, for example, Germain and Larcher 2018, 12). One of the central outcomes of this kind of work may be the addition of other vectors of minority politics, such as coloniality and regional history, to already well-established ones, like race, ethnicity, class, gender, and sexuality. While the Hollywood genres invoked by the films in this book have historically focused much more on questions of the Black-white binary, class, and communities of immigration, part of the argument herein is that these genres are nevertheless often used in France to bring facets of colonial and postcolonial histories into mainstream films.

POPULAR FRENCH GENRE FILMS AS A SPACE OF POLITICS

I suggest that it is impossible to isolate these different senses of American universalism in the analysis of individual events, debates, or cultural texts. In fact, two or more levels can be simultaneously active. The color-blind conception of

French universalism and the different senses of race and ethnic consciousness in what we might call American universalisms both represent different regimes of what Rancière calls *le partage du sensible* (the distribution of the sensible). By this term, he means the shared forms, understandings, and feelings that assign bodies in a given society to particular places or roles. Individuals are either included or excluded in community spaces through shared modes of being, doing, and saying (Rancière 1995, 48). For Rancière, any society contains bodies that are counted and can appear or speak as people and bodies that are not and cannot. In his view, authentic politics in a democratic society takes place when uncounted bodies, what he terms *la part des sans part* (the part that has no part), speak from a position of equality with those who are counted about the social configuration that excludes the uncounted. These moments have the potential to produce a shift in the way that society is organized. This shift is as much aesthetic as it is institutional: "Politics acts on the police. It acts in the places and with the words that are common to both, even if it means reshaping those places and changing the status of those words" (Rancière 1999, 33).

Rancière opposes politics to what he calls the *police*; by this he means the fact that members and parties in a given society have recognized identities, places, functions, and relations with each other (Rancière 1995, 51–52). Rancière suggests that he does not necessarily mean *police* in a violent or repressive sense, though its connotations are hardly positive, something that Delorme's use of the term in his *Cahiers du cinéma* piece on Audiard bears out. For Rancière, modifying the relationships between recognized parties is not politics but simply the work of the police. In his writings about film, Rancière is not particularly attentive to popular forms of cinema. Instead, he focuses on modernist and experimental forms of art cinema, and when he does discuss Hollywood films, it tends to be the canon of films and auteurs championed by the directors of the French New Wave. He would probably agree with Delorme about mass culture's inability to enact true politics, and he would likely view questions of minority visibility in popular French genre films as being more about the police than true politics. Nevertheless, I want to suggest that we can use Rancière's terms to understand what role mass culture and popular films could play in redistributing the sensible.

At a time when minority actors are seen in starring roles, images, and genres in which they are not normally seen, it would be disingenuous to suggest that this is not significant. Furthermore, the regularity of French genre films appearing on French screens is increasing in a context that does not typically expect or want to see them. For many critics and audiences in France, French genre films could be said to represent an example of Rancière's "bruit," the noise of the "part des sans part" that does not count as speech (1995, 52–53). I argue that the genre films examined in this book are sites where politics in Rancière's sense takes place. In these films, excluded and marginalized bodies call attention to inequalities and ask for new articulations of French universalism as much through images as words. At the same time, the sites where these calls take place, namely French genre films about the banlieues, are often themselves excluded and uncounted within the French audiovisual ecology understood as a distribution of the sensible. One of the central arguments of this book is that a politics of style or representation is inseparable from a politics of production—that is, how films are funded, made, distributed, and valued by critics and viewers.

The different senses of American universalism I sketched earlier suggest that even though American histories of immigration, slavery, and cultural pluralism are different from the French contexts of immigration and colonialism, they nonetheless represent essential reference points to think with and against in France. Both Mbembe and Pap Ndiaye have argued that in a universalist country that is officially blind to race, members of France's minority communities have, over the course of the twentieth century, turned toward American mass culture, history, social movements, and theory to identify strategies that might help or hinder them in making their voices heard in the French public sphere (Ndiaye 2009, 363–365, 400–423). In Mbembe's view, when France's dominant culture did not allow a place for second-generation citizens of color (1980–1995) and minorities from former colonies to reflect openly on colonial history and their place in France, it left them to look outside the Hexagon to do so, to the rest of the world and especially to America. He inscribes the arrival of African American popular culture in that same movement of looking outside the Hexagon for models for thinking about racial identity and colonial history (Mbembe 2010, 168–169). I suggest that we can view Hollywood genre traditions as offering similar possibilities in contemporary French films about the banlieues.[9]

Despite the difficulties involved in pinning down what models for understanding difference are at work in French genre films, I do think we can consider Hollywood cinema as embodying certain models for visualizing cultural, ethnic, and racial differences. Many of the films examined in this book return to a mythological sense of genre, or what I would call genre as an engineering of the social imaginary. *Imaginary* is a distinctively French term that does not have the same intellectual currency in the Anglo-American academy (for a history of *imaginaire* as a concept, see Pérez 2014). For a certain kind of Marxist critic, the term is akin to concepts like ideology and mystification, the antithesis of a properly political art or critical practice. Despite this bad reputation, the term has usefulness in the ways that it indexes how a set of images and representations is shared by a community at a particular place and moment in time. Arjun Appadurai has taken the notion of the imaginary seriously and made it speak to the conditions of migration in a globalized world. Appadurai argues that individual acts of imagination, which draw on shared imaginaries, are "now central to all forms of agency" (1996, 31). To come to terms with this new social function of the imagination, Appadurai insists on a need to consider the mechanical production of images in mass culture, to consider the imagined worlds that individuals construct in dialogue with the media images they consume, and to examine the collective and shared dimensions of imagination, something captured for him in the French sense of *imaginaire*. The human faculty of imagination, considered as an interface between the production and consumption of images, offers a means to understand how dominant cultures seek to reproduce themselves and how minority and diasporic cultures resist the dominant cultures in which they live. Appadurai proposes five analytic terms for conceptualizing the imagined worlds that global cultural flows help create: *ethnoscapes, mediascapes, ideoscapes, technoscapes,* and *financescapes*. When it comes to the kinds of imagined worlds found in genre films about the French banlieues, the first three are the most relevant. Ethnoscapes emphasize the shifting compositions of human beings in the world—in effect, the migration of individuals through and between particular spaces. With the term *mediascapes*, Appadurai suggests that the circulation of ethnoscapes is always mediated: "What is most important about these mediascapes is that they provide (especially in their television, film, and cassette forms) large and complex repertoires of images, narratives, and ethnoscapes to viewers throughout the world" (1996, 35). Further, ethnoscapes are always a component of media images and narratives, even if they are not always recognized and discussed as such. They are, nevertheless, a key element that viewers take away from the media they consume. It is in this sense that we can say that Hollywood films and genre traditions visualize ethnoscapes of American-style cultural pluralism that are susceptible to adaptation in the French context. Toward the end of his discussion of mediascapes, Appadurai turns to the question of pragmatics, or what we might also call *reception studies*: "Mediascapes, whether produced by private or state interests, tend to be image-centered, narrative-based accounts of strips of reality, and what they offer to those who experience and transform them is a series of elements (such as characters, plots, and textual forms) out of which scripts can be formed of imagined lives, their own as well as those of others living in other places" (1996, 35). Appadurai leaves open the particular modes this might take—a Ricœurian (1981) version of narrative mimesis or a Certeauian (1990) notion of poaching and tactics—but it does point to how the imagination is an active faculty, both for the migrants and diasporic communities who consume media *and* for members of the dominant cultures that might acquire false and fantastical images of places like the banlieues that they have never visited.

Many films about the banlieues focus almost exclusively on young people. This is not only because banlieue neighborhoods often contain a disproportionately high number of young people but also because young people are often perceived to be negotiating and renegotiating their identity with respect to various cultural images and narratives. Suburban youth may be struggling to create a sense of identity between several different cultures— mainstream French, their familial cultures of origin, and transnational, principally American, media cultures. They are awash in different kinds of images and stories about what it means to be a young person in a globalized world, and so they are looking to the media as well as lived and familial cultures for ways to imagine their identity and belonging. What is more, Lapeyronnie argues that inhabitants of the banlieues are in fact *colonial subjects* in the sense that Frantz Fanon and Albert Memmi give to that term—that is, someone defined by dominant society's external gaze and categories: "They interiorize this gaze and categories and are 'derealized' by the way they are treated." This produces, in his view, "a profound deficit of images" (2008, 17). The spaces of the banlieues are then environments in which it is difficult to demarcate what is true and what is false, and inhabitants have a distorted relationship to language and their own bodies. Ultimately, Lapeyronnie argues, behavior becomes "theatricalized" because of the disconnect between the lived space of the ghetto and the stereotypes and categories imposed by dominant society (2008, 22). While Lapeyronnie's analysis of theatricalized identity in the suburbs comes across as largely negative, other scholars, such as Chantal Tetreault through the notion of transculturality, have argued that suburban youths reimagine belonging through the overdetermined interactions of multiple forms of cultural and linguistic identity (2015, 17–18). Banlieue films often self-reflexively dramatize this imaginative process that Appadurai describes by showing young characters watching movies or consuming different forms of mass culture and then performing and imitating the media images and lived examples that surround them as a *mise en abyme* of the impasses of identity formation in the banlieues.

Finally, Appadurai's notion of ideoscapes helps conceptualize how the contact between French and American universalisms can be read as a process of rearticulating French universalism in an age of globalization and lived multiculture. For Appadurai, ideoscapes are also collections of images, but they are directly related to political struggles, either of the dominant state to impose a particular ideology, especially on its minority populations, or of opposition movements seeking to contest or capture some parts of state power. Appadurai goes on to say that "ideoscapes are composed of elements of the Enlightenment worldview, which consists of a chain of ideas, terms, and images, including *freedom, welfare, rights, sovereignty, representation*, and the master term *democracy*" (1996, 36, original emphases). In addition to debates about the relative values of different forms of mass culture, popular genre films about the banlieues repeatedly stage debates about the ideas and values of French universalism.

If we think of Hollywood cinema over the past several decades as embodying these four different and conflictual notions, or ideoscapes, of American universalism, it is not clear that it represents an external universalism in Balibar's sense, one that competes or conflicts from the outside with an internal French republican universalism. As much as critics or historians in France would like to externalize or *other* Hollywood cinema, it is highly visible on French screens and does very well at the domestic box office, as it does in many distribution contexts around the globe. We could call this something like hegemony or cultural imperialism, but the point I am trying to make is something else. Strictly speaking, it cannot be considered a foreign universalism because it is so present and shared among French moviegoing publics, especially in the banlieues. But this is not to say that Hollywood films are received in just one way, like some kind of univocal multiculturalist propaganda on the model of Sergei Eisenstein's thwarted fantasies of absolutely controlling the meaning of dialectical montage. As Michel de Certeau and others have taught us, local readers and viewers are active and creative in their consumption and appropriation of mass cultural products.

My method here will not be to examine the reception or criticism surrounding Hollywood films in France, though I will occasionally do this as a means of contextualizing how these genres and films are received in France. Rather, it is to examine French attempts to make genre films as acts of translation, indigenization, creolization, and mixing and that seek to visualize spaces and communities that are themselves mixed, whether or not they are framed as such in the discourse of French republican universalism. Balibar ends his book-length meditation on universalism with a section on translation as an example of how universalisms circulate in the global age of multiplicity. For him, this does not mean that translation is not complicit with asymmetrical relations of power, but that translation is an inescapable feature of a globalized world, and it is important to theorize how it works or how it could work. Furthermore, he argues that it is crucial to expand the number of individuals who can translate

(Balibar 2016, 84–85, 122–124). My main contention is that the images and production models of Hollywood cinema, paradoxical as it might seem, allow French filmmakers of many different backgrounds to challenge and re-enunciate what French universalism might mean in a way that preserves—rather than erases—difference.[10] This does not, however, automatically imply the adoption of US models for recognizing racial and ethnic difference. Rather, it is a means of holding a specifically French universalism accountable for its own lofty ideals of equality and inclusivity.

On the one hand, the engagement with an American-style emphasis on particularism and the awareness of race and ethnicity on the part of some French thinkers and filmmakers are not about an imperialist project of cultural hegemony designed to tear the French social fabric apart, as some of France's most reactionary writers about universalism (like Finkielkraut) would have it. On the other, France's deep-rooted culture of equality and unity is Samuels's ideal of social justice, something that is admirable and laudable even if it has perverse effects in how it occludes discrimination. For the filmmakers considered in this book, the transnational space of genre functions as a kind of "contact zone" (Pratt 2008) or "interzone" (Halle 2014, 22–23) between two very different models of understanding cultural difference. At times, Hollywood genre codes bring attention to that which cannot be visualized or felt within France's universalist culture. And at others, French cultural and cinematic codes help temper the American excesses of individualism. This contact zone represents a space where new enunciations of the universal can be explored and tested in France. It is this conflictual and ultimately ambivalent process of imitation, translation, and adaptation that I will trace throughout this book.

In what follows, I analyze individual films, filmmakers, producers, stars, and studios working at the intersection of the French banlieues and Hollywood genre conventions. I mix cultural history with a close analysis of individual films. I examine the ways journalists and critics position individual films within and across national borders, how different studios produce these films, and how directors, producers, and stars conceptualize their work. My approach thus mixes close analysis with industrial and economic approaches to cinema. Genres are an especially iterative mode of organizing film production, and intertextuality across films is an important component of these films' market appeal and meaning. However, rather than simply analyzing how these intertextual references signify, *French B Movies* shows that these transnational genre mixings are part of the ecosystem of the French film industry. In my view, films about the banlieues imagine new identities for French national cinema and create new hierarchies of cultural value in France.

CHAPTER OVERVIEW

The first chapter lays out what I consider to be the two main paradigms for making banlieue films and for understanding how they frame questions of cultural value. I focus on Kassovitz's *La Haine* (1995) and Abdellatif Kechiche's *Games of Love and Chance* (*L'Esquive*, 2003), which establish crucial aesthetic, authorial, and production strategies that are important for the rest of the book. The filmmakers and films considered in later chapters appropriate, adapt, and contest various features of these two models. *La Haine* embraces American mass culture in the form of hip hop, rap, B-boy culture, break dancing, and the Hollywood films of Martin Scorsese, Spike Lee, and John Singleton in order to make the power inequalities between the banlieues and city center visible. *Games of Love and Chance* epitomizes the sociological and documentary approach to the banlieues through its neorealist and quasi–cinema vérité aesthetics (nonprofessional actors from the suburbs, low-budget production values, and the use of digital cameras) and its focus on recording the "authentic" vernacular language of the banlieues. It also stages the possible "integration" of young residents of the banlieues through the traditional vectors of French high culture, including literature and art, something that remains consistent across Kechiche's œuvre. I ultimately argue that *La Haine* is the more important model for the films considered in subsequent chapters, and I use the notion of sampling to theorize Kassovitz's relationship to Hollywood genres and American mass culture.

The second chapter examines the case of Besson, who is something of a lightning rod in France for seeking to rival Hollywood on its own terms. He founded a Hollywood-style studio (EuropaCorp), new film production facilities in Paris's northern banlieues, and even a film school in an effort to challenge the French model of small-scale artisanal and auteurist production. The French suburbs have been a central element of Besson's media strategy in terms of where he locates his facilities, where he produces his films, and even the kinds of narratives he chooses to make. This chapter analyzes the connections between Besson's popular brand of filmmaking and the cultural and geographic spaces of the French banlieues. In particular, it looks at how parkour, a French urban practice of running through the city in simple, yet elegant ways, served as a literal and metaphorical means for Besson and the filmmakers he fosters to imagine alternatives to traditional conceptions of the French film industry, including how genres might operate in French films. Through analysis of EuropaCorp's three parkour films—*Yamakasi* (2001), *District B13* (*Banlieue 13*, 2004), and *District 13: Ultimatum* (*Banlieue 13: Ultimatum*, 2009)—I contend that Besson and the filmmakers who work for him craft utopian tales that both draw attention to neocolonial social relations in the banlieues and argue for a rearticulation of French universalism. They do this by cutting against the dystopian charge of John Carpenter's *Escape from New York* (1981) and *Assault on Precinct 13* (1976), films from which they draw. Finally, I analyze Besson's decision to locate his *Cité du cinéma* facilities and a free public film school in the French suburbs as an attempt to create institutions where a commercially viable popular French cinema about France's multiculture can be imagined and produced.

The third chapter examines suburban gangster films that seek to introduce minority characters into a genre that has some history in the French film industry and enjoys a high degree of cultural prestige. Early Hollywood gangster cinema and the film noir tradition that grew out of it arguably helped launch the French New Wave with Godard's *Breathless* (1960), and from the 1930s onward, French filmmakers have adapted the different periods of Hollywood gangster cinema into distinctly Gallic modes. The classic Hollywood gangster picture is about an immigrant outsider negotiating his own relationship to economic success and upward mobility. However, gangster films, and the crime genre in general, are potentially dangerous to use in connection to the banlieues, as they risk reinforcing perceptions of these spaces as zones of criminality, delinquency, and violence. The third chapter examines how French filmmakers have related to the stylized ultraviolence that characterizes many gangster films from the New Hollywood period.

Here, I examine three films by Bouchareb, Audiard, and Houda Benyamina that draw on the generic language of the Hollywood gangster and mafia film tradition in order to analyze the multiculture of contemporary France and to insert elements of French colonial and postcolonial history into national narratives. Bouchareb has been interested in Hollywood genres across his career; however, his Franco-Algerian film *Outside the Law* (*Hors la loi*, 2010) encountered an ambivalent reception in France because of its subject matter. It sought to memorialize the 1945 Sétif massacre in Algeria through the language of the Western and to represent National Liberation Front activities in and around one of Paris's shantytowns during the Algerian War of Independence through an at times slavish, shot-by-shot restaging of scenes from Francis Ford Coppola's *Godfather* trilogy. Audiard, as I have suggested earlier, has a long-standing interest in genre, and like Besson, he is a director who often coproduces and cowrites films with and for others. In this sense, he is also an important figure trying to create the conditions for French genre cinemas to take root. Audiard's *A Prophet* (*Un prophète*, 2009) and *Dheepan* (2015) explore the social tensions within minority communities by adapting Hollywood gangster tropes to the *huis clos* of a French prison and a French suburban neighborhood, respectively.

Dheepan blends the genre-oriented model of *La Haine* with the quasi-ethnographic approach of *Games of Love and Chance* in a way that did not sit well with critics. Finally, Benyamina's first film, *Divines* (2016), challenges the hypermasculine focus of many suburban gangster films but separates violence from assertiveness and preserves the latter as a possibility for women. *Divines* also reflects on the role of shared video in mediating suburban street violence. All three films seek to explore what kinds of images of suburban and minority communities the Hollywood gangster genre might create.

Chapter 4, on French horror, also considers the question of suburban violence, but from the side of the victim, rather than the perpetrator. Horror is arguably the genre with which the French industry is the least associated. Outside of a few well-known auteurs, such as Georges Franju and Jean Rollin, there are a handful of directors who make films that are recognizable members of the horror genre in the modern sense. However, there has been a small wave of French horror filmmaking since the year 2000, and a significant number of these films have focused on the French suburbs. These Gallic horror films challenge any simple binary between an auteurist art cinema and a genre cinema. On the one hand, they are sometimes considered a part of the hyperviolent art cinema movement that James Quandt infamously branded the New French Extremity. However, films like *Trouble Every Day* (2001), *Irreversible* (2002), and *Baise-moi* (2000) are all set in part in the French banlieues, and they just as easily engage with traditional modes of horror—the zombie film tradition in the case of the first and the rape-revenge film in the case of the last two. On the other hand, French horror films often revel in the genre's excesses; their international reputation is founded, in part, on their extreme violence and their willingness to present graphic images and acts that other national horror traditions, including Hollywood, will not. Several of the best-known examples of French horror are clustered in terms of release dates around the three-week-long protests in 2005 that began in the Parisian suburbs and then spread to the rest of France. Many of these Gallic horror films explicitly thematize suburban street violence in their adaptation of Hollywood slasher and rape-revenge genre formulae. In the wake of then minister of the interior Nicolas Sarkozy's tough-guy persona and securitarian discourse leading up to the 2007 presidential elections, films such as *Sheitan* (2006), *Inside* (*A l'intérieur*, 2007), *Frontier(s)* (*Frontière(s)*, 2007), *The Horde* (*La Horde*, 2009), and *Martyrs* (2008) all explore the social and racial geography of contemporary France through the language of Hollywood horror traditions, rather than European ones. In this chapter, I analyze how these directors rework the race, class, and city-country divides of Hollywood horror for the context of French universalism, debates about national identity, and the very different geography of the banlieues as an in-between space—neither country nor city, but sharing elements of both. The suburbs' uncertain status between city and country in horror calls attention to the violence of universalist discourse on marginalized bodies in France.

Unlike in the case of horror, if there is a genre with which French cinema is arguably well associated, it would be comedy. What is more, France has a tradition of mismatched buddy films that turn around social class and geographic and regional differences. Why, then, would French filmmakers look to Hollywood for inspiration in this arena? The answer, I argue in chapter 5, has to do with the interracial buddy comedy genre that Eddie Murphy first pioneered in the 1980s in such films as *48 Hrs.* (1982) and *Beverly Hills Cop* (1984). This tradition played an essential role in France's second-most successful film of all time and the most successful non-English language film on the export market, the 2011 film *Intouchables*. What is more, the interracial buddy comedy genre played and continues to play a vital role in constructing the star persona of France's first Black film superstar, Omar Sy, who was born and raised in the Parisian banlieues. *Intouchables* is an interracial buddy film about a Black caretaker from the suburbs and a quadriplegic member of the white upper classes. While the film did well with audiences, its critical reception was mixed; some celebrated the film's social conscience, while others denounced its racism. In the first part of the chapter, I analyze the film's representation of race around a Black-white binary, specifically the ways in which directors Éric Tolédano and Olivier Nakache draw on tropes of American blackface, neo-minstrelsy, and 1980s Hollywood interracial buddy comedies. I track how these American tropes align and do not align with representations of the banlieues in France, and I ultimately argue that the film's financial success and ambivalent reception track with the contradictory politics of American tropes for representing Blackness. In the second part of the chapter, I analyze Sy's career as a transnational Black star in France and Hollywood. Sy continues to be the most popular personality in France in opinion surveys, despite his decision to relocate to Los Angeles in 2012 to pursue a parallel career in Hollywood blockbusters such as *Jurassic World*. I end this chapter with an analysis of Sy's role in the 2016 film *Chocolat*, about France's first Black clown at the turn of the twentieth century. I contend that this self-reflexive film offers a meditation on minority stardom in France generally. Sy's star persona offers, I argue, an important case study of how producers, filmmakers, and minority actors have used American comedy traditions to create sustainable career paths in France while at the same time revealing the multiple glass ceilings French minority actors still face at home and abroad. Sy's career as a Black superstar offers a helpful contrast to the practice of casting nonprofessional minority actors in banlieue films.

In the final chapter, I turn to what is arguably France's most well-known banlieue film from the 2010s: *Girlhood* (*Bande de filles*, 2014). Whereas many of the previous chapters discuss an opposition between genre cinema and the art film, Célina Sciamma's film reveals a director who seeks to go beyond such oppositions, even as the French industry continues to be structured by them. I look at some of the Hollywood genres that Sciamma draws on, including the teen movie, the female friendship film, and the music video, and set *Girlhood* briefly in the context of other recent banlieue genre films that work in similar genres, such as Hervé Mimram and Géraldine Nakache's *All that Glitters* (*Tout ce qui brille*, 2010) and Audrey Estrougo's *Leila* (*Toi, moi, les autres*, 2010). Finally, I look at how the film participates, through its production history and stylistic choices, in the codes of French art cinema. Its use of long-take aesthetics and especially the casting of nonprofessional actors were important elements of why the film was taken as a realistic depiction of the suburbs among viewers who praised and criticized the film. I examine how the presence of nonprofessional actors functioned in French writings about Italian neorealism in the mid-twentieth century and then work through the consequences of this history for a banlieue film that purports to universalize Black adolescence.

In the conclusion, I reflect on some of the implications of the Trump era for the United States' image abroad as a supposedly postracial society in the context of renewed transatlantic frictions about the meaning of universalism in France. I then briefly examine Ladj Ly's 2019 banlieue film, *Les Misérables*, and Netflix's Sy vehicle, *Lupin* (2021), as a turn away from American cultural references toward French popular ones while preserving the mainstream address of the other B movies considered in this book. Finally, I consider how the rise of streaming platforms interacts with the French suburbs, and I suggest why services like Netflix and Amazon Prime are internationally distributing some of the banlieue genre films I discuss in this book and investing in filmmakers from the suburbs. The suburbs play an important role in their efforts to localize in France and compete internationally, and Netflix's strategy in France in the late 2010s is in many ways a continuation of the trend of French filmmakers rearticulating the universal that I examine throughout this book.

NOTES

1. Alana Lentin and Gavan Titley use the term *multiculture* to distinguish the fact of people from many diverse cultural backgrounds living alongside each other in contemporary Europe from the more nebulous term *multiculturalism* that has, in their view, come to delegitimize "lived multiculture" (2011, 21).

I follow their suggested usage of *multiculture* throughout this book, and I discuss their analysis of multiculturalism in Europe later in this introduction.

2. See chapter 5.

3. This may change in the wake of the CNC creating a new funding commission in 2018 for French genre films; it is headed by Julie Ducournau, director of *Raw* (*Grave*, 2016). See CNC 2018. For firsthand accounts of how young filmmakers from the banlieues learned to make movies and negotiated French funding and distribution structures, see Diao 2017, 79–147.

4. The first grand ensemble was built in 1951, and construction continued up through March 21, 1973 (Vieillard-Baron 2001, 75; Cupers 2014, 186–187). At the height of their reign in the 1960s, roughly half a million housing units were built each year (Cupers 2014, 275). The villes nouvelles, modeled after the British New Towns project, began in 1965 and continued through the 1970s. The idea was not just to allow for piecemeal construction of mass housing blocks, but to rationally think about urban planning for the whole Parisian periphery. Planners wanted to construct new cities that could get very large and house the projected rapid population growth in the coming years. The villes nouvelles would thus not just be bedroom communities like the grands ensembles, but bona fide urban centers in their own right. This meant that planners sought to create all the cultural life, public services, and commercial businesses that typically emerge organically in cities over decades (Cupers 2014, 185).

5. For an inventory of all the spatial features in the genre's corpus, including pre-1980s films, see Moinereau 1994.

6. I am grateful to Maggie Flinn and Lia Brozgal for first acquainting me with the intricacies of this situation in an Society of Cinema and Media Studies conference panel proposal we drafted in 2018. For journalistic coverage, see Toussay and Montalivet 2018.

7. Emmanuel Todd has called the persistence of this legacy on the left "zombie Catholicism" (2015, 54–57).

8. For historical analyses of the status of art in France and the state's cultural policies since World War II, see Lebovics 1995, 2011; Looseley 1995; Zolberg 2007.

9. Felicia McCarren makes a similar argument with respect to French hip hop (2013, xviii–xix).

10. The spirit of this book is thus similar to Niang's: "It is vital to underline that these new identities are integrated into the French national bloc not in the universalist manner that assimilates by (dis)integrating, but by truly conserving traces of elements inherited from other cultures that enrich the existing cultural patrimony" (2019, 7, translation mine).

ONE

SUBURBAN CINEMA BETWEEN ART AND GENRE

MATHIEU KASSOVITZ'S *LA HAINE* (1995) and Abdellatif Kechiche's *Games of Love and Chance* (*L'Esquive*, 2004) are two of the most influential French banlieue films, and they changed the stylistic possibilities for making films about France's suburbs.[1] The first was a significant domestic and international success, and it led to the codification of banlieue cinema as a genre in the popular and critical press at the time. It remains a foundational reference for banlieue cinema to this day. The second helped launch Franco-Tunisian auteur Kechiche onto the French and later world stage, and he has gone on to become one of France's best-known cinematic auteurs. While neither Kassovitz nor Kechiche would continue making films about the suburbs afterward, *La Haine*, *Games of Love and Chance*, and their directors' career trajectories established important stylistic and professional paradigms for subsequent filmmakers who make movies about the banlieues.

At the level of style, *La Haine* and *Games of Love and Chance* stand in almost complete opposition. *La Haine* is a virtuosic exercise in style and intertextuality that refracts the space of the French banlieues through the sounds and iconography of American mass culture and genre cinema. Its tale of police violence looks back to the stylistic exuberance of the French New Wave, and it updates the New Wave's use of Hollywood genre conventions to include African American music, such as funk, rap, and hip hop. Kassovitz's cinematic influences include New Hollywood directors Francis Ford Coppola, Martin Scorsese, Brian De Palma, Quentin Tarantino, John Singleton, and Spike Lee (Vincendeau 2005, 74–75; Higbee 2006, 76–79; Doughty and Griffiths 2006, 122–123). In interviews, Kassovitz said that he wanted to contest the rough and dirty images that had characterized the banlieues, particularly on

French television. He aspired to make his images of the banlieues beautiful, and consequently he would only begin production on *La Haine* once he had secured a generous budget (Vincendeau 2005, 14). Furthermore, he chose not to use film stock with the characteristic grain and smaller contrast ratio of documentary film.

Games of Love and Chance, by contrast, offers a naturalistic and pseudo-ethnographic account of the lives of school-age suburban youth who fall in and out of love and rehearse a play from France's classical eighteenth-century repertoire, Marivaux's *The Game of Love and Chance*, to be performed at the end of the school year. Kechiche began his career as an actor, and it took him a long time to secure financing for his first two films. To make *Games of Love and Chance*, his second film after *Poetical Refugee* (*La Faute à Voltaire*, 2000), Kechiche persevered through twelve years and fifty rejections to secure financing for the film (Swamy 2007, 64). The film was eventually made on a shoestring budget with then-new digital video cameras, and *Games of Love and Chance* features grainy close-ups and long takes with a handheld camera. The rough quality of the images puts the emphasis on performance and the reproduction of vernacular speech from the suburbs, which dominates the soundtrack.

Both films were successful and critically recognized in their day, though to different degrees. *La Haine* generated significant publicity and drew two million spectators to theaters, which counts as a significant success given that a million tickets sold is the generally agreed-upon threshold for a French film to be considered a domestic box office success. Kassovitz won the Best Director Prize at Cannes that year, and *La Haine* would go on to win Césars, the French equivalent of the Oscars, for Best Film, Best Producer, and Best Editing (Vincendeau 2005, 80–82). *Games of Love and Chance* was also a critical success, winning four Césars in 2005, including Best Film, Best Director, and Best Original or Adapted Screenplay. Sara Forestier took home the award for the most promising actress for her performance as Lydia. However, *Games of Love and Chance* did not do nearly as well as *La Haine* in theaters; it sold 283,578 tickets on initial release, and following its César wins, it picked up an additional 188,468 viewers on a second release (Tarr 2007, 130).

Despite *La Haine*'s success with audiences, Kassovitz' stylistic choices did not sit well with all critics, some of whom detected a lack of authenticity in his insistent use of American cultural references. For example, filmmaker Karen Alexander, writing in *Vertigo* at the time of *La Haine*'s release, remarks that "*La Haine*'s dystopic vision will have a shock value for audiences not used to seeing such 'realistic' images of Paris. This aside, what will probably prompt more cause for concern, especially to the right wing, will be the endless references to and mimicry of African-American culture. This speaks volumes for satellite TV and the globalisation of images of oppression, as a 'style thang,' with its Hood street chic, break dancing and hip-hop. . . . *La Haine* looks like an American film which has been badly transplanted" (Alexander 1995).

Alexander's commentary overlooks the French aspects of the film, which I will return to later, but it pithily sets up the opposition between realism and an American-inflected urban street style that has bedeviled critics of the film who want to assess the extent to which the film's representations of the banlieues are progressive or problematic. For example, director Jean-François Richet, who a couple of years later made the more militant but no less action-packed suburban film *My City's Gonna Crack* (*Ma 6-T va craquer*, 1997) and who would go on to make French genre films like the gangster film *Mesrine* (2008) and the historical action crime film *The Emperor of Paris* (*L'Empereur de Paris*, 2018), accused Kassovitz's *La Haine* of being a science fiction film when it was released (Vincendeau 2005, 89–90). I suggest that there is something about *La Haine*'s exuberant use of American culture that, for some critics, detracts from the film's social engagement with the suburbs. Alexander's assertion that *La Haine* looks like a poor imitation of an American film is a kind of criticism that we will see again and again in subsequent chapters about French genre films that deal with the banlieues.

In *Games of Love and Chance*, Kechiche opts for a diametrically opposed creative approach from Kassovitz, as much for financial exigencies as out of artistic choice (Porton 2005, 47–48). His film evinces a sober and realistic style, and while it is arguably as densely intertextual as *La Haine*, its references are not Hollywood cinema and French and American hip hop, but rather Marivaux's classical eighteenth-century play about four characters who attempt to pass as members of different social classes. Kechiche brings a theatrical eye to the French suburbs, letting characters speak at length in suburban vernacular through long takes that take place in spaces resembling auditoriums. The successful performance of Marivaux's play at the end of the film seemingly makes the case that traditional French culture is just as relevant to suburban youth as it is to those in the city center. Richard Porton, the editor of *Cineaste* who interviewed Kechiche at the time of the film's release, went so far as to write in his introductory remarks that "this ingenious linguistic frisson [of pungent street argot in the film] inadvertently makes a mockery of the arguments proffered by both pseudo-leftists, who proclaim that the work of 'dead white men' are irrelevant to the concerns of a younger generation, and conservatives who contend that the brains of the current generation are hopelessly addled by exposure to bad television and discordant music" (Porton 2005, 46).

However, I caution that Kechiche's use of French culture risks being oppressive rather than liberating, forcing adolescents from many different cultural backgrounds to conform to the supposed universalism of the classical French canon. At the level of style, too, *Games of Love and Chance* anchors its stylistic choices in the conventions of French art cinema. Critics at the *Cahiers du cinéma* connected the film's concern with language and realism back to the films of Jean Renoir, Marcel Pagnol, and Maurice Pialat, rather than the formal exuberance of the New Wave or the Hollywood-inflected style of Kassovitz (Gaertner 2012, 16). Kechiche's choice to cast nonprofessionals through open calls aligns him with the stylistic choices of Italian neorealism as they were received in France in the mid-twentieth century, a history I will examine at great length in chapter 6 in connection to Céline Sciamma's *Girlhood* (*Bande de filles*, 2014), a film that also employs nonprofessional casting.

Games of Love and Chance also corresponds much more closely than *La Haine* to the dominant ways that scholars have theorized political cinema in France. Ginette Vincendeau explains that prior to *La Haine*, the stylistic approaches of films about the banlieues could be divided into two general categories. The first grouping of films took a sociological look at the banlieues often using naturalist, quasi-documentary aesthetics. The second category sought to distance spectators from absorption into a film's image or narrative through techniques of stylistic disruption. Vincendeau's two aesthetic approaches for representing the banlieues overlap with Martin O'Shaugnessey's two conceptions of political cinema in the twentieth century, which, he argues, remain influential today. The first approach looks back to André Bazin's writings on Italian neorealism along with Jean Rouch's conception of cinema vérité and the French documentary tradition. It employs nonprofessionals instead of film stars or trained actors, de-emphasizes plotting in favor of loose, open-ended narrative structures, and prefers long takes over editing because the long take purportedly allows for reality to appear before the camera and later the viewer (O'Shaughnessy 2007, 22–24). The second approach looks back to avant-garde experimental film practices and the formal strategies of Brechtian distanciation that were so essential to post–May 1968 modes of militant filmmaking. These fueled articles in the *Cahiers du cinéma* during the 1970s that criticized the illusionism of the cinematic apparatus and mainstream narrative practices. This understanding of political cinema as stylistic disruption was kept alive in the *Cahiers* during the late 1990s, and its critics used it to find fault with the supposed turn to the social in late 1990s French cinema. The ideal form of political cinema for these writers is the work of Jean-Luc Godard, with its radical subversion of conventional film narrative. For this position, any film that deals with sociopolitical issues through conventional techniques such as narratives oriented around action, character psychology, spectacle, and continuity editing is a priori conservative and even reactionary (O'Shaughnessy 2007, 26–27). Given this schema, *Games of Love and Chance* tracks very well with the neorealist or documentary conception of political cinema, whereas *La Haine* does not, and one of the main tasks of this chapter will be to theorize how style relates to the social engagement of Kassovitz's film.

Despite their stylistic differences, *La Haine* and *Games of Love and Chance* converge around one fundamental point: they are both arguments about the transmission of culture in the context of the banlieues. They frame debates about cultural value that can be mapped onto a spectrum between what French sociologist Pierre Bourdieu calls legitimate or elite culture on the one hand and mass or popular culture on the other. *La Haine* and *Games of Love and Chance* interrogate the ways in which different communities in France both within and beyond the banlieues do or should construct a sense of belonging through culture and, more importantly, which kinds of culture are most appropriate to this construction of an expanded sense of national identity. The debates about cultural value and belonging within the two films also apply to their directors—the ways they present themselves in interviews and their own trajectories in the French film industry.

What is more, all films about the banlieues can be viewed as implicit arguments about competing notions of cultural value, whether this takes place at the scale of individuals, groups, regions, or even nations. Given that France as a nation theorizes social cohesion in part through mastery of the French language and legitimate culture, this should hardly be surprising. Films about the suburbs represent *and* create contact zones between different kinds of culture and hierarchies of taste, and they often thematize the reproduction of dominant social relations through the transmission of culture or the ways in which class mobility might be possible for the popular classes of the banlieues through shifts in how culture is acquired, valued, and used in everyday life.

While *Games of Love and Chance* and *La Haine* are two of the most discussed banlieue films in all of French film history, *La Haine* is generally viewed as the more problematic film because of its director, who did not grow up in the suburbs, and the film's stylized mix of foreign cultural references and genres. The subsequent trajectory of Kassovitz's career, namely his turn from popular social filmmaking to commercial genre productions, whether made in the United States (*Gothika*, 2003, and *Babylon A.D.*, 2008) or in France (*Crimson Rivers* [*Les Rivières pourpres*, 2000] and *Rebellion* [*L'ordre et la morale*, 2011]), might lend credence to the idea that there is something inauthentic about *La*

Haine's representation of the French suburbs. In my view, *La Haine* did not inaugurate a new genre of suburban cinema per se, but it did establish a mode of making French genre films that anchor their Frenchness through suburban iconography. This is not necessarily a shallow attempt at national branding; the social message of these films can be quite genuine, as is the case in *La Haine*. The transnational language of film genres—that is, the recognizable motifs of the gangster film, the buddy cop film, or the horror film, to mention some of the genres I will examine later in this book—is able to bring into focus the problems of discrimination and marginalization in new, imaginative ways. I am not arguing that Kassovitz's choice is *the* way to make films about the banlieues, but it deserves to be recognized as *a* way to do so alongside films like *Games of Love and Chance* that correspond to conventional French modes of auteurist and realist cinema and their attendant cultural politics. This assertion concerns not just Kassovitz's film but also the films I examine in the rest of this book that come after *La Haine* and similarly mix Hollywood genre conventions with the space of the French suburbs.

GAMES OF LOVE AND CHANCE, OR THE SOCIOLOGY OF CULTURAL INTEGRATION

Kechiche's second film, *Games of Love and Chance*, tells two interwoven stories. The first concerns two groups of friends, one of boys and the other of girls, and the sentimental intrigues that bring them together and divide them. Krimo, the ostensible main character, is a shy, withdrawn young man whose girlfriend, Magalie, breaks up with him. Lydia, the film's only white character, is friends with Nanou and Frida, and the latter joins her and another boy, Rachid, as they begin to rehearse Marivaux's play *The Game of Love and Chance* for their French literature class.

This brings us to the second main narrative—the rehearsal and performance of the play. Lydia, Frida, and Rachid are cast in the play, and many of the scenes involve rehearsals in the theater-like spaces of the banlieue courtyard. When Krimo stumbles on Lydia buying her dress for the play from the local tailor, he becomes obsessed with her, going so far as to bribe Rachid with a PlayStation system to let him play the role of Arlequin so that he can be close to her. Krimo does an abysmal job playing the role; he cannot speak the lines or show any emotion. He does declare his feelings for Lydia, but she does not reciprocate. She dodges (*esquive*) Krimo's declarations in the film's only violent scene, when his tall and aggressive friend, Fahti, forces a tête-à-tête between the two in a car that ends with everyone being harassed and then arrested by the police. The role is eventually given back to Rachid, and though the performance at the end of the school year is successful, the final images of the film are of Krimo alone in his room with Lydia unsuccessfully trying to call to him from the courtyard outside his apartment building. Thus, despite the happy ending and double marriage of Marivaux's comedy, Kechiche opts for the open-ended and ambivalent conclusion of a French art film (on the characteristics of the European art film, see Bordwell 2002).

As most commentaries on the film have pointed out, the juxtaposition of the space of the banlieues and a canonical work of French high culture foregrounds the role culture plays in the identity and integration of France's suburban youth, who, in the case of the film's main characters, are primarily of North African descent. Unlike previous banlieue films, in which a trip to the city center is a common trope, in *Games of Love and Chance*, the characters never leave the banlieues except through the imaginative resources of Marivaux's play. Dayna Oscherwitz suggests that the staging of Marivaux's play in the film openly asks whether it, and by extension the Enlightenment heritage for which it is a synecdoche, is about democracy and equality or rather oppression and inequality (2010, 123). Ari Blatt reads the film's staging of the Marivaux play in the marginalized suburbs as an "allegory for a society that is struggling to forge a national identity faithful to its most venerable heritage, while simultaneously striving to come to terms with the growing demographic diversity of its population" (2008, 524). Kechiche's choice of Marivaux does tap into the belief that French legitimate culture is a centripetal, integrating force that informs not only French identity but also French education and cultural policies. For this view, traditional French culture is universalizing within the borders of the nation and offers a significant contribution to world culture as a whole. This view is so pervasive and powerful in the French context that it is worth unpacking at some length before we can appreciate how Kechiche situates *Games of Love and Chance* with respect to it.

The strongest articulations of this belief can be found among conservative thinkers in France, though it is not exclusively found on the right. Leftist philosopher Alain Badiou argues in his 1997 book on universalism that "[identitarian or minoritarian logic] inveighs against every generic concept of art, putting the concept of culture in its place, conceived as culture of the group, as the subjective or representative glue for the group's existence, a culture that addresses only itself and remains potentially nonuniversalizable" (2009, 12). On the conservative side of the spectrum, French historian Marc Fumaroli is less hostile than Badiou to the term *culture*, but in his book-length essay about France's "cultural state" (*état culturel*), he criticizes how the concept as used in France has been expanded from its original associations with high art. He makes the case for French identity not being based on birth but on a knowledge of the French language, literary authors, and history (1992, 33). In making the acquisition of this knowledge elective, Fumaroli extends Ernest Renan's influential conception of the French nation as voluntarist rather than inherited through birth (Renan 1945). For Fumaroli and other conservative thinkers, such as Alain Finkielkraut, basing French identity on an acquired sense of culture has the supposed advantage of being open and egalitarian (Finkielkraut 1987, 136–146). Anyone, anywhere, the argument goes, can become a part of it. However, this sense of identity is based on a defined and almost unchanging set of historical references and texts, and it is often hostile to popular and mass forms of culture. Indeed, one of Fumaroli's principal targets for scorn in his essay is the Jack Lang–era extension that I discussed in the introduction of the term *culture* to include mass forms of culture such as rap and hip hop and even leisure activities such as sports. Fumaroli's book appeared in 1991, at a time when this reorientation of culture under Lang had been underway for more than a decade, and Fumaroli argues that the seemingly egalitarian spirit of this gesture is not at all universal. For Fumaroli, the move toward subsidizing these different forms of art represents a capitulation to the modern capitalist practice of audience segmentation, hardly the means for social unity in a republic. Fumaroli contends that rather than promoting unity, an expanded definition of culture actually serves to fragment French society (1992, 36–37).

French sociologist Pierre Bourdieu wrote the most sustained rejoinder to Fumaroli's view nearly a decade earlier, arguing that elite culture has always been about social segmentation or fragmentation. In this reading, *distinction*, the title of Bourdieu's book, is simply a less pejorative term for segmentation or fragmentation. For Bourdieu, elite culture, which he also calls legitimate culture, is not universal if we understand it to be a natural phenomenon that has no history (1984, 3–4, 16, 28). The distinctions between elite, legitimate culture and popular forms of culture do not preexist or transcend social classes. Rather, Bourdieu argues that it is through the production and maintenance of the social class structure via power and wealth that investments in different kinds of culture are created in the first place. In other words, there is nothing about Claude Debussy that makes him intrinsically affiliated with elite culture. Rather, the exposure to and training in culture that takes place in family circles and school institutions produces this link. The supposed universalism of legitimate culture or of the divide between high and low forms of culture is socially constructed. Bourdieu observes that the bourgeoisie disavow the construction of these class-based hierarchies of culture through a conception of good taste as something supposedly natural that certain people have or lack (1984, 18–28).

Bourdieu would not, however, dispute Fumaroli's assertion that a knowledge of legitimate culture carries social advantages for all classes. In fact, Bourdieu argues that such knowledge is essential for employment, social mobility, and even integration, which we might describe as substantive equality as opposed to formal equality. Even though the French school system is ostensibly designed to give all students, regardless of class origins, the familiarity needed to demonstrate mastery of "general culture" (Bourdieu 1984, 23–25), those students who have the most success at school and in life, Bourdieu argues, tend to be those from bourgeois families who grow up encountering such works directly in their family environment. They thus develop a seemingly natural sense of good taste that is, in Bourdieu's view, a part of the family's wealth that is passed down. For this reason, individuals who acquire cultural mastery at school are often accused of being too scholastic or bookish in their tastes. Autodidacts, meanwhile, achieve some level of cultural fluency on their own rather than in a social framework, and thus they inhabit an awkward category in Bourdieu's scheme (1984, 21–22, 76–80, 328–329). Kechiche, who was born in Tunisia but grew up in an HLM (habitation à loyer modéré) outside Nice, is a classic example of the autodidact, at least in terms of his knowledge of cinema. While he did attend the Nice Conservatory to study theater and acting, his interest in acting and screenwriting came from watching movies. His knowledge of legitimate French cinematic culture thus did not come from film school, but from cinephilia—that is, watching a lot of films beginning at age sixteen. He is careful to mark his cinematic taste in interviews as focusing on French and Italian films rather than American ones (except for Charlie Chaplin). He later learned how films are made by working as an actor on set and observing the process (Mrabet 2016, 149–150).

Bourdieu suggests that individuals who did not grow up with the cultural capital of the bourgeoisie will sometimes opt to orient their tastes around "lesser" art forms—his examples are science fiction and comic books—as a form of compensation for their lack of capital in legitimate culture. Despite the expertise that individuals may acquire in such lesser arts, their choice of art form can relegate them and their objects of predilection to the margins. Though this was not the choice Kechiche made, he did benefit from the fact that the generation just before his (i.e., the French New Wave generation) had largely succeeded in legitimizing the cinema as an art form. The cinema is one of Bourdieu's central examples of the ways in which the choice by a group of individuals to invest their energies in legitimating a lesser art can over time change the hierarchical mapping between what is considered fine arts versus lesser or practical arts (Bourdieu 1984, 87–88, 360).

When an art form like cinema does succeed in climbing the ladder of cultural value, Bourdieu suggests it is often through utilizing strategies adapted from those that valorize so-called legitimate culture. Though he does not ever mention the French New Wave and the original generation of *Cahiers du cinéma* critics like François Truffaut, Jean-Luc Godard, Éric Rohmer, and Jacques Rivette by name, it is likely that Bourdieu had such figures in mind. One can read *la politique des auteurs* and Alexandre Astruc's essay on how the film camera is equivalent to the writer's pen as quintessential examples of revaluing a mass medium as art through the conceptual framework of already legitimate art forms like literature and painting. When this process works, Bourdieu suggests, it is often because its agents have enough cultural capital to understand how cultural value is produced in elite circles, and thus they can apply this knowledge to an emerging or lesser art form. While Bourdieu is talking about how certain kinds of culture acquire new valuations with a nation, his argument cannot be separated from the fact that communities and individuals acquire social value through culture, and this is part of why Kechiche chose Marivaux's play for his film about the suburbs. I will also return to this notion of cultural revaluation later in the chapter, when I discuss Kassovitz's relationship to hip hop. Kassovitz grew up in a bourgeois environment with parents who had significant connections to the elite circles of the French film and television industries, and consequently one could argue that Kassovitz had enough insider knowledge of how culture works to valorize "lesser" art forms like hip hop or Hollywood genre films in *La Haine*.

In a related line of thinking, Bourdieu also suggests that different classes have divergent dispositions toward works of art. The bourgeois aesthetic disposition is one defined by distance—both distance from the artwork as a practical object and distance from one's visceral response to the art. In both cases, the emphasis should be on the cerebral appreciation of form, artistry, and intertextuality, rather than on representation, emotional response, or the object itself. More popular modes of relating to art, which Bourdieu's bourgeois aesthete would call vulgar, relate to art in terms of function—what a photograph represents, what message is expressed, or what immediate feelings are evoked. This often orients the popular viewer toward realistic works, ones that are easy to access and are immediately pleasing. The esthete, by contrast, revels in difficulty and takes pleasure in reflecting on the form of the work of art and the ways in which it reworks its tradition or refers to other works (Bourdieu 1984, 50–60).

In terms of films about the banlieues, these differing aesthetic dispositions can cut both ways. In addition to the privileging of realism in dominant conceptions of political cinema, Bourdieu's analysis of aesthetic dispositions might explain why many filmmakers from the suburbs opt for realism (or more radically, why French producers often expect them to make this choice). This could be because art, for such a disposition, is meant to have a practical dimension. However, it can also become a straitjacket when filmmakers from the banlieues want to work in a stylistic mode different from realism. Alternately, the esthete's distrust of embodied responses to art (i.e., the emotional and affective) explains in part the distrust of popular genres and Hollywood films that I will analyze in connection to *La Haine*. Films that seek to be what they are, convey a simple message, or edify through an appeal to the emotions are dismissed as vulgar, simple, or "merely" entertaining.

Bourdieu's model of cultural value and transmission in *Distinction* has been immensely influential, but it has also been challenged by contemporary sociologists. In an interview dating to around the time of *Games of Love and Chance*'s release, Dominique Pasquier, a French sociologist of culture, discussed his recent book about French high school students and culture. Pasquier references Kechiche's film, and he argues that Bourdieu's model of culture in *Distinction* no longer accounts for young people's relationship to legitimate culture. He suggests that there has been a massive disinvestment in legitimate culture due to changing relationships between children and parents and the omnipresence of media technologies in young people's lives. Most parents, in his view, no longer share legitimate culture with their children through acts of restricting their children's media consumption and exposing them to reading, music, or art. Instead, they respect their children's own cultural choices, discuss what their interests are, and seem to be content to live in a house in which different cultures coexist (Pasquier 2007, 142–143).

The importance of mass culture, which Pasquier terms a "common culture" rather than a legitimate culture, is that it offers a shared set of resources through which young people form social bonds and groups. While this shift from legitimate to common culture brings certain advantages, he is concerned that young people are disconnected from legitimate culture when it is so clearly linked to success in school for everyone. The problem, in his view, is that parents among the popular *and* middle classes have abandoned the vertical transmission of culture in favor of horizontal transmission among peers, something that we will see Kassovitz dramatize in *La Haine* through the kinds of culture the trio consume and discuss. For Pasquier, the school and thus teachers become the only remaining modality for the vertical transmission of legitimate culture in France, and this is precisely what Kechiche explores in *Games of Love and Chance* (2007, 142, 151). Vertical and horizontal modes of transmission represent distinct modes of rearticulating universalism, as we see in the films of Kechiche and Kassovitz.

MARIVAUX AND THE TRANSMISSION OF CULTURE

The question of vertical and horizontal transmission of culture is crucial for understanding the politics of *Games of Love and Chance* as a banlieue film and for understanding how films about the banlieues are implicitly arguments about cultural value. Talking about his career at the time of *Blue Is the Warmest Color*'s (*La vie d'Adèle*) release in 2013, Kechiche opined that "the question of culture and the learning of it are at the heart of my films. At the time of *Games of Love and Chance*, I already wanted to film the world of teaching as a place to observe young people and the intellectualization of the real" (quoted in Mrabet 2016, 196). Kechiche's films are notable for their focus on the dynamics of cultural transmission and for their dense network of intertextual links to what Bourdieu calls legitimate culture. As James Williams puts it, "Kechiche's films display an astonishing density and wealth of historical and cultural sources, references and citations (filmic, literary, philosophical) that are predominantly French or European and often classical in nature" (2013, 189). The choice to focus on legitimate culture in the context of a French school implicitly raises the question of the state's role in cultural transmission. To appreciate the politics of the *Games of Love and Chance*'s representation of young students from the banlieues, we have to come to terms with how Kechiche's cinematic style, intertextual references, and career path relate to the supposed universalism of French legitimate culture.

Critics have tended to celebrate the film's playful use of language and traditional French culture as the main foci of its critical intervention in representations of the banlieues. Blatt, Vinay Swamy, and Carrie Tarr have all championed how the film sets suburban vernacular (*la tchatche*) in relation to the supposedly "classical" French of Marivaux in a way that redefines the value of the type of language used in the banlieues. Tarr, for example, writes about how the suburban vernacular in the film becomes the means of expressing universal problems such as love (2007, 136–137). Blatt takes a different strategy, arguing that Kechiche's film demonstrates just how foreign both the preciosity of Marivaux's classical French and the flourishes of the suburban vernacular are to contemporary mainstream French language (2008, 518). Swamy, in my view, makes the most subtle argument about the film's use of language. For him, Marivaux's language was just as strange for mainstream ears in the eighteenth century as the banlieue vernacular is to those of the twenty-first century. Marivaux's style depended on neologisms and expressions far removed from everyday usage to such an extent that his contemporaries coined a new word, *marivaudage*, to describe just how bizarre this preciosity felt to them. Swamy notes the irony of how this peculiar language has now become synonymous with classical eighteenth-century French and how Marivaux has been enshrined as a part of the classical theatrical repertoire through regular performances at venerable institutions like the Comédie française. Swamy ultimately concludes that the juxtaposition of Marivaux and suburban vernacular offers an invitation for the film's audience to rethink their own assumptions about language and identity in contemporary France (2007, 60–61).

Where I depart from Swamy is in his contention that the film's juxtaposition of Marivaux and the suburban vernacular fundamentally unsettles the division between high and low forms of culture. Yes, *Games of Love and Chance* does bring legitimate French culture into the space of the banlieues, thus letting the young suburban characters encounter it on their own turf. However, it does not automatically follow that such a bringing together, unprecedented though it may be in banlieue cinema, is progressive (Swamy 2007, 61). Making Marivaux the central cultural reference in a film about a school system that seeks to socialize the descendants of immigrants several generations removed as citizens of the French republic could just as easily be about erasing cultural differences in the name of universalism. James Williams puts the interpretative problem posed by Kechiche's use of legitimate culture in *Games of Love and Chance* in its most blunt form: "Does [Kechiche's] method of cultural mediation simply reframe the diasporic experience within a syncretic yet politically complacent conceptual frame based around a cultural memory that is almost exclusively French and gestures irresistibly towards the universal?" (2013, 191). This is the central question about the film with which any commentator arguably must deal.

The role of French legitimate culture in *Games of Love and Chance* points to the main tensions at the heart of the film. First, can the young students from the banlieues successfully perform and imitate a recognized masterwork of traditional French culture? Second, should they have to perform and imitate such a masterwork regardless of whether they can? These questions come to the foreground during the two scenes of in-class rehearsals in which the teacher, who stands in for the authority of the school system, offers feedback on the students' performance and process. During the first in-class rehearsal scene, Lydia becomes annoyed with Frida for being unable to perform as a character from

Figure 1.1 Krimo's teacher gives him feedback on his performance in *Games of Love and Chance*, 2003.

the social class her character is supposed to be from. The teacher takes advantage of Lydia's indirect attack on her friend's acting abilities to offer a teaching moment. Her lesson is that the wealthy characters and the servants cannot truly hide the learned behaviors—linguistic, postural, and gestural—of their social class, which for her are natural and immutable. In the end, despite all the masks and assumed identities in Marivaux's play, the nobles and the servants fall in love with someone from their own social class and marry accordingly. The teacher's commentary frames Marivaux's play in terms of class immobility, and many critics have suggested that Kechiche thus asks viewers to interrogate the extent to which this immobility might also apply to the suburban youth that the film represents.

Critics have challenged the seeming authority of the teacher's interpretation from several angles. Leon Sachs notes that in response to the teacher's commentary, Lydia fires back that they—that is, suburban youth—know how to imitate (*on sait imiter*) (2014, 127). However, the teacher responds by doubling down on her interpretation: "Yes, but it's still imitation. It's nothing but imitation, do you understand?" ("Oui, mais c'est imiter quand même. Ce n'est qu'imiter, tu comprends ou pas?"). The implication here is that imitation is not authentic, and the teacher's conclusion goes unchallenged in the scene. Some critics have interpreted the successful performance of the play that ends the film as an example of how Kechiche contests the teacher's authority, while others have viewed it as the confirmation of her authority (Sachs 2014, 125–126;

Blatt 2008, 524). Still others have argued that the film's own production history subverts the teacher's view. With the exception of the white actress Forestier, who plays Lydia and had previous acting experience, Kechiche cast nonprofessionals found through open calls in the banlieues, and he rehearsed the film with them for several months during weekends and the whole of their summer vacation (Porton 2005, 48). For this line of argument, the performances of these nonprofessionals implicitly challenge the teacher's interpretation of Marivaux's play (Strand 2009, 265). While insightful, this reading does not resolve the purported universalism of Marivaux's play in the film.

Sachs makes the most sustained challenge to the teacher's authority, not through the film's production history nor the students' final performance, but rather through how Kechiche's film stages two opposing relationships to performance and by extension the traditional literary canon. His primary evidence is the second scene of in-class rehearsal. Krimo has now taken over the role of Arlequin from Rachid, and he is doing a miserable job of it. In the scene, Krimo's acting partner, Lydia, does not know how to respond to his utter lack of emotion; reverse shots of the students in the class reveal them to be bored, and the teacher becomes increasingly frustrated. She finally resorts to yelling at Krimo that he needs to get out of himself, have fun, and free himself ("Sors de toi, amuse-toi, libère-toi!"). He is ultimately unable to do so and flees the classroom without explanation. Blatt reads this moment as an embodiment of the authoritarian French state's violence toward its citizens, and he argues that Krimo's failure to perform the role is evidence of the "disenfranchise[ment]" of certain young French people who are unable to integrate into France's dominant national identity as a kind of role they must play (2008, 524). By contrast, Serge Kaganski reads this moment somewhat more generously as "synthesizing in a few minutes the complexity of French society's problems." In his view, the teacher "is right to want to tear this student from the fatalism of his social class and lack of culture [*inculture*]" (2004), thus reiterating the widely accepted view that there is a link between knowledge of legitimate culture and social mobility. Whereas Sachs reads the previous in-class rehearsal scene as one in which French culture seemingly cannot promote social mobility and integration, in this scene, he locates a liberatory potential for legitimate French culture. Through a literary masterwork, individuals might be able to give up their particular background and become other than themselves—and by extension, become free.

Sachs frames these two rehearsal scenes as offering two divergent perspectives on the function of education, the first being the "reformist, progressive position," or what he calls "mere imitation," and the second being the "classical humanist understanding," or "more imitation" (2014, 127–138). The reformist position would argue that the texts of the tradition need to be swapped out for others to reach contemporary youth, and the classical position would argue for more contact with works of the traditional canon. For Sachs, Kechiche ultimately does not choose between the two positions, but rather reveals the conflict between them and invites viewers to make the choice (2014, 136–137). While locating this tension between two divergent relationships to legitimate French culture in the school system is helpful, it does not resolve the question of how to interpret the film's ending, or rather endings. Does the class's successful performance of the film validate or question the importance of traditional French culture? Does Krimo's failure to perform and fall into isolation challenge the relevance of legitimate culture? Krimo's many failures—to become Arlequin, to start a relationship with Lydia, or to be a part of his male friend group—are the most difficult interpretative challenge of the film. One could argue that the "true happy ending" is the performance of the play, but it is difficult to see the film's final images as anything but pessimistic.

Other scholars have suggested that a notion of cultural mixing, variously conceived, might be a way to salvage a progressive politics for *Games of Love and Chance*'s use of traditional French culture. Colin Nettelbeck argues that Kechiche's engagement with the French cultural tradition in his first two films demonstrates how high culture is employed as a means to exclude France's minorities; however, he also suggests that Kechiche "has not given up on believing in the generative power of the French cultural tradition" (2007, 316–317). James Williams, by contrast, contends that Kechiche's use of high culture is generative if we think not just about individual intertexts like Marivaux's play, but rather about Kechiche's films as a whole as spaces where creative cultural mixing takes place. Ultimately, he argues that through self-conscious play with sound, image, and intertextual references, "Kechiche may be said to be reprogramming the 'source-codes' of the French tradition and patrimoine (its texts, images, narratives, symbols) and offering them in turn to his audience for cultural 'open-sourcing,' that is, as an open-access practice of creative modification and regeneration through direct interfacing with culture(s)" (2013, 223). Emna Mrabet comes to a similar conclusion about cultural mixing in Kechiche's films through Edouard Glissant's notion of rhizomatic identity, which she understands as "a mobile identity based on a dynamics of relationality and understood 'no longer as a unique root but as a root going to meet other roots'" (2016, 294).

Sachs makes the strongest case for the specifics of how such "reprogramming" or "relational dynamics" could be said to work in the context of the film's closing performance of Marivaux's play and the subsequent performance of Farid al-din Attar's Sufi poem *The Conference of the Birds* by a younger class of students. Viewers do not see the rehearsals of the Sufi poem, and so its inclusion right at the film's ending risks it being overlooked. *The Conference of the Birds* tells the story of many different birds from around the world who meet to identify a leader who might unify them. As Sachs retells it, the birds go on a long and dangerous journey, only to "discover that the object of their search has been none other than themselves" (2014, 138). For Sachs, the elementary school children's performance thus offers a hopeful message about the future resolution of France's social problems and an example of universalist ideas that is not exclusively French. Indeed, that *The Conference of the Birds* contains a universalist message means, for Sachs, that universalism is not just French, but can be found in texts from all different cultural traditions. Sachs uses this message of hope to counterbalance the hopelessness of the film's final images in which Krimo is alone in his room, having been unable to perform in the play. Lydia calls up to his room from outside the apartment building, but he does not answer, and she simply walks off as the credits roll.

Given the inconclusiveness of *Games of Love and Chance*'s ending, and indeed the endings of Kechiche's films in general, Sachs and James Williams ask viewers of Kechiche's films to take certain political possibilities of his work on faith. In the case of Sachs, it is that Kechiche's choice of *The Conference* "is no doubt meant to express the hope that tomorrow's school will have a more expansive view of the literary canon and literary patrimony" (2014, 139). As for Williams, he argues that the music playing during *Games of Love and Chance*'s credits—upbeat Eastern European songs, rather than rap or hip hop—represents a return to an open, dynamic frame about "performance and process" (2013, 209). Williams also asks us to view Kechiche's larger career in this light, despite evidence to the contrary. Following his third film, *The Secret Life of Grain* (*La Graine et le mulet*, 2007), Kechiche made *Black Venus* (*Vénus noire*, 2010), a film about Saartjie Baartman, the Black South African woman whose body was a fetish object for audiences and scientists throughout the nineteenth century. In Williams's view, this film displays none of the open-source intertextuality and cultural reprogramming of Kechiche's first three films, but Williams nevertheless expresses his hope that Kechiche will return to this mode of working in his next film (2013, 226). Unfortunately, what Kechiche's subsequent career demonstrated is that he has doubled down on making the universalism of French legitimate culture the way to legitimize his own career. Kechiche's next film was *Blue Is the Warmest Color*, which examined a class-crossing lesbian love affair. However, by focusing on two white women, Kechiche elides the questions of race, ethnicity, and diasporic history that previously defined his work. Perhaps unsurprisingly, given its examination of cultural transmission through whiteness, *Blue Is the Warmest Color* was heavily exported on the international art cinema and festival circuit, and it led to Kechiche being recognized at the 2013 Cannes Film Festival with the Palme d'Or.

If I have lingered on the various conflicting interpretations of the politics of legitimate culture in Kechiche's work, it is because I want to make the case that the best way to resolve them is to think about how Kechiche frames his own career trajectory and how his cinematic style interacts with a French critical environment defined by an investment in auteurism. This is one of the main lessons of Bourdieu's *Distinction*: aesthetic choices are not separate from the ways a given geographic and cultural space—what he calls a *champ* or field—values the positions taken by an artist through a work. I am suggesting that what these scholarly debates about the cultural politics of Kechiche's films have failed to consider sufficiently is not the use of French legitimate culture in his films, but how the style of his films and the arc of his career align with dominant modes of French auteurism and art cinema. If *Games of Love and Chance* reveals some equivocation about the film's relationship to legitimate French culture, the film's cinematic style and Kechiche's own subsequent career reveal that he is seeking legitimation through the traditions and career profiles of French auteurism and art cinema. This has consequences, I argue, for the politics of his films in terms of how they represent minority characters and the banlieues.

KECHICHE, THE QUINTESSENTIAL AUTEUR

While much ink has been spilled debating the meaning and function of Marivaux in *Games of Love and Chance* and other classical intertexts like Pierre de Ronsard, Voltaire, and Victor Hugo in previous and subsequent films, most scholarship on and critical reviews of Kechiche's films reiterate just how "French" the cinematic style and references of his films are. Scholars and critics repeatedly stress how Kechiche's films invoke the classics of French cinema, including the cinema of Renoir, Pagnol, and Pialat. Mrabet, in her book-length study of Kechiche's films, has teased out what such comparisons might mean. In the case of Renoir, the comparison seems to refer to the Renoir of the Popular Front years and to Kechiche's use of realism (Mrabet 2016, 263). Pagnol is best known as a writer, but he was also a filmmaker and screenwriter in the early 1930s who made regionalist and heritage films about Southern France that placed a particular emphasis on the distinct forms of language use from those spaces. At the start of the synchronous sound era, Pagnol argued that the cinema should focus on spoken language and theater, something that many film theorists thought cinema had proved unnecessary during the silent golden age of the 1920s. The comparison to Pagnol can indicate Kechiche's concern with regional dialects and sociolects in *Games of Love and Chance*, but it most strongly emerges in the Mediterranean setting of *The Secret Life of Grain*, a film about the effort of a community of North Africans in Sète to start a couscous restaurant.

The comparison to post–New Wave French filmmaker Pialat requires more unpacking. On a surface level, the obvious connection is that Pialat made one of the better-known films about adolescents and the French school system, *Graduate First* (*Passe ton bac d'abord*, 1978). However, the connection is as much about Pialat's understanding of cinema and directorial persona as anything else. Mrabet explains that Pialat is known for a being a particularly exigent director. He believed in a conception of acting as the revelation of truth beyond all social conventions and learned habits. Realism and truth, in his view, would emerge in front of the camera through a combination of difficulty and accidents on set. To force the appearance of truth on set, he was notorious for requiring his actors to do many takes of a scene, often upward of forty or fifty. He would also resort to mistreating his actors to elicit what he wanted from them in terms of performance (Mrabet 2016, 262–263).

Mrabet suggests that Kechiche shares with Pialat this conception of acting as the revelation of truth and that this explains Kechiche's preference for extensive rehearsals, long takes on set, and the use of close-ups to reveal the micro-expressions and emotions of an actor's performance (2016, 261–268). In an interview dating from the 2013 release of *Blue Is the Warmest Color*, Kechiche explained to Cyril Béghin and Jean-Philippe Tessé at the *Cahiers du cinéma* how he understood acting as a form of self-abandonment to "leave to the side imitation so as to appear mysterious, intelligent, or sensual" and to "eliminate all artifice and find in oneself true emotions." In Kechiche's view, actors must "come out of their own prison" and "take off the mask that they wear in life. It is not about self-forgetting but self-liberation" (quoted in Mrabet 2016, 243). While acting may potentially be liberating, it is important to consider the role and power dynamics of the director in that process.

Kechiche's remarks about acting should call to mind the second in-class rehearsal scene in *Games of Love and Chance*, during which the teacher yells at Krimo to let go of himself into the role of Arlequin and thus free himself. Seen in light of Kechiche's own conception of acting, the teacher's words take on a less liberatory and more violent and tyrannical charge similar to Pialat. Kechiche has even suggested in interviews that the teacher in *Games of Love and Chance* is a stand-in for himself as the filmmaker, and the scene echoes Kechiche's own expectations for performance and his working methods with actors (Fevret and Lalanne 2007). Around the release of *Blue Is the Warmest Color*, there was much press coverage about just how cruelly Kechiche treated his two lead actresses, Léa Seydoux and Adèle Exarchopoulos. Both denounced Kechiche in interviews and said that they would never work with him again, but Seydoux later revised her opinion somewhat to say that Kechiche is a great director and she is proud of the film despite the difficulties (Greenhouse 2013; Hay 2013). Kechiche also reportedly mistreated his crew, subjecting them to long hours and violations of labor laws (*Le Monde* 2013). Kechiche's interviews in the bastion of French auteurism, the *Cahiers*, serve to justify his own working methods in the name of art and generally confirm that he has become a genuine French auteur, with the difficult and sometimes negative reputation that the role can entail (Tessé 2013).

Kechiche's path to becoming a world-recognized French auteur has taken place largely through the styles, traditions, artisanal working methods, promotional vehicles, and paths of recognition for auteurs in France. As the outsider autodidact, in Bourdieu's sense, he did not necessarily inherit French legitimate culture, especially film culture, from his family, but rather sought it out through his own cinephilia. In his preference for French and Italian film traditions, he diverges from his contemporary, Rachid Bouchareb, whom I will examine in chapter 3, and from Kassovitz, who both watched and enjoyed a lot of the American movies on French screens. Kechiche is also an outsider in the sense that, not having gone to film school and not benefiting from public state funding at the beginning of his career, it took him many years to secure the funding for his first two films. He notes that the screenplay for *Games of Love and Chance* was written some fifteen years before it was made. When he finally secured the necessary funding, he needed to update the dialogue, so he spent time listening to young people using the suburban vernacular at a McDonald's to ensure that his dialogue was contemporary and accurate (Porton 2005, 48–49). In this, he participates in the tradition of cinematic realism characteristic of Rouch's ethnographic cinema vérité in which Rouch would research his subjects and participate in the filmmaking, often working the camera himself to record ceremonies or semi-fictional scenes (Henley 2009, 140–142, 275–277). Kechiche's casting of nonprofessionals and long work with them in rehearsals would be the rough analogues in *Games of Love and Chance* for Rouch's practice of participatory filmmaking.

Considering his drive to be recognized as a legitimate auteur by the critical establishment, it is perhaps unsurprising that Kechiche foregrounds legitimate

French culture, including cinema, in terms of his stylistic choices, his intertextual references, and the discussion and promotion of his work. Despite his films' cultural mixing, James Williams explains nevertheless that "what specifically Arab influences there are, apart from the occasional use of Arabic, are usually confined to the soundtrack in the form of music which provides a formal tension with the image" (2013, 189). Kechiche, in a 2004 interview, further minimizes the importance of music when he was asked to explain why *Games of Love and Chance* did not feature any rap or hip hop, as many previous banlieue films had. He replied that "hip hop, rap, and slam are powerful forms of expression. But I didn't use them out of fear that they would take up too much space. The film is already talkative [*bavard*], rap is too, it would have been complicated to articulate them together. Besides, I believe that, if one doesn't exist as an image, one doesn't exist at all" (*si on n'existe pas à l'image, on n'existe pas du tout*). He continued, "One can do all the music one wants, it only becomes significant if one appears in the images, and not just music videos, that a society produces of itself" (Lalanne 2004). While I am sympathetic to Kechiche's assertion that minorities need to exist at the level of the image, an assertion I will take up in chapter 3, the minimization of music's importance here only further underscores the importance of legitimate French culture in *Games of Love and Chance*. Despite the degree to which individual scenes may stage moments of cultural mixing or "rhizomatic identity," the model of cultural transmission in *Games of Love and Chance*—and, I suggest, for the rest of his filmography—is predominantly vertical, with French legitimate culture at the apex.

While one might be tempted to view the film and its staging of Marivaux's play as a progressive example of nontraditional casting practices, as Brandi Catanese explains, nontraditional casting practices "risk acquiescing to a hierarchy of valuation, suggesting that their only function is to improve people of color. White theaters and white texts are affirmed as the pinnacle of artistic opportunity in practices that assume that escaping nonwhiteness is the true task of color-blind social progress" (Catanese 2011, 17). *Games of Love and Chance* at least resolves the white theaters question, assuming that we exempt republican schools in the suburbs from their universalizing function, but it does not resolve the question of white texts.

Kechiche has become, as Mrabet points out, a consecrated Franco-Tunisian auteur, fully conversant with the traditions of European high culture and able to theorize and promote his film work in interviews in a way that is recognizable and celebrated by the critical establishment. In a particularly infelicitous phrase, Mrabet suggests in her conclusion that "the prevalence of the aesthetic dimension in [Kechiche's films] testifies to the evolution of a movement [*beur cinema*] that has progressively broken with its sociopolitical rags [*oripeaux sociopolitiques*] to anchor itself more in the furrow of developing a singular writing" (Mrabet 2016, 291). Leaving behind "sociopolitical rags" for "singular writing" is code for a successful transition to a cinema of art and auteurism, one that passes through and celebrates legitimate French culture, rather than challenging it.

I contend that a film like *Games of Love and Chance* ultimately falls victim to Williams's "politically complacent conceptual frame" that "gestures irresistibly towards" French legitimate culture and the universal (2013, 191). Kechiche has established himself as an auteur, and he has valorized the French minority communities he represents on screen and through his own career as a filmmaker. However, he has done this through a relentless appeal to French legitimate culture at the expense of autochthonous, transnational, and even at times diasporic forms of popular culture, including, but not limited to, hip hop, rap, and urban street culture. His films have become an example of diasporic filmmaking, but they have paradoxically done this by speaking in the mode of the universal and by acceding to French legitimate culture as the means through which France's minority communities must assimilate.

There is nothing wrong with this strategy per se, so long as we recognize that it is *one* way—rather than *the* way—to frame the question of cultural value within a film about the banlieues. In my view, *Games of Love and Chance* is not unequivocally progressive. For all of *Games of Love and Chance*'s playfulness, self-reflexivity, narrative openness, and ambivalence, it can be read (or misread, depending on one's point of view) by cultural conservatives as a defense of "dead white authors" and legitimate culture as the means of national cohesion. This is not, I suggest, an accidental feature of the film, but rather it is deliberate on the part of a filmmaker seeking recognition as an insider. With this position come certain advantages; it is easier to talk about politics and cultural value in this film because they align with the values of French legitimate culture. There are also disadvantages; *Games of Love and Chance* does not, I contend, fundamentally unsettle the division between high and low culture. If anything, it reinforces it. *La Haine*, while more difficult than *Games of Love and Chance* to position in terms of politics, nevertheless unsettles this division between high and low more forcefully than Kechiche's film.

STYLIZED ABSTRACTION AND FRANCO-AMERICANISM IN *LA HAINE*

La Haine centers on three friends who live in a suburban neighborhood near Paris, and the narrative follows them as they go about their lives the day after street protests. Residents of the neighborhood were upset when the police accidentally shot a fourth friend, Abdel, and they took to the streets to demonstrate against another instance of a police *bavure* (misconduct). The trio of friends is multiethnic and multiracial, and French commentators refer to the group as *black-blanc-beur* (Black-white-Arab) because Hubert (Hubert Koundé) is Black, Vinz (Vincent Cassel) is Jewish, and Saïd (Saïd Taghmaoui) is Maghrebi. During the protests, a police officer loses a gun, and Vinz finds it and keeps it for himself. As Abdel hangs between life and death, Vinz repeatedly threatens to shoot a police officer in retribution if Abdel dies. Saïd and especially Hubert attempt to dissuade Vinz from further violence as the friends wander through the streets of their *cité* and then later Paris. The film ends with a police officer accidentally shooting Vinz with a gun, thus continuing the cycle of police violence in the suburbs.

The film was received enthusiastically in France, and many viewers found its representation of the suburbs to be topical when it appeared in French cinemas in 1995. Some even related to the film as if it were a documentary or a journalistic exposé on France's suburban minority communities. For example, then prime minister Alain Juppé asked government ministers to view the film, suggesting just how much realism some French spectators attributed to it upon its release (Vincendeau 2005, 84). Yet the film is not realistic in any obvious sense of the term. Phil Powrie finds it difficult to situate *La Haine* with respect to the return of both realism and the political that characterized many French films made by young, up-and-coming directors in the 1990s. In his analysis of *La Haine*, Powrie argues that Kassovitz's film focused on the "contemporary issues of youth alienation" to such a degree that government ministers watched it to "understand" the suburbs, but he cautions that the film is "not particularly representative of 'a return to the real'" (1999, 17). Part of the challenge of relating to the film is that it refuses to fit into one neat category. René Prédal, in his book on the young cinema of the 1990s, calls *La Haine* unclassifiable because it mixes modes as diverse as the allegorical fable, the official government report, anarchist agitprop, and leftist humanism (2002, 116). What does it mean to make a film about the marginalization of the French banlieues through a complex mixing of French and American references, including the *chanson réaliste* (realist song), hip hop, New Hollywood films, US Black urban cinema, and French poetic realism? And how does the film create the perception of realistically engaging with the French suburbs while being so abstract and stylized that it feels timeless? The universalism that we see in *La Haine* is not the mannered spatial authenticity or the legitimacy of traditional French culture that we saw at work in Kechiche's *Games of Love and Chance*. Rather, *La Haine* is a film whose complex layering of French and American cultural and cinematic references enables it to speak to different kinds of audiences, thus suggesting that the space of the suburbs on screen can interface between the social conflicts of a specific time and place (in this case, 1990s France) and more universal struggles related to class and race.

Although the film deals with police violence and social unrest in the French suburbs during the 1990s, *La Haine*'s location in time and space is loosely specified. While *La Haine*'s costumes and production design offer clues about the film's setting, the narrative cannot be pinpointed to a specific week or year, despite the insistent presence of intertitles marking the passage of time and the sound of the ticking clock. *La Haine* deliberately positions itself as a film about the seemingly timeless, cyclical conflict between the forces of order and those living at the margins of society. Even though Kassovitz had very specific instances of police violence in mind while writing the film, he centers the film's narrative around anti-police and antiestablishment sentiments that could emerge from a variety of places and time periods. For example, when I taught the film in the wake of George Floyd's murder on the streets of Minneapolis in 2020, my students in the United States had no trouble making connections between *La Haine*'s representation of police violence and the historical moment they were living. One of the few historical references in *La Haine* is the image of the Bosnian crisis on the train station's TV monitors near the end of the film. This scene does place *La Haine* in the 1990s, but it also broadens the film's themes beyond French borders, suggesting that the film's exploration of police violence might speak to other histories of genocide. During the scene in the Parisian bathroom, when Saïd and Hubert attempt to convince Vinz that he should not murder a police officer, an old Jewish man exits one of the stalls and tells a seemingly incongruous story about the time he and his friend Grunwalski were deported to the Siberian work camps in a cattle car. Grunwalski needed to relieve his bowels but did not do so quickly enough and was left to die in the bitter cold as the train departed. The old man's story also evokes memories of Nazi deportation of Jews during World War II and thus connects the film's representation of police violence in the suburbs to other instances of state-organized genocide. These various references serve not to anchor the film in a specific time and place, but rather to unmoor it so that it can speak to different historical contexts.

Kassovitz's decisions to use black and white and to shoot beautiful, carefully composed shots of the suburban architectural forms similarly distance the film from a specific time and place. Kassovitz shot the film in color, but he chose to print the film in black and white, thus rendering the film's suburban neighborhood abstract rather than realistic for a mid-1990s audience habituated to color film. Kassovitz shot part of his film in a real suburban cité near Paris, Chanteloup-les-Vignes, but *La Haine* never reveals the identity of the cité in which it is set (Vincendeau 2005, 15). Kassovitz's choice to elide specific spatial markers means that the film offers a visual typology of the French banlieues in general rather than a realistic representation of a specific neighborhood. *La Haine*'s images feature HLM apartment buildings, courtyards, playgrounds, deserted parking lots, a grocery store, a police station, and cramped apartment interiors. Even the aerial shot of the cité during the DJ sequence does not offer any terrain markers that would allow viewers to place it in the geography of Paris's suburbs. Kassovitz's purported reason for leaving the exact location of the film unspecified was that the suburban town wanted no publicity about the shooting location (Vincendeau 2005, 15). Yet these details of production history do not fully explain why Kassovitz would make the film's setting at once recognizable (the suburbs) and unspecific.

Unlike the grainy digital video images or handheld camerawork of *Games of Love and Chance*, *La Haine*'s composed cinematography and careful attention to mise-en-scène create painterly images of the suburbs that channel the alienation of those who live there. In a key moment early in *La Haine*, the three main characters sit on stones in a public park while listening to a young boy recount an anecdote about the French version of *Candid Camera*. The dialogue of this scene has no implications for the film's plot, but the framing and composition of the shot tie into *La Haine*'s key themes. In addition to being an arresting image, the oblique lines of the park's building obscure the sky and entrap the trio, suggesting their isolation in the suburbs. Kassovitz also distances himself from documentary realism when he eschews handheld camerawork in favor of the lyrical sweeps that characterize Steadicam and the use of cranes. In a particularly striking example from early in the film, Kassovitz cuts to a tracking shot of the French riot police in the foreground as they approach the trio through a narrow alley between HLM buildings. The characters talk about the protests while evading the cops. The vertical lines of the buildings and windows create a jail-like visual claustrophobia that serves as a metaphor for the sense of entrapment the police bring to the space.

Kassovitz's wide shots are often as desolate and oppressive as his tighter ones. In *La Haine*'s early scene in which Saïd and Vinz find Hubert at his burned-out boxing gym, Kassovitz leaves his camera on the far side of the parking lot as Vinz and Saïd cross a space devoid of cars. On a referential level, the building looks like a dilapidated big-box store. On the level of feeling, Kassovitz accentuates the emptiness of the space by tracking Vinz and Saïd and then fixing his camera in space as if stuck in the adjoining gas station's pump. The camera stays wide, looking at the characters from the outside and transforming the parking lot into a metaphor for the social and economic devastation of the banlieues. No one in the banlieues can move, for lack of cars and gas. Kassovitz composes the image with visually striking foreground and background elements that emphasize the distance Vinz and Saïd must cross. The stylized abstraction of Kassovitz's mise-en-scène places the emphasis on feeling, rather than historical contextualization. By reducing the suburbs to a set of striking architectural forms, Kassovitz enables them to stand for not only the French suburbs in general but also the zones of urban poverty associated with many large cities throughout the world.

While French audiences would of course have matched the film's images of suburban neighborhoods to the French banlieues, *La Haine* offers none of the contextualization that would permit international viewers to relate the police violence to specific historical events in the French suburbs. Furthermore, it does not offer any information about the history of French decolonization and postcolonial migration that led to the concentration of France's immigrant and immigrant-descended poor and working classes in the suburbs. The film's lack of historical contextualization has been explained and connected to the film's politics in various ways. Vincendeau has argued that violent images of the banlieues and the protests saturated television screens and the front pages of newspapers in the early 1990s (2005, 24–25). In this reading, French audiences in the mid-1990s would have made the connection between the film's images and television coverage of street violence in the banlieues without being specifically asked to do so. When generic French images of street protests and conflict between protestors and riot police play in the film's opening alongside Bob Marley's song "Burnin' and Lootin'," French viewers fill in the contextual gaps using their insider knowledge of contemporary political debates and television coverage. For other commentators, the lack of historical context is politically problematic. Ashwani Sharma and Sanjay Sharma argue that Kassovitz's refusal to "situate the racialized crisis of the banlieues as the product of decolonization in France and contemporary postcolonial social relations" as a militant or documentary film might have done fails to produce the historical consciousness necessary for real social change (2000, 111). The implicit assumption behind such criticisms, however, is that the absence of contextual details leaves the door open for audiences to fill in the blanks with harmful stereotypes, a criticism that is often leveled against suburban films that prefer stylization to realism. A progressive film about the banlieues, this line of thinking goes, would be fully contextualized and thus properly realistic so as to avoid the kinds of ambiguity that rely on deleterious stereotypes.

La Haine has also been criticized for its heavy reliance on American cultural and cinematic references, including hip-hop music, break dancing, cartoons, comic books, and genre references, such as citations of the gangster films by Scorsese from the New Hollywood period and Black urban films by Lee. These references at once create the feeling of contemporaneity and also further abstract the film from the specific spatiotemporal coordinates of the French suburbs in the mid-1990s. *La Haine* does employ hip-hop music in the soundtrack, and while this may have created perceptions of topicality for some viewers, these too are partially an illusion. As Sharma and Sharma point out, Kassovitz's soundtrack is not defined exclusively by 1990s gangster rap. Kassovitz does employ some gangster rap, but what predominates is "a thoughtful and knowledgeable mixture of soul, funk, and rap" drawn from the 1970s, the 1980s, and the 1990s (Sharma and Sharma 2000, 113). The film's sartorial choices of track pants, hoodies, and tennis shoes may look to American rap and hip-hop music videos and American urban films such as Singleton's *Boyz 'n the Hood* (1991), but they just as much reference global street culture that is not specific to France or the United States. The French chain store Monoprix created a special clothing line for the film's release, suggesting that *La Haine* received some of the ancillary market tie-in that Hollywood blockbusters typically do (Reader 1995, 14). However, the costume choices we see in the film still signal urban street culture even long after its 1995 release.

The film's many cinematic references to Hollywood films through loose remakes of specific scenes also distance *La Haine* from a specific time and place. These include Kassovitz's riff on the shopkeeper scene in Lee's *Do the Right Thing* (1989), complete with an Asian owner, or the iconic shot of Vinz imitating Robert De Niro's "You talkin' to me?" from Scorsese's *Taxi Driver* (1976). More subtle references include the films Vinz watches at the theater when hiding out in Paris, a scene I will discuss later. This scene, importantly, is also a simultaneous reference to Godard's *Breathless* (À bout de souffle, 1960), in which the main characters, Patricia and Michel, hide out from the police in a movie theater. The hybridity of Kassovitz's influences will be important for understanding the artistic project of *La Haine*.

Many of the scholarly discussions of *La Haine*'s indebtedness to American culture and Hollywood cinema have focused on music and intertextual references to other films. However, it is also important to attend to the ways in which the film's editing, shot selection, and cinematography employ the stylistic norms of post-1960s Hollywood cinema—what David Bordwell has called "intensified continuity." For Bordwell, intensified continuity is defined by four principal stylistic features—"rapid editing, bipolar extremes of lens lengths, reliance on close shots, and wide-ranging camera movements" (Bordwell 2006, 121). Of these, the increased pace of editing has generated the most discussion among scholars, though all four features are intimately related.

After comparing the average shot length (ASL) of a significant number of Hollywood films from the twentieth and twenty-first centuries, Bordwell concludes that the average ASL goes down significantly after the 1960s, meaning that the pace of editing has quickened. ASL is calculated by counting the number of shots in a film and dividing by the film's total running time. It is a crude metric; for example, a single scene of rapid editing in a film that uses longer takes could skew the film's ASL. Nevertheless, ASL remains a useful comparative metric. Bordwell's conclusions regarding ASL in the post-1970s context is that ASLs rarely go above ten seconds and tend to cluster in the five-second to seven-second range, with many averaging four to five seconds (2006, 122). In the post-1960s Hollywood phase, higher ASLs with slower editing or a greater use of long takes tend to characterize lower-budget, independent American films that want to emphasize the performance of ensemble casts or to "create scenes laden with a European gravitas" (Bordwell 2006, 140). When long takes are used in Hollywood cinema, they are typically for scenes of exposition that are delivered on the move in what Bordwell calls a "walk and talk" shot or in a "stand and deliver" shot in which characters remain fixed and talk while the camera spirals around them (2006, 184). These kinds of exposition shots are distinct from the French and European practice of choreographed long takes that emphasize ensemble performance, reflected most powerfully in the French cinematic tradition by the 1930s films of Renoir.

Despite the ways *La Haine* is talked about as a Hollywood film, its ASL places it closer to French norms. Vincendeau calculated *La Haine*'s ASL to be fifteen seconds. She nuances this by saying that some of the scenes are edited more rapidly, such as the car theft scene or the tense exchange between the trio and the television journalists, but the fact is that *La Haine* evinces the slower pace of editing that is more typical of a French film (Vincendeau 2005, 50). However, Kassovitz does employ several of the other stylistic features of intensified continuity, such as opposed lens lengths, manipulation of depth of field, and a highly mobile camera. Bordwell explains that contemporary Hollywood directors often dispense with the establishing shot entirely and cut repeatedly within scenes of exposition, alternating between telephoto and wide lenses that flatten or exaggerate the sense of depth within a shot. Rack focus in shots using long lenses serves as a form of in-camera editing that directs viewers' attention. Furthermore, contemporary Hollywood directors rely less on wide two-shots and more on over-the-shoulder and tightly framed single-person shots, de-emphasizing the performance of actors and increasing the emphasis on how editing constructs performance (Bordwell 2006, 127–128, 137, 130). Many of these stylistic elements are present in *La Haine*, though they are set within a slower pace of editing.

The opening sequence of *La Haine*, following the credit montage of street protests, signals an affinity with intensified continuity from the very beginning. Saïd is framed center in a medium shot with his eyes closed as a gunshot in the soundtrack removes all ambient sound. The camera pushes to a close-up of his face as the background goes out of focus, indicating the use of a long lens. Saïd opens his eyes as the ambient sounds return. Kassovitz cuts on axis to a shot of Saïd's back just a bit more distant from him but still close and using a long lens so that the background is completely out of focus. The camera pushes in again, framing an extreme close-up of Saïd's hair before moving up in an arcing crane shot. Saïd's head disappears out of frame, and the camera freezes and rack focuses to reveal a wider shot of the riot police standing guard outside the local police station. As young children walk in front of the police, Kassovitz holds the final position of the shot for about ten seconds, longer than one would expect in a typical Hollywood film that would move on to the next dramatic beat. He then cuts to a mobile medium close-up of the riot police staged in depth and almost looking at the camera as it tracks right and picks up Saïd, who is tagging the police van. Viewers realize retrospectively that there has been a temporal ellipsis, even though the previous edit feels continuous. Kassovitz cuts to a medium shot behind Saïd so that viewers can read the tag of his name and the phrase "Fuck the police." After Saïd exits the frame, Kassovitz cuts closer twice more in short succession—once to the complete tag and once to an extreme close-up of Saïd's name. The use of the main characters' names as text in a shot to introduce them is a clear nod to Scorsese's *Mean Streets* (1973). *La Haine*'s opening sequence is seventy seconds long and contains five edits, giving an ASL of fourteen seconds. Despite the slower pace of editing as compared to Bordwell's analysis of post-1960s Hollywood cinema, Kassovitz nevertheless places *La Haine* from the very beginning in dialogue with intensified continuity through his expressive use of lens length, close-ups, rack focus, and camera movement.

Kassovitz's use of a mobile, hyperkinetic camera is arguably the most important element of intensified continuity in the film. Bordwell terms this use of camera movement the "prowling camera," by which he means a camera that is constantly on the move through Steadicam rigs, crane and jibs, zoom lenses, or the traditional movements done with physical tracks. The most clichéd usage, in Bordwell's view, is the circling or arcing camera during a scene of dialogue between two individuals, but he also notes the increased importance of the "moving master." Instead of a fixed master shot, contemporary Hollywood directors will use a mobile tracking shot because it gives some of the same information about how space is organized (Bordwell 2006, 134–135). The most conspicuous example of this occurs early in *La Haine*, after all three members of the trio are introduced and they walk through the neighborhood to a rooftop party. The two-minute sequence shot begins with the camera following behind a group of riot police as they walk between two buildings. In the background of the shot, the trio walks toward the police. Viewers hear Vinz telling Saïd and Hubert about how the protestors disrespected the police by spitting on them, but he goes quiet once he notices the police. The two groups go their separate ways, and the camera follows the trio from behind as Vinz finishes the story. The three friends stop in a courtyard, and the camera arcs around them as they debate whose motorcycle they are hearing. As they continue walking, the camera follows in front of them as they catch up on local gossip. Once they arrive at their destination, Saïd and Vinz stay in the background while the camera continues to follow Hubert as he meets a client who then gives him money, ostensibly payment for marijuana. As the three friends enter the building and head for the rooftop, Kassovitz cuts to an overhead shot of Saïd making the final steps on a ladder, eliding the long walk up the stairs. The two-minute sequence shot unfolds in almost complete movement, with the occasional bob left and right that cants the angle of the shot, echoing the instability of handheld. However, the smooth, lyrical movements of the camera make it clear that this is a Steadicam shot, and it combines the "walk and talk" and "stand and deliver" techniques. The different techniques of intensified continuity, in Bordwell's view, "encourag[e] heavy stylization and self-conscious virtuosity" on the part of filmmakers, and they intensify emotional effects throughout the whole film, rather than just in peak scenes of heightened emotion (2006, 180). This is certainly the case in *La Haine*, which is stylized throughout. However, we should not neglect the relatively slow overall pacing of the editing and the languorous long takes that punctuate the film. While *La Haine* signals its stylistic affiliation with Hollywood cinema through its cultural and cinematic references and its use of certain intensified continuity techniques, there are other stylistic aspects and cultural references in the film that point to its embeddedness in French cultural traditions.

In *La Haine*, American, French, and other global cultural references exist side by side, with no clear hierarchical relationship between them. In one scene, Saïd and Vinz debate the relative strengths and weakness of Warner Brother's cartoon duos like Road Runner and Coyote, Tweety and Sylvester, and Tom and Jerry after Saïd goes to see a shady character named Astérix—a clear reference to the famous French *bande dessinée* hero—who owes him money and who answered the door in a towel with nunchaku in his hands, as if he had just stepped out of an East Asian martial arts film. In an earlier scene, the suburban neighborhood's black-market dealer in audiovisual devices, named Darty after the French audiovisual big-box chain store, wears a T-shirt that reads "Elvis killed JFK." Curiously, certain versions of the subtitles translate *Darty* as *Walmart*, and Jonathan Romney was critical of the subtitles used in the 1995 English-language release because of how much they Americanized the French references (1995). Such criticisms are certainly valid, but they also miss how the free mixing among American, French, and other international cultural references enables the film to speak to audiences far beyond those in France during the mid-1990s. The subtitles merely exaggerated the mixing of cultural references already present in the film.

While the many ways *La Haine* abstracts from space and time do detract from a realistic representation of the suburbs, they offer distinct advantages for bringing the French suburbs to mainstream screens and inviting domestic and international viewers to care about the systematic racism and economic marginalization that affect such spaces. Unlike *Games of Love and Chance*, which has not aged well in my opinion, perceptions of *La Haine*'s relevance for the contemporary moment have not waned with time. Kassovitz's film feels as fresh and current as it did when it was released nearly thirty years ago, especially as debates about police violence take on renewed urgency in the United States, France, and other parts of the world. Despite the film being nominally about the French suburbs circa 1995, its stylized abstraction enables it to travel through time and space and connect with audiences around the world. This, I argue, is universalism in a very different sense from what we saw in the context of Kechiche's *Games of Love and Chance*.

La Haine is not about the kind of French universalism in which the school system invites suburban youth to find their place in the universalist republic through French legitimate culture. Rather, *La Haine* abstracts from spatial, temporal, and cultural coordinates through a stylized and free mixing of French and foreign cultural elements in such a way that the French suburbs can speak to audiences around the world. At the same time, the film uses American mass culture and cinema to bring visibility to the forms of racialized exclusion at work in the French suburbs. I contend that *La Haine* represents a horizontal—rather than vertical—mode of cultural transmission, a universalism of mixing beyond borders, as opposed to assimilation within borders. It suggests not only that American mass culture and cinema have universal aspects that are able to speak to the local conditions of the French suburbs but also that a French filmmaker can use American references to craft a distinct discourse of universalism that includes suburban multiculture and that can then speak back to French and international audiences. This is what I mean by rearticulating the universal. Even if *La Haine* remains idiosyncratic within Kassovitz's career, the film represents a specific kind of cultural politics related to the French suburbs and universalism that the other filmmakers examined later in this book will build upon.

THE POLITICS OF FEELING REAL

Appreciating *La Haine*'s politics requires a different kind of theorization and analysis than the models for political cinema that I described earlier in connection to Kechiche's *Games of Love and Chance*. As should be clear from the preceding discussion, *La Haine* is not realistic in any simple sense, yet it is often discussed in terms of some qualified relationship to realism, whether this is what Sharma and Sharma call "aestheticized realism" or "hyper-realism" (2000, 110–111), what Sven-Erik Rose terms "gritty realism" (2007, 484), or what Tarr suggests might be "documentary realism" (1997, 45). All of these qualified uses of the word *realism* seek to clarify how the feelings created by the film's style relate to the French suburbs seen on screen and to its overt desire to challenge police violence. Vincendeau, in her book-length study of the film, argues that "Kassovitz's ability to structure his film along classical lines, rework elements of American culture and deploy an exhilarating style, while respecting the 'local colour' of the *cité*, explain its extraordinary success. Ironically, whereas many films de *banlieue* and *beur* films emerge genuinely from within the *cités*, they have remained home products, whereas the more culturally hybrid *La Haine*, made by a team largely from outside the *cités*, has succeeded in exporting the 'feel' of this territory" (2005, 23, original emphases). Vincendeau's choice to put the word *feel* in quotation marks suggests some ambivalence about how *La Haine* employs feeling. The film acceded to the status of realistic for contemporary French viewers, but it did so principally through its pictorial style and cultural references, which elicited feelings that audiences then mapped onto the spaces of the French suburbs.

How to theorize *La Haine*'s use of feeling has proved to be a difficult task. Kassovitz's film corresponds to neither of O'Shaugnessey's two positions on political cinema that I described earlier. While Kassovitz wants *La Haine* to be an intervention into debates around the marginalization of the French banlieues, especially in connection with police violence, his stylistic choices make it difficult to locate a critical realism or a critical aestheticism in the film. Though Kassovitz's use of the long take is arguably related to the realist position, his use of black and white and carefully composed shots draws attention to stylization, rather than a referential relationship to real space. One could argue that such stylization seeks to create spectatorial distance along the lines of the experimental position. And yet, the lyrical quality of such long takes puts the emphasis more on pictorial beauty and feeling than critical distance. On the experimental side of the debate, Kassovitz's self-conscious intertextuality could be read as a form of distanciation. Yet, the film diverges in important ways from the model of French New Wave filmmakers like Godard and Truffaut. *La Haine*'s intertextuality does not necessarily distance the spectator. For example, if one does not recognize Vinz's reference to *Taxi Driver*'s iconic "You talkin' to me?" line, this lack of knowledge does not affect *La Haine*'s narrative development nor the film's characterization of Vinz as playing with different kinds of identity.

Intertextuality in *La Haine* is more about style than critical commentary, and this positions Kassovitz less as a descendant of the French New Wave and more as a follower in the footsteps of New Hollywood directors like Scorsese and Coppola. Film historian Robert Ray has analyzed the ways many New Hollywood films post-1967 absorbed the experimental techniques of the French New Wave, including disjunctive editing that breaks continuity, unmotivated flashbacks, extreme close-ups, freeze frames, self-conscious intertextuality, ironic uses of music, and abrupt shifts in tone and genre. However, Ray argues, filmmakers like Scorsese and Coppola ultimately made such techniques subservient to conventional modes of Hollywood narrative and characterization. Such usage merely added expressive techniques to mainstream narrative cinema, rather than disrupting its codes altogether (Ray 1985, 272–295).

Ray ultimately concludes that this subordination of formal experimentation to the conservative goals of conventional narration and genre pleasure allowed New Hollywood films to speak to audiences on the right and the left in the politically volatile period of the 1960s and the early 1970s: "The industry's solution to this new division [between naïve spectators who wanted straightforward genre films and ironic spectators who wanted art films and revisionist reworkings of Hollywood] was the 'corrected' genre movie, a film like *Butch Cassidy*, which could provide enough straight action to appease the traditionalists and enough self-consciousness to satisfy the iconoclasts. In effect, the wide appeal of both the Left and Right films derived from their double nature: all, in fact, were 'corrected' genre pictures, capable of being taken two ways" (Ray 1985, 327). Ray's account of a "corrected" genre picture is a helpful framework for understanding the politics of style in *La Haine*, as the film is open to multiple readings: naïve and ironic, sincere and cynical, realistic and stylized.

However, the film's self-conscious layering of cultural references and focus on the shared feelings of culture originate not in the New Hollywood period or in the Tarantino-esque play of postmodern pastiche. The sincerity of Kassovitz's representation of the suburbs in *La Haine* connects back to an older tradition of popular social filmmaking in France: the films of the 1930s Popular Front, including those belonging to the category of poetic realism. Both Vincendeau and Oscherwitz hint that Kassovitz's film might be related to older models of French filmmaking prior to the New Wave, such as poetic realism, but they do not develop these connections in any depth (Vincendeau 2005, 75; Oscherwitz 2010, 108). Kassovitz noted the importance of 1930s French cinema for *La Haine* in a 1995 interview with the French magazine *Les Inrocks:* "It certainly wasn't American cinema that invented social cinema, but rather the French, the English, the Italians. . . . It's not the Americans who would have made *They Were Five* [*La Belle Équipe*, 1935] and all the films about the Popular Front" (Kaganski et al. 1995). I contend that *La Haine* in fact represents a carefully calibrated synthesis of the French New Wave's formal exuberance, New Hollywood's absorption of the New Wave's techniques in service of conventional genre and narrative filmmaking, and the naïve sincerity of French poetic realism that sought to offer simple moral fables about France's urban, working-class poor.[2] A brief consideration of how feeling operates in French poetic realist cinema will offer a helpful framework through which to understand why *La Haine* felt real to audiences even though it manifestly is not.

Poetic realism, as a style or tendency, has never enjoyed the same degree of critical visibility or theoretical interest as other movements in French film history. Dudley Andrew defines poetic realism as "maintain[ing] contact with social experience analogously, not directly; it models social experience by means of a cinematic experience that chemically transforms whatever facts make up its climate" (1995, 15). Marcel Carné is arguably the most emblematic poetic realist filmmaker from the 1930s, and while his films have lost something of their power to affect viewers the way that they did in the 1930s, both *Port of Shadows* (*Quai des brumes*, 1937) and *Daybreak* (*Le jour se lève*, 1939) were "explosive" films upon their release. Critics and politicians went so far as to blame their bleak pessimism for the debacle of the French capitulation to the Germans at the start of the Occupation. Such a statement is clearly exaggerated and even ridiculous if thought of as an accurate statement of historical cause, but it does index the e/affect of his films in their historical moment and the extent to which they figured into the social anxiety and unease of late 1930s

France. In response to such claims, Carné famously retorted that one does not blame the barometer for the storm (Turk 1989, 114–115).

Carné's image of the cinema as barometer is a helpful way to understand how feeling operates in stylized films that are not self-evidently realistic in their representation of the world. Taken metaphorically, it gestures to the relationship Carné imagines between his films and the social world of 1930s France. The barometer points to an indexical relationship between his films and the social world, but not in the way indexicality has typically been thought of in film and media studies. Charles Sanders Peirce's semiotic conception of indexicality has a long history in classical theorizations of the cinematic image's relation to realism. In the tradition of classical film aesthetics that descends from Bazin, film celluloid captures reflected light from the event before the camera lens, also called the pro-filmic, and records traces of this light through a chemical reaction in celluloid's material substrate. These same light patterns are then recreated by the light of the projector shining through a film print back onto the screen, thus supposedly giving cinema the closest relationship to reality of an aesthetic medium. However, this literal sense of indexicality oriented around light does not help us understand Carné's image of the cinema barometer. The barometer is indexical in the sense that its mechanism responds to actual atmospheric pressure in the world around it. However, the barometer is not a prosthesis for the eye in the way the camera is. Rather, it translates pressures or feelings that the human body may or not may not register into a form that is perceivable. This is why Andrew characterizes poetic realism as an analogical mode.

The ways a barometer registers felt atmospheric pressure and translates it into visual form suggest that film style and the cultural references with which a film engages serve to register the feelings engendered by social conflicts and translate them into a recognizable form that audiences can then feel. In "The Analysis of Culture," Raymond Williams defines culture as a "structure of feeling" that is the "living result of all the elements in the general organization [of the culture of a period]" (2006, 36). Williams understands culture as a shared experience, made up of conscious and unconscious knowledge, memories, and feelings, by particular groups of people. The structure of feeling is temporally bound in that it is tied to the people who grew up together at a particular moment in a particular place. Structures of feeling evolve over time, and critics can never operate fully outside their own moment and their own structures of feeling; they can only be aware of their own experience and how it colors their views of the past (Williams 2006, 36–38). Lawrence Grossberg translates Williams's structure of feeling into a broader conception of affect:

"[Everyday life] is not always the same, but a historical articulation of that realm of 'how one lives.' Everyday life is not simply the material relationships, it is a structure of feeling, and that is where I want to locate affect. This is what I call 'territorializing.' It is about how you can move across those relationships, where you can and cannot invest, what matters and in what ways" (2010, 313). Grossberg speaks to how the feelings that circulate through culture enable individuals and communities to invest in spaces and communities and decide what is important. Territorializing is another way of characterizing how *La Haine*'s focus on feeling permitted mid-1990s French audiences to match Kassovitz's film to the French suburbs. Furthermore, it helps explain how *La Haine*'s stylized abstraction allows international and subsequent audiences to relate the film to their own historical contexts. It enables, in other words, the kinds of differential viewing and localization that have become a common way to talk about transnational forms of cinema.

Grossberg's territorializing is already operative in the French poetic realist films that I mentioned earlier, though fully arguing this point would take us too far afield. What is important to note here is that we find 1930s poetic realist films being criticized as inadequately realist, just like *La Haine*. For example, Bazin criticized Carné's *Daybreak* for its lack of any reference to the political events of the day in terms of verbal allusion, discussion among characters, or visual records such as posters, newspapers, and the like (1998, 93, 96). Yet this kind of criticism misunderstands how films that focus on feeling in the manner I have been discussing can be political. In the case of *La Haine*, a rap song or an intertextual reference to *Taxi Driver* may not document the historical causes of a particular suburban street protest in France, but such moments do build relationships based on feeling among viewers who might not have shared historical experience in common. *La Haine* invites viewers who do and do not come from the French suburbs to care about the banlieues on screen for themselves through the feelings elicited by the dense network of cultural references. It is not about introducing suburban characters into legitimate French culture on screen, but about introducing viewers into cultural references that can mediate the suburbs and that are themselves connected to other cultures and places.

The origins of Kassovitz's own interest in the societal difficulties facing the banlieues testify to how the shared feelings of culture can build relationships across social divides. Kassovitz grew up in a privileged middle-class family, and his parents had extensive experience in the film and television industries. He first became interested in the difficulties of the French suburbs when he began frequenting the underground hip-hop scene in France in the 1980s and 1990s, which heavily drew on the conventions of American hip hop and gangster rap. American hip-hop culture, including its expressions both in music and in cinema, provided him a way into the challenges that second- and third-generation French citizens in the Parisian suburbs were facing. It is easy to call this inauthentic, but I prefer to see it as a point of entry. Through the film's style and intertextual references, Kassovitz attempts to recreate his own personal trajectory into the suburbs. We can see this most directly in *La Haine*'s complex, nonhierarchical layering of cultural references, which is a compositional approach adapted to the cinema from hip-hop music.

NONHIERARCHICAL LAYERING: HIP HOP MEETS THE CHANSON RÉALISTE

Hip hop can be understood in terms of ethnicity, race, or national belonging; however, I argue that its compositional strategies are the most essential for understanding *La Haine*. Cultural and legal theorist Richard Schur has recently criticized Anglo-American hip hop scholarship because it "downplays [hip hop's] production to focus on the violence, misogyny, or cultural nationalism of its lyrics" (2009, 46). For Schur, hip hop as a form of music and performance art is based on sampling, the layering of samples, the flow and rupture of rhythms created through layering, and a use of parody and irony (2009, 43). Sampling and layering are modes of creative recontextualization that seek to transform and comment on preexisting source materials without destroying the pleasures of listening to a song or dancing to a break. In a 2019 interview, Kassovitz implicitly suggests this reading of *La Haine* in retrospect when he argues that a popular social cinema is no longer possible in France: "For decades, cinema was at the center of debates. But that's over. This idea that one could make cinema like one makes hip hop, wake people up while entertaining them. This utopia of edutainment by cinema is completely obsolete" (Lalanne and Joyard 2018). While the term *edutainment* carries pejorative connotations, Kassovitz's formulation—"wake people up while entertaining them"—offers important clues for understanding how *La Haine* engages with both French and American cultural references.

Discussions of the impact of American hip hop on *La Haine* have tended to concentrate on Kassovitz's use of rap, soul, and funk music in the soundtrack and his selection of recognizable visual markers from hip-hop culture, including B-boy clothing, graffiti/tagging, and break dancing (Vincendeau 2005, 30–31; Tarr 2005, 63–64; Higbee 2006, 79). Vincendeau notes that the film's audiences thought they heard more hip-hop and rap music in the soundtrack than they actually did (2005, 56–57). In part, this is because of the French hip-hop compilation album that was released simultaneously with the film, but it is likewise because hip hop is *also* about image, dress, movement, and gesture, and *La Haine*'s audiences saw all of these in the film. However, I argue that Kassovitz's hip-hop aesthetic is fundamentally about the sampling and layering of cultural borrowings from both American *and* French culture. The DJ scene, which incorporates a well-known chanson réaliste into a rap song, represents the best way to theorize Kassovitz's project in the film.[3] *La Haine* appropriates, blends, and layers samples of many kinds of culture to create a popular, transnational French cinema appropriate to suburban multiculture.

Sampling involves the exploration and reinterpretation of the past to produce new, hybrid meanings. The performance in the DJ sequence reflects the collaboration between DJ Cut Killer (who is the person mixing on screen) and the French hip-hop group Suprême NTM (NTM stands for *Nique ta mère* [Fuck your mother]). Cut Killer is wearing a Cypress Hill T-shirt, which references a West Coast hip-hop group that formed in the early 1990s. The song itself, "Nique la police," is primarily a French-language cover of American rap group NWA's 1988 song "Fuck tha Police." In fact, the French song's title is a literal translation of the American one. The DJ sequence incorporates two other samples, one from KRS-One's "Sound of Da Police" (1993) and one from Édith Piaf's iconic "Non, je ne regrette rien."

Kassovitz's use of Piaf solicits distinct forms of recognition from different audiences. "Non, je ne regrette rien" is Piaf's most recognizable song, both in France and abroad (Bret 1988, 122), and thus its use in *La Haine* suggests a concern with international accessibility. Piaf sang and recorded it in late 1960 at the height of the Algerian War, when French citizens were grappling with the question of what France would look like without its vanishing colonial empire (Burke 2011, 194). Members of the Organisation de l'armée secrète (Organization of the Secret Army [OAS]) reportedly sang the song instead of "La Marseillaise" as they returned to France at the end of the war (Crosland 2002, 209). The OAS was a subset of French Army officers who committed acts of terrorism to slow the process of decolonization when it became apparent that then president Charles de Gaulle favored Algerian independence.

However, the song and its singer signified more than the difficulties of the Algerian War. As Vincendeau points out, Piaf looks back to—and indeed represents the culmination of—the French chanson réaliste from the early twentieth century as figured by an earlier generation of singers, including Damia and Fréhel. Vincendeau notes that the chanson réaliste tradition and French poetic realism shared a common stylized iconography of working-class neighborhoods, with their rainy cobblestone streets, village dances (*bals musettes*), unassuming buildings, and accordions (1987, 107–108). Keith Reader characterizes the chanson réaliste and French poetic realism as parallel phenomena, both nostalgic for a vanishing France. He interprets Kassovitz's citation of Piaf's song in *La Haine* as an ironic gesture to the tradition's obsolescence (2003, 207). In a similar vein, Powrie argues with respect to contemporary French cinema in general that the use of French songs from "historical periods" serves to evoke nostalgia "for a lost way of life under the pressure of Americanization, nostalgia for the family that fragile 'tribal' communities are replacing" (2015, 542). I suggest, however, that the presence of "Non, je ne regrette rien" in *La Haine* marks not the chanson réaliste's decadence, obsolescence, or nostalgia, but rather its ongoing relevance for the late twentieth century as an example of how the feelings at work in popular music like the chanson réaliste or poetic realist films from the Popular Front era can potentially model new forms of community and belonging.

If Piaf's song were entirely obsolete, rap music would supplant it; rather, the opposite is true in *La Haine*. The DJ's performance begins with rap, and Piaf's song later takes over the foreground with the occasional "Nique la police" in the background. It is important to note that Kassovitz inverts the song's associations from the Algerian War period. While it once was used to signify a lack of regret about the violence of the Algerian War and about the French colonial enterprise generally, in Kassovitz's film, the generations of French citizens descended from France's former colonial subjects suggest that they have no regrets about street demonstrations as a form of protest against a government and a dominant culture from which they feel excluded. Piaf's song marks their knowledge of French culture and situates their struggle within French history.

Moreover, the presence of the chanson réaliste underscores the importance of feeling in *La Haine*'s representation of the suburbs. Here, the song's evident nostalgia comes into play. It is true that images of large-scale apartment block housing have replaced the pastoral, small-town iconography of working-class *faubourgs* or neighborhoods, familiar from poetic realist films like *Daybreak*. However, the emotional tonalities of mid-twentieth-century popular traditions nonetheless inform Kassovitz's representation of suburban alienation in late twentieth-century France. With the interpolation of a sample from the chanson réaliste tradition, Kassovitz suggests an analogy between the historical struggles of the early and mid-twentieth-century working class and those of the unemployed suburban youth of the 1990s. Fundamentally, both groups share a lack of access to self-determination, solidarity, acceptable living conditions, and adequate employment in the wake of the pressures of modernization, urbanization, and now globalization.

The song, while quintessentially French, suggests that it is difficult to disentangle French and American references in *La Haine*. Piaf's song came out in 1960, a time of transition in French popular music. The chanson réaliste began to diminish in importance as jazz, rock, and the blues flowed to France from the United States. Johnny Hallyday, often called the French Elvis, said that he loved Piaf and that her emotional style influenced him, even though her work seemed antithetical to the rock and jazz that were taking over pop music and that he himself was using in his songs (Burke 2011, 200–201). In an analogous manner, Kassovitz uses the song for its emotional mixture of melancholy and defiance. The staging of the DJ sequence in *La Haine* suggests rap's ability to link people and urban space through music, and Kassovitz's DJ performs a similar function to the DJ in Lee's *Do the Right Thing*. However, the scene also harks back to Jean Gabin's musical number on the rooftops of the Kasbah in Julien Duvivier's *Pépé le Moko* (1937), which creates a sense of community among the Kasbah's inhabitants. In the DJ sequence, the strategic use of samples and the scratching together of songs and beats is itself a live performance that fosters community. According to David Looseley, rap's sampling aesthetic was originally intended to allow would-be rappers to make music with minimal training and equipment (2003, 55). In this reading, sampling is a democratic musical form that does not require years of study in order to master instrumental, vocal, or compositional techniques, like more elite or legitimate forms of classical or jazz music. *La Haine*'s sample of Piaf taps into both the chanson réaliste's perceived democratic nature and its nostalgia for "authentic," community-forming feelings created through live performance.

The DJ encapsulates the film's hip-hop compositional approach and its focus on feeling, but these define the film as a whole and work alongside its engagement with melodrama, another cinematic form that emphasizes feeling. Here, melodrama enables Kassovitz to create feelings of innocence and guilt and moral outrage and virtue around police violence. Sharma and Sharma argue that *La Haine* contests stereotyped media representations of violence in the banlieues through an intensified realism that emphasizes affect, rather than through a modernist or self-reflexive realism. They suggest that *La Haine* most resembles classical melodrama in that "the mise en scène attempts to present the anxiety of exclusion and the alienation of the violence" (2000, 110). In her influential analysis of the racial politics of melodrama, Linda Williams has argued that melodrama is not "a submerged, or embedded, tendency, or genre, within classical realism, but that it has more often itself been the dominant form of popular moving-picture narrative," especially when "[literature, stage, film, and television] see[k] to engage with moral questions" (2001, 23, 17). For Williams, melodrama is not simply one genre among many, but rather the mode of moral legibility that defines many popular Hollywood genres, from action to science fiction and from comedy to musicals. Williams argues that "the emotional content and vivid style regarded as excess, in other words, much more often constitutes the mainstream even as it continues to be perceived as excess. And most important in this mainstream are the entertainment needs of a modern, rationalist, democratic, capitalist, industrial, and now postindustrial society seeking moral legibility under new conditions of moral ambiguity. In other words, the ongoing loss of moral certainty has been compensated for by increasingly sensational, commodified productions of pathos and action" (Williams 2001, 23). To return to Bourdieu's terms, melodrama challenges the bourgeois aesthetic disposition of distance and distaste for embodied responses to art, which might help explain why some commentators on *La Haine* express uneasiness with the film's politics.

The turn to feeling resulting from the loss of moral certainty is especially true, Williams suggests, for forms of American popular culture that deal with questions of race and class. She argues that in the post–civil rights era of color blindness, race assumes within "the melodramatic 'text of muteness' . . . a heightened mode of expressivity as a dialectic of feelings—of sympathy and antipathy—that dare not speak its name" (2001, 16–23, 300). It is hardly surprising, then, that the supposed excesses of spectacle and feeling that characterize melodrama in all its forms might also have currency in a country like France that is even more rigidly color-blind than the United States. Yet, the representation of class conflicts through melodrama was already how poetic realist films in the 1930s operated. However, these turned around class rather than race, and this is where the stakes of Kassovitz's layering of American and French references lie. By turning to American hip hop, New Hollywood films, and Black urban films, Kassovitz can activate the melodramatic tradition in French poetic realism but use American references to bring race and ethnicity into view in a cultural context defined by color-blind universalism. However, Kassovitz's use of Hollywood references is not a simple question of wholesale appropriation, but rather one of adaptation and transformation for the particular needs of a French social context, specifically the importance of solidarity over individualism. Through Vinz in *La Haine*, who reflects the excesses of individualism that characterize some masculine American genres like the action film or the gangster film, Kassovitz reorients these genres toward a collective social vision, a gesture that we will see repeated in many of the films examined later in this book.

VINZ AND THE VAGARIES OF LIVING GENRE FILMS

La Haine rearticulates American film genres in relation to French suburban communities primarily through the character of Vinz. Didier Lapeyronnie has argued that young people from the banlieues are often "derealized by the gaze of dominant society" and thus suffer from a lack of self-images, leading to theatrical modes of behavior (2008, 17). Saïd and Hubert also perform different kinds of identity in the film, but Vinz is the most self-conscious in his imitations of the tough-guy forms of masculinity found in American action and gangster films. Following Judith Butler's influential account of gender as inherently performative (1999, 33), Todd Reeser has argued that masculinity in general possesses no original, authoritative model; instead, it is an individualized and shared performance that draws on previously existing models circulating within a given culture or space. Akin to a style, masculinity takes shape through the ritualized repetition of corporeal practices and codes by individuals over time (Reeser 2010, 81–85).

These codes are learned horizontally in the film through peers and media, rather than vertically through families and fathers. The absence of father figures in *La Haine*, with the possible exception of the older Jewish man in the bathroom scene, has often been noted (Vincendeau 2005, 65). Lacking models of masculinity that are passed down vertically through generations, characters in the film orient their search horizontally toward other men their own age, toward men slightly older than them, and, most importantly, toward mass culture, especially the cinema. Unlike in *Games of Love and Chance*, we never see the school system in *La Haine*, so it is through performances of suburban masculinity and media consumption that Kassovitz's film explores questions of cultural transmission and mixing. Media representations are especially important to understanding masculinity as performance because, as Reeser explains, they simultaneously "reveal a form of masculinity that already exists in culture" and "construct (or help construct) the masculinity that they depict in culture" (2010, 25). This is why I have been suggesting *La Haine*'s relationship to American cultural references is dynamic, not passive.

Posters of action heroes Sylvester Stallone and Arnold Schwarzenegger adorn the wall of Vinz's bedroom, indicating the importance of American cinema for the construction of his masculinity. This influence is even more pronounced in *La Haine*'s original script than in the final film. Myrto Konstanarakos points out that according to the script, Vinz was supposed to see American movies featuring Schwarzenegger and Stallone during his peregrinations through the Parisian multiplex. The script also mentioned an older but no less virile model of masculinity, Clint Eastwood, and the Disney film *Bambi* (1942), a choice perhaps meant to suggest that Vinz has a sentimental side beneath the tough exterior (Konstantarakos 1999, 164). The actual scene in the film when Vinz hides from the Paris police in a movie theater preserves the juxtaposition of violence with animation. Toward the end of the sequence, Kassovitz cuts to an image of Vinz sitting next to a mother who has taken her young son to the film. The disjunctive cut dilates time in such a way that the viewer is not sure how long Vinz has been there or how many films he has watched. The image of mother and son conspicuously draws attention to the lack of father figures. Vinz, ignorant of their presence next to him, forms a gun with his hand presumably in imitation of the film, a gesture he repeats several times over the course of *La Haine*. The young boy a few seats over then proceeds to imitate this same gesture. The scene illustrates how models of masculinity are transmitted horizontally from young men to young men, rather than vertically from father to son. The models transmitted, moreover, are triangulated through movies, television, hip hop, rap, and other forms of mass culture.

Vinz's attempt to imitate film heroes is most strongly felt in the scenes when he threatens to shoot a police officer. His desire to literally enter into the movies he has been watching places him in the lineage of the Jean-Paul Belmondo character in *Breathless*, who, in Barry Keith Grant's words, goes "to the literal extreme of attempting to live generic conventions directly" (2012, 134). In Godard's film, the literalness of these genre conventions was intended as satire. For Kassovitz, Vinz is a meditation on the positive and negative consequences of individuals actually trying to live out the models they receive from media. Though Vinz proves perfectly capable of pulling the imaginary trigger in the Cineplex, he cannot do so in real life. When he stumbles upon an overtly racist skinhead played by none other than Kassovitz himself, Vinz draws his gun and considers the possibility of finally making the cinematic images he has consumed into reality. While Vinz has the gun trained on the skinhead, Hubert urges Vinz to go ahead, all the while knowing that his friend is either unable or unwilling. After a dramatic pause, Vinz withers and lets the skinhead flee. Hubert's unmasking of Vinz's tough-guy persona exposes the vulnerability beneath the posture—the same vulnerability that would have led Vinz to cry in front of Disney's *Bambi*. When Vinz's heroic path to self-affirmation by becoming a suburban Stallone or Schwarzenegger falls apart, *La Haine* shifts the tone of its final part from the outward-directed violence of the gangster or action film genres to the inward-directed suffering and pathos of melodrama.

The film's ending carries a tragic inevitability that is signaled from the beginning and marked throughout by the ticking clocks that punctuate the film.

Figure 1.2 Vinz at the movies. *La Haine*, 1995.

Hubert's opening monologue about a man falling from a fifty-story building foreshadows the ending: the viewer will spend the film waiting for the inevitable end of a long, slow fall. Vincendeau quotes an interview with Kassovitz in which he explains, "I knew the ending before I knew the storyline. Everything is about the end, the last five seconds" (2005, 44). Tom Conley and Jenny Lefcourt suggest that the film's pathos has its roots in a "residual classicism," which is another way of characterizing what I have been calling abstraction in the film. They write, "The gun ... becomes the 'floating signifier' of violence, like a letter of fate," and "the film obeys the Aristotelian 'unities' in its circumspection of time, space, and action" (1998, 231). The ticking clock in *La Haine* morphs into the sounds of an alarm clock during the police repression midway through the film, but the ticking resumes just after. Vinz's murder, not the second street protest, is the film's true paroxysm.

Kassovitz's film ends in a martyrdom that is symbolic of the social and economic forces oppressing the suburban poor. In *La Haine*, a sincere lament about the futility of violence underlies the masculine posturing of the police and the suburban trio. The final scene takes place after the trio returns to the suburbs from their night in Paris. Vinz gives the gun he found over to Hubert for safekeeping. As Vinz walks away from Saïd and Hubert, a police car arrives out of nowhere. The train station is devoid of people and activity, again suggesting that viewers are in a timeless space. The three policemen immediately begin roughing up Vinz. One of the cops ostentatiously holds a gun to Vinz's head in a way that echoes Vinz's earlier performance of the tough-guy cinematic hero. Kassovitz films this moment in an intimate two-shot that accentuates the size of the phallic gun. The framing of the shot makes it somewhat visually ambiguous whether Vinz or the cop is holding the weapon, suggesting that the ongoing escalation of violence is in fact a form of collective suicide. The gun goes off by accident, and so the cycle of violence completes itself once more. When the cop shoots Vinz, the other two policemen vanish. With their disappearance, the narrative relinquishes any remaining semblance of chronological time and verisimilar space. Hubert, who has advocated nonviolence throughout the film, now pulls the gun Vinz just gave him on the police officer, and the final shot is of Hubert and the officer each pointing a gun at the other. *La Haine* ends with the sound of a gunshot but cuts to black before viewers see who pulled the trigger. Through this ambiguity, Kassovitz suggests that the logic of violence exceeds the psychology or motivation of any one person, and *La Haine* thus echoes the stakes of the racialized forms of melodrama that Linda Williams has analyzed in the US context. Drawing on the work of Lauren Berlant, Williams argues that at a time when citizenship under the promise of formal equality does not guarantee substantive equality, "a second model of citizenship has emerged around the visible emotions of suffering bodies that, in the very activity of suffering, demonstrate worth as citizens" (2001, 24). Through modulation of feeling, *La Haine* transforms Vinz into a martyr of police violence that demands the recognition of those excluded from dominant society, much like the murders and suicides that ended poetic realist films from the 1930s.

La Haine's ending can be read in this light as a gesture that inscribes Vinz's death within a marginalized community whose boundaries are not fully specified. An ethics of solidarity replaces the American gangster's unbridled self-interest and quest to affirm himself through decisive action. Early in *La Haine*, viewers see *Scarface*'s iconic slogan "The World is Yours" (*La vie est à vous*) written on a billboard advertisement. Near the end of the film, Saïd rewrites this slogan with spray paint to read "The World is Ours" (*La vie est à nous*). Conley and Lefcourt read this rewriting as a reference to Renoir's 1936 militant Popular Front film of the same name (1998, 235). Though Renoir's and Kassovitz's films differ at a stylistic and thematic level, the reference further suggests that *La Haine* attempts to evoke memories of French Popular Front cinema alongside those of Hollywood films. While one could argue that *La Haine*'s rewriting of *Scarface*'s slogan is ironic, Hubert takes up Saïd's inscription of an *us* in the final retelling of the fall story that closes the film. Crucially, it is no longer the

Figure 1.3 Saïd rewrites *Scarface*'s famous line from the individualistic *you* to the collective *us*. *La Haine*, 1995.

story of a man falling from a fifty-story building, as in the prologue, but that of a whole society falling. By changing the individualistic slogan from Howard Hawks's *Scarface* to embrace the collective destiny of a society, Kassovitz sets the deaths at the hands of the police at the scale of France as a whole. This rescaling of Hollywood genres from the level of the individual to that of society is one that we will see repeated in the other films that pair Hollywood genres with the spaces of the banlieues, discussed later in this book.

Despite the film's engagement with the question of police violence in the French suburbs, its abstraction from a specific time and place and its engagement with an international set of cultural references enable it to speak to various contexts. The film serves as a barometer for many different storms made up of race and class conflicts in peripheral spaces, and that is why it can still feel so real and relevant some thirty years after its release. As long as there is police violence against minority communities in France or elsewhere, *La Haine* will feel realistic, even though it is not. In this aspect, the film represents an innovative blend of localization to France and transnational address that manages to be politically engaged with the challenges of the French suburbs while also understandable and relevant to international audiences. *La Haine* does not sacrifice the pleasures of genre and style for realism and historical contextualization, nor does it see French cultural references as opposed to American ones. Rather, it suggests that it is possible to layer and mix them together in a film that is socially engaged and expresses an inclusive sense of universalism.

CONCLUSION

Two of the most important banlieue films made in France, *Games of Love and Chance* and *La Haine*, represent very different approaches to making a socially engaged film about France's suburban peripheries. They employ distinct aesthetic strategies and articulate divergent notions of cultural value. If critics accept the categories of realism and experimental aestheticism as the primary forms of political cinema, then *Games of Love and Chance* is arguably more progressive, not just because it was made by a director of minority origins, but because it corresponds to one of the more generally accepted categories of political cinema, namely realism. It also frames the integration of France's minority communities through the legitimate forms of culture that characterize France's dominant national community. However, this can also be viewed as a problematic gesture of assimilating France's minorities to the tradition of republican universalism and erasing or minimizing their own cultural backgrounds. Kechiche, though an industry outsider in terms of his origins and his autodidacticism, chose to fit himself and France's Maghrebi communities, which he represented, into the recognized traditions and career paths of French art and auteurist cinema.

Kassovitz, by contrast, made very different choices. While he is arguably an insider in terms of the cultural capital he inherited through his family, his early films focus on multiculture and suburban communities. While still working loosely within the tradition of auteurism in the cinema that descends from the French New Wave, Kassovitz nevertheless looks to Hollywood cinema and American and African American mass culture to redefine the place of the suburbs on screen. Not all suburban youth, the film suggests, must assimilate to the dominant culture in order to have value or virtue, to use the language of melodrama; mixing and coexistence are possible. Kassovitz sought to make this distinction even during the promotional events surrounding the film. When *La Haine* won an award at the Cannes Film Festival, Kassovitz did not serve the traditional champagne and canapés at the celebratory party; instead, he served Coca-Cola, beer, and merguez sausages as a means of calling attention to the different kinds of food eaten in the banlieues (Vincendeau 2005, 81). Though it was possibly a pedantic gesture, it nevertheless reveals that Kassovitz's ambition in *La Haine* was as much about changing the kinds of cinema that the French industry valued as it was about shifting the images of France's suburban communities on screen. I contend that these two aspects go together, as they do for many of the other films examined later in this book.

Kassovitz, however, quickly grew tired of the ways critics and commentators alike overemphasized and interpreted *La Haine*'s social meanings. Despite his clear concern for the police violence and marginalization in the French banlieues, he did not want to be pigeonholed as the voice of the suburbs for the rest of his career. As he put it in an interview, he did not see himself as a French Ken Loach (Vincendeau 2005, 96). What has puzzled many critics about Kassovitz's subsequent career is his turn to genre pictures more overt than *La Haine*: *Assassin(s)*, *Crimson Rivers*, *Gothika*, and *Babylon A.D.* Those with bemused reactions forget that despite his cinephile pedigree, Kassovitz originally began his career as a genre filmmaker. His early influences included Steven Spielberg and George Lucas, and his first Super 8 films were genre exercises: horror, science fiction, and action-adventure movies (Higbee 2006, 9, 12). I suggest that his films have always sought to balance entertainment and genre with social engagement. The disappointment some might feel at Kassovitz's subsequent career trajectory toward making films that more openly espouse genre and feature less social engagement, especially in his Hollywood films, is understandable. However, if one views this as a betrayal of *La Haine*'s promise, I suggest this reaction indicates a misunderstanding of what *La Haine* was. Even his last film, the largely unsuccessful *Rebellion*, returns to *La Haine*'s type of popular social filmmaking in representing separatist violence in New Caledonia during the 1980s through the action-adventure genre. I am not trying to recuperate Kassovitz's post–*La Haine* films—far from it. Rather, I have brought into view *La Haine*'s particular blend of genre tropes, stylization, social engagement, and moral feeling so that we can then see how this paradigm has a future not in Kassovitz himself, but in the other films and filmmakers that I will examine throughout the rest of this book.

Unlike *Games of Love and Chance*, *La Haine* traffics in spectacle, Hollywood genres, and highly stylized images whose purpose is to elicit some of the strong moral feelings and legibility that characterize melodrama. This technique is not unequivocally progressive, because it cannot be read in just one way. Linda Williams, in the conclusion to her book about the "melodrama of black and white," writes that she does not want to conclude that all melodrama is reactionary, though she admits that it sometimes, and possibly often, is. She ultimately speculates that melodrama may well define an American sense of social justice, and in her view, it is more important to understand how it works in culture so as to recognize when and where its "insidious" power operates. Unlike other scholars, she is under no illusion that it will imminently disappear or that scholarly commentary or critical filmmaking practices could end it (Williams 2001, 308–310). I come down more strongly on the side of her argument that views the stylistic resources of Hollywood genres, which often draw on the spectacle and excess of melodrama, as sometimes being progressive. This is the case, I argue, of a film like *La Haine*, as it continues to be an inescapable reference in banlieue cinema and still speaks to audiences today. It is a film that manages to be eminently universal in its address to viewers at home and abroad. Other films considered later in this book do not necessarily work as well as *La Haine* in terms of their popularity, critical success, or progressive engagement with French suburbs, but they do seek to build on *La Haine*'s use of the stylistic resources of popular cinema and genres, especially Hollywood genres, to deal with questions of ongoing race-, ethnic-, and class-based exclusion in contemporary France, as much through the feelings embedded in shared culture as through argument and discourse.

In this chapter, I have not been arguing that *La Haine* is necessarily a better strategy for representing suburban multiculture on screen than that represented by *Games of Love and Chance*. Kechiche's move from autodidact outsider to recognized establishment auteur is an important path to legitimacy, both for himself and the communities he represents. I will consider the opposite and potentially more problematic trajectory from auteur to banlieue filmmaker in the sixth chapter with Sciamma's *Girlhood*. Rather, I have been suggesting here that *La Haine* is *another* strategy, one whose artistic genealogy and afterlives have been less appreciated because of the anxieties *La Haine* raises about mass culture and Americanism in a country that often defines itself against them. My own position is pragmatist, and I contend that *all* strategies for bringing visibility to France's multiculture and the marginalization of the banlieues can be complementary. The pragmatist would try to develop and encourage all of them, for one cannot know in advance where they may lead and what kinds of films might result from them. If there is an a priori to this book, it is that filmmakers who take up questions of suburban marginalization through mainstream French, American, and global genre vocabularies should be taken as seriously as filmmakers like Kechiche, who do so through the traditional parameters of French legitimate culture and auteurist art cinema. It is the knowing and unknowing descendants of *La Haine*'s blend of genre filmmaking and social engagement with the suburbs that I will analyze in the rest of this book.

NOTES

1. Kassovitz's film is best known through its original French title rather than *Hate*, even in English-language scholarship, and consequently I will refer to it as *La Haine* throughout this book.

2. For a longer discussion of French poetic realism and its connections to *La Haine*, see Pettersen 2015.

3. Kelley Conway defines the French chanson réaliste tradition as songs sung by "world-weary," "knowing," and sexualized women about "prostitution, urban poverty, and female desire." Active around the turn of the twentieth century, *chanteuses réalistes*, whom Conway characterizes as "ancestors" of Edith Piaf, were figures capable of uniting working-class communities (2004, 2).

TWO

LUC BESSON'S EUROPACORP AND PARKOUR IN THE SUBURBS

WHILE MATHIEU KASSOVITZ, WHOM WE considered in the previous chapter, continues to act, most recently in Canal+'s successful spy TV series *The Bureau* (*Le Bureau des légendes*, 2015–2020), his difficult personality and his focus on genre-oriented filmmaking when he does direct have reduced him to something of an isolated figure in the French film landscape. He has not achieved the same explosive success as he had with *La Haine* (1995) with his subsequent films in France or in Hollywood, and his difficult personality online and in interviews reveals him to have several of the enfant terrible traits of some French auteurs. *La Haine* represented a pathbreaking fusion of commercial genre filmmaking, auteurist intertextuality, and social interest in the banlieues; however, it would take another filmmaker and producer, Luc Besson, to attempt to give institutional form to what the style of Kassovitz's film implied.

Besson came of age with the same cocktail of Hollywood movies that Kassovitz did, and he shares some of the same investments in genre filmmaking and mainstream audiences. Besson began making movies a decade before Kassovitz, and some of Besson's early films helped show Kassovitz that genre movies could work in France (Higbee 2006, 12, 39–40). However, Besson had none of Kassovitz's family pedigree in the media industry, and he began his career in movies as a young, diploma-less autodidact observing film sets through internships, much as Abdellatif Kechiche did. Besson is internationally known for his work as a director both in France and Hollywood. The films that established his reputation include *Subway* (1985), *Nikita* (*La femme Nikita*, 1990), *Léon: The Professional* (*Léon*, 1994), and *The Fifth Element* (*Le cinquième élément*, 1997). Not content to be a misunderstood filmmaker in the wilderness, Besson, unlike

Kassovitz, sought to institutionalize a uniquely Gallic brand of commercial filmmaking, one that both competes and collaborates with Hollywood studios.

While Besson is still well known as a director, since the early 2000s, he has devoted more time to producing films and developing the business offshoots of his European studio than to directing. Taking as his model the vertically integrated Hollywood studio, Besson thought to bring all aspects of the production process to the French banlieues. After some thirteen years of negotiation, fundraising, and delays, the Cité du cinéma, a French version of England's Pinewood Studios or Italy's Cinecittà, finally opened outside Paris in the French banlieues on September 21, 2012. Besson and his collaborators chose to locate the Cité du cinéma in the Seine-Saint-Denis region: the so-called *ninety-three*, nicknamed for the first two digits of its postal code. This area was one of the flash points of the 2005 suburban protests that spread well into Paris. In the city of Saint-Denis, Besson's team renovated a 1930s art deco power station to house soundstages, postproduction facilities, corporate offices, and two different film schools. Education, we might say, is the uniquely Gallic addition to the American tradition of vertical integration. EuropaCorp, a company Besson had founded in 2000 as a French rival to and sometimes collaborator with the American major studios, moved its headquarters to the Cité du cinéma campus. The École nationale supérieure Louis Lumière, one of France's two top state film schools, also relocated, and Besson opened a free two-year film school for those without financial means or formal degrees.

The choice of the culturally and economically marginalized space of the French suburbs is part of a broader strategy on the part of Besson and EuropaCorp to harness the countercultural charge of the banlieues to reorient the values of French cinema and French culture more broadly. While Besson's efforts to establish a commercial model of filmmaking have been regularly noted in the secondary literature, the importance of the French suburbs for these efforts has not been systematically analyzed.[1] France's deep-rooted cultural exceptionalism (*l'exception culturelle*) has historically emphasized elite culture over popular, high forms over low and a culture of distinction over an egalitarian one (Bourdieu 1984). Besson and EuropaCorp's efforts over the past two decades seek to carve out alternate spaces and paths for commercial French film production within the constraints of Hollywood's strong performance at the domestic box office, French critical tastes that scorn the popular, and state funding mechanisms that favor small-scale auteurist films. While many European filmmakers who have shared Besson's desires have left for Hollywood, Frédéric Sojcher suggests that "the specificity of Luc Besson . . . is his desire to reach the world film market without expatriating" (2002, 151). EuropaCorp seeks to create industrial and cultural shifts in France, confirming Valentina Vitali and Paul Willemen's observation that cinema is both an industry and a "cluster of cultural strategies" (2006, 2). Besson and EuropaCorp's cultural strategy in the 2000s and 2010s is not a negation of French culture, but rather a creative adaptation of Frenchness to the constraints of global film markets.

This cultural strategy extends to certain of EuropaCorp's films, for, as Elena Oliete-Aldea, Beatriz Oria, and Juan A. Tarancón point out, "films are both agents and expressions of globalization" (2015, 5). Three of the films produced and cowritten by Besson and distributed by his company—*Yamakasi, the Samurai of Modern Times* (*Yamakasi, les samouraïs des temps modernes*, 2001), *District B13* (*Banlieue 13*, 2004), and *District 13: Ultimatum* (*Banlieue 13: Ultimatum*, 2009)—have become cult hits in France and abroad. All three focus on the banlieues and foreground the urban sport and martial art of parkour as a means of Gallicizing commercial and popular genre cinema. The cultural messaging of these films, I argue, helped create the mythology of EuropaCorp's distinct popular brand of filmmaking, one rooted in the banlieues.

With Besson's mini-major studio, this strategy has produced mixed results in terms of the studio's finances and the longevity of the various institutions that have grown up around it. Besson's own personal volatility has played its part in the ups and downs of the company, and the 2018 accusations of sexual assault against Besson in the age of #metoo have not helped matters (*Le Monde* 2018b; *Le Monde* 2019). This chapter does not seek to recuperate his reputation, but rather to demonstrate that not all his initiatives have been categorically negative. Ultimately, the institutions are more interesting than the man in what they have enabled for other filmmakers in France, some of whom will be examined later in this book.

In what follows, I disentangle the complex function of the banlieues, both real and imagined, for understanding Besson and EuropaCorp's institutional projects. Opening a mini-major studio was always a significant financial risk, and unfortunately, EuropaCorp's finances collapsed in 2019. Besson's *Valerian and the City of a Thousand Planets* (*Valérian et la Cité des mille planètes*, 2017) did not perform well enough at the box office to pay back its 198-million-euro budget, the highest ever for any French blockbuster. Controlling interest in EuropaCorp's stock was sold to an American holding company, and Besson has been reduced to the studio's artistic director rather than chairman of EuropaCorp's board (Vulser 2020a). What these changes mean for the studio's future is unclear. However, Besson and EuropaCorp's interlocking production, institutional, and education projects in the first two decades of the twenty-first century nevertheless reveal important lessons about the role the French suburbs can play in expanding audiences for French cinema internationally. The films that EuropaCorp produced that mix transnational genres, commercial filmmaking, and the banlieues represent important templates for other filmmakers in France who seek to make socially engaged genre films about the suburbs, rather than auteurist art films that privilege realism.

PARKOUR AS CULTURAL POLITICS

Parkour, or free running, as it is called in some parts of the world, is a physical practice that combines elements of sports, martial arts, gymnastics, and running. As parkour practitioners—*traceurs*, as they are known in French—run through the suburbs, they move through and over rather than around such architectural obstacles as buildings, fences, stairs, and benches, and they always look for the simplest and most efficient way to get between two points. The results are singular expressions of grace and freedom, often captured and shared on streaming platforms like YouTube (Archer 2010). With its roots in the French banlieues, parkour combines an autochthonous sense of Frenchness, a countercultural street credibility, and a social conscience.[2]

Parkour is often analyzed through Michel de Certeau's influential concept of tactics (Archer 2010; Marshall 2010). By tactics, Certeau means quotidian practices like reading and walking that use spaces and texts in ways other than those their creators intended (1984, 37–38). In the case of parkour, this involves using the constraints of the occasionally bland architecture in ways different from those that urban planners imagined for suburban neighborhoods. Such uses subvert established configurations of power without altering the built environment. We can extend the reading of parkour as an example of Certeau's tactics to see in the spatial practice a model of the ways Besson's producing activities and French genre films more broadly seek to negotiate the complex national and transnational pressures on French cinema and identity.

Transnationalism has been a contested term in film and media studies, and many scholars have criticized the simultaneous ubiquity of the term and the conceptual imprecision that often characterizes its usage. Nataša Ďurovičová and Kathleen Newman suggest that the term is best understood as a scalar reference situated above the level of the nation and below the level of the global or the world. In this, it is roughly equivalent to the word *international*; however, it does not imply the sense of equality that the latter term does. Instead, they argue that the prefix trans- gestures to inequalities, "unevenness," and "mobilities" (2010, ix–x). As a metaphor for transnational French film production and distribution, parkour gestures toward a similar creative negotiation

Figure 2.1 David Belle leaps from building to building in *District B13*, 2004.

of shifting local and global economic and cultural obstacles in imagining a popular national cinema.

EuropaCorp's interest in parkour and the physical spaces of the banlieues within and beyond their films constitutes, to speak in Marxist terms, an intervention in both the infrastructure and superstructure of the French film industry. As we will see, these two levels of intervention cannot be neatly separated and are mutually reinforcing. To consider both levels together, we need a mode of analysis that combines aspects of both auteurist and industrial approaches to film history. Beyond Susan Hayward and Phil Powrie's edited volume (2006), studies of Besson's work have tended to adopt an auteurist lens, meaning that they limit their scope to the films that Besson himself directed. Such an approach minimizes both Besson's institutional activities (EuropaCorp and the Cité du cinéma) and his work as a producer. Another important exception to this trend is Joshua Gleich, who argues that Besson should be viewed as a producer-auteur akin to Warner Brothers' Darryl Zanuck in the classical Hollywood period. However, Gleich makes this case through a stylistic analysis of the successful English-language action films that Besson has directed, written, or produced, thus separating him from the French industrial context of which he is also a part (2012).

Given that Besson is principally a producer and writer, these activities seem important in thinking about his place in French film history. At the same time, a purely industrial approach to EuropaCorp or to French commercial cinema more broadly also has trouble capturing the cultural stakes of Besson's recent activities. Isabelle Vanderschelden's two articles about the economics of French commercial cinema go a long way toward addressing the relative neglect of French popular cinema, particularly genre cinema (2007, 2008). However, they share some of the limitations Jerome Christensen attributes to industrial approaches to film history.[3] In addition, the specific deployment of suburban space in these films cannot be separated from the cultural politics of the banlieues in contemporary France or from Besson's choices to locate EuropaCorp and the Cité du cinéma in Saint-Denis. By opening the Cité du cinéma in a postindustrial suburban neighborhood, Besson believes that his "cinema city" will bring the area jobs, tourism, urban development, transportation connections to the rest of France, and perhaps even racial and economic integration.[4] In the case of EuropaCorp, the politics of production aligns with the politics of style.

What is more, Besson's use of the banlieues to imagine an alternative French popular culture has created a template for other producers and filmmakers to follow, and not just those associated with Besson or EuropaCorp. Besson's vision for EuropaCorp and the Cité du cinéma is part of an attempt at a broader reconfiguration of the power and taste structures that define French film culture. He employs his own megawatt star personality, cultivated over several decades of directing films on both sides of the Atlantic, to shift ideas about what French film and culture is or should be. For Besson, the marginalized banlieues serve as an alternative space within France, one that creatively fuses autochthonous and transnational forms of popular culture into a uniquely French brand.

Besson's recent work as producer exemplifies this new trend, but it also extends far beyond him and EuropaCorp. An investigation of Besson's work suggests that this tendency is not simply a question of film style as representation and the politics associated with it; rather, it is a model of thinking in which the means of production and the kinds of practices involved in making these films must be equally considered. Only this integrated form of analysis will allow us to understand what is taking place in these commercial banlieue genre films and why they might have important political resonance while still being examples of resolutely popular cinema. The figure for EuropaCorp's cultural politics of working creatively within constraints is the traceur, and the countercultural ideology of parkour can help us understand the spirit of Besson's interventions in the French film industry and how they relate to the French suburbs.

BESSON'S CERTAIN TENDENCY OF FRENCH CINEMA

Like the traceur's relationship to the built environment of the banlieues, Besson's production strategies seek neither to overturn Hollywood hegemony nor to accept it. The same could be said of his relationship to French culture. Even though Besson is often accused by French critics of being the harbinger of doom for French high culture, he wants to preserve a space for popular films in the French language and to bring the money of international film productions to France. Besson's strategy is a complicated dance of push and pull, much like the athleticism of the traceurs, who use the urban space that confines them to create beautiful expressions of movement and grace.

The relationships of various national cinemas to Hollywood have often been theorized in terms of power and metaphors of colonization. However, in an increasingly globalized, transnational age, other power centers, such as Bollywood, Nollywood, or East Asia, create a more distributed field of activity for film production. Nevertheless, Hollywood and the commercial big-budget mode of filmmaking for which it stands structure much of the discourse surrounding transnationalism in film and media studies. In their discursive analysis of how scholars have mobilized the term, Will Higbee and Song Hwee Lim point to two categories of usage: descriptive and proscriptive (2010, 8–9). I would add that taste hierarchies between elite and mainstream modes of film production often implicitly subtend proscriptive usages that seek to divide the ways scholars frame good and bad forms of transnationalism. In these accounts, Hollywood cinema, standing in for commercial and spectacle-oriented modes of production, functions alternately as American national cinema—that is, somehow not transnational—or as the hegemonic transnational cinema par excellence. For Mette Hjort, Elizabeth Ezra, and Terry Rowden, Hollywood and its mode of commercial filmmaking is one against which good forms of transnational cinema might be defined. Ezra and Rowden admit that non-Hollywood industries do in fact make "American-style action films" (2006, 3), and Hjort, in her typology of transnationalisms, makes space for a "globalizing transnationalism" that produces expensive films and seeks global markets to recoup production costs (2010, 21–22). Nevertheless, the remaining categories of her typology explicitly valorize experimental practices like Dogma 95, Nordic Film initiatives, and their imitators elsewhere (2010, 16–18). Ezra and Rowden, for their part, talk problematically about transnational cinema as if it were a self-evident category of films somehow "opposed to Hollywood" and "possessing a destabilizing potential" (2006, 11). Here, transnational cinema is synonymous with oppositional film practices and set against popular commercial filmmaking. In this kind of reading, EuropaCorp's parkour films would be either the antithesis of transnationalism or a bad version of transnationalism.

Anxiety about power differentials between Hollywood and other national cinemas is particularly acute in French critical discourse, especially after Hollywood films began to dominate the French box office in 1986 (Powrie 1997, 1). Since that time, and with few exceptions, Hollywood films have outperformed

French films. The French have long believed their culture to be exceptional rather than popular and to be deserving of legal protections to ensure its continued existence. Cinema plays a significant role in cultural pride in France, thanks in part to the international renown of the French New Wave. Early diplomatic and political maneuvers that sought to preserve this place include the renegotiation of the Blum-Byrnes accord around the end of World War II and the establishment of government subsidies for film production under Culture Minister André Malraux. As I explained in the introduction, the popular turn of cultural policy during the Jack Lang years in the 1980s and the negotiation of the General Agreement on Tariffs and Trades (GATT) treaty in 1993 reveal how France has persistently advocated in favor of economic exceptions for French cultural products, particularly films (Looseley 1995, 79, 197–209). The cultural legacy of the French New Wave and the economic legacy of funding structures have solidified a certain idea of what French cinema was, is, and should be.

As Jonathan Buchsbaum has argued, the conception of cinema that justified many of France's protectionist efforts during the GATT negotiations is the idea that it should be culturally and linguistically specific (2017, 90–96). Cultural specificity has been a point of contention in many of the debates surrounding the usefulness of the term *transnational*. For Hjort, Ezra, and Rowden, *global* might be the preferred word to talk about commercial films with "transnational appeal" like EuropaCorp's, because these films often shed cultural specificity. Similarly, Higbee and Lim take a position against the kinds of transnational films and scholarship that elide questions of cultural specificity and context. Indeed, they suggest that the kinds of transnational filmmaking that do this might be better approached using scalar concepts like *region* (Europe) or *supra-national* (2010, 9–11). Writing specifically about France, Martine Danan avoids the term *transnational* altogether, preferring to talk about a "post-national" turn in French cinema. By this, she means films that downplay any national distinctiveness except perhaps in terms of the local color afforded by production design. For her, such post-national films are those that focus on "excess spectacle," which seems to mean big-budget French films that would rival Hollywood on its own terms (2006, 177). Such sorting of transnational films into good objects (artistic, experimental, or culturally specific films) and bad objects (bland, decontextualized, and commercially oriented ones) betrays an investment in an auteurist art cinema framed largely in national terms. Tim Bergfelder has helpfully suggested that this positive valorization of art cinema depends on viewing it as a "quasi-ethical framework of cultural practice" (2005, 317).

French critical discourse has long scorned Besson as an Americanized director who focuses on making stylized yet vapid commercial fare for young audiences (Maule 2006, 23). Besson and his films often are vilified as the deplorable *other* of an authentically French auteurist art cinema. In a particularly vicious article that elicited a defamation lawsuit from Besson, Hervé Deplasse characterized him as a mere businessman and a cinematic "sponge" who recycles the meager dreams of an infantilized young consumerist audience. Deplasse's Besson is not an artist, and he does not possess any knowledge of film history; his films are mere marketing machines. In Deplasse's estimation, a true French cinema, or a true cinema *tout court*, should be surprising, timely, anticommercial, and countercultural—in short, composed only of works of "art." Deplasse compares Besson to an exaggerated Georges Lucas who thinks only of money and carefully calibrates the "parameters" of his films to maximize profits.[5]

Film historian and critic Antoine de Baecque articulates the dangers of a figure like Besson more bleakly in an op-ed piece responding to a flash point in the culture wars of the early 2000s. During a press conference in December 2001, the president of Vivendi-Universal, Jean-Marie Messier, was asked about the risks of the Americanization of French cinema, to which he replied that French cultural exceptionalism was dead (Riding 2001; Poirrier 2008). These words unleashed a torrent of anxious and irritated commentary in the French press from defenders of French exceptionalism and a certain notion of French cinema (Raphaël 2001; Sorman 2002). In de Baecque's own reaction to Messier's remarks, he defines French cinema in relation to what it is not, namely Besson. French cinema, for de Baecque, is a cinema of culture, diversity, and auteurs. French films are made through traditional methods of production with small companies and state funding. Besson and his studio, EuropaCorp, function for de Baecque as a "big bad wolf" with a completely different mode of production and, by extension, cultural identity. By imitating the vertically integrated Hollywood studio with its factory line of "efficient and effective competencies," Besson is concerned only with commercially successful products. For de Baecque, "this Hollywood dream ... could turn out to be French cinema's worst nightmare" (2002).

These caricatures of Besson in the press mask a more complex reality. Despite the difficulties inherent in navigating French institutional structures and cultural discourses, Besson has managed to retain a degree of creative independence, whether working in Hollywood or in France (Maule 2006, 23–24). EuropaCorp can also be understood as an attempt on Besson's part to maintain autonomy and foster his own vision for a different kind of French cinema. His conception of French cinema has progressively taken institutional form, both through EuropaCorp and the Cité du cinéma campus in Saint-Denis. Though his personal involvement with EuropaCorp's projects varies, his influence is considerable. Besson's cultural capital and institutional power have created, directly and indirectly, the conditions that made many of the French genre movies in the 2000s and 2010s viable.

PARKOUR FILMS AND THE ORIGINS OF EUROPACORP

EuropaCorp's first parkour film that Besson produced and cowrote, *Yamakasi: The Samurai of Modern Times*, inverts the stereotypes commonly associated with banlieue characters in popular mainstream cinema or in ethnically specific modes of *beur*, or French Maghrebi, cinema from the 1980s. *Yamakasi* was one of the first two films that EuropaCorp produced after Besson founded it with Pierre-Ange Le Pogam, a former Gaumont studio executive, in September 2000 (Pogam 2007, 32). This choice suggests something of its importance for the company's emerging corporate identity. The film is a hybrid thriller/heist movie, and its main plot, the story of a group of banlieue residents looking after their own, contains a minimal level of social awareness. It uses a naturalistic cinematography, and its look evokes documentary, but its stylized editing rhythms locate it closer to action and thriller genres.

Yamakasi tells the story of a young child from the banlieues with a frail heart who tries to imitate the traceurs by climbing a tree. When he falls to the ground, he injures his heart so severely that if he does not receive a transplant within a few days, he will die. No compatible donor is available in France, so his family must find four hundred thousand francs to have an acceptable heart shipped from Switzerland. Because this is an impossible sum for a poor family, the traceurs decide to rob the rich Parisian doctors who run the organization that deals in transplant organs. The traceurs explicitly refer to themselves as latter-day Robin Hoods, explaining to the viewer the black-and-white, class-inflected morality that pits the poor banlieue residents against the rich Parisian doctors who live in palatial homes in the city center.

Yamakasi transforms the parkour founders into heroic, almost mythic figures. The film's title clearly indicates the interpretative lens through which Besson and his collaborators styled parkour for a mass audience as a French form of martial arts. The film's narrative also evokes Akira Kurosawa's *Seven Samurai* (1954) as a means of portraying the traceurs as reluctant heroes who will defend the weak. Given the film's genre references, one might expect multiple fight sequences. *Yamakasi*, however, focuses more on the acrobatic gymnastics involved in daring heists and escapes than on violent confrontations. In the end, the film's narrative premise and its opposition between heroes and villains feel like a pretext for spectacular stunts.

Yamakasi was a popular success but a failure with critics. The film sold 2,484,292 tickets over eleven weeks, and it was shown in 504 theaters during its opening weekend, which counts as a wide release for a French film in France.[6] It was not distributed in the United States, though it has a cult following in parkour circles outside France. French critics panned it as a film designed to please a young audience without serious intellectual engagement. Didier Péron, who calls the film's social critique "too stupid for words" (*bête à pleurer*), does admit that the one incontestably positive dimension of the film is "its capacity to make of second- and third-generation immigrant kids something different from sociological fiction or ethnoparodic comedy" (Péron 2001). The parkour founders who play the traceurs also note that the film marks one of the first times French audiences saw young people from the banlieues playing heroes in a film.[7] The film's chief interest, then, is contesting conventional representations of suburban characters, be they positive or negative. *Yamakasi* refuses the naturalistic, sociological, and documentary conventions of much beur and banlieue cinema. It also challenges the comedy or action genre stereotypes of many suburban characters. *Yamakasi*'s traceurs are not the violent, idle youth of *La Haine*, nor are they the comedic figures in what Péron terms "ethnoparodic comedy" or the comic stereotypes seen in the five films of Besson and EuropaCorp's *Taxi* franchise (1998–2018). *Yamakasi* does not create figures of great complexity, but it does invert the typical ethical distribution of racial, ethnic, and class categories in action cinema. The traceurs remain melodramatic, oversimplified characters. Yet, as stand-ins for ordinary banlieue residents, they become the heroes, while upper-class French bourgeois become the caricatured villains.

Despite the film's noteworthy depiction of banlieue heroes, *Yamakasi* did not enjoy international success. It relied too heavily on an implicit knowledge of the social situation in the banlieues, French political structures, and Parisian geography to be easily intelligible to foreign audiences. Even though it references Kassovitz's *La Haine* by featuring a banlieue-born cop torn between loyalties, *Yamakasi* was not as accessible to a global audience as its predecessor. *Yamakasi* was not given even a limited release in the US market, confirming that the film's producers knew of its indeterminate status vis-à-vis international markets. It was not enough of an action movie to succeed in mainstream international theaters, and it also differed significantly from the usual French entrants in the international art cinema marketplace (auteurist films, heritage pictures, and light social comedy), putting its exportability in doubt.

Yamakasi nevertheless represents an important attempt to frame the challenges facing France's poor, suburban diasporic communities for a mainstream audience. In their analysis of transnationalism, Higbee and Lim go beyond the opposition between commercial mainstream cinema and culturally specific forms of noncommercial cinema to anchor their notion of transnationalism in the supposed authenticity of diasporic filmmakers. For them, a critical transnationalism requires scholars to frame films through engagement with the fields of diaspora studies, cultural studies, and postcolonial studies. However, they come out strongly against the "ghettoizing" of transnational films that has characterized some scholarship on diasporic filmmaking. Higbee and Lim suggest that diasporic filmmakers can and do address the mainstream. However, in terms of imagining what kinds of cultural exchange and mixing might be possible in such mainstream transnational films, Higbee and Lim opt for the identities of which diasporic filmmakers are a part. In the context of French North African filmmakers, they argue that such filmmakers might address the French nation, the Maghreb, or both (2010, 9–12). What this account leaves out is the possibility that diasporic and dominant filmmakers might use film cultures that are not "theirs" to address shared contemporary social and political challenges.

This possibility is alluded to elsewhere in the debates surrounding transnationalism, but first we must consider what has obscured it from view. Willemen reminds us that while we can think about cultural specificity in terms of gender, class, history, or other axes of difference, cinema is primarily an industry, and consequently institutional factors are especially important in the context of film and media studies (2006, 33). It is for this reason that many countries, especially in Europe, have opted to create protectionist structures that seek to fend off Hollywood films and foster national production. John Hill, in the context of British cinema, offers one of the most oft cited defenses of this logic. For him, while a national cinema may be a conceptually unstable category, it can in fact examine and challenge the cultural, social, and political complexities within a national space (1992, 16–19). In a similar vein, Willemen argues that British minority filmmakers can make films that are uniquely British that also deal with concerns about the British nation. He makes a distinction between films that are national, which can include minority voices, and films that are nationalist, which in his view are homogenizing (2006, 34–36).

Andrew Higson questions the national distinctiveness model that scholars like Willemen and Hill have proposed for protectionist conceptions of national media industries. For him, borders are never fixed and impenetrable, and so national cultures are always hybrid and impure. Furthermore, he argues that the desire for culturally specific national films in the British context is in fact "a call for a very specific type of film: social dramas set in contemporary Britain, attending to the specificities of multiculturalism and employing a more or less realist mode of representation" (Higson 2006, 22–23). In his view, so-called foreign films can contribute just as much to the mediation of contemporary social concerns as national ones. While the "foreign films" Higson mentions are largely international—he mentions the work of Spike Lee and Jane Campion as examples—we can, I argue, extend his reasoning to suggest that the shared language of popular cinemas like Hollywood can also do this work.

In their analysis of post-1980s French films by diasporic filmmakers, Higbee and Lim do allude to this possibility by giving the example of Rachid Bouchareb's *Days of Glory* (*Indigènes*, 2006) as a film that revisits colonial memory in a mainstream mode.[8] However, when discussing the film's use of tropes from the Hollywood war film, they are careful to call this "transatlantic dialogue" as opposed to *transnational* (2010, 13). While a small detail, this word choice nevertheless suggests that calls for cultural specificity risk falling prey to notions of authenticity, ones secured by biographical and community origins or the affirmation of belonging on the part of a filmmaker. Higson's point that foreign films from outside one's personal cultures can speak just as much to contemporary social concerns is, I suggest, more radical and useful for understanding some of EuropaCorp's films. Taking into account Higbee and Lim's caution that "cross-border film-making activities" may in fact represent "new forms of neocolonialist practices in the guise of popular genres or auteurist aesthetics" (2010, 18), we can nevertheless think about Hollywood film genres as a positive feature of commercial transnational films that deal with the challenges of multiculture in contemporary France.

DISTRICT B13 AND THE BALANCE BETWEEN LOCAL AND TRANSNATIONAL ADDRESS

In EuropaCorp's second parkour film, *District B13*, filmmakers found a more exportable balance of commercial appeal, genre conventions, and social engagement. In discussing EuropaCorp's production philosophy, Pogam explains that they view each project as a prototype, with the implication being that if a prototype is successful, they will attempt to iterate it (2007, 37). *District B13* arguably represents the next iteration of the *Yamakasi* formula. Besson produced and cowrote *District B13* with Bibi Naceri, the brother of Samy Naceri, who anchored Besson's *Taxi* franchise. Besson had the idea for the film's basic concept and then called Naceri into his office to help him write the screenplay because Naceri grew up in the banlieues and spent some time in the French prison system before becoming an actor and screenwriter. Besson entrusted the project to first-time director Pierre Morel, who had previously worked as a cinematographer on the first *Transporter* movie (2002), written and produced by Besson.

District B13 did prove exportable, but not because it successfully removed the "Frenchness" from a parkour film. On the contrary, *District B13* explicitly and consistently foregrounds the social issues confronting the French suburbs. While *District B13*'s aesthetic vocabulary is drawn from a variety of national cinematic traditions, its narrative refers specifically to contemporary France. Vanderschelden attempts to smooth over some of the polarization in debates around transnational cinema by defining it as those films that "through a combination of national, international and post-national elements, at both a production and a textual level, deliberately blend nations and cultures, rather than simply erasing cultural specificity" (2007, 38). While the notion of blending is more attentive to hybridity, it risks being purely descriptive. Rosanna Maule locates the problem precisely when she explains that Besson's films, in seeking to be global, must be adaptable to individual national markets (2006, 37).

In terms of *District B13*, we might speak of an independent coexistence between national social context and international aesthetic styles and narrative tropes. The film succeeds at allowing multiple points of access within different contexts of reception. These multiple levels of meaning coexist and do not interfere with the film's genre pleasures. *District B13* can be appreciated as a sci-fi martial arts film without any understanding of the contemporary French social contexts behind it; yet, for those in the know, it reads as an explicit commentary on the social marginalization of the French banlieues. Nevertheless, this social commentary is not located at the level of social realism; instead, it appears through the film's use of genre tropes. *District B13*'s generic references to American cinema (John Carpenter's *Assault on Precinct 13*, 1973; *Escape from New York*, 1981; and *Escape from L.A.*, 1996; and Brian De Palma's *Scarface*, 1983) are not just winks meant for action movie cinephiles. Rather, they call attention to how *District B13* rewrites and inverts the source material. It is in this rewriting that we can locate the film's social engagement.

District B13 tells the story of a dystopian future Paris in which the impoverished banlieues have been separated from the bourgeois city by means of an impenetrable wall. In this tense environment, an idealistic Parisian cop (Damien, played by Cyril Raffaelli) and a man from the banlieues (Leïto, played by David Belle) team up to locate and disable a nuclear bomb that has been stolen by a suburban gang. The government refers to this weapon as the "Bombe propre" or "Clean Bomb." Over the course of the film, we learn that the French minister of the interior orchestrated the whole affair as a means to destroy the banlieues once and for all. In the end, Damien and Leïto expose the plan on national TV, and a chastised government votes to destroy the wall. Leon Hunt writes that *District B13* was the first film to match a specifically French action and movement vocabulary with a thematic context where parkour makes sense. In effect, the film found "indigenous" French action heroes, bodies, stories, and styles (2008, 228–229). The director, Morel, decided to use a combination of Asian martial arts forms, American sci-fi and action film conventions, and an indigenous French movement vocabulary to articulate a more hopeful vision than one would typically see in French banlieue cinema. Parkour, in *District B13*, becomes a literal and figurative means of liberation, both for suburban residents and French forms of commercial genre cinema.

At the level of its narrative, *District B13* offers an idealistic fable about the suburbs and democracy, conspicuously refusing pessimism for optimism at nearly every turn. Science fiction, despite its seeming orientation toward the future, is primarily about exploring the implications of the present when pushed to an extreme. *District B13* borrows the same basic narrative premise as Carpenter's *Escape from New York* and *Escape from L.A.* In all three movies, a section of the country is separated from the rest of the nation by a wall or a body of water. The isolated territory becomes the home (or prison) for the nation's undesirables: criminals in *Escape from New York*, opponents of Moral America in *Escape from L.A.*, or the French immigrant and working classes in *District B13*. While Carpenter transposes the contradictions of the American dream onto an imaginary dystopic future, *District B13* literalizes a geographic and cultural divide that already exists in the minds of many French people, something that actors Raffaelli and Dany Verissimo note in interviews on the DVD release (Morel 2006).

The filmmakers refuse to create a suburban antihero modeled after Snake, the protagonist in both Carpenter films. Instead, *District B13* adopts the formula of a buddy film, splitting the central protagonist into two characters. Within that pairing, *District B13* does not simply set an idealistic hero in opposition to a world-weary skeptic and pessimist. Instead, it differentiates the cop (Damien) and the suburban native (Leïto) in terms of class and geography but casts both as republican idealists who, over the course of the film, realize that they are fighting for the same values and goals.

When they first meet, it seems that they could not be more different. To earn Leïto's trust, Damien poses as a fellow banlieue native. Leïto sees through Damien's ruse because his fighting style is too "clean." He does not have the improvisation that being raised with "hate" gives someone who grew up there; this remark almost certainly references Kassovitz's *La Haine*. In an exchange that offers a clear example of what Arjun Appadruai has called *ideoscapes* (1996,

Figure 2.2 The wall separating the banlieues from the center of Paris. *District 13: Ultimatum*, 2009.

36), Damien immediately retorts that he did not learn hate in school, but rather liberty, equality, fraternity, and a respect for law (i.e., the basic tenets of French universalism). As I explained in the introduction, the term *universalism* refers to France's particular version of the Enlightenment philosophical heritage in which all markers of individual or communal difference should be invisible in the public sphere when people act as citizens. The law and the school figure here as two of the classic republican institutions that mediate French national identity.

Equality, for the government functionary Damien, is a question of a common social contract and the laws that define it. Leïto immediately fires back that more immediate needs, like water, gas, and electricity, must come before such lofty ideals. He notes that he respected every law and that it brought him nothing. The government erected a wall and closed all the schools, post offices, and police stations in the banlieues, evidence of what Étienne Balibar calls the "recolonization of social relations" characteristic of globalization (2004, 38–42). Leïto sees in Damien a pit bull sent to do the will of his master, who is not a paragon of French republicanism. However, it is the framework of French universalism that ultimately unites them against a common enemy. Based on a belief that the law should be the same for all, they agree to work together to defuse the bomb.

As the film progresses, the recurring disputes between Damien and Leïto focus on whether the current French government actually lives up to its supposedly republican values. Leïto is suspicious of the bomb and Damien's noble "rescue mission." Damien was allegedly sent to enter a code that will disarm the bomb, but Leïto thinks the government is plotting to blow up the banlieues themselves. Leïto concludes that Damien's role is to ensure that the bomb explodes in the right place, the French suburban ghetto. Leïto compares the government's project to destroy the banlieues to the Nazi extermination of the Jews as the *ne plus ultra* of discussions around discrimination and racism. Damien refuses to believe Leïto, but when the timer expires and the bomb does not explode, Damien finally accepts the truth.

After this revelation, the film again refuses a pessimistic, dystopic ending, rejecting the Carpenter model. Damien and Leïto directly confront the minister of the interior. After threatening to explode the bomb right there in his office, the minister screams that the banlieues are uncontrollable and cost the state a fortune. The state's taxpayers, presumably the middle and upper classes, are fed up with paying for "cette racaille" (that scum). This turn of phrase received much press attention when Nicolas Sarkozy, the French minister of the interior from 2002 to 2007, used it to describe protesting banlieue residents in 2004 and 2005. When Sarkozy assumed that office (and later the presidency), he proposed to be the tough guy who would "clean up" and secure the suburbs. *District B13* predates Sarkozy's remarks and prefigures the protests, but it imagines the final implications for his policies when pushed to their logical extreme. Besson notes the irony of this prefiguration in a *Première* interview just after Sarkozy's remarks, wondering "whether Kärcher the First [Sarkozy] stole *District B13*'s dialogue" (Loustalot 2006, 63). At the end of the film, Damien tells the minister that there are far more democratic means that do not depend on violence to resolve the problems of the banlieues. By explicitly televising exposé coverage of the minister admitting he wanted to level the banlieues because he did not know what else to do, the film again returns to the rhetoric of French universalism. The final scene suggests that decisions about places and peoples should be made collectively and publicly, thus reinforcing the Enlightenment idea of a democratic public sphere as essential to the survival of a modern, inclusive nation.

It would be easy to say that *District B13* simply adopts the conventional happy ending common to much popular cinema as a way of avoiding engagement with ideological contradictions. However, the extent to which the film repeatedly emphasizes an idealistic, optimistic narrative reveals the way it engages social problems through the language of American genre cinema. Contrary to de Baecque's accusations that Besson's brand of commercial films has no sense of film history, *District B13* very much does; it is simply a different history from that which de Baecque expects. While less self-conscious and less experimental than Jean-Luc Godard's reworking of early Hollywood gangster films in *Breathless* (*À bout de souffle*, 1960), *District B13* nevertheless represents a new iteration of a long familiar French film practice, particularly in the ways it stages its relationship to Hollywood cinema. While the film most obviously imitates and modifies the dystopic world of Carpenter's *Escape* films, it opts for a rhetoric of optimism through a reversal or *bricolage* of American genre cinema tropes.

District B13's depiction of drug lords and gangsters offers a commentary on one of the urtexts of contemporary American gangster cinema, De Palma's 1983 remake of *Scarface*. The film is a fundamental reference point not only for banlieue cinema in its more "serious forms" but also for banlieue youth.[9] *District B13* does not make reference to the film's famous dictum, "The World is Yours," but instead parodies Al Pacino's portrayal of drug lord Tony Montana. Of course, Pacino's Montana was himself already a kind of parody, but the performance of co-screenwriter Bibi Naceri as Taha in *District B13* satirizes Montana's cocaine snorting, his explosive temper, and his quick recourse to violence. Taha's office, a pathetically small corner of a warehouse, is filled with gold statues and a leather chair that evoke Montana's estate on a much smaller scale. Taha's fall in the film results not from killing too many people, but from running out of money to pay his gang members, as if they were simple employees.

District B13 critiques the excess of the destructive American gangster figure by contrasting Taha with his lieutenant, the quieter and more enlightened K2 (played by the late Tony D'Amario). Though physically a brute, K2 acts upon reflection rather than sheer impulse. When K2 and the other gang members return without Leïto or the drugs he stole, Taha begins shooting them one by one until he points his gun at his second in command, K2, who throws his hands up and tells Taha that he has figured out how to capture Leïto. Later in the film, when Taha tries to murder all his gang members rather than pay them, he comically runs out of bullets and asks K2 for his gun. K2 refuses, and the rest of the gang members gun Taha down in a parody of Montana's spectacular death.

K2 takes charge of the gang and decides to capture Damien and Leïto. However, when finally confronted with them, K2 first asks them how much time remains until the bomb explodes. K2 initially wants to keep one of them hostage while the other disarms the bomb, but after some debate, he decides to let both Damien and Leïto go to the top of the building, where the bomb has been placed. The uncertainty in his voice and gestures betrays his discomfort with the role of the tough American-style gangster. When Damien and Leïto return, K2 does not execute them. Instead, he gives Damien five minutes to get out of town. This final moment shows that K2 can think beyond mere self-gratification for the good of his community. As we saw earlier, the banlieues are represented as a neocolonial space in which Taha's gang stands in for the unenlightened savages who need France's *mission civilisatrice*, or civilizing mission of education, health care, infrastructure, and economic development. K2's shift from Taha's violent instincts and pursuit of self-gratification toward reason and a concern for the suburban community reinforces the film's optimistic fable that republican communities can be created in the banlieues. In other words, the savage American-style gangster can be civilized and thus become a true member of the French republic. In effect, *District B13* replaces the caricature of the self-destructive American gangster with the caricature of the noble outlaw, choosing Robin Hood over Scarface. It is as if K2 had learned the lesson of *La Haine*'s ironic rewriting of *Scarface*'s slogan: "The world is ours, not mine."

The optimism of the ending, however, is not without a certain irony. When Damien tells Leïto in the final scene that the government plans to destroy the wall and reopen the schools, hospitals, and police stations, it is not clear that this is a positive development. After all, the community in Leïto's building in the beginning of the film seemed to work well under his protection. Only Taha's drug trade disturbs its stability. With Taha gone, who is to say that K2 might not run a better community on a decentralized, local model than a centralized, national model? The return of republican institutions to the banlieues might just as well establish a neocolonial situation of systemic inequality. In any case, within *District B13*, the optimistic, utopian revision of American genre tropes is intimately tied to a consensual myth of French universalism.

The mildly defensive tone of the film's promotional materials, which seems to apologize for the social content of *District B13*, should dispel any remaining doubt that the film itself ties social commentary to genre tropes. Concerned that the pronounced emphasis on the problems of the banlieues might detract from the film's pleasures as an action movie, *District B13*'s filmmakers repeatedly stress that the movie is primarily an action picture and that any social commentary is an afterthought or background. Bibi Naceri, co-screenwriter, notes that the film is "an action film before being a social film," and in the film's official press kit, Morel distances himself from the social dimensions of more committed banlieue cinema (Sauvion 2004). When asked if the expression *banlieue film* suited him, he replied, "I don't know what it means. *District B13* is first and foremost a pure action film which takes place in a suburb, set a few years into the future. The initial screenplay pitch was a 'political fiction' about what the suburbs might be in a few years if we don't change things and make the wrong decisions" (EuropaCorp and Magnolia Pictures 2004, 5). It is as if the marketing department worried that promoting the film's social conscience would lead to charges of oversimplification—which French critics made anyway—or that it would alienate the film's key intended demographic: youth audiences in France, particularly those in the banlieues. Ironically, such extensive apologies only drew attention to the film's social agenda.

The film's production history and actors tell a story that contrasts sharply with the promotional disavowal. As Bibi Naceri recounts, the banlieue context was always fundamental to the articulation of the film. Talking about the real social context behind the film, Naceri explains that the film's conspiracy is plausible given the level of distrust toward the banlieues (Sauvion 2004). The actors, in their special features interviews, also seem to understand that they were making more than a simple action movie. D'Amario, K2 in the film, explains best the complex balance the filmmakers maintained between creating an action film and a film with something to say about French society: "There were moments [in French history and in the history of the banlieues] when [the separation between the banlieues and Paris] was worse than [what we see in the film]. This film is useful. And maybe it's to avoid falling again into moments like that [that] this film has a use, a social dimension" (Morel 2006). Bill Marshall reads these claims to a social message as disingenuous because "this dystopian future is outlandishly more 'other' to the present day than it is the 'same'" (2010, 171). In effect, he argues that the banlieues' problems in the film bear little relation to actual problems. Marshall's claim assumes that realism is the only way to portray social problems in cinema, especially with respect to marginalized spaces and peoples. However, the reception of *District B13* problematizes this assumption.

Bibi Naceri talks about how banlieue audiences identified powerfully with the film's two heroes at advance screenings in Mantes-la-Jolie and Saint-Denis: "Before the film, they only applauded the rapper MC Jean Gab'1 and myself.... After the screening, we didn't exist anymore. They were completely taken with David Belle and Cyril Raffaeli. That's what's beautiful. These banlieue kids aren't different from any other kids; they like heroes who save the world" (Sauvion 2004). French rapper MC Jean Gab'1, who plays a small role in *District B13*, also stresses the film's unique place in French cinema during an interview:

> It's a real action film. It really gets going. French cinema today is filled with rich kids who take up all the space. Or it's swashbuckling costume dramas as if France were lost in its history. With *District B13*, we're in the realm of fiction and not pseudo-documentary and we get a [gentle] lesson. What is it? When one doesn't know what to do with people, one locks them up. It could happen. They're building a lot of prisons right now and they're going to have to find

some delinquents to put in there. I have the impression that our generation isn't represented in cinema. When you see the banlieues, it's pure caricature. (Catroux 2004)

When asked what films he was thinking of, Gab'1 responds with a list of "classic" mid-1990s banlieue films: "*Raï* [1995], *La Haine* and, worse yet, *Ma 6-T va crack-er* [*My City's Gonna Crack*, 1997]." As he imagines his ideal banlieue cinema, he goes on to advocate what sounds like a neorealist aesthetic: "If these guys [the directors of those other films] had really wanted to show the banlieues, we would have seen people working and living normally" (Catroux 2004). *District B13*, of course, does not show suburban youth working, and furthermore, the cultural associations of naturalistic realism and high culture often prevent youth from recognizing themselves within the films. Gab'1 reminds us that it is precisely because of their own identifications with action heroes in patently "unrealistic" films that something like *District B13* can serve as a more effective form of self-recognition.

District B13 performed respectably at the French box office. It was released on 428 screens and stayed in theaters for six weeks, selling 961,850 tickets. While it was less successful in France than *Yamakasi*, it was exported to the United States and did relatively well. Magnolia Pictures released it to 151 theaters, including some multiplexes. Most French popular mainstream successes, including comedies, are released abroad on the art house circuit. Besson's *Taxi* was one of the first exceptions to this distribution strategy (Mazdon 2001, 1–4). *District B13* did not remain long in theaters, and by the third week of release, the number of screens dropped 62 percent; however, the film did gross $1,200,216 in its US release.

District B13 does not fit neatly into traditional categories like commercial cinema, art cinema, French cinema, genre cinema, or even banlieue cinema. It falls into the unusual category of a popular social genre film. In the end, it may be reductive. The government officials are simplistic villains, and viewers are told that the wall will come down. The banlieue residents go back to the banlieues, the cop goes back to Paris, and K2, we imagine, goes back to selling drugs. But even in its failure or its inadequacy, *District B13* remains an interesting example, or unfulfilled desire, of what a French genre cinema could be: an internationally successful popular cinema with a social conscience that anchors yet disturbs its Frenchness.

The film shows that cultural specificity and transnational address are not as opposed as some scholars would have us believe. Cultural specificity does not automatically imply an appeal to realism, ethnography, or personal authenticity.

Social problems specific to a national space can also be engaged with through the shared resources of the imaginary, such as myth and heroic figures. What is more, these resources can be shared across national borders. EuropaCorp and the filmmakers of *District B13* balance local and global ambitions, and in this they correspond to what Charlie Michael has called the professionalist and pragmatist positions in the French film industry. In his book on the history of French blockbusters, Michael elaborates a tripartite typology of positions that individuals take with respect to defending the French film industry: exceptionalists, professionalists, and pragmatists. Exceptionalists are people invested in notions of cinema as art and cultural patrimony. A professionalist, by contrast, is someone who argues that attempts to secure the future of the French cinema "must remain grounded in the realities of a competitive, changing industry" and be "primed to compete within the logic of global flows and to respond quickly to the advent of new media platforms." For Michael, these are not necessarily mutually opposed positions, and indeed what he calls the "pragmatist" freely draws on both (2019, 22–24).

This strategic mixing of positions is something that several commentators have identified in how the industry and government regulations simultaneously support auteurist and commercial filmmaking. France's automatic aid gives loans to producers for their next film as a means of supporting commercial forms of French filmmaking. Selective aid, by contrast, awards funding based on a jury's attribution of artistic merit to a project as an attempt to subsidize noncommercial, elite forms of art and auteurist cinema (Danan 2006, 175). When trying to account for how these two seemingly opposed logics of state funding can coexist, Danan suggests that in fact they represent an opportunist strategy in a "synergetic battle for international visibility within an integrated approach in favour of global economic expansion" (2006, 181).

For the pragmatist or the opportunist, both French auteurism and commercial filmmaking help preserve a national industry. Stephen Crofts has suggested that the category of national cinema functions in part as a brand that countries use to market their films on the export market. Generally, this is, in his view, subtended by the rhetoric of universal humanism, cultural specificity, or aesthetic beauty. In this way, most national films are circulated in festivals and released in European and North American markets as art films (Crofts 2006, 52–53). While the branding of French cinema internationally is oriented around art cinema and auteurism, even for large-budget heritage films, commercial French filmmaking is nevertheless crucial for the overall health of the industry.

In the case of Besson and the parkour films, I would add that pragmatism can also mean balancing national cultural specificity and transnational appeal.

While this may be difficult and rare, even across EuropaCorp's body of films, *District B13* nevertheless shows that it is possible. Crofts argues that framing national cinema as distinct from Hollywood's claims on film entertainment effectively inhibits the circulation of films from other national industries. For Crofts, this does not mean that other national cinemas do not produce genre-based films or that they should export them. Rather, it produces a distribution environment that encourages films to be framed in terms of national "distinctiveness" or "chauvinism" or in terms of "imperial aggression" (Crofts 2006, 52–53, 55–57). Bergfelder makes the same point in terms of European national cinemas. For him, circling the wagons around national art cinema does nothing to refute the dominance of Hollywood at what he calls a conceptual level. If anything, it reinforces this dominance by giving European national cinemas a rigidly defined place (Bergfelder 2005, 324). Through EuropaCorp's parkour films, Besson seeks to destabilize this sense of French cinema having a rigidly defined place. By creatively negotiating the constraints of the French industry and the global marketplace, a film like *District B13* is similar to a traceur in that it seeks the freedom to move through a space it did not wholly create.

DISTRICT 13: ULTIMATUM AND GRAND PARIS

The sequel, *District 13: Ultimatum*, preserves both the utopianism and the didactic exemplarity of the original. If the original *District B13* was a fable about the limits of gangsterism, the sequel focuses more on unity within a racially divided suburban neighborhood and on cooperation between the political elite and the banlieue residents. The two principal actors returned for the sequel, but Besson hired a different director. Patrick Alessandrin first interned with Besson on *The Last Battle* (*Le dernier combat*, 1983), and his directorial efforts prior to *District 13: Ultimatum* were comedies and dramas. With the *District B13* sequel, Besson takes sole writer credit, whereas he came up with the original idea for the first film but passed script-writing duties to Bibi Naceri. The sequel performed about as well as the original at the French box office; it sold 1,106,804 tickets over seven weeks of release. Magnolia Pictures again picked up the US distribution rights, but the film saw a very limited theatrical run in a small number of cities. *District 13: Ultimatum* grossed only $36,136 at the US box office before being released on DVD.

District 13: Ultimatum opens three years after the close of the first film. The government did not fulfill its promise to destroy the wall. The film's first sequence rhymes with the visually spectacular opening of the first film, using a fluid moving camera that imitates parkour as it maps the architectural and human geography of the banlieues. Echoing director Jean-Pascal Zadi's contemporaneous remark that the banlieues of the late 2000s and early 2010s are more racially segregated than those of the 1990s, the sequel's first images reveal that B13 has been divided into five areas controlled by ethnic or racial gangs: Black, Asian, North African, Romany, and skinhead (Zadi and Binet 2011). The representations of the people in the banlieues were rather limited in the first film; in the second, each neighborhood teems with ethnically and racially marked individuals as they move through the shared spaces of open-air markets, stores, trailers, and project housing.

Through clever digital effects, the camera effortlessly moves through the human map of the banlieues, penetrating interior as well as exterior spaces that are meant to be reserved for their respective ethnic groups. The camera's gaze is quasi-ethnographic, and there is the sense that the camera visits places that the viewer does not necessarily belong. These initial images depict the banlieues as an underdeveloped, non-Western country within France's borders. The exoticism of the production design paradoxically makes the banlieues seem less French and more generically global in the sense that it is closer to the cliché cinematic images of urban squalor and tribal shanty towns in Hollywood spy and action film franchises, from Bond to Bourne to *Mission Impossible*. In this way, the film positions the subject of the gaze as those people who live outside the banlieues. The speed of the camera's movements and the hip-hop beats of the soundtrack give the sequence a hallucinatory, oneiric quality. The representation of the banlieues in the opening sequence is not realistic in any sense of the term; it corresponds more to French fantasies and anxieties about the cultural otherness of the banlieues. The camera, like the traceur, overcomes the obstacles that would demarcate the space of the banlieues. The opening sequence's visual path through the banlieues puts these spaces into relation to each other and prefigures the gang unity that ends the film. As in the first *District B13* film, the banlieue residents here will turn out to be better defenders of French universalist values than those who live on the other side of the wall.

The camera movements in the opening sequence are inseparable from the ideological meanings of parkour, and they once again anchor the film in the tradition of French universalism. Besson and Alessandrin return to the narrative structure of *La Haine* in orienting the dramatic conflict of the film toward a standoff between the police and the banlieue residents. A multinational conglomerate has paid off the French chief of special services, Walter Grossman, to convince the president to raze the banlieues so that a new middle- and upper-class neighborhood can be rebuilt, complete with high-rise apartment buildings to replace the project housing. The focus of the second film is less on law and order and more on economics and the politics of humanitarian aid. Damien remarks that this conspiracy represents the first time that the Iraq and Afghanistan destruction-reconstruction model of economic development has been attempted in France. In the end, the five gangs rally around a notion of banlieue solidarity and expose Grossman's plan to the president.

The twist at the end of the film betrays the same utopian orientation of the first film. Following the dispatch of Grossman, a humbled president promises more aid money for the banlieues. Leïto refuses, arguing that the patchwork of aid money does not get at the real problem. Instead, he proposes that they carry out the plan to level the suburban neighborhood to start from scratch and build "green spaces" and jobs. After some hesitation, the president agrees to give the order. In the final scene, Damien, Leïto, the president, and the gang leaders sit around a table smoking cigars. The president asks them if they know the famous French architect Jean Nouvel. They do not, but the reference inserts the film into the context of Sarkozy's failed plans to remake and modernize Paris and its banlieues on a mass scale, the so-called Grand Paris project announced in 2008. Sarkozy got as far as soliciting and publicly debating proposals from architects all over the world, including Nouvel, but the project stalled because Sarkozy refused to work with local political authorities, preferring instead to impose changes from on high. This final utopian moment of the film, then, suggests that banlieue residents want change as much as everyone else, but only when they are included in the political process.

HOLLYWOOD-SUR-SEINE-SAINT-DENIS

If Besson's third parkour film satirizes Sarkozy's own pale imitation of former president François Mitterrand's Grands Projets to rebuild Paris, Besson intends his own symbolic move to the banlieues to be closer to the spirit of solidarity dramatized in the *District B13* films. The realization of this vision has been uneven, but its populist pretensions are inseparable from the ideological messages of EuropaCorp's parkour films. Besson's studio project came about in the late 1990s, when he decided to make the transition from directing to producing. He first considered venturing out on his own when Gaumont refused to fund two of his projects, the first *Taxi* film and *Yamakasi*, both of which would go on to become domestic hits, and had the idea for the Cité du cinéma during the production of *The Fifth Element* in the mid-1990s (Carrière 2003). When Besson's team began to plan where to shoot, France did not have adequate soundstages and facilities for big pictures, forcing him to film in England despite his preference to spend that money in France (Chebil 2012).

Besson's EuropaCorp studios commenced operations in 2000 with the modest goal of producing ten films per year. The overarching goal was to produce profitable films with mass, and even global, appeal so that the studio could in theory sustain itself rather than depend on state money. There are conflicting accounts of the extent to which EuropaCorp depended on state funding for its projects. Vanderschelden suggests that in financing its films, EuropaCorp rejected the traditional support of the *avances sur recettes*, or automatic aid, in favor of private funding sources, banks, and American partners (2008, 96). Such a choice would be ideological as much as economic, rejecting the CNC's (National Center for Cinema and the Moving Image) implicit ideas about what a culturally specific French cinema should be. However, Fabrice Lalevée and Florence Lévy-Hartmann argue that EuropaCorp, along with other consolidated media companies such as Gaumont and Pathé, regularly drew on automatic aid for close to 50 percent of a film's production costs during the 2000s. In their view, such commercially successful companies should be able to rely on the market alone for financing, whereas state support should be reserved for smaller companies and projects that are struggling to secure funding (quoted in Heinich 2008, 64). EuropaCorp's annual reports reveal the levels of funding drawn from the CNC's automatic aid. Between 2010 and 2018, the amount of state funding varied from as low as 4 million to as high as 11.6 million euros per year across all of EuropaCorp's various projects.[10] For Nathalie Heinich, such a use of public funding is ironic when, in her view, companies like EuropaCorp could simply rely on the market, their cash reserves, and private funding (2008, 64). Based on Geoffrey Le Guilcher's analysis of Besson's methods throughout his career, his overall strategy is resolute pragmatism: he is willing to draw on whatever public and private funding resources could be available to him at any given moment.[11] Through these different financing efforts, Besson and his company sought to build alternative economic structures to fund commercially viable French productions and international coproductions. The change in economic structure enabled a shift in the kinds of films they made; some were even able to compete with popular Hollywood movies within and outside France.

It would be easy to imagine, as de Baecque does, that EuropaCorp's model simply replicated Hollywood's interest in producing commodities. However, Besson insists that he does not believe in or practice the mass-production model of Hollywood. Besson sought the autonomy of the EuropaCorp model to realize his artistic visions with sufficient freedom, money, and quality facilities (Maule 2006, 26). These visions are profoundly transnational. As Besson has explained, "We're not trying to Americanize French cinema, but to internationalize it. Besides, my biggest hits, like *The Fifth Element*, worked less well in the United States compared to elsewhere. I direct and produce international films, not American ones" (Vadjoux 2007). Yet the EuropaCorp projects did not always gauge the domestic and international markets accurately. The last EuropaCorp blockbuster that Besson directed himself, the comic book adaptation *Valerian and the City of a Thousand Planets* (2017), performed much worse than expected overall, given that it was the most expensive French feature film ever produced, at a colossal budget of 198 million euros. It was especially unsuccessful in the US market; however, it did surprisingly well in China, with 11.6 million tickets sold (Vulser 2017, 2018).

At the level of economics, internationalizing is easy to understand. Part of what makes Hollywood financially viable is that the United States possesses a large enough domestic audience to allow films to recoup most of the initial investment before they are distributed to international markets and other secondary windows. According to Hayward, this situation has existed since at least the 1920s (1993, 26–30). Internationalizing, for EuropaCorp, meant international coproductions, but it also meant securing presales for international distribution and television rights before green-lighting a movie. EuropaCorp's policy was to secure 80 percent of such funding before entering production, thus ensuring an acceptable level of risk whereby one underperforming film would not sink the studio (Vadjoux 2007).

The company's fortunes were up and down during the 2000s and 2010s. Three main franchises, *Taxi*, *Taken*, and *The Transporter*, were responsible for boom years in the early 2000s and the mid-2010s. The underperforming *Arthur and the Minimoys* trilogy in the late 2000s and the 2007–2008 global economic depression made for lean years (Le Guilcher 2016, 189–191). Success returned with *Taken 3* (2014), *Transporter Refueled* (2015), and especially Besson's *Lucy* (2014). Besson began a process of recapitalization for EuropaCorp in 2013, but he nevertheless wanted to retain creative control. The recapitalization was part of an attempt to further vertically integrate the company and expand into TV production and film exhibition (Gonzalès 2013). However, the luxury multiplex market in Paris and Marseille did not provide EuropaCorp the stability it sought, and the fact that *Valerian* did not make back its production costs meant that EuropaCorp had too much debt relative to its capitalization on the stock market (Sallé 2018). Unfortunately, the financial turmoil caused by *Valerian* proved too much for EuropaCorp, and as of February 2020, Besson and his company agreed to a financial reorganization plan with the American company Vine Alternative Investments, who will own 60 percent of EuropaCorp's stock. As a condition of this new plan, Besson will no longer have full control of the company but will serve as its artistic director for a period of five years

(Vulser 2020a). Ironically, as a company now controlled primarily by Americans, EuropaCorp is no longer eligible for CNC funding (Vulser 2020b). The changing fortunes of Besson's company prove just how difficult it is to achieve stability in a notoriously unpredictable global media industry. And yet despite all this uncertainty, EuropaCorp's films, for better or worse, dominated the French industry's performance on the export market during the 2000s and 2010s, accounting for over 40 percent of all foreign spectators who watched French-made films during those decades (Sallé 2018).

In addition to obtaining funding and administrative structures, Besson also wanted to be able to source technical infrastructure and expertise in France. The Cité du cinéma is a collaboration between the producer-writer-director, other French media companies, and the French government. Much of the money for the project came from the Caisse des dépôts et consignation, a public bank that invests in the long-term economic future of France (Henni 2020). While court proceedings were started in 2013 about the suspicious use of public funds during the Sarkozy years for the benefit of EuropaCorp, the investigation concluded in 2018 with no further actions to be taken (Le Monde 2018a).[12] The Cité du cinéma, which bills itself as Hollywood sur Seine on its website, includes nine sound stages, editing suites, scene shops, camera and light shops, and two auditoriums for projection.[13]

It is possible to argue that Besson's Cité du cinéma project is just a form of neoliberal gentrification of suburban neighborhoods. Gillian Jein, in her examination of several initiatives to bring art exhibits and cultural organizations to the banlieues, has argued that such efforts do not break down "class and cultural barriers." Rather, they "tend to reproduce the visibility regime of dominant cultural elites." In her view, such initiatives seek to make the banlieues compatible with "neoliberal market logic" and "republican ideas of the social regeneration of place," and thus gentrification through the art and culture industries is simply the "state's most recent civilizing mission" (Jein 2016, 95). However, I argue that Besson's efforts with the Cité du cinéma do not quite fit this account for several reasons. First, the films EuropaCorp produces do not reproduce the types of art and auteurist cinema that France is already known for; they produce Gallic versions of the kinds of global entertainment-oriented media many suburban youth already watch. Second, EuropaCorp's goal is not just suburban revitalization, but also the creation of an economic engine that would benefit local business through all the support services contracts that come with large-scale film production. Finally, Besson's creation of a new film school at the Cité du cinéma reveals a desire to give suburban youth who lack the usual academic background a potential entry into the industry.

The Cité du cinéma campus in fact includes two film schools. The first, École nationale supérieure Louis Lumière, is one of France's most well-known state film schools that relocated to Saint-Denis as part of the Cité du cinéma project. The second is Besson's own creation, called École de la Cité, with the word *cité* again playing on its multiple meanings as a way of signaling the school's populist ambitions. It is part of his desire to create a popular and commercially viable French cinema by shaping the next generation of filmmakers, including those from the banlieues who might not find a place in traditional educational institutions.[14] Like Louis Lumière or La Fémis, France's other well-known state film school that I will discuss in more detail in chapter 6, Besson's school is free. Unlike the other two, acceptance into the École de la Cité does not require the high school baccalaureate. It does, however, require an entry exam that is every bit as competitive as the ones for Louis Lumière or La Fémis, with approximately six thousand candidates competing for sixty spots each year (Diao 2014). The subject matter of the exam's three components, however, is quite different. Louis Lumière and La Fémis expect that candidates have already done at least two years of university-level coursework in film history, theory, and analysis and that they can demonstrate a mastery of their basic craft through written and oral exams. For its part, the École de la Cité exam emphasizes creative exercises for which previous preparation is not necessary, asking students to perform such tasks as coming up with a film idea from a newspaper, dubbing a film excerpt with new dialogue, and describing oneself without using words.[15]

The model of the auteur remains influential in the curricula of state film schools like La Fémis and Louis Lumière, though this, too, is starting to change. The orientation of Besson's school marks a break with this model in its pragmatism and its strong focus on internships with the media companies that sponsor the school. Despite the school's arguably noble ambitions, it has not escaped the financial turmoil surrounding EuropaCorp and Besson. The École de la Cité risked closure in 2018, allegedly due to reduced public and private sponsorship, but has since stabilized and accepted new entering classes (Bourdon 2018; Blanchard 2018).

Through a vertically integrated studio, sophisticated production facilities, and even educational institutions, Besson attempted to remedy what has repeatedly been a weakness in the history of French film production. After the globally dominant French film industry was obliterated during World War I, it rebuilt itself based on an artisanal approach to filmmaking with small, often financially risky production companies. The French New Wave turned this approach into a dominant aesthetic value. In addition, at different moments, the French industry failed to sufficiently centralize and invest in technological infrastructure, leaving it to pay higher licensing costs from foreign companies, most notably during the early days of sound (Hayward 1993, 21).

Through investment in the technological expertise and infrastructure necessary to produce sophisticated cinema and other media in France, Besson sought to redress these historical oversights. As Violaine Hacker explains, in the age of commercial digital filmmaking in Europe that requires expensive practical and special effects, a production company whose country of origin lacks sufficient industrial infrastructure often must farm out much of the specialized work to small firms around the world. Such outsourcing fragments the financing and reduces the profits for a film's producers. It also puts these films at a disadvantage on the global export market (Hacker 2011, 38–39). Besson's postproduction center for sound and special effects in Normandy, Digital Factory, the Cité du cinéma, and EuropaCorp are efforts to create the kind of industrial infrastructure in France necessary for this kind of filmmaking. According to some, this centralization of infrastructure also has creative advantages. Eric Rochant, the creator and showrunner of Canal+'s successful quality television series, *The Bureau*, which was produced at the Cité du cinéma, explains how helpful it was for him creatively to be able to meet with all the different members of the production team, from writers to postproduction technicians, on the same day at the same physical location. Rochant said that he learned the "virtues" of this "unity of place" in the United States (2017, 25). While Besson is generally hostile to the French discourse of cultural exceptionalism, he nevertheless appears to be working for French national interests in terms of the projects he produces and his desire to create French infrastructure. In this, he is every bit the professionalist, to return to Michael's terminology.

Ultimately, Besson wants to prove that it is possible to negotiate the frontier between art and business in a way that returns autonomy to French filmmaking and inverts the direction of influence between Hollywood and Europe. As Maule explains it: "With EuropaCorp, the 'post-Hollywood' Besson is proving that successful movies can be made and distributed outside of the constraints and limitations of Hollywood's global control and France's stance for cultural exception. Conceived from within a national-popular perspective, the film production and distribution company targets the international film market and thrives on the ideological inconsistencies of France's pretensions about its 'cultural' specificity" (Maule 2006, 32). EuropaCorp's wide-ranging efforts, extending beyond the narrow purview of individual films, are in fact typical of a French emphasis on the importance of cultural and artistic identity as a fundamental dimension of national identity.

This mix of cultural specificity and transnational flexibility is an attempt to resist the place that contemporary Hollywood would assign European national cinemas. In her analysis of Hollywood's global ambitions in the twenty-first century, Nolwenn Mingant has shown how the kind of containment I discussed earlier with respect to Crofts's work can take place through coproduction agreements across borders. Mingant notes that Hollywood was originally leery of international companies investing in their projects because they feared that such coproduced films might lose their "American" qualities. However, this fear turned out to be unfounded, as companies such as the French pay channel Canal+ were interested in these films' financial success in the United States, on their domestic pay channels, and in other markets around the world. Mingant suggests that since such companies' interest was primarily financial, they did not seek to change how Hollywood handled questions of cultural specificity—in this case, Americanness—as a globally generic brand. When finance capital flows in the opposite direction—that is, when Hollywood companies invest in international coproductions abroad—they take the opposite tactic: they tend to favor types of films that are "typical" for each country. This investment strategy leaves the direct imitation of Hollywood models and genre formulae to national companies like Besson's EuropaCorp, though Mingant argues that this should not be viewed as a simple case of "Americanization," but rather of what she calls "hybridization" and "creolization" (Mingant 2013, 6–7).

Through EuropaCorp's stylistic, narrative, and institutional strategies, Besson and his collaborators attempted to craft a youthful, banlieue-inflected identity for his films and his company. The outcomes of these choices are uncertain and ambivalent, whether one views them in terms of financial numbers, cultural import, or even institutional reforms. A skeptical critic for the left-leaning magazine *Marianne* argued that Besson's Cité du cinéma would fall short of its lofty social goals but acknowledged it as an attempt at social engineering (Charles 2009). Despite the project's critics, the article admits, Besson did have the Communist mayor of Saint-Denis on his side (Beier 2010). Michel Guerrin puts it perhaps most helpfully when he talks about Besson in terms of a "pas de deux" between self-interest and avowed patriotism (Guerrin 2016). One could argue that self-interest wins out over helping others or helping France, but one could also suggest that his self-interest is at times aligned with "patriotic" goals. In any case, regardless of how one views EuropaCorp and the Cité du cinéma's larger implications, Besson's various initiatives illustrate the extent to which his vision for French media in the twenty-first century was political and ideological as well as economic.

The nature of Besson's relationship to the banlieues has also been difficult to establish conclusively. Writing for *Le Monde* in 2008, Luc Bronner explains that Besson first learned about the difficulties faced by France's impoverished suburban neighborhoods during film shoots in the banlieues and through the hip-hop artists that created original soundtracks for EuropaCorp's films. Besson has personally sought to form connections in the communities and build local organizations. In the late 2000s, he funded a documentary about protests in Villiers-le-Bel, and he brought the films from Cannes to screen at festivals in several suburban neighborhoods (see Diao 2017, 241–242). Bronner captures Besson's contradictory image when he writes that Besson "the liberal, not well known for his kindness in business matters, has come to develop a quasi-Marxist discourse on the origins of the crisis [in the banlieues]" (Bronner 2008a).

We see these two sides of Besson's relationship to the banlieues in his decisions regarding the shooting locations for Morel's third post–*District B13* EuropaCorp film, *From Paris with Love* (2010), which was supposed to be an attempt to align the politics of production with the politics of style. The film features a special agent (John Travolta) and an embassy assistant (Jonathan Rhys Myers) who uncover a terrorist plot to bomb an African trade summit in Paris. One short exterior sequence does take place in the banlieues, but the film's Frenchness consists mainly of a collection of American clichés and stereotypes about French culture. The trip to the banlieues is a case in point. When the two protagonists arrive, Travolta's character remarks that this ramshackle place is not in any of the Paris guidebooks. The banlieues are more a part of the film's production mythology than its narrative. Unlike *District B13* and *District 13: Ultimatum*, which were shot in Romania and Serbia respectively, *From Paris with Love* was supposed to be shot in the Parisian banlieues at the Cité des Bosquets de Montfermeil in Seine-Saint-Denis, one of the epicenters of the 2005 protests (*Le Figaro* 2008). At the time, EuropaCorp's publicity campaign, picked up in French press coverage, focused on how the film's two big American stars were coming to the French banlieues (*L'Express* 2008). When ten vehicles were torched the week before the film was to begin principal photography, Besson halted production, angering local residents who were supposed to appear as extras. He eventually moved the film to a more secure part of the Parisian periphery, Poissy in the northwestern suburbs.

This ambivalent relationship has continued in the years since. In an op-ed piece in *Le Monde* written a few days after the January 2015 terrorist attacks at the *Charlie Hebdo* editorial offices and the Hyper Cacher kosher market in Paris, Besson argues that the banlieues are the real problem France needs to solve. His piece carries a split address, speaking on the one hand to suburban youth through the informal second person (*tu*) and repeated uses of "my brother" and on the other to France's business and political elites in the second-person formal plural (*vous*). To the former, he suggests that study, hard work, and the democratic process, rather than violence, are the answer. To the latter, he exhorts them to help this "humiliated young generation" and to create a more equitable French society (Besson 2015). The piece is filled with sentiment and calls for sweeping change but is short on ideas. Most problematically, it implicitly blames both sides for the violence. These kinds of gestures make it impossible to establish the exact nature of Besson's relationship to the banlieues. In her analysis of Besson, journalist, blogger, and writer Claire Diao has brought together the contradictory perspectives on Besson's actions and words from those living and working in the banlieues. While she recognizes his power in the media industry, she ultimately leaves him as a question mark in terms of whether he helps or hinders the banlieues and those who live there (Diao 2017, 233–251).

CONCLUSION

Despite Besson's slipperiness, we cannot separate EuropaCorp's genre films from Besson's broader social and economic strategy. Besson's vision for an alternative French cinema is inextricably linked to the space and culture of the French banlieues, and it informs French genre pictures that he did not direct or even produce. Besson describes this vision in the following terms: "I greatly admire the banlieues. Today, the most creative place in France is the banlieues. People there are in a situation of such precariousness that they must get out. For twenty years, all stylistic and artistic innovations come from there: rap, tagging, hoodies, baggy clothes, tennis shoes, and a thousand other things. It doesn't come from the 16th [one of the richest neighborhoods in Paris] where three-quarters of young people dress like they lived in Stains [a suburban cité in Seine-Saint-Denis]" (Loustalot 2006, 63). This vision, part of the corporate mission of EuropaCorp, has gradually taken institutional and spatial form, as Besson has moved the studio's operations to the French suburbs. Besson prefers to characterize his role in terms of being a *facilitator*, but this term coyly occludes his central role in fostering people, projects, and even on-set creative decisions during production (Maule 2006, 35). If some of the early accounts from directors who have worked with him are to be believed, Besson takes a very active hand in all aspects of the films EuropaCorp produces (Sojcher 2002, 152–153). Within his larger economic and cultural strategy, parkour offers an important visual and narrative style around which to build a global French brand of action cinema using a hip, countercultural banlieue identity. However, Besson's interest in the banlieues and its residents is not merely opportunistic; in fact, it is arguably sincere, though at times perhaps flawed or misguided in its execution.

EuropaCorp's strategies during the 2000s and 2010s have often been misunderstood as an attempt to import a Hollywood-inspired, commercial, and industrial model into France and thus destroy what makes French filmmaking properly French. This misrecognition is the result of France's long-standing critical distaste for popular and industrial modes of production. Ironically, despite Besson's significant institutional power in the global media industry, EuropaCorp's brand of commercial filmmaking signifies within France as a kind of independent, marginalized cinema despite its big-budget, profit-motivated orientation. EuropaCorp's films and the Cité du cinéma project represent not just a move toward vertical integration, but a specifically French mode of cultural politics, one that seeks to create the institutional conditions for a popular and commercial mode of filmmaking that defends, in its way, the national specificity of French cinema.

In the same way that the multiculture of the French banlieues contests narrow conceptions of what it means to be French, Besson, through his companies and his films, harnesses this space to expand what French cinema is or should be. Rather than defending an authentically artisanal French cinema as the pure negation of the industrial Hollywood model, these films and filmmakers trace singular and complicated paths through the various cultural and economic forces acting on the French film industry, much like the traceurs who caught Besson's imagination in the late 1990s.

Besson and EuropaCorp did not go on to specialize in making parkour or genre films that deal with the specificities of the French banlieues, except perhaps for the English-language remake of *District B13*, *Brick Mansions* (2014), which is a poor imitation of the original. Bronner suggests that Besson ultimately views the banlieues as a center of creativity in France, one that he hopes EuropaCorp will be able to use (Bronner 2008a).[16] Other media companies, such as Netflix, share this view, and I will return to this question in the book's conclusion. One can debate to what extent the idea of the banlieues as a hub of creativity is true, but we can say that parkour is one of the most powerful forms of culture to emerge from the banlieues, and it has become a shared global movement practice and cultural imaginary. Even though we do not see or hear about parkour as much in the 2020s as we did in the 2000s, I suggest that it is one of France's biggest cultural exports of the early twenty-first century. Parkour has not disappeared; it has simply grown into a ubiquitous part of our physical and visual culture throughout the world. Parkour has become part of the movement vocabulary for action stunts in general, and it has turned into one of the dominant means of navigating three-dimensional virtual worlds in video games. Parkour gyms and clubs have formed all throughout the world, and at a time when young students in the junior high and high schools in the wealthier neighborhoods where I live in Pittsburgh can regularly do parkour summer camps, it is fair to say that parkour is seemingly nowhere because it is now everywhere.

Films like the two *District B13* movies use the Hollywood (and even global) cinematic imaginary in the same way that the traceur uses urban space—as a set of constraints that can be creatively redirected to other ends. Rather than accepting such constraints as a kind of prison, a film like *District B13* attempts to find a way to move through them, to make them expressive of uniquely Gallic social and political concerns related to the suburbs within the language of commercial entertainment. Like the spirit of parkour, *District B13* winds its way through the traditional notions of French cinema, French funding structures, and US entertainment-oriented media to create an instance of cinematic bricolage that emblematizes EuropaCorp's cultural strategies during the first two decades of the twenty-first century. While EuropaCorp failed as a company due to financial overreach, it nevertheless remains a powerful template for a different kind of French cinema, one that seeks to rearticulate what the universal means in economic and cultural terms. Besson's producing activities suggest that one way to defend the Frenchness of French media against foreign competition is not to fall back on historical models of cultural prestige, but to see how popular global film formulae could look in and from France. Besson may never be celebrated by the French critical establishment because he has aligned his identity so much with genres and commercial filmmaking. However, his example has created space for other filmmakers to attempt the pragmatic balance among art, cultural specificity, and genre codes. In the next chapter, I examine three filmmakers with very different profiles from Besson's who seek to strike a similar balance in the context of suburban gangster films.

NOTES

1. For an overview of the previous scholarship on Besson, see Michael 2019, 114–126.

2. Bill Marshall reminds us that parkour's origins are not so indigenous (2010, 167; Bloom 2008, 183–198). Georges Hébert, naval officer and physical educator, developed the *méthode naturelle* after admiring athletic Black bodies

in Martinique at the turn of the twentieth century. The méthode naturelle is an early twentieth-century version of French gymnastics training that focused on everyday movements and used obstacle courses. The méthode naturelle was later adopted by the French military to train soldiers and firemen. Belle's father, Raymond, was trained in this method, and David learned it through him.

3. According to Christensen, industrial models of film analysis ignore differences in the production strategies, and ultimately the films, of individual studios. Christensen's solution to the auteurist/industrial divide is to posit the corporation as an intermediary body every bit as intentional as an individual person. A studio's corporate mission and identity can be discerned by looking for "the pattern of studio productions that define its identity, represent its objectives, and that endeavor to achieve those objectives" (2008, 177).

4. For an analysis of new efforts to reuse former industrial sites in the suburban periphery, see Djament-Tran 2015.

5. See Deplasse 2003. The site is inactive since 2012, but the archived page can be accessed here: http://web.archive.org/web/20111218202357/http://www.banditscompany.com:80/Bessontxt.html (accessed May 27, 2022).

6. French box office figures are from CBO Box Office (https://www.cbo-boxoffice.com [accessed November 15, 2013]) and US box office figures are from Box Office Mojo (https://www.boxofficemojo.com [accessed November 15, 2013]). Yamakasi's performance is good for a French film. Comparatively, *La Haine* sold 2,042,070 tickets in theatrical release, but only opened in 118 theaters. The most successful French film of all time, *Bienvenue chez les ch'tis (Welcome to the Sticks*, 2008) opened in 793 theaters. The second most financially successful French film in French film history, *Intouchables* (2011), was released on 508 screens before the distributor ratcheted it up to 898 theaters at the height of its popularity. The second figure is closer to an opening weekend screen number for a typical Hollywood blockbuster.

7. See the interviews in the documentary *Génération Yamakasi* (2005).

8. See my discussion of Bouchareb in chapter 3.

9. Ginette Vincendeau, in her monograph on *La Haine*, cites director Mathieu Kassovitz as saying that everyone in the banlieues knows De Palma's film (2005, 74).

10. EuropaCorp's annual reports to investors in French can be consulted on the studio's website: http://www.europacorp.com/fr/espace-investisseurs/rapports-financiers-periodiques (accessed May 1, 2021).

11. See chapters 10–20 in Le Guilcher 2016, which deal with the EuropaCorp years.

12. For an account of the Cité du cinéma's financing, see Le Guilcher 2016, 245–262.

13. See the Cité du cinéma's website (http://www.citeducinema.org/ [accessed May 1, 2021]) and the École de la cité's website (https://www.ecoledelacite.com/lecole-de-la-cite.html [accessed May 1, 2021]).

14. Besson's name and image feature prominently in the promotional materials on the École de la cité's website, including the following quote: "I created this school as an alternative for passionate young people like me when I was young who haven't found their way by the traditional route," (https://www.ecoledelacite.com/lecole-de-la-cite.html [accessed May 1, 2021]).

15. See Oui 2007 and Diao 2014.

16. For a similar account of the banlieues' possibilities, see Chombart de Lauwe 2008, 112–113.

THREE

SUBURBAN GANGSTERS
Screen Violence and the Banlieues

THE FRENCH FILM INDUSTRY HAS long been known for its crime films, called *films policiers* or *polars* in French, which can include films noirs, police procedurals, thrillers, and gangster films. While not quite on par in terms of numbers with comedy, crime cinema is the third most common genre in the French film industry after the biopic and enjoys a high degree of cultural prestige. French crime films have also long been in dialogue with Hollywood crime and gangster cinema. Early Hollywood gangster cinema and the film noir tradition that grew out of it arguably helped launch the French New Wave with Jean-Luc Godard's *Breathless* (*A bout de souffle*, 1960), and from the 1930s onward, French filmmakers have adapted the different periods of Hollywood gangster cinema into distinctly Gallic modes.

The tropes of the crime film and gangster cinema have been repeatedly used to represent the suburbs and France's marginalized communities, arguably as early as French poetic realism in films such as Marcel Carné's *Port of Shadows* (*Quai des brumes*, 1938) and *Daybreak* (*Le Jour se lève*, 1939).[1] New Hollywood gangster films from the 1970s and 1980s by filmmakers such Francis Ford Coppola, Martin Scorsese, and Brian De Palma have been particularly influential on the history and style of banlieue films, especially after Mathieu Kassovitz adapted them so compellingly in *La Haine* (1995). However, even though *La Haine* is very much a film about violence, it is not a film whose style is especially violent. There are none of the extended action sequences, kinetic editing, or practical effects like squibs, blood packs, or special effects makeup that define violence and gore in contemporary cinema. Squibs are small explosive devices that can be layered into costumes or objects on set and then detonated remotely to simulate the impact of bullets. Squibs can be combined with packs of fake blood to create particularly visceral sensations for viewers of how bullets tear into bodies. Unlike *La Haine*, whose violence was more verbal than physical, the three films that I examine in this chapter—Rachid Bouchareb's *Outside the Law* (*Hors la loi*, 2010), Jacques Audiard's *Dheepan* (2015), and Houda Benyamina's *Divines* (2016)—all take up in different ways the question of physical violence in films about the suburbs. They do this through a sustained engagement with the gangster films of the New Hollywood period, including the increasingly sophisticated forms of on-screen violence that these films innovated.

The New Hollywood period is generally thought to have begun in 1967 with the release of Arthur Penn's *Bonnie and Clyde* (1967) and to have continued through 1976. It was characterized by a willingness on the part of Hollywood studios to experiment with young, relatively unproven filmmakers and new types of self-reflexive narrative even in genre films meant for wide release. The period also witnessed an increase in the explicit sex and violence that could be shown on screen due to the end of the Motion Picture Association of America Production Code that had regulated censorship in Hollywood since the 1930s (Krämer 2005, 1–2, 47–58). Stephen Prince, in his now classic analysis of screen violence, coined the term *ultraviolence* to refer to the new level of explicitness that characterized this period. In his view, there are essentially two types of ultraviolence: *montage-slow motion* and *graphic mutilation*. The first type tends to employ spectacle sequences that focus on bodies in conflict, such as one-on-one combat, shoot-outs between groups, and large-scale battles. Slow-motion violence, which Prince defined as "squib-work, multicamera filming, and montage editing utilizing differential rates of slow motion," emerged from Hollywood in the 1960s with filmmakers like Samuel Peckinpah and Penn (2000a, 17, 13). It found expression in genres like the Western, the gangster film, the martial arts film, and the war film, and it was imitated throughout the rest of the world in contexts as diverse as 1980s Hong Kong martial arts cinema and contemporary Hollywood action and war films. The second type of ultraviolence focuses on images of bodily mutilation and harm, and it tends to occur in individually focused sequences of penetration, evisceration, and self-harm. Graphic scenes of bodily mutilation emerged during the late 1970s and throughout the 1980s in Hollywood horror films, especially slasher films, and would impact French horror films in the 2000s and 2010s, some of which I will examine in the next chapter. The emergence of cinematic ultraviolence has been variously explained, including as a response to televisual coverage of the Vietnam War in which scenes of real violence and carnage were so widely and regularly distributed as to become horrifyingly banal.

Pervasive French media images of the banlieues as violent spaces offer one possible explanation for why gangster cinema has so often been used in films about the banlieues, including the genre's penchant for stylized violence. Indeed, one of the most pernicious and deleterious negative media stereotypes about the French banlieues is that they are spaces in which violence—both self-destructive violence in which residents kill each other and violence against the state, as in the mediatized images of banlieue protests during the past five decades—is endemic. Ginette Vincendeau has argued that television coverage of sensationalized violence in the banlieues was already widespread at the time of *La Haine*'s release in 1995. As much as the critical discourse surrounding *La Haine* stresses the film's revelatory power at the time of its release, it was simply arranging images, sounds, and tropes that were already present in many viewers' minds (Vincendeau 2005, 24–25). In a related vein, French historian Annie Fourcaut contends that French media have never captured the reality of the banlieues. Rather, they select and frame events in specific ways to present the banlieues alternately as a place of violent protestors or as the future of French society. In her view, banlieue residents would likely prefer more "ordinary" representations of their communities (2008, 125). By ordinary, I take her to mean representations of the banlieues as spaces in which people live, work, and play.

The centrality of media representations to how the banlieues are perceived suggests that viewers' memory is an important component of how films about the banlieues are made and received. Genres share with media representations an emphasis on memory, as using genres to make sense of a film requires viewers to pay attention to repetition and difference in how an individual film manipulates the codes of genre. However, the films I examine in this chapter also employ genre and memory in a different sense. They seek to create cinematic images that place minority characters within specific genres and even specific images from individual genre films. This is part of how such films rearticulate the universal through a process of accretion in which images of minority characters and communities are added to viewers' memories of a particular genre.

Mikhail Bakhtin's writings about genre can help us understand how the process of accretion works. While his reflections on genre focus mostly on speech and literature, they can be productively applied to cinema as well. Bakhtin understands genres as impersonal collections of concepts, behaviors, events, and worldviews. Rather than view each work in a genre as a repetition of the past, he argues instead that each work generates something new and unrepeatable. Genres for Bakhtin represent a patchwork of uses, imperfect but good enough for the purpose at hand (Morson and Emerson 1990, 290–293). They both carry a history of the past—what he sometimes refers to as "genre memory"—and they open onto a future of unintended usages. This future potential is what enables genres to rework the present. As Gary Saul Morson and Caryl Emerson explain, "because genres are so often adapted from previous genres, they may carry the potential to resume their past usage and so to redefine a present experience in an additional way. Some genres easily lend themselves to this kind of 'double-voicing'; they recover old contexts or intimate the possibility of new ones" (1990, 293). Genre films may thus reactivate the historical contexts of genres such as the gangster film and make them speak to a new context, whether this is the events of the Algerian War or social divisions in the contemporary suburbs. Morson and Emerson characterize this process as one of double-voicing and reaccentuating: "The unsuspected potential of a genre may also be used to 'reaccentuate' a voice. This process is a common part of both individual psychic life, in which we arrive at our own inner discourse through reaccentuating the discourses of others, and of collective social life, in which it serves as a method for adapting the lessons of one kind of experience to another" (1990, 293). All three of the films I examine in this chapter are defined by the gangster genre and its attendant violence, but they also employ gangster tropes in combination with other genres and modes, including epic cinema, the war film, romantic comedy, the female friendship film, and the dance film. Taken together, the complex mixing of genre in these three films is an attempt to adapt the lessons of the gangster genre to the suburbs as a means of nuancing and even criticizing the violence with which such spaces are often associated in the French popular imaginary.

One of the principal objections to using the spectacular aspects of certain genres like the violence of gangster cinema in films about the banlieues is the dangerous divide they establish between the quotidian aspects of life in the banlieues and the seductive violence of images on screen. The emotional charge of cinematic spectacle can reinforce violent stereotypes about the banlieues in French citizens who do not live there or who do not have regular contact with those who do. What is more, these negative stereotypes about violence can be racialized—that is, they can be activated with respect to minority bodies regardless of where they live and work in France.

It should thus come as no surprise when banlieue residents, filmmakers, or scholars call for more realistic, ethnographic, or even documentary films that challenge the negative and violent stereotypes about the banlieues (see, for example, Niang 2019, 6). And yet, films about the banlieues continue to use stylized violence and the genres that anchor them to reach audiences, even for goals that the filmmakers believe are progressive. It is important, then, to analyze how cinematic violence, including ultraviolence, functions in banlieue films both to render palpable the violence of social exclusion that many feel and to challenge viewers' complicity with social systems that are maintained through violence inflicted on minority bodies.

The gangster's seductive criminality and penchant for violence have always carried an ambivalent politics. On the one hand, violence on screen can arguably serve to denounce the exclusionary violence of capitalism and shock viewers from apathy. On the other, screen violence can also reinforce preexisting negative media stereotypes about the banlieues and justify law-and-order policies that only increase repression. Why, then, would a wide range of filmmakers from different positionalities—dominant and minority, from and not from the banlieues, men and women—turn to the cinematic violence of gangster films and other proximate genres like the Western and the vigilante film, especially the ultraviolent forms of cinematic spectacle that emerged from the United States during the New Hollywood period in the late 1960s, in their bids to represent the banlieues on mainstream screens?

All three films considered in this chapter use the violence of the gangster genre to different degrees as a means of reflecting on the mappings between the spaces and bodies of the banlieues and the various kinds of violence that are perceived to operate on and in them. Bouchareb's *Outside the Law* is not a banlieue film, per se, but it focuses on the infamous immigrant shantytown at Nanterre during the 1950s and early 1960s, as it was an important antecedent to contemporary marginalized suburban spaces. What is more, by focusing on events from the shared French and Algerian colonial past, the film explores how history can be added to the French public memory of decolonization using cinematic genre. Audiard's *Dheepan*, about a family of Tamil refugees who flee political violence in Sri Lanka and move to a French banlieue, does not focus on specific historical events to the same degree that *Outside the Law* does. However, it does bring attention to France's very real Tamil immigrant communities, who are not always as visible as Black or Maghrebi communities in the banlieues. The film, which Audiard presents in interviews as a loose remake of Peckinpah's *Straw Dogs* (1971), balances a quasi-ethnographic focus on everyday life in the banlieues with genre tropes that run the gamut from the romantic comedy to hard-hitting gangster and vigilante cinema. In interviews, Audiard discusses how this combination of genre and Tamil characters is meant to introduce heroic images of minority communities to French audiences. Finally, Benyamina's *Divines* focuses on a young woman who wants to get rich as quickly as possible by adopting a gangster's lifestyle. Benyamina questions the gendered parameters of violence in the banlieues, ultimately separating violence from agency and assertiveness when expressed by women characters. She explores the dangerous ease with which smartphones and streaming platforms circulate images of violence as a means of challenging such representations of the French suburbs. Taken together, these three films demonstrate that gangster cinema and its violent style can be used to rearticulate the different kinds of images that mediate the French suburbs in mainstream films.

THE CONTROVERSIES OF HISTORY AND GENRE IN *OUTSIDE THE LAW*

Franco-Algerian director Bouchareb is a central figure in the so-called *beur* generation of French Maghrebi filmmakers who came of age in the 1970s and 1980s. This loose grouping includes filmmakers like Mehdi Charef and Abdellatif Kechiche, who were either born in France to immigrant parents or who were born in former French colonies and immigrated to France at a young age. Bouchareb has made many kinds of films, from small-budget auteurist projects like *London River* (2009) to expensive mainstream genre films like *Belleville Cop* (*Le Flic de Belleville*, 2018), an homage to 1980s Hollywood buddy cop films such as *Beverly Hills Cop* (1984) and *Lethal Weapon* (1987). He is best known in France for two big-budget films that revisit neglected moments in the history of French colonialism and decolonization: *Days of Glory* (*Indigènes*, 2006) and *Outside the Law* (2010), the latter of which will be my focus in this chapter because it draws heavily on the gangster genre. While not a banlieue film per se, *Outside the Law* nevertheless tells the prehistory of the suburbs in the bidonvilles or shantytowns where Algerian immigrants lived in the 1950s and 1960s. Through an anachronistic reference to the banlieue, the film suggests that it targets the present in addition to the historical past.

Outside the Law follows three brothers who are displaced from their farm in rural Algeria, first to the city of Sétif and then to the Nanterre shantytown outside of Paris. The brothers witness firsthand the colonial land expropriations of 1925 and the Sétif massacre of 1945 before two of them become militants for the Algerian National Liberation Front (FLN) party. Saïd, played by Jamel Debbouze, works first as a pimp and later as a nightclub owner and boxing promoter. Abdelkader (Sami Bouajila) is the most idealistic and political of the three brothers, and he eventually becomes the FLN cell leader in the shantytown and later the Paris region. Messaoud, played by Roschdy Zem, fights for the French forces in the Vietnamese war of decolonization and then becomes one of Abdelkader's key enforcers as the militants fight for liberation from France. The film ends with the deaths of both Abdelkader and Messaoud; however, the police colonel in charge of the antiterrorist squad recognizes that it is only a matter of time until Algeria becomes an independent country.

Outside the Law was controversial when it premiered at Cannes due to its violence and its representation of history. Far-right politicians from the surrounding region publicly criticized the film (Donadey 2014, 15–16). War veterans—including former French soldiers, Algerians who had chosen to fight with France (the *harkis*), and former French residents of Algeria who had to leave upon independence (the *pieds noirs*)—protested the film outside the festival. Many of these critical voices had not even seen the film, but this did not stop some from calling the film anti-French (Jørholt 2016, 50–51). Lionnel Luca, a right-wing politician and member of Nicolas Sarkozy's conservative party, objected in part to the liberties Bouchareb's film takes with history. Luca went so far as to send the film's script to the French Defense Ministry's Historical Services department to identify inaccuracies. In a similar gesture, Hubert Falco, an undersecretary of defense for veterans' affairs at the time, questioned why the French government would help finance a film whose version of history was "barely credible" (Adi et al. 2010). The reactions in Algeria focused mainly on the film's reception in France, and some critics argued in favor of the film as a means of defending the Algerian film industry. However, as Nedjib Sidi Moussa has shown, some critics in Algeria challenged the film's simplistic representation of history and poor quality as a crime film (2012, 120–121). Critic Olivier Barlet views the film as essentially being about the fratricidal violence between the FLN and the moderate Algerian National Movement (MNA) party and the violence between the French state and those who resist it. Consequently, he finds the film's lack of historical context and its stereotyped characters understandable (2010).

The film was also widely criticized for its supposedly clumsy use of genres. Interviewers, critics, and Bouchareb himself invoke a wide-ranging set of genres and individual films to make sense of *Outside the Law*: the gangster film, the Western, the boxing film, and the epic film. Intertexts include Sergio Leone's *Once upon a Time in America* (1984), Jean-Pierre Melville's *Army of Shadows* (*L'Armée des ombres*, 1969), Scorsese's *Raging Bull* (1980), and, most prominently, Coppola's *Godfather* trilogy (1972–1990). Not all critics viewed the film's engagement with genre films as positive. For example, Moussa writes that the film's many borrowings from Coppola's *Godfather* films are "as obvious as they are clumsy," and he quotes approvingly an *Elle* journalist who remarked that "Rachid Bouchareb must have watched a lot of *Once upon a Time in America* and *Raging Bull*, but he's neither Sergio Leone nor Martin Scorsese" (2012, 125). For

Moussa, *Outside the Law*'s refusal to represent tracts, newspapers, meetings, or protests and its use of "mob movies" rather than political or revolutionary cinema is a betrayal of the film's subject matter, one that puts the question of violence above all other historical concerns (2012, 125).

Bouchareb responded to criticisms about the film's representation of history by reiterating repeatedly across interviews that the film is cinema rather than history or documentary, by which I take him to mean it is fiction (Irbah 2010). Further, he explained that he used archival research and oral interviews to generate a narrative that would be largely cinematic. While the film does offer "historical reference points" (*repères historiques*), he emphasizes that the film is primarily cinema and meant to entertain through its spectacle and genre pleasures. As such, in his view, audiences can take up the historical references or not, but they are not the film's primary focus (Bouchareb 2010b). How, then, are we to think about the film's use of genre to represent history, especially genres like the gangster film that emphasize violence? We first need to consider the film's engagement with history, not in terms of documentary or even the heritage film, but rather in terms of the epic mode that seeks to create a sense of being in history through the stylistic excesses of cinematic spectacle. Second, we must examine the film's rather restrained use of violence in the context of the epic mode as mainly about expressive effects and the action of individuals, rather than the overwhelming shock of New Hollywood ultraviolence. Third, we must connect the film's epic mode and use of violence to Bouchareb's project of creating cinematic images of Maghrebi gangsters. Here, Bakhtin's concept of genre memory will demonstrate how *Outside the Law* uses genre references to insert minority characters and the history of FLN militant activities in Paris into preexisting memories of cinematic images. It is here that *Outside the Law*'s project of rearticulating the universal lies.

OUTSIDE THE LAW AND THE EPIC MODE

One of the principal criticisms leveled against *Outside the Law* is the extent to which the film departs from the historical record in favor of cinematic spectacle (Merkel 2013; Jørholt 2016; Moussa 2012).[2] In answering such criticisms, Bouchareb has said that his film is not a political film, but rather an "epic with a romanesque form" (quoted in Genty 2011, 170). The French word *romanesque* is especially challenging to translate into English. It can mean novelistic, as *roman* is the French word for novel. It can also refer to the fanciful flights of fiction and adventure, gesturing back to the word *romance*, as in romance of chivalry. The words *epic* and *romanesque* highlight the emotional and affective appeals of the film's use of style, including the monumentality of the epic and the imaginative and page-turning appeal of the romanesque. Like some film scholars have done with melodrama, I prefer to think about epic more as a mode than a genre. The sense of production scale, image quality, focus on individual action, and engagement with history that define the epic in cinema can mix with other genres, be they the Western or the gangster film in the case of Leone's *Once upon a Time* films or sword-and-sandal films (*péplums* in French).

When it comes to the epic mode, the production history and scale of the film matter just as much as the historical events represented. Writing about epic cinema in the Hollywood context, film historian Vivian Sobchack argues that the "temporal excess of historical events" to which epic films refer must be confirmed by the material excess of production in terms of cost, scale, and labor (1990, 30). Consequently, films in the epic mode often test new means of production, be they special effects or widescreen cinematography. Sobchack suggests that this explains why the epic films depend so heavily on extratextual elements, such as promotional materials, publicity, interviews, and coverage of the film's production in the popular press. Sobchack ultimately argues that the "laborious struggle" of the film's production serves to repeat formally the struggle of the historical events themselves (1990, 30), and this is why we must consider both together in the context of *Outside the Law*.

The promotional materials surrounding *Outside the Law* draw attention to the film's production history and especially its production scale. The number of times that Bouchareb emphasizes in interviews the film's expense in terms of costumes, production design, set design, and cinematography suggests that the epic mode defines the film's overall approach to genre. *Outside the Law*'s budget was twenty million euros, which does not even come close to rivaling expensive Hollywood blockbusters from the same time whose budgets can begin at around a hundred million dollars (Studio Canal 2010, 21). However, it was an enormous figure for a French film, as the average French film budget in the late 2000s was $7.4 million, compared to $70.8 million for a North American production (Michael 2015, 75). When asked about the film's epic "breath and sweep," Bouchareb does not deny his emphasis on spectacle: "I constructed the film like a fresco covering forty years of history with large sets, action sequences, and meticulously worked costumes" (Studio Canal 2010, 7). This interview is included in the film's press packet, which means that it is a part of how the film's distributors wish to position it to exhibitors and journalists. Bouchareb's film is a Franco-Algerian coproduction that was shot at Tunisian producer Tarak Ben Ammar's studios at Ben Arous in Tunisia. As *Outside the Law*'s press kit reminds readers, these are the same studios where films like

Georges Lucas's *Star Wars* and Steven Spielberg's *Raiders of the Lost Ark* were filmed, thus inserting Bouchareb's film into a venerable lineage of Hollywood blockbusters (Studio Canal 2010, 21).

Bouchareb turns to the epic mode in *Outside the Law* not just because the neglected history of FLN militancy in Paris deserves to be represented on screen; rather, it deserves to be represented with all the cinematic excess that the production scale of the epic genre can muster, like any other historical period or set of events represented in a French historical film or *film patrimonial*. The pairing of the gangster genre with the epic mode suggests that unlike other French historical films, *Outside the Law* is not just about a trip to the past, where one can contemplate the past as a nostalgia-tinged image in a coffee-table book. Rather, this is a film in which viewers experience the actions that moved history forward. Representing the events of the FLN militancy in this manner is a part of how Bouchareb uses genre to rearticulate the universal. When one argues that films about contemporary multiculture should only be handled in a low-budget, realist manner, one is effectively relegating them to a cinematic "ghetto" where they are not worthy of the same stylistic attention as other parts of French history or other kinds of big-budget films. Cinematic style and production scale are thus just as important for Bouchareb's project of rearticulating the universal as the historical events themselves, if not more so.

Sobchack argues that detailed criticisms of an individual film's representation of historical events miss the point of the epic mode. The goal of such films, in her view, is not an accurate account of specific events, but rather the "narrative construction of *general historical eventfulness*" and "the *general* possibility for re-cognizing oneself as a *historical subject* of a particular kind" (1990, 28–29, original emphases). *Outside the Law* asks its viewers to spend time with these ignored and repressed historical events at the scale of cinematic spectacle that only a film in the epic mode can offer. As film scholar Robert Burgoyne puts it, "the sublime spectacle offered by epic cinema becomes ... a way of accessing the somatic, physical apprehension of being in history, the burning in of experiences in a way that links us to other times and other places" (2010, 93). Unlike Leone's *Once upon a Time in America*, Bouchareb's *Outside the Law* does not retell events through retrospective narration saturated by melancholy, but through the present-tense narration of the epic mode that focuses on action rather than memory, even when dealing with historical events. As Dina Iordanova explains, epic films typically feature a "heroic protagonist compelled to make choices that affect the course of history" (2010, 102). The gangster genre's violence in the film serves to highlight action and demarcate the causes and effects of such action. Unlike the New Hollywood films' style of ultraviolence,

Bouchareb's use of violence in *Outside the Law* is rather restrained and is ultimately subservient to epic mode's goal of creating the sense of being in history for spectators by emphasizing the individual actions of the FLN militants.

OUTSIDE THE LAW'S RESTRAINED VIOLENCE

Despite the centrality of violent acts and spectacle in *Outside the Law*, when compared to ultraviolent Hollywood films such as *Once upon a Time in America* or Peckinpah's *The Wild Bunch* (1969), Bouchareb's film is much less violent in terms of how its images and sounds are put together. Anne Donadey argues that *Outside the Law* does not present a "heroic" or "Manichean" view of the Algerian conflict in France, but rather an attempt to "bring the fragmented memories of the war together for a short time" (2014, 23–24). In her analysis of the film's violence, she contends that during the opening Sétif protest scene, Algerians are only shown to use violence in self-defense and that in general, the violence, while spectacularized, does not "linger on gushing wounds" or feature "gory sounds" and thus is more properly considered as an example of pre-1970s Hollywood war cinema's "sobriety and restraint" (2014, 20). I would add that while Bouchareb's film does not often emphasize the embodied aspects of violence—what Donadey calls *gore*—its use of violence is not so much a rejection of ultraviolence as a careful nuancing of how it is used. Bouchareb's use of fast montage editing and bouncing handheld and Steadicam shots during sequences of crowd violence have more to do with post-1970s Hollywood representations of violence than classical-era ones. To understand the use Bouchareb makes of violence, we must look at the specifics of the film's editing, staging, and practical effects in several of the sequences of spectacular violence.

Of the three elements that Prince argued define the slow-motion montage style of ultraviolence, Bouchareb only uses montage editing and squib work in *Outside the Law*. There are no slow-motion insert shots during scenes of violence that would give a balletic quality to the violence. There is significant squib work, but it only rarely features the use of the spraying blood packs that are so striking in Peckinpah's or Leone's films. Squibs with blood packs in *Outside the Law* are mostly used in single-person medium shots when an important character is killed, such as the scene in which Abdelkader and Messaoud execute the police captain Picot with two quick gunshots or the scene in which the police shoot Abdelkader in a metro station at the end of the film. There are a few other squibs in the film during sequences of crowd violence, such as the Sétif massacre in which French soldiers murder the protesting Algerians or during Abdelkader and Messaoud's escape from the police station. However, these crowd sequences rarely feature blood. We repeatedly see and hear guns firing (muzzle flares and sound effects), but we do not often see the direct impacts of the shots. The bodies being struck are hidden behind the tarps of military vehicles, as in the scene when the FLN cell murders a caravan of *harkis*, or there are simply too many bodies to see the shots' effects, as during the Sétif massacre. If we do see squibs in scenes of collective violence, they tend to be environmental rather than corporeal, as in the aforementioned truck scene or the final shoot-out with Colonel Faivre's squad, when we see the glass windows on cars and trucks shatter and bullets tear through the vehicle frames.

Blood is rare in the film, which means that it takes on more of an expressive effect than it would in ultraviolent sequences from New Hollywood films that are literal bloodbaths. For example, when Saïd executes Kaïd, the Algerian who collaborates with the French colonial authorities and dispossessed the family of their land in the opening sequence, Bouchareb uses blood packs. Saïd first stabs him with the knife, and viewers do not see the blade entering; they only hear the sound. Bouchareb focuses on Kaïd's surprised face as the blade enters his torso, then he cuts to a close-up shot of Saïd's face with rage on it. After this initial shot/reverse shot construction, viewers do get a cutaway shot of the blade in the body with blood all over Kaïd's shirt. What is more, it is matched with a sound effect of a new stab, showing Saïd doing the action. Bouchareb then cuts back to the close-up of the torso as Saïd pulls the blade out and looks at his handiwork, and viewers see the blood on Kaïd's body as Saïd takes his wallet. Sustained moments of bloody violence like this, however, are infrequent in the film. When Messaoud dies at the end of the film, his blood gets all over his body and Abdelkader, accentuating just how far the latter was willing to push others in service of the revolution. Other moments with blood are more punctual, such as the scene in which the MNA-affiliated café owner outside the shantytown slaps Abdelkader for promoting the FLN or when the police antiterrorist squad shoots one of the French FLN sympathizers on the street. In the latter scene, viewers see a spray of blood on the wall timed with the gunshot, but the impact of the bullet is not shown, as the target is hidden behind a metal structure on the sidewalk.

Instead of showing the rather anonymous balletic spectacles of violence that one finds in Leone's or Peckinpah's films, Bouchareb focuses much more on the individuals committing or receiving acts of violence. In this, Bouchareb reveals the influence of Jean-Pierre Melville's *Army of Shadows*, an unconventional and slow-paced gangster film about the French Resistance that is more a meditation on the reasons for violence than a glorification of it. Donadey is right to point out that *Outside the Law* represents the violence the brothers commit more than the violence of French police against Algerians as a means of inviting a debate about whether violent means can justify the ends (2014, 20). Bouchreb's use of violence is thus as much ideological as it is embodied. A brief discussion of the Sétif massacre will make this clear. I do not mean to suggest that the Sétif massacre is not a massive spectacle sequence, given the number of actors and extras running through the images and the layered density of the sound design. However, the violence is more about effects than cause. We see bodies lying on the ground or the two women who were murdered on the stairs of the family's home. However, rarely does Bouchareb connect the cause and effect of violence through a shot or reverse construction or through two bodies interacting in a single shot.

When Bouchareb does connect them in this way, the effect is brutal. In a shot toward the end of the Sétif massacre, a handful of Algerians are positioned up against a wall. Soldiers stand in a line behind the Algerians, one for each that is about to be executed. The soldiers shoot simultaneously, and blood packs explode onto the wall as the Algerians slump down together, creating a row of irregular red circles that stand out against the intense tans and beiges of the set design. This moment's strong charge depends on its evocation of the method by which the Germans executed the French, especially Resistance members, in Occupied France. In fact, the Sétif massacre took place shortly after Victory-Europe day, and *Outside the Law*'s early use of archival footage of French Liberation that then transitions seamlessly into the first image of the Sétif street protest accentuates the disconnect between liberation and ongoing colonial oppression. In a later scene in which Abdelkader, leader of the Paris FLN cell, meets with Colonel Faivre, the former makes a direct equation between the FLN and the Resistance that Faivre participated in. Now, Abdelakder notes, Faivre is on the wrong side of history (Jørholt 2016, 58–59). Violence in *Outside the Law* is used not to create the shock effects of ultraviolence, but rather to connect individual action and the sense of being in history, and in this, its use is more properly understood through the epic mode than through gangster cinema.

ALGERIAN GODFATHERS

The importance of the epic mode in *Outside the Law* does not, however, mean that the gangster genre is unimportant to the film. Rather, Bouchareb is trying to do something other than shock viewers with violence through his use of the gangster genre. Instead, he seeks to insert Maghrebi characters and the events of FLN militancy in Paris into French public memory through very specific images taken from well-known Hollywood gangster films. In an interview included with the DVD release, Bouchareb commented on the significance of making a Maghrebi gangster film: "When have we seen a gangster film with Maghrebi men? In the 1950s, with Borsalino hats, vests, ties, cigars? . . . Where does that exist?" (Bouchareb 2010a). Bouchareb suggests here that creating enduring images of Maghrebi gangsters is at least as important as anything he wants to express about the historical context of the conflict, yet the references to other films could hardly be said to interrupt the film's narrative. In another interview, Bouchareb describes *Outside the Law* as "partly about the management of a revolution and how you must go to great lengths, further perhaps than you originally wanted, to commit violence to achieve your ends. In that respect both Abdelkader and Messaoud are like Michael Corleone. . . . Of course, the criminal aspect is not the same but there is a parallel with regards to their management" (Jaafar 2011, 39). Bouchareb's discussion of Coppola's *Godfather* trilogy suggests that it played a significant role in how he conceived of *Outside the Law*.

The affinity between them lies partly in how the *Godfather* films and *Outside the Law* create quasi-ethnographic images of the past within a genre film. Messaoud's marriage in the film and the corresponding scene that lingers on how immigrant Algerians celebrate in the Nanterre shantytown strongly evoke the spirit of Coppola's recreation of early Italian American marriage customs in the opening scene of the first *Godfather* film. However, the connection goes beyond a generalized stylistic affinity, because *Outside the Law* quite literally recreates several scenes and images from the first *Godfather* film, as I will detail below. These serve to explore the justification or lack thereof for certain forms of criminal behavior and violence. Among the three brothers, Saïd is the one who most directly embodies the classic cinematic gangster's desire for easy money and the rich life. While Abdelkader and Messaoud make a living by working in the Renault factory, primarily to recruit FLN militants, Saïd refuses such drudgery. On his first day exploring the shantytown, Saïd notices a well-dressed man sitting across from the grocery store and immediately strikes up a conversation with him. Saïd presses the man on how to make easy money, and the man sets him up as a pimp near Pigalle. Viewers do not see images of Saïd's rise from small-time pimp to nightclub and boxing gym owner, but they do see the money he repeatedly offers his mother, which she refuses. The shantytown residents talk of Saïd as a "bandit," and his mother and two brothers harshly judge his criminal lifestyle.

Tensions between the violence of gangsters motivated by greed and the violence of FLN militants motivated by revolution come to a head during a debate among the brothers just over a half hour into the film. Abdelkader speaks about

Figure 3.1 The FLN cell in Paris holds court in a visual nod to Don Corleone's office in *The Godfather*. *Outside the Law*, 2010.

wanting to organize the revolution in the shantytown, whereas Saïd argues that they should form a gang and lay down their own law. Abdelkader objects and says the Algerian revolution is the only cause worth serving, and Messaoud sides with him. Saïd leaves, and relations are tense between the three until the very end of the film. Despite the fact that the FLN cell indirectly forces Saïd to close his nightclub and stop promoting boxing, he rescues his two brothers from the final shoot-out at the end of the film, even if he does not ultimately succeed in saving their lives.

However, despite the way this early conversation seems to separate Saïd's version of gangsterism from FLN militancy, Bouchareb quotes from *The Godfather* to suggest that the difference is not so clear-cut. The scene in which Abdelkader first demonstrates leadership of the FLN cell through violence is a loose remake of the Italian restaurant scene in which Michael Corleone (Al Pacino) chooses the criminal life by killing the gangster who attempted to assassinate his father. In *Outside the Law*, there is a café next to the shantytown where the Renault factory workers from Algeria gather for drinks. The café owner is a supporter of the MNA, one of the moderate parties that sought to free Algeria through democratic rather than violent means. When Abdelkader attempts to recruit FLN members in the café, the owner roughs him up and throws him out, threatening him with death if he returns. Abdelakder, Messaoud, and a third man, who heard his speech and joins the FLN, return later. The owner sits at a table eating noodles with a large, checked napkin tucked into his shirt, a clear visual echo of the *Godfather* scene I just mentioned. Abdelkader attempts to choke him with a clothesline, but he does not have the strength, so Messaoud finishes the job.

Abdelkader and Messaoud have now chosen the violent path of what the French police in the film consider domestic terrorism. As Abdelkader settles into the role of leading the shantytown FLN cell (and later all of Paris), he becomes the cell's "godfather," something that Bouchareb marks through other visual rhymes with Coppola's film. As Abdelkader sits in the café's back room, collecting fees from local Algerians and meeting with them, the line forming in the other room evokes the image of Don Corleone's office in *The Godfather* and the supplicants waiting outside. Later, after Abdelkader first kisses a French costume designer, Hélène, who works for the FLN cause, the latter is viciously killed during a car explosion that visually echoes a similar scene in the first *Godfather* film in which Michael's Sicilian wife, Apollonia, is killed by a car bomb. These quite literal citations of visual motifs and plot elements from *The Godfather* highlight the parallels between the FLN militant cell and an organized crime gang. As much as Bouchareb would like his film's engagement with gangsters to be only about "organizational management," visually, it is also— perhaps even predominantly—about violence. The French secret police admit as much when, following the murder by the FLN of a French police captain who had been torturing and executing Algerians, Colonel Faivre forms a new secret group called the Red Hand, an organization that really existed (Donadey 2014, 23). Faivre explains that they will imitate the methods of criminal terrorists and that they have legal immunity from the French government. They begin executing FLN supporters on the streets, just like any criminal gang and the film's FLN cell itself.

Outside the Law's final climax in the spectacular confrontation between the FLN cell and the Red Hand group near Valenciennes also draws significantly on the iconography of shoot-outs in gangster cinema. The FLN militants have just successfully trafficked automatic guns and ammunition across the border from Germany, and the Red Hand learns of this by capturing and torturing one of the FLN militants. After the extended shoot-out sequence that I analyzed earlier, Messaoud and the FLN militants are all killed. Abdelkader escapes but is shot shortly thereafter during a clash between pro-independence Algerian protestors and the police in a Parisian metro station. Colonel Faivre finds his dead body and admits that Abdelkader has won.

Bouchareb's persistent reworking of narrative tropes and images is not accidental; it is an essential part of what *Outside the Law* contributes to a politics of representation of France's minority communities. In the same interview on the film's DVD release that I mentioned earlier, Bouchareb says that he and his collaborators "had the impression they were creating something. . . . I'll take the example of African American cinema in the United States. We're not making a communitarian cinema, we're making a cinema that is new [*vierge*]" (Bouchareb 2010a). *Communitarian* in French usage is often understood as the opposite of universalism, so Bouchareb's interview suggests that his decision to make a Franco-Algerian gangster film about decolonization is a universalizing gesture in which he seeks to add Algerian decolonization to the storehouse of images that film genres accrete.

Adding images of Maghrebi gangsters to the genre memory of the gangster film is a different kind of memory work related to ongoing efforts in France to integrate historical memories of the French-Algerian war of decolonization into national narratives. Benjamin Stora, a well-known French historian of France's relationship with North Africa, remarked in an interview at the time of the film's premiere that France's collective national memory had yet to integrate the end of the Algerian War (quoted in Lherm 2010). It is precisely the recognizability of film genres that allows a filmmaker like Bouchareb to present historical events that arguably have yet to be fully integrated into national memory as nevertheless already a part of the genres' historical memory and, by extension, the memory of viewers.

Bouchareb's remarks in interviews suggest that he is aware of using genres in this way, even if he does not speak about their use explicitly through the terms I have laid out here. For example, during the Q and A session at Cannes, Bouchareb calls the film a "trip [voyage] into the colonial past" and goes on to explain that if there is controversy surrounding the film, it is because the film "has resonance with the present" (Irbah 2010). This statement could be taken to refer to the ongoing memory process discussed above or to the contemporary challenges of multiculture in France. While the focus in the film is on the shantytowns that are precursor spaces to the banlieues, a character does use the word once in a scene that takes place in 1955, and its usage is arguably anachronistic. As I explained in this book's introduction, it was not until French white working-class and pieds noirs communities began to move out of the banlieues in the 1960s that former colonial subjects, now immigrants and migrants, started relocating to them. In fact, as Paul Silverstein has shown, the building of permanent housing blocks in banlieue neighborhoods was in part meant to combat FLN recruiting success in shantytowns like Nanterre (2004, 92).

Before then, many immigrants from the French colonies lived in bidonvilles or shantytowns outside French cities and near the factories and construction sites that fueled France's postwar modernization. In *Outside the Law*, this is a Renault factory near Nanterre. Bouchareb spends a significant amount of the film's screen time and production design budget to visualize the Nanterre shantytown for audiences, and this is part of the production "excess" of the epic mode that seeks to place viewers in history. The first images of it in the film reveal a decrepit set of shacks built with discarded wood and insulated with broken-down boxes against the winter's cold. And yet, the wide shots of the shantytown are hauntingly beautiful, such as the first one in which snow falls, calling attention to the extreme climate difference for newly arrived Algerians. The shots are beautiful for their composition and for the minute details of production design. In this, they visually echo the studio reconstructions of Algiers and working-class Parisian neighborhoods that one finds in 1930s French poetic realist films such as Julien Duvivier's *Pépé le Moko* (1937) or Marcel Carné's *Daybreak*.

The word *banlieue* is not uttered in the shantytown but rather during the years Abdelkader spends in a French prison between the time of the Sétif massacre and his release in 1955. On his last day, one of the other prisoners, ostensibly an FLN leader, tells him that he must "[speaking in French] organize all Algerians in the suburbs" and "[speaking in Arabic] those in Paris." The use of the word *banlieue* rather than *bidonville* unmoors the film from its reconstructed historical setting and makes it as much about the humiliations of the present-day banlieues as about those the first generation of Algerian immigrants faced in the 1950s and 1960s. It marks the ways in which the film functions as a visual prehistory of the banlieues, connecting the current banlieues back to the French colonial history of land dispossession, independence, and immigration, at least for French Algerians, but also by extension for other postcolonial communities in France. The answer to the marginalization of the suburbs is arguably the same then as now—organize and demonstrate—and perhaps what so unsettled white French audiences is the film's implication to take up armed resistance if these other democratic options fail, especially given the memory of the 2005 suburban protests five years before *Outside the Law*'s release.

Through the excess of cinematic spectacle, the use of violence to create a sense of action, and a careful manipulation of genre memory in *Outside the Law*, Bouchareb introduces Algerian characters, history, and settings into the global tradition of gangster genre. At the same time, he invites neglected events from a shared history of decolonization into the memories of mainstream French audiences. *Outside the Law* thus bears witness to the power of cinematic genres to make demands on the universal—that is, to shift mainstream representations of France's minorities and make visible the histories they share with the French nation.

JACQUES AUDIARD AND FRANCE'S "HEROIC" MINORITIES

The impulse to renegotiate what universalism means in France through cinematic spectacle, violence, and film genres can also be also found in the work of Audiard in films such as *A Prophet* (*Un prophète*, 2009) and *Dheepan* (2015). Unlike Bouchareb in *Outside the Law*, Audiard was not restrained in his use of violence, and *Dheepan* in particular suggests that screen violence is not always the best means of introducing minority communities onto mainstream screens through genre memory. *Dheepan* was conceived as a loose remake of Peckinpah's *Straw Dogs*, though as I will argue, it engages with several different genres beyond the gangster or vigilante film. Nevertheless, the excessive violence of its ending somewhat undoes the rest of the film's efforts to place France's Tamil community into mainstream cinematic images, suggesting that the cinematic style of ultraviolence cannot be viewed as unequivocally progressive. *Dheepan* combines the stylistic approaches to the suburbs of Kechiche's *Games of Love and Chance* (*L'Esquive*, 2004) and Kassovitz's *La Haine* that I analyzed in chapter 1. Audiard casts nonprofessional actors and shoots the suburban neighborhood with a quasi-documentary camera. However, he also employs the ticking time bomb narrative of the vigilante film and the stylized ultraviolence of the gangster genre in the final confrontation sequence. The combination of these two distinct stylistic approaches ultimately proved unpalatable for many critics.

Despite their shared interest in the power of genre images to bring minority communities onto mainstream screens, Bouchareb and Audiard come from very different backgrounds and have taken different trajectories through the French film industry. Jacques Audiard is the son of Michel Audiard, one of the most bankable dialogue writers from the mid-twentieth century who wrote populist, slang-filled scripts in a variety of genres that focused on France's "popular" (i.e., working) classes. In many ways, Audiard the father is a descendant of French poetic realism, and he has commented that Jacques Prévert's stylized language first inspired him to seek a career in the film industry. He believed that carefully written dialogue was the most important element of a good film. The antithesis of the emerging French New Wave, Michel Audiard traded barbs in print with the culturally bourgeois *Cahiers* critics (Chabrol 2001, 26, 90, 115–116, 118–125, 131–134). His work has largely been forgotten and neglected outside of France. Jacques Audiard takes from his father an interest in genre, language, and the everyman, though he positions his work within the auteurist tradition that descends from the New Wave, and he was canonized as one of France's preeminent auteurs when he won the Palme d'Or at Cannes for *Dheepan* in 2015. As I discussed in this book's introduction, the reception of *Dheepan* was mixed despite the critical accolades at Cannes, especially among the new generation of critics at the *Cahiers du cinéma* who objected to the film's use of genre.

Dheepan tells the story of three refugees—a former Tamil Tiger soldier (Dheepan), a woman (Yalini), and a preteen girl (Illayaal)—who seek to flee the civil war in Sri Lanka. They receive the passports of a dead family, and they decide to pretend to be that family so they can relocate to France. The French government eventually grants them visas, and they settle in the Paris suburbs, where Dheepan works as the building supervisor, cleaning public spaces, fixing broken elevators, and sorting the mail. Everything seems to be going well: Dheepan develops a solid reputation among the residents of the *cité*, Yalini finds work cooking meals for an older North African man, Illayaal fits in at school, and a love affair between Dheepan and Yalini takes shape. Yet life in the neighborhood is not without challenges. A gang controls one of the other apartment buildings, and its members engage in drug trafficking. Audiard gives us little information about the gang, so knowledge of genre codes must fill in the gaps. The refugees' lives worsen when a rival gang attacks the neighborhood. Although they try to keep their distance, Dheepan and Yalini become involved in the cycle of violence, and Dheepan brutally executes the gang members to save Yalini's life. The "family" ends up fleeing to the English suburbs in an epilogue where they seem to lead a middle-class life within a Sri Lankan expatriate community.

As this summary indicates, the film is characterized by several genres. The style of the first half of the film is neorealistic and even quasi-ethnographic in its approach to the Tamil family. This filiation is signaled by Audiard's choice to cast primarily nonprofessional actors, like Kechiche did in *Games of Love and Chance*. However, Audiard's casting of nonprofessionals is even more radical than Kechiche's, as most of the dialogue within the family is in Tamil, a language that Audiard does not even speak. Audiard in *Dheepan* thus gives significant creative control to his Tamil-speaking actors, and in interviews, he suggests that the choice to use Tamil with French subtitles is the film's most radical political gesture in its portrayal of minority characters (Libiot 2015; Romney 2016). Interviews in which filmmakers or actors discuss the film's production history are another way the film's promotional materials signal its status as quasi-ethnographic. I will analyze at greater length the stakes of advertising a suburban film as a partial cocreation between filmmaker and nonprofessional actors in my analysis of Céline Sciamma's *Girlhood* (*Bande de filles*, 2014), but suffice to say that involving nonprofessional actors in the creative process does unproblematically guarantee authentic realism.

The first half of the film also signals as quasi-ethnographic through a focus on quotidian details of family life: Dheepan works, Yalini works, Illayaal goes to school and does her homework, and all three discover France. It is not until the final half hour that violence erupts, which led film critic Jean-Philippe Tessé (2015) to characterize Audiard's film as a bait and switch in which a family drama masks a vigilante film. In a related vein, Julia Dobson writes that "the disproportionate scale of the violence creates the awkward appendage of a war or vigilante film ending to a largely realist film" (2016a, 266), and elsewhere she calls *Dheepan*'s ending "atypically clumsy for Audiard" (2016b, 188). However, in my view, the film's final third is not so much an awkward shift but rather the slow-burn explosion of generic tensions that Audiard establishes clearly from the beginning.

Through self-reflexive camera work and framing, *Dheepan* highlights inescapable mediation rather than unmediated realism. Audiard's Steadicam camera is hypermobile as it shifts between different internal points of view that are both those of family members and those of city residents. Everyone is scrutinizing each other: Who are you and what do you want from me? Within the buildings and the family's apartment, Audiard insists on the uncertainty of human relationships through staging choices organized around doors, windows, and walls. No gaze is without mediation and framing. In one scene, Dheepan looks into the bathroom where Yalini is taking a shower, and he wonders about a potential romance. Yalini is also curious about romance, but with the gang leader, Brahim. Dheepan notices Yalini surreptitiously reading a woman's celebrity magazine, which serves as a means for her to learn about the kinds of lives women can have in this new country. Several times throughout the film, Dheepan watches the gang activity across the courtyard through his window as if he were watching a gangster movie. In fact, when Yalini joins him at the window in one scene, she says to him, "It's funny, it feels like we're at the movies" (*C'est drôle, on se croirait au cinéma*). The phrasing is ambiguous: on the one hand, Yalini's remark refers to the spectacle they are watching on the other side of the window; on the other, this is the moment when Yalini takes Dheepan's hand and offers to have sex as if they were in a romantic comedy. Later, after the gang's trafficking and violence increasingly dominate neighborhood life, Dheepan paints a white line in the courtyard, establishing a "no fire zone" line between his building and that of the gang. In an interview, Audiard speaks about this white line as a genre shift: "The film shifts with its characters, it crosses into different genres as the genres unfold. Beyond this line that

Figure 3.2 Dheepan draws a line between his building and the gangsters. *Dheepan*, 2015.

[Dheepan] traces, we change genres. For a while, it becomes a *vigilante movie*" (Rouyer and Tobin 2015, 12, original emphasis). Figuratively, this line can also be understood as an attempt to draw a genre boundary around the kind of film he wants his family to live in. On this side, we are living in a romantic comedy; on the other, pretend it is *The Wire* (2002–2008).

Rather than talking about a shift towards genre in the film's final third, I suggest instead the film was not realistic from the beginning. *Dheepan* is defined by a nonnaturalistic aesthetic in which genres are constantly shifting. It is at once a quasi-ethnographic neorealist film about refugees, a film about France's republican schools, a romantic comedy, a comedy of remarriage, a gangster movie, a vigilante movie, and even, at times, a Western. What is more, the choice of genre is also an identity choice. It is as if *Dheepan*'s characters were asking themselves two questions: Through which genres do people see me and by which genres can I assert myself in this suburban neighborhood? *Dheepan*'s use of various genres seeks to add the Tamil characters to the genre memory associated with them through accretion.

To appreciate how Audiard understands genres and how he uses them in the context of the banlieues, it is crucial to consider his previous film, *A Prophet*, because it shares the same relationship to genre and multiculture as *Dheepan*. *A Prophet* tells the story of a French Maghrebi man, Malik, who receives a six-year prison term. Although the film presents Malik as an "Arab," there is a certain ambiguity in his ethnic background and self-presentation that allows him to come across as white—or at least to make people forget that he is meant to be Arab. A traditional Corsican mafia godfather takes him under his protection after Malik murders another Arab man. Malik rises in prison society and then, upon release, begins to run a trafficking operation in the Parisian suburbs due to his intelligence, his cleverness, his willingness to get an education, and his ability to learn "foreign" languages such as Corsican.[3] Malik ultimately replaces the Corsican godfather as a new kind of gangster for changed times.

When *A Prophet* was released, several international critics noted the influence of American gangster films such as those directed by Scorsese or Coppola, and, as a kind of facile shorthand, they referred to Audiard as a French Scorsese (Aftab 2010; Nelson 2010; Pulver 2012; Solomons 2009). These characterizations recognize that Audiard draws on the codes of genre films, a phenomenon that is often associated with Hollywood cinema and marked as an instance of Americanization. The implication for Audiard's reception in France is that there is something inauthentic about a French filmmaker who chooses to manipulate genre without a sense of artistic difference or ironic distance. When *Dheepan* won the Palme d'Or at Cannes, film critic Jérôme Momcilovic characterized Audiard's filmography as "the fantasy of 'auteurifying' recruiting commercials for the French army" (Momcilovic 2015). Stéphane Delorme's comments about *Dheepan*'s violent ending are also symptomatic in this regard: "[*Dheepan*]'s whole ending awkwardly replays *Taxi Driver*'s climbing of the staircase then the calm ending that was so ambiguous and debated in Scorsese's film. Audiard cannot have it both ways: playing at the 'auteur' and cutting and pasting genre films" (2015, 8). Delorme's derogatory comparison of using genres to cutting and pasting suggests the view that this practice does not display the artistic labor required for recognition as an auteur.

In an interview from the time of *A Prophet*'s release, Audiard expresses his exasperation with this type of criticism and its insinuation—that his films are not sufficiently French. Audiard acknowledges that what he calls "the reference to genre" has not been and still is not easy in French cinema. When he clarifies his relationship to American cinema, especially his shock at critics who speak of his films in terms of "Americanness" (*américanité*), he explains that he will not deny this influence. However, he clarifies that what interests him in American cinema is neither a place nor a tradition, but what he calls "the mythological use of cinema" (Kaganski 2009). Genre traditions in his view can "call on characters that are immediately recognizable to the viewer" (Mandelbaum 2009). Here, Audiard's remarks echo what Bouchareb said about making films that feature Maghrebi gangsters and what Kechiche said in the context of *Games of Love and Chance* about minority characters needing to exist in cinematic images and not just on the soundtrack. Audiard goes on to explain that in *A Prophet* he wanted to "transform actors," especially unknown Arab actors, "into icons of genre cinema" (Kaganski 2009). Genres, for Audiard, make it possible to call upon, iterate, and reconfigure cinematic images that circulate widely in a shared imaginary for the benefit of communities that have so far been excluded from these genres and, by extension, mainstream cinema.

For Audiard, the goal of using genres to create images in *A Prophet* was not to turn Arabs into heroes or to show the coexistence of different languages on screen, but to posit a radical equality among the different characters and communities in the film: "I wanted to make the 'after' film. The one where we are no longer in these questions about integration where we have been going nowhere for years. In *A Prophet*, this question is resolved, there are only problems of power, territory and the sharing of objects. 'I want what you have' is at once a relation of strength and equality. This is also what genre does, place us immediately somewhere else other than in temporary sociological questions" (Kaganski 2009). Whether or not one believes that making the "after" integration film is possible or desirable, Audiard's remarks emphasize the iconographic power of genre traditions and the memories that genres carry, to speak in Bakhtin's terms. Further, he indicates genres' capacity to create and iterate shared images through the bodies of minority actors in France.

In an interview on *Dheepan*'s DVD release, Audiard talks about his use of genres in that film in terms reminiscent of those with which he discussed *A Prophet*. He explains that what interests him about genres is their ability to "grab the viewer," by which I take him to mean emotional engagement. *Dheepan* evinces the same desire for egalitarianism in representation that we saw in *A Prophet*, which took the form of the decision to film Tamil actors in widescreen Cinemascope and thus, in his view, to transform them into heroes. Audiard also explains how the conventional dialogues of genre films foster an unusual kind of cinematic equality. He suggests that some viewers might believe that a dialogue between two Tamil actors would not be the same as that between two American actors in a genre film. However, he argues that when you give the dialogue of American actors to Tamil actors, it works very well on screen. Audiard in *Dheepan* seeks to reconfigure a global cinematographic imaginary in which refugees can now occupy leading roles and heroic images in several film genres.

However much Audiard speaks about heroism in interviews, he does not fully clarify what that word means for him, especially in the context of a film like *Dheepan* that features vigilante violence. What is more, Audiard does not exercise restraint in his use of violence like Bouchareb did in *Outside the Law*. In fact, he employs in the film's final sequence all the techniques of ultraviolence that Prince identifies as characteristic of the style: slow-motion shots, fragmented montage, and squibs with blood packs. Audiard's film is not as relentless as Peckinpah's *Straw Dogs* in using each moment in the narrative to give the screw one more turn that will eventually cause the paroxysm of violence at the end. As I have argued above, Audiard deploys many different genres in *Dheepan* that serve to help viewers make sense of the Tamil family and to reveal how the family makes sense of itself. However, the gangster storyline does persist throughout.

The final buildup in *Dheepan* begins around seventy minutes into the film, when a group of gangsters get on motorbikes to conduct a raid in the neighborhood. Yalini and Illayaal are walking home with grocery bags and are caught in the cross fire. Here, the violence is predominantly implied through off-screen sound effects and the occasional image of muzzle flare. Audiard sticks to close-ups of the two women to emphasize their disorientation as they seek shelter. The local gang gets together and heads off on a raid, presumably in response to the violence they just endured. Viewers do not see this violence, but they presume it is successful because the gangsters return, and Dheepan watches them from his window as they fire their guns into the air in celebration. The next day, the gangsters light fire cans and set up checkpoints to secure their territory. Yalini, understandably disturbed by what she witnessed, tries to leave to flee to England alone by train. Dheepan catches her, and a violent domestic dispute ensues on the station platform. The couple eventually returns, and the gangsters attempt to search Yalini's bag as they reenter the neighborhood. Dheepan goes mad with rage and pushes one of the men to the ground before another can defuse the situation. At this point, Dheepan tells Yalini, "I'm not moving from this spot," and this is when he paints the line in the courtyard to separate the buildings the gangsters control from the others.

The violence slowly escalates on both sides until the moment when a rival gang comes to kill Brahim. Yalini has finished cooking lunch for Brahim's uncle and is preparing to leave when the doorbell rings, and then the sounds of automatic weapons erupt in the soundtrack. The camera stays tight on Yalini as she attempts to figure out how to leave. Brahim is lying on the ground with gunshot wounds in his chest, but he is still alive. He asks her to help him, and when she goes to leave, he entraps her foot and eventually puts a gun to her head, perhaps a distant echo of the sexual violence and domination of women in *Straw Dogs* that are that film's narrative motor for vengeance. Brahim makes her call Dheepan, thus launching the ultraviolent sequence that follows. The sequence demonstrates Dheepan's competence at violence: unlike the "small-time hoodlum" (*petit voyou*), as Dheepan calls Brahim, he is a hardened leader of men with experience in a violent guerilla civil war. Dheepan grabs a machete and a screwdriver and seeks to close the distance between his building and the one where Brahim is holding Yalini. He distracts the men by pretending to be just the building supervisor and then he attacks the first man from behind, cutting his leg with the machete and driving the screwdriver into his chest. Audiard films this moment from behind Dheepan in a medium shot, so viewers see and hear the blows and the spray of blood packs. Audiard then cuts forward in time to a different shot of Dheepan as he fires the gun he has presumably taken from the first man into the head of a second man sitting in the passenger seat of a car. Viewers do not see the blood pack explode, but as the bouncing Steadicam camera tracks left, we notice blood all over the car's dashboard. Özlem Köksal and Ipak Rappas have argued that Audiard's choice to have Dheepan carry a machete marks the violence—and, by extension, the banlieues—as a foreign space, the "jungle" of the Global South, coming to France (2019, 263). While this point about the machete's symbolic resonance is well taken, it is also important to note that after the first murder, Dheepan acquires a handgun and primarily uses this weapon to kill the other men. By the time he climbs the stairwell, he has discarded the machete, suggesting that the machete was perhaps just a practical choice until he could acquire the gangsters' guns.

Audiard begins using slow-motion shots a moment later, when Dheepan commandeers the car and proceeds to drive it toward the building. He takes fire as the car starts, and as he drives, a shot grazes his ear. Viewers see a blood pack go off in the medium close-up shot, and suddenly the camera speed slows down and the images begin to blur slightly. The ambient sound effects and the loud sounds of gunshots disappear, and viewers hear a single musical note played on a synthesizer, rather than the sound of the flesh opening, to mark the impact of the bullet that grazes Dheepan's temple. The sound design here is anchored by a car engine that has been processed to sound as if it were underwater, placing viewers in Dheepan's momentary subjective disorientation. As Dheepan collects his wits, the ambient sounds and score music resume, and the car engine returns to the previous, natural-sounding processing. Throughout, the sound of the car revving remains in real diegetic time despite the slowed-down image, and this mismatch is a central element of how Peckinpah stylized ultraviolence in his films. Audiard repeats this subjective slow-motion technique a moment later, when Dheepan crashes the car. Along the way, he crashes into one of the men, and we see and hear this body as it flies by the driver's side window.

Once Dheepan enters the building and begins his ascent to the top floor where Brahim holds Yalini hostage, Audiard focuses predominantly on a medium shot of Dheepan's upper legs and lower torso. This shot rhymes with the earlier framing of Dheepan walking with the machete and screwdriver in hand. The sequence also echoes the ending stairwell sequence in Scorsese's

Taxi Driver (1976) in its narrative premise. However, the sequence in *Dheepan* is both longer and more subjectively disorienting in its visual style than the final shoot-out in Scorsese's film. Before Dheepan starts the climb, he wipes a drop of blood from his nose, and viewers hear faint echoes in the score of the Tamil Tigers song Dheepan listened to earlier in the film. The stairwell is filled with smoke, which serves to highlight the dreamlike nature of this sequence and to create a sense of slowed motion even for the shots that take place in real time. The smoke also visually accentuates the flash of the gun going off as Dheepan murders several men on the way up. Most of the violence takes place off-screen, and the time and space of the actions are not clear, evoking some of the modernist fragmentation of space that Prince argued was a hallmark of Peckinpah's ultraviolent style. The subjective time dilations, the musical echoes of the Tamil Tigers song, and the smoke in the stairwell all serve to highlight the present tense of Dheepan's unresolved trauma from the Sri Lankan civil war and how it has been activated by the "petty hoodlums" in this French suburban neighborhood. When Dheepan reaches the top-floor apartment, he points the gun at Yalini. Brahim bled out during Dheepan's ascent, and Yalini must slap and then embrace Dheepan to bring him back to reality.

Returning to Audiard's suggestion that genres create heroic images, it is not clear in *Dheepan* what exactly is heroic about the violence in the vigilante sequence. The film's epilogue hardly resolves the matter and proved controversial. Following the spectacular shoot-out, the film fades to black and then fades up on a suburban street somewhere in England. The wide street and single-family homes serve as a stark contrast with the French housing projects. To the right of the image is a flowering cherry tree, a visual rhyme with the shots of tall trees through which Dheepan, Yalini, and Illayaal first see the apartment blocks when they move to the Le Pré neighborhood, whose ironic name means *field* or *prairie*. *Dheepan* ends with a domestic idyll: Yalini hands Dheepan a baby, presumably theirs, as they spend time in the backyard with other Sri Lankan families living in England. Illayaal plays with other children, and the film ends with a close-up of Yalini's hand strokingCed 's hair from behind his head. Earlier in the film, Yalini resisted believing the story that they are a family, and here at the end, viewers get a happy ending of sorts, almost a gesture toward romantic comedy. For some French critics, the film's geographic shift to England was somehow anti-French, perhaps suggesting that the problems of the French suburbs cannot be resolved; the only solution is to leave (Haddad 2015). This is a plausible interpretation, but it overemphasizes the realist components of the film. Despite the quasi-ethnographic style of the first half of the film that invites viewers to see it as an intervention in the real,

Dheepan's politics is, in my view, primarily about the different kinds of images that mediate the banlieues, and *Dheepan* ultimately demonstrates the risks of employing the cinematic style of ultraviolence.

The risks are the same as those that Prince identifies in the work of Peckinpah, who believed that highly stylized violence on screen would awaken people to the horror of violence in real life. Peckinpah and other filmmakers such as Scorsese, who used the style of cinematic ultraviolence in *Taxi Driver*, became distressed when some viewers found pleasure and gratification in screen violence. In fact, for some viewers, violent sequences have provoked desires to imitate violence instead of creating critical distance from it. Prince explains this contradiction by arguing that such responses result from the aesthetic concerns of filmmakers who carefully craft sequences of violence and thus transmit pleasure to viewers. In his view, filmmakers who use ultraviolence are complicit "in stimulating the aggressive reactions of their viewers," and ultimately ultraviolence does not permit sufficient space for viewers to think about the "meaning and consequences of violence" (2000b, 197–200). Prince's point is important, but it risks falling into the same binary essentialism as Peckinpah's belief that screen violence awakens viewers from the slumber of complicity. The truth likely lies somewhere in the middle—namely that ultraviolence has unpredictable and contradictory effects on viewers that operate independently of a director's intentions. The effects of ultraviolence, in other words, cannot be reliably controlled; ultraviolence may have a progressive effect on some viewers and the exact opposite on others. What is more, the visceral exhaustion that ultraviolence can induce in viewers risks overshadowing other aspects of a film that might seek to complicate, challenge, or criticize that violence.

This is what happens in *Dheepan*, in which the spectacular violent finale overshadows the play with genre that came before. Nowhere is this clearer than in the film's epilogue. Narratively speaking, the film's ending in England is as improbable as the escalating violence and spectacular shoot-out that invite no government or police response. As I have been arguing throughout this section, Audiard's film is stylistically and generically mixed, and no one genre is more anchored in reality than another. *Dheepan* seemingly invites viewers to see the film through a realist framework, as many viewers do when watching films about the banlieues and other kinds of cinema about minority communities. Audiard then moves to the antipode of this kind of cinema: the ultraviolence of the shoot-out. The stark contrast between these two styles seems to have generated the most controversy, yet the problem with the turn to violence is not its rupture with the real, but that it has occluded the film's thoroughgoing play with images and genres. When Dheepan turns out to be such a competent killer, viewers forget that they have also seen him working, learning to tell a joke, playing at being a lover, and becoming a father.[4] Audiard frames the film in interviews as being about putting minority bodies in the kinds of images and genres they have not previously occupied, especially heroic ones. This includes gangster cinema but also less violent genres, such as comedy or romantic comedy. Ultraviolence is excessive by design, and its excess in *Dheepan* overwhelms and ultimately caused some viewers to forget the rest of the film, which is a central reason why the film's shoot-out seems like a compromised representation of the Tamil family and why the epilogue feels so improbable. The very feeling of improbability is what calls attention to how risky it is for a filmmaker to use ultraviolence, however much they might try to contain it through the rest of the film or through the exegeses they might offer in interviews.

DIVINES AND THE CIRCULATION OF VIOLENT IMAGES

Bouchareb's *Outside the Law* and Audiard's *Dheepan* reveal the possibilities and limitations of how a filmmaker might use violence and genre to create cinematic images of the banlieues that seek to change how French audiences view minority communities in mainstream films. By contrast, in *Divines* (2016), Benyamina takes up the mixing of multiple genres we find in *Dheepan* and *Outside the Law*, but she ultimately questions violent representations of the banlieues through the specific ways she manipulates the gangster genre. Her use of genre to reflect on suburban violence was especially important in the mid-2010s, when individuals could take pleasure in filming acts of violence (including themselves committing acts of violence) and in watching the violence of others through cell phone cameras and streaming platforms. *Divines* tells the story of Dounia, a young French Maghrebi woman, and Maimouna, a young French Black woman, who grew up in the banlieues and are best friends. Dounia's mother is an alcoholic who cannot keep a job, and she, Dounia, and Dounia's brother live with an uncle in a "Romany shantytown" (*camp de Roms*) adjacent to their banlieue neighborhood's apartment blocks. With this setting, we have come full circle back to the 1950s Nanterre shantytown, though Benyamina shoots this latter-day version with none of the visual poetry that Bouchareb used in *Outside the Law*.

Maimouna's father is the local imam, and she grew up in a strict household. Dounia's confrontational choices get both women in trouble with the law. Dounia wants to make lots of money by any means necessary, and she adopts the gangster lifestyle, apprenticing under Rebecca, the leader of the local drug trafficking gang. Toward the end of the film, Dounia steals money from a supplier that Rebecca considers hers, and Rebecca inadvertently kills Maimouna to get it back. The film ends on a bleak note, with the neighborhood residents protesting the cause of Maimouna's death in a standoff with police and firefighters.

In terms of its production history and reception, *Divines* is situated somewhere between auteurist art film and genre film. *Divines* did benefit from the CNC's (National Center for Cinema and the Moving Image) selective aid. It premiered at Cannes in 2016 in the Director's Fortnight series (Quinzaine des réalisateurs) and even won the festival's Golden Camera award for a promising director (Arbrun 2016). However, the success of her first film belies the fact that Benyamina's entry into the film industry was not nearly as easy as it was for Audiard and Bouchareb. As Mame-Fatou Niang explains, Benyamina was not the best student, and the French education system tracked her for a vocational degree. She was eventually able to transfer to a literature program, where she did very well (2019, 246). Though Benyamina had the idea for *Divines* at around the time of the 2005 suburban protests, the film took nearly ten years to finance and complete. In addition to making short films, Benyamina also founded and ran the 1000 Visages association to teach filmmaking to would-be filmmakers from the banlieues who did not have the money or the connections that come from attending one of France's state film schools like La Fémis (see Niang 2019, 246–250).

Whereas Bouchareb and Audiard sought to create heroic images of individuals drawn from France's contemporary multiculture, Benyamina walks a fine line between creating images of strong women through the tropes of gangster cinema and calling into question the general obsession with gangsters in banlieue cinema. *Divines* is arguably a more "authentic" film than *Dheepan* in the sense that Benyamina grew up in the Parisian suburbs; however, it is also a film that is as unrealistic as Audiard's in its representation of the suburbs through the tropes of the gangster film and other genres. Furthermore, the filmmaker shares many of the same Hollywood references as Audiard and Bouchareb, especially the work of Scorsese. According to Steve Rose (2016), Benyamina has even compared Dounia and Maimouna to Robert De Niro and Harvey Keitel. She also likens them to Laurel and Hardy. Benyamina does distance her film from the hypermasculine suburbs represented in *Dheepan* or *Outside the Law*. It puts women characters at the center of the various genres she employs in the film, and it seeks to separate violence from power, allowing a place for positive expressions of women's assertiveness. Mixing the codes of the female friendship film, dance film, and teen movie with those of the thriller and gangster cinema, *Divines* examines the capitalist and neoliberal imaginary of young people in the banlieues and the difficulties that arise when they confront the realities of capitalist exploitation and violence.

In an interview with *Le Monde*, Benyamina explains that the film emerged from the context of the 2005 suburban protests, which, unlike the events of May 1968, did not change much about France, especially in terms of the treatment of its suburban poor. The character Rebecca, in Benyamina's view, embodies what French politics have become: "Individualism, the god of money, and the search for power without any values" (Carpentier 2016). Benyamina's description of politics reads like a summation of the gangster's motivations in classic and contemporary Hollywood cinema, and this is arguably why the gangster figure has been so salient for young people in the banlieues.

Franco-Tunisian writer Mehdi Belhaj Kacem has suggested that the shared imaginary of the gangster played a particularly important role at the time of the banlieue protests in 2005. He argues that it is not surprising that disaffected youth in the banlieues were attracted to the figure of the gangster and especially a film like De Palma's *Scarface* (1983). In his view, youth who do not have the means or opportunities to participate in consumer society turn to illicit means to participate either imaginatively or in reality. However, Kacem is careful not to say that this fascination makes De Palma's film somehow progressive. Instead, he views it as a secretion of capitalism that gives a perverse kind of pleasure to those who are excluded from its benefits. Kacem goes on to say that the gangster imaginary was also important at the time of the 2005 protests because of the tough-guy persona of Sarkozy, then minister of the interior before he was elected president in 2007 (Belhaj Kacem 2006, 25–26, 28–29). In widely mediatized interviews around the time of the 2005 protests, Sarkozy characterized banlieue youth with the lexicon drawn from the gangster imaginary, including hoodlums (*voyous*), scum (*racailles*), gangs (*bandes*), and big man or gang leader (*caïd*) (*Le Monde* 2005). Benyamina works through the legacy of gangster imagery for the French suburbs in *Divines*, but in the context of women characters rather than men. Her use of gangster cinema explores how the genre relates to the banlieues from three different angles: how the media represent the banlieues, how banlieue youth see and represent themselves, and how those in France who do not live in the banlieues view those who do.

From the opening credits, Benyamina reveals a similar desire to that of Audiard in *A Prophet* and *Dheepan*: to film France's minorities, in this case banlieue residents, in widescreen Cinemascope. However, what Benyamina adds to this project is a reflection on the reality that young people living in the banlieues during the 2000s and 2010s were immersed in a reservoir of shared images and video clips that circulated via the internet, smartphones, and other small screens. Alternating between shots framed in widescreen and shots framed with the vertical aspect ratio of smartphones, Benyamina calls attention to the importance of mediation in an even more striking way than Audiard did in *Dheepan*. Through shared videos, the young people in the film construct the space around them and imagine a bigger world outside their banlieue neighborhood.

Fantasies of the gangster life are first transmitted through a video clip that shows the pleasures of conspicuous consumption awaiting those who have a lot of money. After the scene in which Dounia's mother loses her job, Benyamina cuts to an image of a young Black woman partying who viewers later learn is Rebecca, the local gang leader. Background music and reverberation give viewers the impression that they have left the world of the banlieues to arrive on an idyllic beach and then a nightclub. The images look like they came from smartphones due to the subject matter and framing, but Benyamina chooses to show them in widescreen. It is only when viewers hear men's voices commenting on the images off-screen that they realize that this is a video clip of Rebecca on vacation in Thailand. The immersive quality of the camera—it travels underwater to observe Rebecca swimming in the sea, and it sits next to Rebecca as she parasails above it—suggests Rebecca's embodied experience of pleasure on vacation even as it alternates between seemingly subjective point-of-view shots and shots of Rebecca herself. Rebecca brags to the other residents about her plans to return after making enough money to open a bar, which is the neoliberal fantasy of combining work, leisure, and consumption. The framing of Dounia looking with admiration at Rebecca and their exchange of glances reveal the mimetic circulation of desire through shared videos (on mimetic desire, see Girard 2011).

Dounia's primary goal in the film is to realize these fantasies of wealth, status, and consumption for herself, and throughout *Divines*, Benyamina uses conspicuous camera movements to highlight how shared video is the interface between fantasy and reality. After Maimouna and Dounia begin to work for Rebecca as lookouts, Maimouna quickly becomes bored, so Dounia invites her to think about the future. Imagine, she says, that they are already in Phuket. Dounia gets into an imaginary Ferrari at the same time that the actress steps onto a camera cart that viewers do not see off-screen. After some coaxing, Maimouna joins her. Dounia then makes the sound of a car engine starting, and the camera begins to move through the concrete courtyard as if the two really were in a Ferrari. Dounia declaims that they are on the beach with cocktails, beautiful men with washboard abs, and especially money. Viewers hear

Figure 3.3 Dounia and Maimouna ride in an imaginary Ferrari. *Divines*, 2016.

nondiegetic sounds such as a car engine, car horns, music from the car's radio, the voices of people at a party, and the clinking of glasses, which serves to break down the separation between reality and fantasy. The distance between camera and actors and the framing are reminiscent of those of a selfie, transforming the sequence into a selfie shot in cinematic widescreen.

While the earlier video of Rebecca's vacation suggested her embodied point of view, how are we to make sense of the camera's position and movement in the Ferrari sequence? It is an unrealistic point of view in what is arguably the film's most unrealistic sequence. Daniel Morgan has argued that theorizations of camera movement have gone astray by overemphasizing the question of how the camera relates to the film world and enables viewers to access that world. For him, this type of thinking views the camera as a perceptual anchor for embodied experience in the world on screen, either taking the place of a character in the narrative or the place of an observer independent of the narrative. Morgan contends that instead of this view, we need to accept the fact that cameras do not reproduce human modes of perception or human forms of movement through the world. Accepting this fact, however, does not prevent viewers from wanting to be "at the position of the camera" and to be "moving with it," something he terms "epistemological fantasies" (Morgan 2016, 242). Morgan argues that filmmakers exploit these fantasies to create a wide range of expressive effects in fictional cinema. To avoid the simplifications of reducing the camera to a simple access point to the world on screen, Morgan turns to the British philosopher Richard Wollheim's notion of an "internal spectator." For Wollheim, an internal spectator is a figure within a painting that views the world of the painting in an expressive manner that differs from that of the external spectator who looks at the painting. Adapting this concept to cinema,

Morgan suggests that one important function of camera movements is that they create internal spectators within the world of the film: "The recurrent presence of characters within camera movements ... establishes positions from which we can imagine how that world is being experienced" (Morgan 2016, 232–233, 240–242, 237–238). Crucially, the sense of how the film world is being experienced includes emotional colorations that are transmitted through the various elements of film style.

The self-reflexive positioning and movement of the camera in the Ferrari scene from *Divines* places viewers at the level of the imaginary dashboard, but in fact we are seeing the world as Dounia and Maimouna see it as internal spectators. What we are seeing is not the reality of their suburban neighborhood, but neither are we in Thailand. Rather, we are feeling the emotional coloring of their shared fantasy of going to Thailand through the exuberant camera movement and Benymaina's use of diegetic and nondiegetic sound. In addition to this fantasy—and this is the crucial point—viewers see how Dounia, Maimouna, and others in the film interact with shared video in general. Smartphone video in *Divines* shares the basic epistemological fantasy Morgan analyzes in the context of camera movement, namely the sense of being at the place of the camera, experiencing that world. The ebullient emotions of the Ferrari fantasy scene that viewers and characters both experience contrast starkly with the concrete slabs of the courtyard, highlighting just how difficult it is to close the gap between reality and fantasy for many living in the banlieues. As the film unfolds, the sense that the smartphone video is there in place of the camera hints at danger as Dounia's fantasies become violent.

The real violence in the film that counterbalances the escape into the imaginary is linked to the 2005 suburban protests. However, I contend that the film is not so much about the reality of these protests as it about the function of another kind of shared image. Media coverage of protests and violence in the banlieues has become a television genre in its own right (Sedel 2009, 31–53), but it is one that can produce effects in reality. As political philosopher Étienne Balibar reminds us, there was a feedback loop of mimicry during the 2005 suburban protests among different neighborhoods. One neighborhood would see images of what was happening in another neighborhood through television reporting and imitate what was happening. In Balibar's view, such televisual mimicry took the place of political organization (Balibar 2014, 237–238; Mauger 2006, 46).

In both sequences of protest in *Divines*, Benyamina examines the incommensurability of an individual desire to act violently for self-gratification and the collective demands of a community. The first sequence takes place after

Samir, Rebecca's second in command, has sex with Dounia's mother as an act of revenge against Dounia. When Dounia catches them in the act, she decides to burn Samir's car as her own act of revenge. Dounia and Maimouna sit on the scooter as they watch the spectacular image of the burning car. Dounia uses the new iPhone 6 she got from Rebecca to film it, and she alternates between filming selfies of her and Maimouna enjoying the moment and images of the spreading fire. When the fire truck arrives, she hands Maimouna the phone and asks her to keep filming, then goes in search of a Molotov cocktail. Like she does in the scene with the Ferrari, Dounia attempts to bring a visual genre she knows—that of the protest video—into reality. The police and other residents from the neighborhood arrive, which triggers a violent confrontation on a small scale. Dounia gets on the back of the scooter, and Maimouna drives away while Dounia keeps filming, turning the scooter into a camera cart. Benyamina shifts the framing from widescreen to smartphone as she cuts between shots, and Dounia flips the phone back and forth between the police pursuing them and Maimouna driving. Benyamina intercuts the smartphone footage with hyperkinetic mobile shots of the chase as Dounia screams in exhilaration. The two friends finally crash in a frenzied, abstract montage of fast-moving lights; then the police arrest them. Camera movement in this sequence introduces the same disjuncture between Dounia's emotional experience of the chase as an internal spectator and the reality that she almost killed her best friend and both are now going to jail.

The second protest sequence that ends the film does not allow Dounia any escape into the realm of fantasy. Instead, it forces her to leave with the reality that her desire for money at all costs has led to the death of her best friend. Right before this sequence, Dounia finally realized her gangster dream: she stole a hidden stash of money from the higher-level gangster who provided Rebecca with drugs to sell. However, Dounia decides to keep the money for herself instead of giving it to Rebecca as previously agreed. In retribution, Rebecca kidnaps Maimouna and threatens to kill her if Dounia does not hand over the money. Dounia returns to their neighborhood to save her friend, but she refuses to reveal the money's location to Rebecca. Rebecca douses the basement with gas and threatens to light it on fire as a means of increasing the pressure on Dounia to relent. After a heated exchange, Rebecca accidently drops the lighter, and the basement begins to burn. Maimouna dies because she cannot fit through the window to escape. The firefighters refuse to intervene before the police's arrival because of the hostile welcome they have previously experienced when coming to suburban neighborhoods. A violent confrontation breaks out again, but this time because of a real collective grievance regarding the breakdown of social services. However, Dounia watches the scene without taking action. She neither sees through her iPhone nor is she seen through its recorded video. Benyamina uses shot/reverse shot constructions at this moment to show Dounia frozen in tears amid the violence erupting around her. George Frideric Handel's *Dixit Dominus* dominates the score during this ending to highlight the sadness of what is taking place. This final moment, which can be read as the fall of the gangster, is not due to murder or suicide, as in traditional or parodic versions of the genre. Rather, it results from Dounia realizing that the true cost of the gangster's hyper-individualism is losing one's friends, community, and society.

Divines' narrative ends at the moment of the protest, as if to suggest that French politics and society have yet to process the outrage that the 2005 protests represent. However, the film ends with a sequence of Maimouna and Dounia hugging and gleefully whirling in the local mall. The camera dances around them at a slower rhythm than their movements, and then Benyamina cuts to a final shot at the height of the characters' heads, suggesting their point of view as they look up and spin in joy. This is another moment in which camera movements in *Divines* create a position of internal spectatorship and share the feelings associated with how characters view their world. I would add that the mixing of genres in *Divines* is another central element of film style that serves to create different kinds of internal spectatorship. Benyamina's play with the genres and the emotions associated with them in *Divines* ultimately critiques the violence of the gangster genre, challenges banlieue films that spectacularize violence, and suggests that other genres might bring into view a different emotional coloration of the banlieues.

One of these other genres is the teen dance movie that also serves as the occasion for Benyamina to stage an opposition in the film between genre and art. The opposition is focalized through the character of Djigui, a young banlieue man who works as a mall security guard but really wants to be a dancer and successfully auditions for a dance company. Djigui talks about dance as something sacred and explains that when he dances, he feels open to the world, a stark contrast to the lesson Rebecca gives Dounia about being tough and hiding your emotions. Dounia's money stash is in the catwalk of the theater where the troupe rehearses, and Dounia watches Djigui dance from above. She is attracted to him, and the two dance together at two different moments in the film in an energetic choreography that explores issues of violence and sexual desire that the film also examines through the gangster genre. The second dance scene takes place in the store Djigui works for, and after the two dance, Dounia eats junk food—chips, M&Ms, and cookies—a far cry from what Djigui must eat to maintain his chiseled physique. As characters do in *Intouchables* (2011), which I will discuss in chapter 5, Benyamina uses junk food as a metaphor for popular forms of mass culture, indicating that Dounia's investment in the gangster lifestyle is somehow lesser than Djigui's pursuit of a dance career. Djigui invites Dounia to the premiere of the troupe's show, but Dounia does not attend because Rebecca has sent her to get the money from her supplier. Benyamina intercuts the scene in which the supplier violently beats Dounia in his apartment with the premiere of Djigui's dance performance. This juxtaposition suggests different ways of relating to violence, implying that the path of art has more of a future for suburban youth than the path of the gangster.

Benyamina's use of the gangster genre in *Divines* serves two functions. On the one hand, the film creates images of women gangsters through references to a hypermasculine film genre, which aligns with the egalitarian impulse I analyzed earlier in Audiard and Bouchareb. However, Benyamina also undertakes a feminization of the gangster genre at the level of the gaze. In a near complete reversal of Laura Mulvey's analysis of gender and scopophilia, Dounia and Maimouna both become women who look at men along with the film camera. We see this in the scene when the two women first visit Rebecca's apartment and meet the latter's kept man. He answers the door without his shirt, and the two young women admire his washboard abs. Later in the film, as Dounia watches Djigui dance from the catwalk without his shirt, she similarly looks approvingly at his glistening body and even takes a video of his solo dance rehearsal, presumably so that she can rewatch it later. In addition to flipping the male gaze, Dounia also knows how to manipulate the male gaze to her advantage, as in the scene in which she gains access to the apartment of Rebecca's supplier by seducing him through dance in a Parisian nightclub.

On the other hand, the emotional contrast among the different genres Benyamina uses through *Divines* makes viewers feel the risks to society of the extreme capitalist individualism represented by the gangster. From this perspective, the female friendship film, the dance film, and the teen movie serve to delimit the emotional stakes of what is lost when Dounia becomes a gangster. By extension, these other genres suggest the potential limits of inverting the gendered framework of a heavily masculine genre like the gangster film. In other words, simply putting women in the roles previously played by men does not automatically lead to a progressive film.

Divines' criticisms of the violence inherent in the gangster genre do not mean that the film challenges assertiveness as a legitimate form of agency and identity expression for suburban women. Instead, the film draws a distinction between violence and assertiveness. Here, I build on the work of Mehammed Mack, who has articulated an understanding of virility as a neutral, rather than stereotypically masculine, category to describe the agency and identity performances of gay men and women in the suburbs who undertake actions and behaviors that are stereotypically associated with heterosexual men. In his view, rather than "female virility" being some kind of "false consciousness, or internalized machismo" that hides a supposedly more natural femininity, Mack contends that it is rather an inherently queer category, one that marks "urban belonging" rather than "gender belonging" (Mack 2017, 39–46). Though Mack reclaims "virility" as a neutral concept, I find the word too intrinsically gendered at the level of etymology to use it in that way, so I prefer here, in the context of *Divines*, to speak of assertiveness as a mode of agency and suburban belonging, rather than virility.

The problem in *Divines* is not that Dounia learns assertive behaviors from Rebecca but that she seeks to express them in the context of the gangster lifestyle. Instead, assertiveness is prized throughout the film, perhaps nowhere more so than in one of the film's cult lines, when Rebecca admiringly tells Dounia that she "has clitoris" (*T'as du clitoris, j'aime bien*), using the expression as a women's equivalent of a man "having balls." Benyamina also valorizes this kind of assertiveness in her own self-presentations to the French film industry, most famously when she used this line from the film in her acceptance speech of the Golden Camera Award at Cannes. In her speech, she stressed how important it was for her face and the cast's faces to be at Cannes and how the industry needs more women making decisions to have more women making films. At the end of her speech, she thanked her producer by repeating the line from the film—"T'as du clitoris"—further emphasizing that anyone can and should be assertive in advancing who can make and star in French films (Canal+ Cinéma 2016). *Divines* thus differs from *Outside the Law* and *Dheepan* in the ways that it criticizes the violence of the gangster genre while celebrating the agency and assertiveness it enables for certain characters, especially suburban women.

CONCLUSION

Outside the Law, *Dheepan*, and *Divines* share a commitment to exploring what kinds of images can or should be created of minority characters on mainstream screens. They all engage most heavily with the tropes of the gangster genre, and this genre's penchant for spectacular violence allows each filmmaker to come to a different conclusion about how violence may or may not support progressive agendas in films about suburban communities. For Bouchareb, violence serves to create a sense of the eventfulness of history, especially the felt sense of the effects of violence committed by FLN militants and the French government. In *Dheepan*, Audiard sought to place minority actors in a wide variety of heroic images, but by revealing Dheepan to be so skilled at violence, he risks reinforcing, rather than subverting, fears of France's violent suburbs. Benyamina parses the distinctions between violence and agency in banlieue cinema and, through criticisms of the gangster lifestyle and videos of street violence, ultimately suggests that other genres might better mediate images of suburban women, a question I will return to in chapter 6. Each of the three films mixes minority characters and the gangster genre with a multiplicity of other genres, suggesting that the goal is not simply to make a suburban gangster film. Rather, they use what I have been calling *genre memory* to accrete new images of minority characters into film genres in ways that suggest possibilities for how these genres can rearticulate the universal in films about the banlieues.

However, the question of how appropriate the cinematic style of ultraviolence is for films about the French suburbs has not been completely resolved. In this chapter, I have primarily focused on the gangster genre, which features ambivalently seductive characters from marginalized communities who commit acts of violence. What about when minority characters are on the receiving end of violence, either literal police violence or the more subtle forms of everyday discrimination? This question is more properly considered through the second type of cinematic ultraviolence that Prince characterized as the embodied violence of screen gore that emerged from Hollywood horror cinema in the 1970s and 1980s. Just as there are French suburban gangster films, there are also French suburban horror films. At times these films channel fears of violence emerging from the suburbs that could impact the city center, but more often than not, they represent minority characters as victims of excessively brutal forms of violence that result from all-too-human monsters and spatial marginalization. These suburban horror films are the focus of the next chapter.

NOTES

1. See Pettersen 2016, 62–108; Met 2018.
2. For an analysis of the ways in which the film does reflect the historical consensus about some of the events depicted, see Donadey 2014, 16–19.
3. Dayna Oscherwitz characterizes Malik as a new type of gangster for a time in which transnational flows of money and power are more important than

state-centered ones (2015, 270–271). Gemma King argues that linguistic code switching is an important component of Malik's rise to power (2014, 83–86).

4. When Köksal and Rappas argue in the context of *Dheepan* that films about European refugees need to go beyond crisis and the idea that refugees' only agency is "that born in violent acts," the implication is that Dheepan's only true agency in the film is the violent shoot-out (2019, 266–267). This reading neglects the other kinds of agency we see in Dheepan over the course of the film.

FOUR

SUBURBANOIA AND FRENCH BANLIEUE HORROR FILMS

FRANCE'S NATIONAL FILM TRADITION IS not known for horror. If one looks at which genres have recently defined the French domestic box office, comedy is at the top of the list, followed by biopics, crime films, animated films, and documentaries (Deleau 2016, 4). While there are a few twentieth-century French horror films known internationally, such as Georges Franju's *Eyes Without a Face* (*Les Yeux sans visage*, 1960) or Jean Rollin's 1970s and 1980s exploitation soft-core horror films, these are generally viewed as exceptions in a national film industry that has other specializations. Since 2000, there has been a significant yet still small increase in the production of highly explicit and violent French films that engage with horror. These range from films that position themselves in the lineage of classic 1980s Hollywood slasher films, such as *High Tension* (*Haute tension*, 2003), *Frontier(s)* (*Frontière(s)*, 2007), or *Martyrs* (2008), to extreme art house films—for example, *Trouble Every Day* (2001), *In My Skin* (*Dans ma peau*, 2002), or *Personal Shopper* (2016)—that engage with horror tropes and motifs but in the context of an auteur's personal preoccupations or aesthetic concerns.[1] Other films, like the internationally successful *Raw* (*Grave*, 2016), situate themselves somewhere between the two poles, suggesting a flexible relationship to horror on the part of many French filmmakers that does not fit neatly into an opposition between genre films and art house cinema.

Some of these films have garnered visibility on the festival circuit, but rarely have they done well at the domestic box office. The exception to this trend is *Deep in the Woods* (*Promenons-nous dans les bois*, 2000), which sold 740,000 tickets in France (Deleau 2016, 38). However, Frédéric Gimello-Mesplomb notes that only one post-2000 horror film, *Them* (*Ils*, 2008), sold more than 200,000 tickets (2012, 37). French horror has fared slightly better on the export market, though even those numbers remain small. Between 1995 and 2014, French horror netted only 2.2 million ticket sales internationally; however, 84 percent of those ticket sales come from two films: *High Tension* and *House of Voices* (*Saint Ange*, 2004) (Deleau 2016, 36–39). While *High Tension* did well internationally, it sold only 107,853 tickets in France (Gimello-Mesplomb 2012, 37).

Given the relatively small corpus of French horror films in the twenty-first century as compared to France's average annual number of films produced (several hundred), it is notable that several French horror films from the mid-2000s deal with the French suburbs, suburban street violence, and interactions between the suburbs, the city, and the French countryside. In contemporary French horror, one might expect to find a privileging of whiteness, given France's long-standing republican tradition of color blindness in the public sphere. Yet, several contemporary French horror films visualize minorities, and not just as monsters or threats but primarily as victims. Kim Chapiron's *Sheitan* (2006) tells the story of four young people from the suburbs who travel to the countryside looking for fun and sex and who find instead an inbred family of devil worshippers looking to steal their body parts. Xavier Gens's *Frontier(s)* (2007) focuses on a group of suburban youths who commit a bank robbery in the midst of ongoing street demonstrations and seek to flee to Belgium, only to be massacred by a family of Nazis living in the French countryside. Yannick Dahan and Benjamin Rocher's *The Horde* (*La Horde*, 2009) forces gangsters and cops to work together to repel zombified suburban youth in a rent-controlled housing project. Finally, Alexandre Bustillo and Julien Maury's *Inside* (*À l'intérieur*, 2007) features a pregnant journalist whose suburban home is invaded by an unknown woman seeking to take her baby on the same night that the streets are filled with protestors. If one adds three art house films associated with the New French Extremity (NFE) in the early 2000s—Gaspard Noé's *Irreversible* (2002), Claire Denis's *Trouble Every Day* (2001), and Virginie Despentes and Coralie Trinh Thi's *Baise-moi* (2002)—to the mix, then in the years just before and just after the 2005 suburban protests, there are no fewer than seven French horror and horror-adjacent films that deal more or less directly with questions of street violence and how the French suburbs fit into the cultural landscape of the nation.

Film scholars writing about French horror, however, have not viewed the social settings of French horror films from the mid-2000s favorably. This corpus of genre films has been criticized for the films' simplistic and reactionary politics and their allegedly slavish relationship to Hollywood horror genre tropes. Film scholar Ian Olney writes that French horror films from the 2000s are too derivative of American horror to be of interest when compared to the more auteurist examples of what he calls *Euro horror,* such as the work of Franju, Roman Polanski, or Dario Argento (2013, 219–220). Another film scholar, Philippe Met, argues that *Frontier(s), The Horde,* and *Inside* are disappointing films because they manage to transmit "a suspect or irresponsible ideology to say the least" by mixing a "vague sociological contextualization" with the traditional genre pleasures of horror (2012, 40).

Denis Mellier is even less generous to the category of 2000s French horror films, which he terms *neohorror.* These films, in his view, share a vague "naturalist ambition" to stage conflicts between worlds: countryside, forests, and, in the case of *Sheitan* and *Frontier(s),* the suburbs. However, he finds such naturalist ambitions to be "schematic" and unable to reveal national monsters. The violence that such films depict against young residents of the suburbs reveal only their "nakedness" and "nullity" when they venture outside the projects (Mellier 2010, 156, 158). In a formulation that echoes film critic James Quandt's influential denunciation of the NFE as all provocation and no politics (2013, 24–25), Mellier concludes that French horror films from the 2000s only offer silent cries of terror and not any kind of progressive politics (2010, 162). The exception to this general critical tendency is Alice Haylett Bryan, who argues that films like *Sheitan* and *Frontier(s)* offer a "counter voice" that "trouble[s] the calls for assimilation and integration that are so often directed at the descendants of immigrants in France." Building on Jacques Derrida's notion of hospitality, Bryan focuses her analysis on "hosting locations"—"hotels, cafés, and even homes"—that she reads as "microcosms of the nation itself: a place that should welcome the foreigner, but instead threatens their liberty" (2021, 235–236).

While I agree with some of Mellier and Met's criticisms of these French horror films' simplistic politics, I am not ready to dismiss entirely the attempts of French filmmakers to Gallicize Hollywood horror through an engagement with contemporary sociopolitical debates about the suburbs. However, I am not prepared to move fully to the opposite position that Bryan takes when she argues that these suburban horror films represent a relatively unproblematic form of counter discourse. There is much that is troubling and potentially reactionary about the politics of these films along with the space they do open to consider questions of belonging and identity in the French suburbs through the genre of horror. Finally, I do not view these films' use of the suburbs as a necessary or unfortunate consequence of making horror in France. Film scholar Guy Austin suggests that many French horror films in the 2000s opted for forms of social horror as a means of offering the realism that many spectators have supposedly come to expect of French films in general (2015, 277). The critical success of Julia Ducournau's *Raw* seems to confirm how pairing horror with a sense of realism and a touch of personal style on the part of the director provides a path for French horror films to be taken seriously by the industry at large. *Raw* was the film that led the CNC (National Center for Cinema and the Moving Image) to start a specific funding program for French genre films, and horror was the genre twice, first in 2018 and again in 2020 (CNC 2019).[2] Yet, it would be a mistake in my view to attribute the presence of social context in French banlieue horror films to mere opportunism on the part of filmmakers in an industry that tends to privilege realism and auteurism.

The French suburbs do serve the important function of localizing Hollywood horror tropes to the French context. However, these films also demonstrate a recognition that horror has always been political and that the genre can in fact be used to engage with contemporary social debates. Such engagement does not take place through a reflectionist conception of realism or the personal voice of the director, but at the level of the imaginary—that is, the shared repository of images that maps bodies, identities, and spaces onto each other within a culture. With respect to Hollywood horror in the 1970s and 1980s, Carol Clover argued in *Men, Women, and Chainsaws* that "horror operates in an allegorical or expressionist or folkloric/mythic mode, whereby characters are understood to concretize essences" (1993, 231). In her view, horror films can be less restricted in what they represent than more realistic forms of cinema. I would not go so far as to suggest that allegorical readings are the best way to understand these French banlieue horror films. Instead, these films *hypersignify*, to use Matt Hills's term (2005, 65), their relationship to the French suburbs about which they hope in some measure to comment (Austin 2015, 279–280). However, an understanding of banlieue horror cinema in France must contend with how French filmmakers transform the imaginary of the horror genre as it has been imported from Hollywood to correspond with the social imaginary of cultural, racial, and spatial differences in contemporary France.

Clover's analysis of the rape-revenge subgenre of horror and specifically what she calls the city-revenge or urbanoia film is especially helpful for understanding the social contexts of these mid-2000 French banlieue horror films. While Clover's book is a foundational work for examining gender and sexuality in Hollywood horror from the 1970s and 1980s, it is arguably underappreciated for the tools it offers for thinking about how space, class, and race relate in horror cinema. For Clover, a divide between the city and rural spaces defines much of Hollywood horror in general and typically involves urban or suburban characters who travel to the uncivilized and wild countryside. In her reading, the geographic limits of cities and suburbs represent the boundaries between the state and the no-state, between civilization and the primitive, and between the rule of law and a Darwinian state of nature. When urban characters travel to the countryside in horror films, the undereducated and poor economic underclasses who live in rural areas exact revenge for the economic resentments they feel and for the humiliations forced on them by city residents and the corporations that act on their behalf. This is where Clover's terms *city-revenge* and *urbanoia* (urban paranoia) film come from. The form of this revenge is usually physical and/or sexual violence that comes to an end only when an avenging woman—what Clover terms *the final girl*—finishes off the killers or rapists through spectacular acts of revenge. In Clover's analysis of the rape-revenge film, feminism operates as a safety valve to resolve narrative tensions that in fact turn centrally around economic guilt and spatial divisions. Seen in this light, Clover argues, rape-revenge films extend implicit colonialist features of Hollywood Westerns from the 1940s and 1950s into the closing decades of the twentieth century, replacing "redskins" with "rednecks" who stand in for other ethnic and racial minorities and who can be safely neutralized in a film's narrative because they are white. Clover ultimately concludes that the embodied forms of violence in rape-revenge films make explicit the forms of colonial exploitation that classic Hollywood Westerns would not show directly (1993, 131–133, 134–136, 163).

The challenge of using Clover's class- and race-based resentment model of the rape-revenge and urbanoia film to make sense of recent French banlieue horror films is that the ways in which class and race map onto spatial divisions between countryside, suburbs, and city center differ significantly in France. Single-family suburbs in the United States tend to be aligned with the city's dominant social groups when it comes to their cultural belonging and economic interests, to the point that it makes sense to speak of US horror in terms of a (sub)urban/rural divide. However, this model does not hold for spatial divisions in the French context. There are of course single-family suburbs surrounding French cities—the so-called *banlieues pavillonaires*—but when they are used in a French horror television series like *The Returned* (*Les Revenants*, 2012, 2015), the effect feels nonspecific and non-French, as if viewers were in a strange American suburb that had somehow been transplanted into France (see Pettersen 2021). The banlieues of the French imaginary as spaces of multiculture and project housing simply do not map onto American suburban spaces as the US horror genre has visualized them. These banlieues belong neither to the city center nor to the countryside. Instead, they share elements of the city and the countryside but also remain quite distinct from both.

The French suburbs' mixture of city and countryside can be traced back to the early days of their urban planning and construction in France. For example, psychoanalyst Jean-Jacques Rassial has argued that an important way to understand the utopic *villes nouvelles* projects from the 1960s and 1970s was as a way to bring the ideals of city and country together (2002, 9). These spaces could mix housing density, access to transportation, services, and cultural activities along with access to green spaces, nature, and close-knit communities. Geographer Jérôme Dunlop explains that most rural areas around cities have either seen the culture of the countryside erased as residential, industrial, and recreational functions replace agriculture—what he calls *rurbanization*—or they have maintained some autonomy as peri-urban spaces but still depend to some degree on a nearby city center. The banlieues, however, differ in Dunlop's view from these rurbanization or peri-urban models of rural development in that the suburbs were urbanized against their will due to nearby urban growth that gradually took over the countryside. For this reason, Dunlop calls the banlieues "the only true cities that were former villages" (2019, 54–58, 56). However, Dunlop notes that even though the banlieues are less diverse than city centers in terms of ethnic, racial, or class composition, they are quite diverse among themselves, even as an individual banlieue neighborhood may be relatively homogenous when it comes to who lives there and what types of employment are available (2019, 57, 59–60). This means that the banlieues can have a stronger sense of locality than the city center, a feature that paradoxically aligns them with the countryside and notions of *terroir*—that is, the specific environmental factors that make a place, its people, and its goods distinctive.

In a related vein, Dayna Oscherwitz has argued that the general phenomenon of banlieue films is part of the reemergence of regionalist discourse in French culture, and she goes so far as to call banlieue films "a multicultural reappropriation of the logic of regionalism" (2010, 105). Banlieue films, like rural films, stress the importance of local space in constructing a sense of collective identity, with suburban residents identifying with their specific neighborhood or even specific apartment block. In the same way that regionalism contests notions of a homogenous national identity, so too does banlieue cinema challenge monolithic conceptions of French identity and thus rearticulate the universal.

To understand the social meanings of the banlieues in mid-2000s horror films, we first need to understand the differences between French horror films and NFE films that represent the suburbs and class resentments. Second, we need to attend to how specifically French forms of spatial identity and resentment operate in French banlieue horror films with respect to characters from the country, the city, and the suburbs. To mark the importance of Clover's model of the rape-revenge and urbanoia film for my analysis and the ways in which I seek to modify it, I will refer to these French banlieue horror films as an instance of *suburbanoia* or *suburbanoia films*. Their sense of paranoia can be found in both the suburban characters when they travel to the countryside and in the country residents who interact with suburban characters. Finally, we need to examine how the extreme violence inflicted on minority bodies in French horror films relates to questions of discrimination and color-blind universalism in contemporary France. French banlieue horror films stage the dislocation of suburban spaces and residents within the shared cultural imaginary of France but in ways that are not always progressive.

SPATIAL RESENTMENTS AT THE MARGINS OF NEW FRENCH EXTREMITY FILMS

What the NFE is and how it relates to horror has been a matter of much debate. Quandt first coined the moniker *New French Extremity* as a derogatory term (2013). He was puzzled by the explosion of excessive violence in French art house cinema at the turn of the twenty-first century, especially because this extreme violence was divorced, in his view, from any kind of emancipatory framework that gave the stylistic excesses of earlier European avant-garde movements in the interwar or post–World War II periods an anchor in political engagement. In his view, the excesses of films like Noé's *Irreversible* (2002), Denis's *Trouble Every Day* (2001), or Despentes and Trinh Thi's *Baise-moi* (2000) are superfluous, shock for shock's sake, or art house directors "slumming it" in B-genre territory. Quandt's polemical formulation led to a wave of exegetical commentaries on films of the NFE, creating a cottage industry among scholars who sought to explain their stylistic excesses in various ways that ranged from phenomenological, aesthetic, or affective terms to sociohistorical context and production or reception histories.[3] Others, such as Maxime Bey-Rozet, argue that NFE films set out to be irredeemable, beyond recuperation to any final politics of meaning (2020). It should come as no surprise that the banlieues are represented obliquely in such films if they are represented at all.

The debates surrounding the meaning of violence and stylistic excess of NFE films have tended to downplay their connections to horror as a genre. While I do not agree with critics who view the horror genre as incidental to NFE films, the three that do engage with the banlieues—*Irreversible, Baise-moi,* and *Trouble Every Day*—do so in such an indirect manner that I will not consider them at great length here except to signal briefly why they are not central to this book's project. *Irreversible* and *Baise-moi* self-consciously engage with B-movie traditions of the rape-revenge films, and whether this category of film is a subgenre of horror or a distinct genre in its own right has been a matter of debate. Emily Brick notes that prior to Hollywood horror films like *Saw* (2004) or *Hostel* (2005), sexual violence was symbolic rather than implied or literal. With the move to what has been misleadingly called *torture porn*, sexual violence has increasingly become part of what many contemporary horror films engage with directly (Brick 2012, 100). *Trouble Every Day*'s tale of biotech research in former French colonies gone wrong invokes the zombie film subgenre of horror with its two characters whose uncontrollable sexual impulses can only find fulfillment through cannibalism and murder. Yet, the gore and shock effects in all three of these films subvert the typical narrative patterns of the rape-revenge film or the zombie film. NFE films amplify the traditions of narrative ambivalence that characterize European art cinemas generally, and so the shock effects of gore and sexual violence are not anchored in the traditional genre patterns of horror cinema. Of the three, *Baise-moi* engages most self-consciously with B-movie tropes, both in its narrative construction and highly stylized, grainy handheld images, but the film's artistic conversation is more with exploitation films and pornography than horror.

Irreversible, *Trouble Every Day*, and *Baise-moi* engage with the economic marginalization and class resentments of the banlieues in a very circuitous manner. *Irreversible*'s tale of revenge and then rape (reverse order in the film) does not clearly indicate where viewers are in the city, in part because of Noé's disorienting mobile camera. Tim Palmer suggests that the space where the party and the rape take place are somewhere beyond the peripheral boulevard that encompasses the city center. The film's characters do not travel to the banlieues per se, but to the city's imprecise outskirts, where poverty, criminality, and danger lie (Palmer 2011, 125). Denis differs from Noé in that she has arguably made a banlieue film, *35 Shots of Rum* (*35 rhums*, 2008). However, in *Trouble Every Day*, where viewers are spatially is not always clear. Coré's (Béatrice Dalle) first kill takes places when she hitchhikes somewhere outside Paris and then murders a truck driver in a field at night. We see high-rise apartments like those north of Paris, but the banlieues are not thematized. When Coré's husband, Léo (Alex Descas), locks her in a house for her safety (and that of others), it is in a suburban single-family home. Of the three films, *Baise-moi* has the most explicit connection to the banlieues. The source material for the film is Despentes's novel by the same name that begins explicitly in the banlieues, where the two main characters are from. The first part of the novel before their revenge spree details their lives there. However, in the film adaptation, the spatial context of the banlieues is not mentioned directly. Their neighborhood in the film is portrayed as generically crime ridden and racially diverse, but these scenes look to have been shot near the Place d'Italie neighborhood within Paris, and thus the film does not feature the recognizable cinematic iconography of the banlieues.

All three NFE films deal with forms of economic, cultural, and racial marginalization, but they do so in an indirect way, leaving the social meanings of violence and identity fluid. The violence may be literal and extreme, but the social backgrounds of the characters and places are not fully fleshed out. They are thus distinct enterprises from the other genre films examined in this book that seek to fuse genre codes with the recognizable places, characters, and narrative tropes of banlieue films. It is for this reason that I will not consider these NFE films in this chapter, preferring instead to focus on French horror films that engage directly with the banlieues. By invoking the codes of horror and banlieue cinema directly, these films will allow us to understand how their filmmakers seek to adapt the spatial geography and class structures of post-1970s Hollywood horror to France.

NO-HOLDS-BARRED PROVOCATION IN *SHEITAN*

Sheitan (2007) was the first feature by Chapiron, a member of the short-film collective *Kourtrajmé* (French *verlan* or backward slang for *court-métrage*, short-film); some of the group's members starred as the film's three male protagonists. Vincent Cassel and Éric Nevé produced the film, with the former making an explicit link back to arguably the most important banlieue film of the mid-1990s, Mathieu Kassovitz's *La Haine* (1995). *Sheitan* focuses on three twenty-something young men—a white man named Bart, a Vietnamese man named, surprisingly, Thai, and a West African French Muslim man named Ladj. The film begins at a nightclub in the Parisian suburbs as the three men seek to find sexual partners for the night. Ladj charms the club's bartender, Yasmine, a French woman of Algerian descent, played by a young Leïla Bekhti. Thai meets Eve, a libidinous white French girl from a small country town near Paris. When Bart gets himself ejected from the club, Eve suggests that they all go to her family's home in the French countryside to "have a little fun." There, they meet a mix of oversexed young women, bored young men, and physically deformed characters who suggest the clichés of an inbred French countryside filtered through Hollywood horror films like *The Texas Chainsaw Massacre* (1974). Cassel plays Joseph, the housekeeper of Eve's family home, who has made a pact with the devil, as viewers eventually learn. In the context of Islam, the film's title, *Sheitan*, means alternately Satan, any evil spirit, or a vicious person or animal. Joseph has slept with his sister, Marie (a corpulent woman played by Cassel wearing a fat suit), and fathered a child who will go on to be the devil. Joseph needs to make a doll using human parts to ensure a successful birth at the stroke of midnight on Christmas Eve, and the film suggests that Eve is complicit in his entrapment of the young group from the city. With its pairing of stereotypes about rural spaces and suburban characters, the film literalizes the excesses of stereotypes in images, language, and genre tropes and thereby seeks to destabilize them.

Sheitan is arguably not a banlieue film in the sense that we never see its main characters in suburban spaces. There is, however, a rap video set in the suburbs that I will return to in a moment. Viewers meet the group of young people at a Parisian nightclub, rather than the suburbs, before they decamp to a house in the countryside. While the script originally called for a mountainside location, the scenes were shot in the countryside of Île-de-France, the region that contains Paris. Nevertheless, there are reasons to consider this an instance of a banlieue horror film even though viewers do not spend significant screen time in the recognizable iconography of suburban neighborhoods or project housing. First, there is the multiethnic cast of characters, a clear nod to the trio in *La Haine*. Their sartorial choices and slang-filled language reflect street culture and indicate that they are hardly *fils de*, or sons of well-respected bourgeois families playing at being from the suburbs. Furthermore, Chapiron admits that he wanted to offer "a portrait of his generation" (Valo 2006, 30). By *generation*, I take Chapiron to be referring both to his own unique childhood and to the Kourtrajmé collective's connections to contemporary French multiculture and suburban spaces.

Chapiron's career echoes Kassovitz's in that Chapiron came from a bourgeois but artistic and politically engaged family, one that allowed him to connect with suburban spaces and culture through friendships and music. Chapiron's father, punk media artist Kiki Picasso (artistic alias of Christian Chapiron), had his own leftist collective, Bazooka, for many years. Chapiron's father was a member of one of several bourgeois but leftist-sympathizing filmmaking families who decided to move out of Paris's bourgeois neighborhoods into Ménilmontant, a Parisian working-class neighborhood, where they lived in a converted warehouse starting in the late 1960s and 1970s. This network of media artists and filmmakers included Peter Kassovitz and his wife, a television producer, Left Bank New Wave filmmaker Chris Marker, Kiki Picasso, and Alexandre Gavras, whose father, Costa-Gavras, was one of the most important political filmmakers of the 1970s (Higbee 2006, 7–8; Etchegoin 2017).

Chapiron met a key Kourtrajmé collaborator, Romain Gavras, Alexandre's younger brother, in the apartment building where Chapiron grew up. Chapiron's mother is Vietnamese, and much of her family lived in the suburban neighborhood Cité des Bosquets in Montfermeil in the Seine-Saint-Denis. It was here that the young Chapiron met another key collaborator, Ladj Ly, the future director of *Les Misérables*, the prize-winning 2019 adaptation of Victor Hugo's novel into a banlieue crime film that I will discuss briefly in this book's conclusion. Chapiron's father had a significant collection of hip-hop music on vinyl, which allowed him to discover France's emerging suburban street culture in the 1980s and 1990s. Chapiron was born in 1980 and is thus thirteen years younger than Kassovitz, who was born in 1967. Nevertheless, the two grew up in the same building, and the example of Kassovitz and Cassel in *La Haine* proved to Chapiron and his friends in Kourtrajmé that one did need to come from a wealthy family, attend France's state film school La Fémis, or be a devoted cinephile to become an important filmmaker (Goldszal 2019).

Along with Gavras, Ly, and others, Chapiron cofounded the filmmaking collective Kourtrajmé in 1995, and it was best known in its early days for the provocative short films and music videos that they distributed on VHS cassettes and through their website in the early 2000s, just before YouTube arrived on the scene in 2004. The collective is now reputed to have some 135 members, and their vision has expanded beyond filmmaking to include film education. Ly took the lead in helping Kourtrajmé found a film school at Montfermeil in Seine-Saint-Denis in 2018, again confirming the importance of film schools in democratizing access to the means of production for suburban and working-class youth and in allowing space for different kinds of French cinema to emerge (*Le Monde* 2018).[4] Ly also plays the Black character, Ladj, in Chapiron's *Sheitan*, suggesting a dense network of mutual support for filmmakers from working-class and suburban Paris that are all politically engaged with French multiculture and suburban communities in their own unique ways.

In addition to contextual details surrounding the filmmakers and actors that link *Sheitan* to the suburbs, some critics wrote about it as a banlieue film upon its release in 2007. Film critic Stéphanie Belpêche refers to *Sheitan*'s characters as "suburban youth" (*jeunes de banlieues*) in her review in *Le Journal du Dimanche* (2006), and Stéphanie Binet in *Libération* describes the film as "banlieue labeled" (*étiqueté banlieue*) about the "other France" of the 2005 protests (2006b). Finally, the film features Cassel, whose role as star and producer are intimately connected to French suburban cinema. In fact, without Cassel's help, the film might not have seen the light of day. In an interview, Cassel explains that *Sheitan* is not an obvious banlieue film like *La Haine*, despite the importance of suburban street culture in Chapiron's film. Instead, Cassel argues that *Sheitan* is notable for breaking taboos in suburban communities around sexuality (Binet 2006a). Cassel's account of the production process reveals the extent to which Chapiron relied on guerilla filmmaking techniques. Chapiron did not wait for a funding subvention from the CNC to make his first feature film, and some of the cameras used for the film were stolen (Belpêche 2006). These details suggest that *Sheitan* is the most underground of the banlieue horror films considered in this chapter, even though it ultimately premiered at the Cannes Film Festival.

While *Sheitan*'s characters do not travel to the suburbs, the film does feature an embedded rap video, "Bâtard de barbares" ("Mongrel or Illegitimate Barbarians"), that is set in the banlieues and showcases the Kourtrajmé collective's history of making confrontational short films and music videos. Many of Kourtrajmé's shorts are known for their wild humor and willingness to push boundaries through provocation and a complete lack of respect for any kind of political correctness. *Sheitan* has a short-film aesthetic in that its narrative contains three sections that are stylistically and narratively distinct. The first section in the nightclub presents an extended version of the encounter between suburban youth and urban party culture that we also find in *All That Glitters* (*Tout ce qui brille*, 2010) and *Divines* (2016) and that I discuss elsewhere in this book. *Sheitan*'s second section, about the arrival of the main characters in the countryside, draws on the tropes of the teen sex comedy and 1980s Hollywood slasher films. Finally, the third section, which is about entrapment and violence, is the most horror-inflected section of the three, but horror's sense of unease and menace pervades the whole film.

The French suburbs are portrayed as a place of extreme violence through the film's fictionalized terrorist French rap group, also named Sheitan, whose music video features prominently in the film. Thai and Bart watch the video with Eve on the television at her parents' country manor, and it features an Arabic-looking rapper dressed in the trappings of a sheik who incites the suburban youth to acts of extreme violence and hatred. In shots that resemble televised images of Arab extremists, the rapper brandishes a machine gun, another person wears a suicide bomb and blows himself up, one person lights another on fire, and the rapper himself fires a handgun into a man's mouth, making his head explode, among other gruesome acts. Whereas *Sheitan* the film is otherwise restrained in its gore and splatter effects when compared to *Frontier(s)* or *Inside*, the rap video shows the violent acts of the rapper's entourage in gruesome detail.

Furthermore, the song's lyrics link sexual coupling and terroristic sadism with images of suburban street violence: "I dig up your grandma and rape her like a dog / and if you're not happy, I rape your dad / When your whore blows me I lose some weight" (*Je déterre ta grand-mère et la viole comme une chienne / Et si t'es pas content je viole ton père / Quand ta pute me suce je perds des kilos*) and "Terrorist, public enemy / I blow up trains, towers, and schools / I shoot myself up with glue / I'm a human bomb in an elementary school" (*Terroriste, ennemi public / J'fais sauter les trains, les tours et les écoles / Moi j'me shoote à la colle / Je suis une bombe humaine dans une maternelle*). When Thai and Bart cheer along with the song, they seem unaware of the violence depicted. It is simply one more outlet for their disaffection and frustration along with chasing women and getting into fights. While meant as a parody of the violence in American rap videos and as a delirious satire of French fears of domestic terrorism in the banlieues, it clearly connects *Sheitan* to televised images of street violence seen during the 2005 suburban protests. Furthermore, at a time when Nicolas Sarkozy was earning political points during the 2007 presidential campaign for using offensive language about the suburbs and the people who live there, *Sheitan* literalizes just how dark stereotypes can be on both sides of the cultural divide between the suburbs and dominant French society.

These connections are far from accidental, even though the rap video sequence predates the 2005 protests. Chapiron notes in an interview that they shot the rap scene in Clichy-Montfermeil a year before the street protests that took place in that very neighborhood (Valo 2006). For Chapiron, these excessive images serve to make literal the words of the rap song. Yet, Chapiron also disavows the excessive violence of the rap video's images and words. In a common refrain that we will encounter repeatedly in interviews with the French horror filmmakers considered in this chapter, Chapiron argues that "only reality is violence" (*seule la réalité est violence*) (Valo 2006). His film, by contrast, is for laughs. Nevertheless, *Sheitan*'s excessive images of violence and sexual coupling combined with a refusal of all political correctness reflect on how France imagines its suburban youth and the kinds of cultural mixing taking place in contemporary France.

The film's shots of the countryside's wide-open spaces contrast with the constricted framings and graffiti-filled images of project neighborhoods that we see in many films about the banlieues, though much of *Sheitan*'s depiction of the countryside turns on stereotype. The group's car becomes stuck in the mud after they stop for a herd of goats blocking the road, suggesting rural backwardness. This moment is when the group first meets Joseph, who, in a possible parody of the affected swagger from his performance in *La Haine*, ambles up to meet the protagonists dressed as the unhip country bumpkin with his plain sweater, functional pants, and oversized galoshes. Joseph helps them get unstuck with his bare hands, and as the group pulls away, Thai tells Ladj to stop messing around because "it's not your country [*bled*] here" *Bled* here is the Arabic word for country that has been imported into French. It simultaneously means the countryside in Africa and Maghreb, but French youth whose families immigrated at some point in the past also use it pejoratively to refer to

Figure 4.1 The group of young people from the suburbs cozy up to Joseph (Vincent Cassel) as they drive to the country manor house. *Sheitan*, 2006.

the backwater town that their parents left in search of better fortunes in France. Thai's line marks the suburban youths' disjuncture from their rural surroundings. While the French countryside might imaginatively, if not literally, be the home for a city dweller whose family has lived in France for generations, for the film's suburban characters, the countryside is not "theirs."

Sheitan's exploration of how race, class, and nationality map problematically onto the countryside and the suburbs continues when the group first sees the country manor house where Eve's family lives. It serves as the film's gothic mansion, a horror genre staple filled with hidden rooms and dark secrets. As the group exits the vehicle, Bart admires that Eve is in fact "a rich girl," ostensibly a reference to the size and spaciousness of her family's house. However, as they explore the interior, they see that several of the house's wings are just as dilapidated as some suburban neighborhoods. Clover's model of how city-country resentment functions in urbanoia films does not quite work here in *Sheitan*. In what I am calling *suburbanoia*, the city does not represent the rich and those in the countryside are not the marginalized or the exploited. Rather, the materially poor suburban youth, who do not even have enough money for gas to get to the countryside, meet a group of materially well-off yet off-kilter country residents.

Furthermore, in *Sheitan*, the French countryside, not the city, is represented as sexually permissive and promiscuous. Whereas Bart could not find himself a willing woman in the nightclub, when he eyes a young woman in the town square, Joseph calls her over and she immediately begins flirting with Bart. The group shortly thereafter goes skinny-dipping in the local hot springs with the town's youth, both beautiful and deformed. Most of the rural dwellers seemingly ignore the racial and ethnic composition of the suburban group and pick on them because they are outsiders to the countryside. Only Joseph seems to notice the group's mix of cultural and ethnic backgrounds, repeatedly calling Yasmine "my camel driver" (*ma petite turque*) and Ladj "le nègre." In creating the doll that will supposedly aid the devil's birth, Joseph cares only for Bart, the ostensible white man in the group. Joseph intentionally mispronounces his name as Marc to make it sound more French. Joseph is not the serial killer seen in Hollywood film franchises like *Halloween* (1978) or *Nightmare on Elm Street* (1984). He does not seem to care when the rest of the group escapes, as long as Bart is still there. Instead, Joseph is interested in maintaining a certain kind of racial purity for his family, rather than killing everyone from the suburbs. *Sheitan* is ultimately more interested in combating stereotypes of the country and the suburbs by pushing everything as far past the point of political correctness as possible. Incest, deformity, and the birth of monsters, then, are the flip side of fears of miscegenation, but at the same time, it seems that the countryside needs the suburbs if it is to have a future. While this idea that the rest of France needs its suburbs to survive is largely implicit in *Sheitan*, Gens makes it one of the main themes of his banlieue horror film *Frontier(s)*.

UNCERTAIN BORDERS IN *FRONTIER(S)*, OR WHAT ARE FASCISTS DOING IN THE FRENCH COUNTRYSIDE?

Like *Sheitan*, Gens's *Frontier(s)* (2007) stages a collision between a group of young men and women from the Parisian banlieues and the French countryside, and it imitates *The Texas Chainsaw Massacre* even more explicitly than *Sheitan* does. What Gens's protagonists find is not an incestuous clan of white devil worshippers, but rather an incestuous family of Franco-German Nazis who have taken control of an old mining town and its surroundings. However, the film diverges from Clover's model of the urbanoia film in which country residents take violent revenge on city dwellers for the latter's neglect and exploitation of the countryside. In the form of suburbanoia we find in *Frontier(s)*, the suburban protagonists are dislocated from city center and countryside, something Gens emphasizes by setting the film in the context of suburban street violence. Whereas *Sheitan* evoked street violence indirectly through its embedded rap video, Gens opts for a more direct representation in *Frontier(s)*.

The film opens with ultrasound images of a baby as the main character and the film's final girl, Yasmine, wonders in voice-over whether she can bring a baby into a world defined by violence in the banlieues and the recent election results in which an extreme right-wing candidate advanced to the second round. This subplot in the film is a thinly fictionalized version of National Front leader Jean-Marie Le Pen's success in 2002, which would be repeated by his daughter, Marine Le Pen, in 2017. The film was released in 2007, and it also anticipates the 2007 presidential elections in which former minister of the interior Sarkozy was elected on a law-and-order platform. Radio and television reports in *Frontier(s)* identify the extreme right-wing candidate in the diegesis as the current minister of the interior, a clear nod to Sarkozy.

The sequence following the ultrasound images invokes the opening of Kassovitz's *La Haine* through Gens's use of news footage of street protests, including confrontations with police, the torching of cars and dumpsters, and the throwing of Molotov cocktails. The film gradually transitions into a fictionalized sequence about the protagonists—four men and one woman who have committed a robbery and seek to flee the banlieues to Holland. Whereas Kassovitz's earlier film only suggested violence with police, Gens's opening sequence stages a full-blown action sequence in which one of the main characters violently assaults a police officer during their group's attempt to escape the city. The sequence employs shaky handheld camerawork, sped-up images, and rapid-fire editing to such a degree that it can trigger nausea. The excess of violence here, which is arguably like the ultraviolence I analyzed in the previous chapter, prefigures the excessive violence of a different type, the gore and human mutilation that will define the protagonists' encounter with the fascists in the French countryside.

Gens's sympathies are clearly with the suburban protestors in the opening sequence, if perhaps not with their violence. During the news footage sequence that interlaces with the opening credits, Gens cuts to an image of a stocky dog wearing a sign in the middle of the protests that reads "I eat fascists and shit them out" (*Je bouffe du facho et je le chie*). Later, while Tom and Farid await Alex and Yasmine's arrival in the hotel, they watch coverage of the election results about the Sarkozy figure's success. Tom calls the candidate a "faggot" (*pédale*) and France a "country of fascists" (*pays de fachos*). Tom goes on to claim that France is ten years behind the United States and has just elected its own George W. Bush. The repeated references to fascism are clearly meant to set up the presence of a latter-day Nazi family in the French countryside, though the analogy between contemporary French right-wing politics and historical Nazism muddles the social fable Gens seemingly wants to tell.

Before dealing with the question of why there are Nazis living in twenty-first century France, we need to attend to how Gens imagines the countryside. It is important to stress that despite its use of news footage of suburban protests, *Frontier(s)* is not sociological or realistic in any meaningful sense. Even though viewers know that the film's countryside is situated somewhere between Paris and France's northern border, there are no meaningful geographic markers in the opening sequence in the banlieues or the rest of the film. We are in the countryside of myth and folklore, rather a specific rural zone. The film is similarly vague in its representation of suburban geography. When Karl, a local cop and the family's second in command, asks Tom and Farid where they are from, Farid refers to the Parisian suburbs in the singular (*banlieue parisienne*), a choice that, as I argued in the book's introduction, is reductionist by implying all banlieue neighborhoods are the same. *Frontier(s)*, like the other banlieue horror films considered in this chapter, examines questions of spatial inequalities and multiculture at the level of the collective social imaginary and not at the level of realism.

Gens visually and aurally marks the French countryside as radically different from the banlieues and from any kind of authentic France (*la France profonde*) that might be found there. Tom and Farid are the first to arrive in the countryside, and Tom jokingly asks Farid if they are even still in France. Farid answers, "Yeah, we're in the Middle Ages. We were better off in our apartment blocks" (*Ouais, on est au Moyen Âge. Sérieux, on est bien dans nos HLM [habitations à loyer modéré]*). Aurally, the opening action sequences employ tense orchestral scoring, but as Tom and Farid drive out of the city, Farid switches on rap music that accompanies their trip to the countryside. Farid's ringtone is also a rap song, and when his phone rings at the hotel, it offers an aural marker of their being out of place and contrasts with the death metal soundtrack that Gens uses to define the pseudo-Germanic, neo-Nazi space of the northern French countryside. The family members' first names are predominantly Germanic and spelled with *K*s to mark them as non-French. When Tom and Farid arrive at the hotel, they meet the clan's two beautiful young women, Gilberte and Klaudia, and Tom begins flirting with Gilberte as if they had stumbled into the sexual tourism plotline of Eli Roth's 2005 film *Hostel*. Later, as the four have sex, death metal music blasts in the soundtrack to aurally distinguish the countryside from the banlieues.

Tobe Hooper's 1974 film *The Texas Chainsaw Massacre* (*TCM*) is the most direct influence on the *Frontier(s)* narrative construction as a whole, although Gens's scenario does not reach quite the same integration of horror formulae and social context as Hooper's film. In *TCM*, unemployment drives former cattle ranchers to cannibalism and the slaughter of travelers, whereas the slaughter

Figure 4.2 The fascist family of cannibals gathers for dinner. *Frontier(s)*, 2007.

and cannibalism in *Frontier(s)* have no clear narrative motivation. Both families, however, seem to engage in the slaughter and butchery of humans and animals. As with *Sheitan*'s rural family, the neo-Nazi family in *Frontier(s)* does not seem to be poor, but rather relatively well-off and obsessed with creating the perfect race. The film's references to Islam and French Maghrebi cultures also turn on stereotype. Viewers learn that Farid's family is originally from Algeria, though he grew up entirely in the banlieues and only left once to attend his parents' funeral in Bilda. During the first family dinner sequence, when Farid refuses a dish cooked in pork fat, Goetz asks him if he is Jewish, and Farid replies that in fact he is Muslim and does not like pork. However, Farid is hardly the model Muslim. He drinks alcohol and reluctantly lets Klaudia remove his shirt and grind up against him in bed after protesting that he has a girlfriend and would prefer to film the group sex instead. Tom insulted his manhood earlier during the car ride, suggesting that masculinity is more at issue than religious identity and thus aligning the film with horror genre tropes, rather than sociological realism. Karl calls Farid a *métèque*, a generic xenophobic term for immigrants, especially those who look vaguely Mediterranean. Images of Tom, Alex, and Yasmine's captivity shot in the family's slaughterhouse are juxtaposed with the sounds of pigs squealing, again evoking but not developing the topic of shared dietary restrictions between Jewish and Muslim traditions. Through this and other juxtapositions, Gens narratively assimilates the plight of contemporary French Maghrebi communities in the banlieues to that of European Jews during World War II.

In case the film's comparison of unrest in the French suburbs, police violence, and right-wing election results to the extermination of European Jews was not already abundantly obvious, Gens visually likens the clan's slaughterhouse hotel to a concentration camp. As the family chases Tom and Farid through the countryside, Gens cuts to an image of Klaudia, who tosses Farid's cell phone into a box alongside many others. The neatly stacked boxes of eyeglasses, cell phones, watches, and passports recall famous imagery of prisoner intake and execution procedures at German concentration camps. Later in the film, Farid is boiled alive in a steam chamber deep in the mines before being shot in the head, visually evoking the gas chambers. Finally, in a visual transition that looks back to the famous tracking shot in Alain Resnais's *Night and Fog* (*Nuit et brouillard*, 1956) that moves from the Polish countryside to reveal Auschwitz's barbed wire fences, near the end of *Frontier(s)*, Gens cuts from a bucolic time-lapse image of the countryside during the day to a cloudy shot of a similar landscape with a barbed wire fence in the foreground, suggesting that the repressive logic of World War II concentration camps is somehow alive and well in the French countryside.

Gens's choice in the film to locate the lineage of French fascism in Germany can be read in two ways. On the one hand, it occludes France's own history of repressive violence in its former colonies and on colonial subjects living in France during decolonization, both of which are in part responsible for the marginalization of the banlieues. It is as if Gens were suggesting that the forms of discrimination that characterize fascism were a foreign import, rather than a homegrown phenomenon. This choice conveniently lets French viewers off the hook for their country's own historical complicity with the violence of the colonial period or with contemporary discrimination in the banlieues. On the other hand, the German reference also returns viewers to the origins of France's constitutional provision for color-blind universalism as a reaction against the collaborationist Vichy government's racial laws that were responsible for the deportation of French Jews during World War II. It could thus be argued that *Frontier(s)* recognizes French complicity in historical genocide that led to color-blind universalism as a means to protect the nation against such violence in the future. As these two divergent interpretations should make clear, the film does not take a coherent position on the origins of discrimination in France, despite the many references to fascism.

The film suggests that France may well need its contemporary multiculture to assure its own future or it risks becoming like the inbred family of *Sheitan* or *Frontier(s)*. One of the central themes of Gens's film is racial purity, though ironically, the father of Gens's neo-Nazi family argues that they need Yasmine's blood to renew their own bloodline and prevent the birth of more deformed blind children like those living in the mines, the probable result of incest among family members. Yet any sustained reflection on the benefits of cultural diversity falls by the wayside in the final bloodbath prescribed by the genre codes of the slasher film. Yasmine is the film's final girl, and she escapes the family after a lengthy struggle but is then stopped by French police officers at a roadblock for unknown reasons. Karl himself was a police officer, and during her earlier escape attempt, she flagged down Goetz only to be brought back to the family mansion in a moment that replays a similar scenario from *TCM*. This final scene, shot with a low-angle camera that accentuates the wide expanse of the French countryside, offers no neat resolution to the question of where Yasmine can find a future in France. She exits the vehicle with her hands raised, not sure if the police are there to help her or arrest her.

The meaning of this final shot is far from clear, and the same could be said of any kind of social message the film carries. Met reads the social context of *Frontier(s)* as mere pretext for an explosion of violence. The characters escape what he calls "social violence" only to fall into a "fantasmatic" form of violence (2012, 41). In his view, *Frontier(s)*' thinly developed sociopolitical storyline simply "goes down the drain under dump trucks filled with guts" (2012, 43). Bryan views the film more positively than Met as a "call for white France to question the direction in which it is moving politically" (2021, 229). Gens attributes the incoherence of his first feature-length film to youthful exuberance, though he looks back on it fondly. He views *Frontier(s)* as an adolescent exercise into which he tried to pack everything he appreciated from growing up on 1980s Hollywood cinema. In an interview, Gens explains that he wanted to prove that a French horror director could do as well as Hollywood ones with much less funding: "The film is very teenage in its approach, a bit reckless and irreverent, but when you watch it, you say to yourself, this guy stuffed himself with 1980s cinema his whole life. He loves gore and trash, but he's sincere and in that I'm very happy" (Nicolet 2020). The film was promoted in the United States on film posters as the French response to *Saw* and *Hostel*, suggesting a direct rivalry with American forms of horror. The excess of its violence includes exploding heads, the cutting of Achilles tendons with branch trimmers, and table saw executions, among other gory confections. The point of the film's violence might simply be to "shock the Americans" in a contemporary genre cinema twist on the early twentieth-century avant-garde's desire to shock the bourgeois (*épater le bourgeois*).

However, viewing *Frontier(s)*' extreme violence as a mere shock effect sells short the film's attempt to imagine how the French suburbs could fit into the codes of Hollywood horror cinema. I do not disagree with Met's cautions about the incoherent social meanings of *Frontier(s)*, nor do I want to defend Gens's first film against accusations of stylistic awkwardness. And yet, I think the film represents an important though flawed exploration of how to Gallicize horror through the suburbs and multiculture of contemporary France. The film's stylistic imperfections point to the places where the class parameters of the Hollywood slasher film or the rape-revenge subgenre that Clover analyzes do not map onto the realities of contemporary France. At the same time, through the Manichean plot conventions of the slasher film in which only the final girl should survive, the forms of social exclusion that characterize the French suburbs become legible for international viewers to a small but not insignificant degree. While we may still be waiting for the cinematic masterpiece of French banlieue horror, *Frontier(s)* has the merit of assuming that the horror genre might be able to express visceral feelings of social exclusion and the violent logic of some forms of discrimination in contemporary France to audiences outside the suburbs. The suburbanoia we find in Gens's film dramatizes in a spectacularly violent fashion the dislocation of the banlieues in the French imaginary—neither countryside nor city, seemingly far away and intimately close, and very French.

THE FRENCH SUBURBS AS A GLOBALIZED SPACE IN *THE HORDE*

Whereas *Frontier(s)* largely elides the impact of France's own history of colonial violence for contemporary social problems in the suburbs, Dahan and Rocher's *The Horde* (2009) makes direct if incoherent references to French colonial history. The filmmakers also go one step further than Gens in that they do not only make the French banlieues legible for international audiences; they also show that the French suburbs are connected to other marginalized spaces, such as contemporary urban megaslums, and the global flows of human migration that helped create them. A key feature of what I am calling the suburbanoia film is not just economic resentment and suspicion, but also the fear that the rule of law does not hold in suburban spaces or the doubt that such spaces are even French. Étienne Balibar has characterized the French banlieues as global cities "whose demographic composition and movements reflect the contradictions of globalization and their local projection" (2014, 234). The French banlieues thus often channel anxieties about globalization in the French imaginary. The genre conventions of Hollywood horror that circulate internationally can, I argue, bring attention to local inflections of the pressures of globalization in France, including local histories of migration, suburban inequality, and contemporary multiculture.

Figure 4.3 One of *The Horde*'s (2009) protagonists in a standoff with suburban zombies.

Unlike *Sheitan* and *Frontier(s)*, the horror in *The Horde* is not about suburban residents traveling to the French countryside, but rather about a group of angry cops seeking to avenge a fallen colleague by killing the gang members responsible for his death in a run-down, dilapidated suburban apartment block. The gang members in the film are quite nationally diverse, having come to France from Eastern Europe and the African continent at some point in the past. Once the zombies descend, the cops and the gang members realize they must work together if they will have any hope of living out the night. This time, the suburban residents are not the victims; rather, they become the monster in the form of clambering throngs of hungry zombies, embodying through genre imagery French fears about unrest in the French suburbs.

Zombies are among the most polyvalent of the horror genre's repertoire of monsters. Sarah Lauro explains that zombies are figures of hybridity in that they are both "creolized" and "creolizing." They bear witness to a "colonial and postcolonial history of oppression" originating in the experiences of slaves. What is more, Lauro argues that zombies embody two seemingly different meanings: they "incorporat[e] a people's history of both enslavement and political resistance" (2015, 3–4, 8). The throngs of zombies in *The Horde* undoubtedly echo televised images of 2005 suburban protestors demanding change. French-Tunisian writer Mehdi Belhaj Kacem compared seeing the 2005 news coverage of the protests to watching Michael Jackson's "Thriller" video, suggesting that the zombie is a shared cultural trope through which to make sense of suburban street violence (2006, 22–23). Furthermore, the zombie's usual lack of speech also echoes some of the reactionary criticisms around the 2005 protests that this generation of suburban youth, unlike that of 1968, could not voice political demands or even organize themselves politically into a movement (Mauger 2006, 90–91). I argue that in *The Horde*, the zombie's presence reflects the tangled history of French colonialism in the banlieues. Over the course of the film, Dahan and Rocher situate the banlieues not as an intermediary space between the city center and the countryside, but as a liminal space as much connected to France's colonial past as it is to the contemporary Hexagon.

The film's references to French colonial history are baroque almost to the point of incoherence. René, the crazy and overweight old white French man the group meets halfway through the film, anchors the film's connections to French colonial history. Played by Yves Pignon, an actor better known for his comedic roles, René explains that he has been living in the banlieues for many years following his return to France after fighting in the French-Indochina War. He repeatedly calls the zombies outside "the yellows" (*les jaunes*), and he imagines himself to be defending one of the last outposts of civilization. He specifically invokes the battle of Dien Bien Phu, comparing the cops and gang members' fight against the zombie horde to the French standoff with Vietnamese troops that ended the war. The reference to the French war of decolonization in Vietnam, as opposed to the more protracted and arguably more painful one in Algeria, might seem incongruous, especially because migration from North Africa has been more consequential for the cultural makeup of the French suburbs than migratory flows from Vietnam or Cambodia. However, the French loss at Dien Bien Phu in 1948 marks the beginning of decolonization throughout France's disparate colonies.

Dahan and Rocher's choice to link the suburban neighborhood in the film to French Indochina, however obliquely, has important consequences for how the film imagines the geography of the banlieues and their relationship to the rest of France and the world. *The Horde*'s opening image of the apartment block or HLM where the standoff will take place is a dark nighttime shot in which only the faint gray outline of the building is visible, along with a few illuminated windows near the top. It differs from the more conventional representations of HLMs in French banlieue films to the point of being a generic image of urban war zones. When the cops and gangsters later make it to the top of the building and contemplate the fires burning in the center of Paris, the gang's leader, Adé, remarks that he might as well be in his home city of Abuja in Nigeria. Adé ostensibly came to France with his brother, Nola, seeking a better life; however, what they find is not all that different from what they left. With this comment, Dahan and Rocher connect the geography of suburban Paris to impoverished megaslums in cities of the Global South.

It is not until the end of the film that the relationship between Dahan and Rocher's imagined banlieues and the French countryside becomes clear. Adé and the cop Aurore are the only two left standing, and they escape the zombies and the apartment building into the daylight. Dahan and Rocher filmed the apartment block exteriors in Clichy-sous-Bois, once again the *cité* where the 2005 protests began. They frame their protagonists' escape against the backdrop of the tall, thick forest that begins just beyond the building's parking lot. Aurore and Adé run toward the forest, thinking it might offer an escape. However, in the final scene, Aurore shoots Adé, thus escalating the cycle of vengeance that provoked the zombie outbreak in the first place. When Aurore pulls the trigger, Dahan and Rocher match cut to a long shot looking back at the scene with the burned-out HLM building in the background, suggesting that there is no escape.

The imagery of tangled trees and leaves bordering the cité further connects the film's banlieues to stereotypes about France's colonial empire. Dahan and Rocher effectively imagine the surrounding countryside not as escape, but as a menacing jungle in which unruly hordes or France's marginalized citizens lie in wait. The film's references to Indochina and the battle of Dien Bien Phu that took place in the jungles of the Mường Thanh Valley suggest that the forests bordering the cité do not necessarily connect to the French countryside, but rather to phantasmatic memories of the jungles of Vietnam and violent wars of decolonization. The film's suburbs become a dangerous liminal zone, the site of ongoing neocolonial struggle. Paris is cut off from its own rural spaces, the so-called France *profonde*, and instead opens out onto a neocolonial jungle in which it cannot escape its own colonial past, and the hordes of discontent citizens and immigrants possibly wait to storm the city. The banlieues in *The Horde* are not a real space; rather, they are an imaginary space whose visual connections to other urban megaslums and to the history of French decolonization make explicit the colonial memories that still condition how France imagines its banlieues.

This is not to say that *The Horde* is a progressive film in the manner of George Romero's zombie film cycle. I agree with Met's claim that *The Horde*'s simplistic characters and wild bloodletting reinforce racist stereotypes about the lawlessness of some suburban spaces (2012, 41–42). Dahan and Rocher admit in the making-of documentary included on the DVD release that they were less concerned with constructing a fable about social inequalities in the banlieues than with crafting particular kinds of cinematic images, again excusing the political meanings of their film by saying it is fiction. They explain that even though they are using the iconography of zombies, they actually wanted to make something closer to a 1980s Hollywood action movie in the vein of *Conan the Barbarian* (1982), complete with tough-looking actors (Rocher and Dahan 2010). Yet I still hold that *The Horde* reveals the suburbs to play a localizing function when filmmakers adapt Hollywood horror tropes to a Gallic context. In Clover's model of the rape-revenge and urbanoia film, economic resentments drive the filmic narrative, even as the colonial history of violence required to conquer the Western United States remains unrepresented in the background. By contrast, the colonial and neocolonial history that drives economic resentment in some contemporary French suburbs is very much on the surface in *The Horde*. Even though the film risks the most reactionary readings, *The Horde* confirms that one important function of the horror genre in general has long been to visualize social inequalities through the representation of space. Dahan and Rocher's film highlights the extent to which the banlieues are often imagined as globalized spaces that interface with other zones of poverty around contemporary cities throughout the world. This interconnectedness is an important element of how transnational film genres like horror can move in and out of the Hexagon and how horror can help visualize the racial dimensions and colonial histories of discrimination that fuel inequality in a color-blind country.

DECONSTRUCTING SUBURBAN BORDERS IN *INSIDE*

Whereas *The Horde* took a global perspective on colonial history and the French suburbs, *Inside* (2007) focuses on the most intimate levels of home and body. Bustillo and Maury's first feature film tells the story of a pregnant woman, Sarah, whose husband was killed in a tragic accident and who now doubts she wants to be a mother. As Sarah is about to give birth sometime on Christmas Eve or Day, an unknown and unnamed woman enters her home and tries to take the baby by force. *Inside* is thus an instance of the home-invasion subgenre of horror that seeks to disrupt the safety of domestic spaces and challenge how individuals and communities define home. Other examples of this subgenre include horror films like Wes Craven's *Last House on the Left* (1972) and Michael Haneke's *Funny Games* (2007), though Michael Fiddler suggests that the home-invasion film is not limited to the horror genre, as Sam Peckinpah's vigilante film *Straw Dogs* (1971) or Chris Columbus's slapstick comedy *Home Alone* (1990) illustrate (2013, 282).

At the end of *Inside*, the intruder performs an impromptu C-section with scissors on Sarah, and in the final scene, the blood-soaked woman is shown rocking the newborn in an image of a monstrous Madonna. There really is not much more to the plot. There are minor peripeteia involving the gruesome murder of the police officers and friends and family who come to check on Sarah and the various means Sarah uses to thwart the woman's designs, including locking herself in the bathroom for a significant portion of the film. However, these narrative anchors are mainly meant to motivate the meticulously crafted and excessive images of blood and gore. Given *Inside*'s focus on anxieties surrounding motherhood and the female body, it is not surprising that Adam Lowenstein considers the film an instance of feminine horror even though it was directed by two men (2015, 484). Despite the centrality of motherhood, there is nevertheless an important emphasis on the French suburbs and specifically the 2005 suburban protests that take place at the same time as the home invasion in the film.

Characters reference the 2005 protests throughout the establishing phase of the narrative before the intruder enters Sarah's home. Sarah is a photojournalist by trade, and Jean-Pierre, her boss at the newspaper and possible lover, implies that Sarah is excellent at her work, perhaps the best at covering the French banlieues. Sarah also happens to live in or near a neighborhood where street violence is taking place, though the film plays with audience expectations about what such spaces look like. When we see Sarah return home after her hospital visit, it is to a single-family home, making viewers think that she perhaps lives in the safety of a banlieue *pavillonnaire*, or single-family-home suburb. However, as the film unfolds, it becomes clear that she lives in some unspecified proximity to the cités where protests are taking place. Before the intruder's first appearance, Sarah watches news coverage about the street violence, and it references the 2005 protests directly. Furthermore, the film shifts the historical timeline of the 2005 protests forward by one month so that *Inside*'s narrative can take place on Christmas Eve (the street violence in the film begins on November 27). As Sarah dozes on the couch, viewers see images of the protests on her television, and the news anchor explains in voice-over that the "nocturnal riots" were caused by the "accidental death" of two young French citizens "from an immigration background" (*issus de l'immigration*). The demonstrations have spread from the Paris suburbs to other provincial cities, tracking the spread of events in 2005. The TV report also mentions the inflammatory comments made by an unnamed minister of the interior that is a clear reference to Sarkozy's governmental role during and after the 2005 protests.

Viewers might assume based on the kind of home Sarah lives in that such violent events are at a safe distance from her house or at least behind the relative safety of the television screen. However, the police during their first visit indicate that the street violence is closer than viewers originally thought. After searching Sarah's house for the intruder the first time, the police tell her that they will send a team later to check on her and not to worry because "everyone is mobilized in the suburban neighborhoods," implying that she lives in such a neighborhood. When the night patrol returns to check on her, they have with them a young French Maghrebi man whom they arrested for allegedly throwing Molotov cocktails at cars. One of the officers tells him that after checking to see if this nice lady is safely asleep, they plan to go back to the streets and arrest the rest of his friends, suggesting that the dangerous streets are but a short car ride away from Sarah's house. Similarly, when Jean-Pierre comes to see how Sarah is doing during the night, he justifies his visit to the intruder, whom he mistakes for Sarah's mother, by explaining that with the street violence taking place nearby, and he wanted to make sure Sarah was safe.

The film is careful to avoid the word *banlieues*, preferring instead to use somewhat more precise terms like *cités* and *quartiers pauvres*. For example, Jean-Pierre uses the phrase *bordel dans les cités* (charged slang for *mess in the projects*) several times during the film to describe the protests. While this phrase reinforces stereotypes of chaos and violence in suburban spaces, it at least links them to the specific word for neighborhoods and not the catchall category of *banlieue* in the singular, which can mean all peripheral spaces outside the city. The word *banlieues* is used only once in the film during the TV report about the protests, but even there the reporter is careful to qualify that it is only the "poor suburban neighborhoods" (*quartiers pauvres des banlieues*) where violence is taking place. The police use the more neutral *quartiers* throughout, suggesting some measure of attention to sociological detail on the part of the filmmakers and a desire not to stigmatize.

Inside's representation of the banlieues differs from the previous banlieue horror films that I have been categorizing as suburbanoia. It is possible to view the suburban setting as a convenient backdrop for the film's gore, which is focused primarily on gender, motherhood, and the body. However, I contend instead that *Inside* represents the most sophisticated use of the banlieues in the French horror films considered so far. To understand this, we must appreciate the metaphorical equivalences the film makes between violence to the body and violence in the banlieues through the tropes of the home-invasion film. Bustillo and Maury use the conventions of the home-invasion subgenre of horror to deconstruct how viewers relate to the French suburbs, upsetting spatial parameters about inside and outside, near and far, and what is safe and what is dangerous. *Inside* may be a home-invasion film, but it does not end with the restoration of the home's borders or safety. Rather, these are utterly destroyed. To appreciate this aspect of the film, we need to leave behind a desire to see the questions of the French suburbs represented through sociological details or cinematic realism. Despite the film's attention to the terminology it uses to describe the spaces of the cités, its representation of the banlieues takes place at the level of a shared imaginary, rather than realism.

What is more, unlike the Hollywood urbanoia film that stages the violence of contact between different social classes as they circulate in spaces that are not typically theirs, *Inside* breaks down the very notion that spaces and people are or can be separated. When the intruder first speaks to Sarah, she stands outside the sliding glass door to the porch, a visual rhyme with the television screen on which Sarah and viewers have just watched the TV report about the protests. The street protestors are in a sense like the intruder in that they want to disrupt the seeming safety of domestic neighborhoods or homes by bringing street protests from the suburbs into the city. The analogy between the two is admittedly clumsy, as viewers ultimately learn that the intruder was in the other car during the accident and miscarried her own baby due to the crash. In the film's most haunting line, the intruder commands Sarah to "open your door to me" (*ouvre-moi ta porte*) as she hides in the bathroom. This line is both about the literal bathroom door and the borders of Sarah's body that the woman will cut into in the monstrous C-section delivery that concludes the film. However, I read this line as being about other kinds of borders as well. Unrest in poor neighborhoods as a form of social protest asks for France's dominant communities to open their doors, pay attention, and change the traditional ways of the country. The film's use of tropes from the home-invasion subgenre suggests that the seeming safety of borders, whether of one's domestic space or surrounding neighborhood, is ultimately illusory. In the film's most radical deconstructive gesture, disturbance, whether individual or social, is revealed to always already be within whatever barriers we might erect to keep it out. Consequently, *Inside* does not simply remap Clover's class resentment model in the urbanoia film for the French context of spatial difference. More radically than in the previous three banlieue films, the home invasion and attendant violence break down the distinctions that might allow viewers to position themselves with respect to resentments fueled by class, race, or space.

Inside's violence and gore are extreme, but how they relate to the film's deconstruction of suburban borders is less clear. Bustillo and Maury admit in interviews that they had a social agenda related to images of violence in mind when they set *Inside* in or near the suburbs and the 2005 protests. In a *Critikat* interview dating from the film's 2007 release, Audrey Jeamart asks them to explain the meaning of the images of the 2005 protests in the film. Bustillo replies that the film does not contain a message about the banlieues. Rather, he argues that the images of street violence constitute the real violence and draw attention to the falsity of the film's extreme violence: "For us, the image of the suburbs on fire that we see at a specific moment was a way of showing what real violence is now. We knew that certain people might criticize us for the film's violence because we try to go as far as possible, but we have no problem with fictional violence in cinema" (Jeamart 2007). In their view, the only real image of violence is the three men throwing Molotov cocktails. *Inside*'s actresses, Dalle and Allyson Paradis, are not experiencing real violence, however much it might look that way on screen. According to Bustillo, Dalle even went so far as to say that the film's "most abominable images ... will never be as trashy as the nightly news" (Jeamart 2007).

Bustillo goes on to suggest that fictional violence on screen can nevertheless evoke forms of real-life violence. He argues that the level of violence in American horror films has long tracked with the mediatization of real-life historical violence, whether in the case of 1970s New Hollywood cinema and the Vietnam War that I discussed in the previous chapter or the early 2000s US war in Iraq and the violent horror cinema of that decade. Bustillo remarks, "When you watch *Hostel*, you have the impression of seeing Abu Ghraib or Guantanamo" (Jeamart 2007). In Bustillo's view, France also experienced a similarly violent period during the 2005 protests, and, by implication, *Inside* gives viewers the impression of seeing it. While the historical equivalence of Abu Ghraib and the 2005 French suburban protests is debatable, what is important is the social reflectionist model Bustillo sketches out to motivate the social meaning of the violence of *Inside* and its use of images from the 2005 protests.

Bustillo's comments about horror and real-life violence echo the debates about the supposed realism or stylization of cinematic ultraviolence that I considered in the previous chapter. For Stephen Prince, who coined the term *ultraviolence*, "graphic imagery of bodily mutilation" first began in Hollywood slasher films in the 1980s due to improvements in special effects such as prosthetic limbs and latex (2000a, 13–14). This is the type of Hollywood horror with which these French banlieue horror films most closely engage, and the same cautions about realism that Prince applied to ultraviolent New Hollywood filmmakers like Peckinpah also apply to French horror films like those examined in this chapter. Peckinpah's ultraviolence was not "real," but rather highly stylized and intended to unnerve viewers who, in Peckinpah's view, had become anesthetized to "bloody death" (2000b, 175–176). Bustillo's claims about violence in *Inside* echo Peckinpah's beliefs about the emancipatory possibilities of screening fictionalized ultraviolence, without going so far as to say explicitly that cinematic ultraviolence somehow resensitizes viewers to the violence from real life that they can no longer feel. However, in the case of horror,

Prince's warning about the unpredictability of cinematic ultraviolence's effects on spectators is even more relevant than it was for the gangster and vigilante films I discussed in the previous chapter. Horror fans often laugh or talk back to the screen when seeing images of horror violence, especially at public screenings with other horror fans. The reception of horror films arguably offers the best example of how difficult it is to generalize about the effects of violence on screen. This indicates that it is equally difficult, if not impossible, to attribute specific social meanings to the ways viewers receive on-screen violence.

However, Bustillo's comments about fictionalized violence are disingenuous on another level, because as sensitive as he is to all the art and artifice that go into constructing images of violence in horror films, he assumes that television images of street violence are unproblematically real or somehow unmediated, a point I already challenged in my analysis of *Divines* (2016). *Inside* engages with the suburbs and street violence without reflecting on what it means to create or circulate images of violence that involve or are inflicted on minority bodies. The same could be said of *Sheitan*, *Frontier(s)*, and *The Horde*. For an example of a French horror film that does reflect on the forms of violence inflicted on minority bodies, both the violence of discrimination and the violence that color-blind universalism enacts when it erases difference, we will turn to Pascal Laugier's 2008 film *Martyrs*.

MARTYRS: THE VIOLENCE OF MAKING IMAGES IN THE PLACE OF THE UNIVERSAL

One of the most extreme French horror films, Laugier's *Martyrs* (2008) lacks any overt references to banlieues, street violence, or multiculture. And yet, the film nevertheless explores how the production of certain kinds of images requires violence for minorities to occupy the supposedly unmarked place of the universal. *Martyrs* is about a secret society that tortures those on society's margins to produce the experience of spiritual ecstasy. Their only "success" is a young French Maghrebi woman, Anna Assaoui, whose entire skin is literally removed. By success, her torturers mean that she lived through the extreme experience and was able to talk about what she witnessed on the other side. Laugier shoots the moments after this peeling procedure in a series of luminous full-body shots and close-ups of Anna's face in seeming spiritual ecstasy. These images oscillate between violent context and sensuous image and between a contradictory set of affects: revulsion and disgust and beauty and transcendence. In this final section, I will argue that these unstable images ask us to consider the tensions between the personal and the impersonal aspects of racial marking in contemporary France and in cinematic images of horror more broadly.

Most of the scholarly commentary on Laugier's film thus far has tended to focus either on gender or on the affective responses that the film's extreme images of violence provoke. Amy Green finds in the film a reflection on the circulation of images that show violence against women in the age of the internet (2011, 22). Several commentators take *Martyrs*' representation of gender in a different direction, noting how the film's final scene "ungenders" Anna's body and, for Ruth McPhee, transforms it into something "inhuman and transcendent" (2016, 50). In a similar vein, Michael Kerner and Jonathan Knapp approach the film through Kristeva's notion of abjection and argue that Anna's final "unsexing" takes her body back to a pre-gendered human form, the same kind of limit to which abjection is supposed to take us (2016, 61). Xavier Aldana Reyes, who approaches the film through the lens of affect studies, argues that the "unsexing" and "ungendering" of Anna's body in fact evacuates a priori the possibility of any "political" or "social" reading of the film. Ultimately, for Reyes, *Martyrs* is "an effective exercise in negative affect," one that works "regardless of the gender of its main characters" (2016, 70). I want to argue instead that far from evacuating the possibility of a political reading, the "unsexing," "ungendering," *and* "unracing" of Anna's body expose the violence at work in the assimilationist discourse of French republican universalism that seeks to inscribe a neutral image of the body on its citizens when they circulate in the public sphere. By neutral, I mean the erasure of particularity or difference in the name of a radical egalitarianism, one that elides cultural difference while removing the very grounds for struggle against discrimination. *Martyrs* offers, I argue, an important reflection on how the body functions as a medium for images both in the act of perception and in the act of inscription—quite literally images written on the flesh through the violence of the surgeon's knife.

By calling the body a medium for images, I have in mind the work of Hans Belting, who has argued for an anthropological conception of the relationship among image, medium, and body. In Belting's view, many semiotic accounts of images, including cinematic ones, risk reducing images to something so abstract that they have neither a body nor a medium. The advantage of this approach's abstraction, according to Belting, is that it allows for visual signs to function in ways analogous to linguistic signs. Alternately, materialist accounts of media that seek to redress this abstraction run a different risk—that of focusing exclusively on technology at the expense of the way technologies are used by bodies and cultures. For Belting, the way out of this impasse involves an understanding of the human body as "that which is aware of being and acting like a medium," both a consciousness that gives life to, or animates, images in acts of perception and memory and a literal surface on which images are inscribed in the case of masks and tattoos (2014, 30–31). Belting thus talks about the body as a medium and as something mediated by images. His reflection on the body and its inclusion in a circuit that contains cultural representations and their various material supports offers us the best way to understand *Martyr's* dramatization of the violent production of images.

It is crucial to remember that the film's secret society tortures young women to produce *images* of ecstasy, and in a key scene, Mademoiselle shows Anna the historical photographs that inspired the society's mission—and, we assume, some of the actual pictures that they have managed to produce. The scene begins when Anna awakens in a long corridor in the society's complex chained to the wall in front of several horrific images of violence and ecstatic gazes. Laugier begins with a wide shot of the corridor at ninety degrees, highlighting an axis between Anna's gaze and the photographs on the wall that are the object of her gaze. Anna is an unknowing spectator, animating through acts of consciousness, to use Belting's terms, the kinds of violent images that the society will ultimately seek to inscribe on and materialize through her body. Mademoiselle then enters and comments on a set of images inscribed on a very different material support: physical photographs pasted on the pages of a worn album. The first of these photographs is of a Chinese criminal in 1904 being put to death by *lingchi*, variously translated as "death by a thousand cuts," "death by slicing," or "the lingering death" (Brook et al. 2008). The practice, outlawed in China in 1905, involved slicing flesh off the breasts, biceps, and upper thighs, stabbing the condemned person to death through the heart, and then methodically cutting the body to pieces. This practice became famous in Europe as a marker of Chinese society's otherness through several photographs that French soldiers took during the practice's final days and that Georges Bataille's final published work, *Tears of Eros* (1961), introduced into world memory. In the closing pages of that text, Bataille—or his editor, as it is not entirely clear who had final authorship over the text—explained how "this photograph had a decisive role in my life. I have never stopped being obsessed by this image of pain, at once ecstatic (?) and intolerable" (1989, 206). Bataille's remarks about the image's effect on him points to the importance of how viewers animate images through the act of perception.

Other commentators on *Martyrs* have noticed Laugier's connection to Bataille. Jean-François Rauger, in a review in *Le Monde* upon the film's release, notes the reference as a way of disparaging the film's pseudo-intellectualism (2008). Kerner and Knapp also make the connection between the film and

Tears of Eros but use it as a way of connecting *Martyrs* to Bataille's theory of transgression and the sacred (2016, 56). No one has yet worked through the materiality of that text in connection to the film, namely *Martyrs*'s exploration of the material support of images. Laugier admits in an interview in Italian that he read *Tears of Eros* and was inspired by it for the film (Allucineazioni 2009; Becattini 2009), and in fact, of the fifty or so photographs of lingchi that exist in archives, the one he chooses to show in the film is the same one that Bataille did in *Tears of Eros*; it is housed in the collection of the French Musée de l'Homme. In Bataille's work, the violent photographs of lingchi come as something of a shock after a text that focuses primarily on cave drawings and paintings of violence and eroticism in the Western tradition. In their history of the book's gross historical inaccuracies and troubled composition, Sinologists Timothy Brook, Jérôme Bourgon, and Gregory Blue argue that what Western readers saw in that lingchi image as "ecstatic suffering" was ultimately the projection of Western conventions for representing Christian ecstasy onto an exceptional image. This projection, they contend, interprets the image in a way that disappears the victim's body and the historical and social context. Bataille's gaze—and the one he transmitted through *Tears of Eros*—traps the person in the image within a "mask of suffering" (Brook et al. 2008, 236).

Unlike the other famous French horror film about skin peeling, Franju's *Eyes Without a Face*, Laugier's film spends very little time on the surgical operation of peeling. Instead, Laugier devotes most of the third section to violent images of a brute beating Anna to a pulp, a metaphor we can understand literally in the sense of reducing her body and herself into a pulpy soup onto which the image of ecstasy can then be inscribed. Laugier spends significant time building up anticipation for the skin peeling and the meaning of such images. Mademoiselle offers an extended commentary of her collection of ecstatic images that functions both as an inelegant information dump about the secret society and as a verbal double to the role of written text in Bataille's *Tears of Eros*. The Bataille of *Tears of Eros* and of the photomontages of his short-lived 1930s interdisciplinary magazine, *Documents*, always hoped the images would speak for themselves. However, he could not help also commenting on them as if to explain how they should work while insistently reminding his readers that what he wanted to express was somehow beyond language. After explaining the difference between a martyr and a victim, Mademoiselle opens a photo album on whose pages have been affixed images of what she considers to be martyrs with ecstatic expressions inscribed on their faces. The first is an enlarged detail of the Long Shen torture victim photograph from Bataille's *Tears of Eros*, and it is followed by a succession of other similar images of bodies, mostly of women, in the paroxysm of violent and painful experiences. Compounding the violence of the images themselves, the sequence dramatizes the violence of decontextualization.

Mademoiselle tells the story of each image but then returns Anna and the film's spectators to the purported ecstatic affect in the eyes and face of the martyrs. Mademoiselle asserts that the Long Shen torture image is about a woman who had stolen a chicken. This story does not correspond at all to Bataille's, but it does gender the martyred bodies as female. The next image is a medium shot of the violent retribution against a French woman who slept with a German soldier during World War II, suggesting rather flimsily that a side benefit of historical traumas is the production of ecstatic images. The contexts of the subsequent images are comparatively more banal—terminal illness, horrific car accident—but they are gradually elided as the filmmaking accelerates through the compression of jump cuts and a dim roar in the soundtrack that suggests Anna's response to them. These photographs hit her like the physical blows she will go on to receive, and any context the images might have recedes behind the violence of the images themselves. Like the pictures in Bataille's *Tears of Eros* that are reduced through the juxtaposition of text and image to violent eroticism, the photographs Mademoiselle shows Anna are gradually reduced to a decontextualized, violent, and ecstatic state that is mediated through the violated body in the image and the violated body of the spectator who looks.

In the actual scene of peeling, Laugier only offers a medium shot of Anna's back as the scalpel is inserted and then cuts to her face as she registers the pain. Laugier then cuts to the aftermath of the operation; Anna sits in a wheelchair wrapped in a white sheet, suggesting her martyrdom. It is only when her torturers strap her into what (for lack of a better term) I will call a crucifix-gyroscope that viewers learn that she has been fully peeled except for her face. Whereas the mask in Franju's film drew attention to Christiane's disfigured face, in *Martyrs*, it is the rest of Anna's body that has been laid bare, and only the skin of her face remains. It is at this point that she attains what the secret society considers the ecstatic experience of the martyr in what Bataille calls the beyond of the "last instant."

Unlike Robert Bresson, who marks the cinematic unrepresentability of Catholic grace by cutting to an abstract image of a cross over a white background in *Diary of a Country Priest* (*Journal d'un curé de campagne*, 1951), Laugier chooses to represent the ecstatic movement through a digital effects shot. From there, he uses a cosmic zoom that begins and ends on Anna's face. Laugier zooms in on Anna's iris and then through a white tunnel and a white light toward some approximation of infinity before zooming back out to a close-up of Anna's now shuddering body over a glowing white background that was not there in the

Figure 4.4 The secret society's leader contemplates the image they have produced. *Martyrs*, 2008.

beginning of the shot. In *Tears of Eros*, Bataille talks about how prohibition confers a "wicked glow," a "transfiguration," or an "illumination" on certain transgressive actions (1989, 67, 70, 207). For Bataille, this glow is metaphorical; it indexes an affect or feeling that a transgressor might experience but that would only be visible to an observer in metonymic form—perhaps a certain glimmer of pain in the facial expression or a certain alacrity in the transgressor's gestures. Laugier, by contrast, literalizes this glow in the material support of the images the secret society has created and does create with Anna.

Cosmic zooms are typically used to define human scale with respect to the macro levels of the universe and the micro levels of the human body. Here, the cosmic zoom is more about the expanse of inner space, which might or might not overlap with the infinity of the universe. The important point is that this shot situates Anna within the cosmic scale of the universe. Anna has gone from being a marginalized, tortured French Moroccan woman to being an image of the infinite at the price of her gender and her racially marked skin. Indeed, for this image to be written on her body and for her body to mediate this image of infinity, her racially marked skin must be removed. In the context of racial politics in contemporary France, this violence allegorizes that inflicted on bodies when they must disappear aspects of themselves to signify as a universal citizen in the public sphere. I am thinking especially of accounts of white French women violently removing headscarves and full-body coverings from French Muslim women. If race matters in Laugier's film, it is not as a contest between society's marginalized victims and its normative monsters. Rather, it is about the violence with which the universalist cast of French public discourse seeks to make the bodies of its citizens mediate a particular kind of image of the universalist citizen over and against markers of difference.

If Laugier's film forces spectators to witness the violence with which such images are produced, it ends by holding open a space in which such images carry a disruptive force that cannot be contained and ultimately subvert the normative order that produces them. In the final moments of the film, Laugier cuts to a series of shots that narrate Mademoiselle's arrival at the facility. As she walks in to where Anna is being held, we see that Anna has been moved from the gyroscope to a bed of blue water illuminated from below and is lying on a plastic frame contoured to her skinless body. She has now become the physical body that mediates the illuminated images she first saw in the corridor at the beginning of her torture. Mademoiselle kneels down to hear Anna's witnessing of the beyond. Unlike Bataille's photographs of lingchi, this image can talk back. Viewers hear only muttering, and shortly after this scene, Mademoiselle shoots herself in the head for reasons left unclear. There are many possible interpretations for this scene, but I prefer to read it as allowing for a disruptive force against the universalizing kind of image the torturers sought to produce, one that undermines the very logic that set its production in motion to begin with. Laugier's handling of race does not see the color of skin as a signifying parameter within a semiotic network of meanings, but rather as a surface that can be made to mediate certain universalizing images through extreme violence, even, and perhaps especially, when it is peeled away altogether. Laugier's film departs from the position espoused by the directors of *Sheitan, Frontier(s)*, or *Inside*, who explain away the violence of their banlieue horror films by saying that they are just images; real life is where violence lies. Returning to Prince's point about the potentially unmediated realism some viewers claim to find in cinematic ultraviolence, violence on screen is never unmediated, whether fictionalized on film screens or supposedly real on television or YouTube. *Martyrs* reminds us that when viewers see violent images, they need to think about—and, more crucially, feel—the violent histories and cultural contexts in which such images are situated and through which they are produced.

CONCLUSION

The French suburban horror films examined in this chapter seek to adapt the conventions of what Clover calls the urbanoia film to a French geography of difference in what I have called the suburbanoia film. The sense of mistrust, jealousy, or persecution in such films is not, however, unidirectional from countryside to city, as in Clover's urbanoia film. Rather, jealousy and mistrust can run in both directions in suburbanoia films, whether this is fascist families committing genocide on suburban minorities, suburban residents protesting police violence, suburban characters envying the wealth of rural families, or rural characters resenting the extent to which multiculture represents the future of France. *Sheitan, Frontier(s), The Horde, Inside,* and *Martyrs* examine the archetypal positions of monstrosity and victimhood that residents of the French countryside, city, and suburbs variously occupy when they interact with genre conventions inherited from Hollywood horror cinema. While Clover's analysis of urbanoia films in the US context suggests that they disappear economic resentments that result from racial discrimination and colonial exploitation behind class or gender, *Sheitan, Frontier(s), The Horde, Inside,* and *Martyrs* all foreground the forms of racial profiling, discrimination, exploitation, and violence that suburban residents can encounter when they move beyond the suburbs. By exceeding the limits of political correctness or polite discourse, they expose the dark underbelly of stereotypes about the banlieues.

The films do not all necessarily rearticulate the universal, as they run the risk of reinforcing reactionary stereotypes about the suburbs just as much as they may hope to challenge them through exposure. The suburban characters of these suburbanoia films are doubly dislocated from countryside and city center, and the suburbs are represented as neither country nor city but a singular combination of both. The French suburbs embody the logic of regionalism with a strong sense of local identity in France, and they are simultaneously connected to spaces and histories outside of France, whether this means other contemporary global spaces of urban poverty or the unresolved legacies of French colonialism. This mixing may seem monstrous to some conservative commentators in France, and these French banlieue horror films do indeed channel some of those fears, but as Jeffrey Jerome Cohen has argued, monsters are always "our children." By this he means that any society creates its own monsters who "ask us to reevaluate our cultural assumptions about race, gender, sexuality, our perception of difference, our tolerance toward its expression" (1996, 20). These banlieue French horror films, for all their flaws, dive into the viscera of France's shared cultural imaginary of difference, including the perception and expression of difference in various types of spaces.

In French horror, the suburbs serve simultaneously to interrogate the French imaginary of difference and to localize Hollywood conventions of horror to France. Consequently, it is possible to think of them as examples of glocalization or the interconnection of local and global concerns. Not all these films self-consciously reflect on what it means to make or view images of cinematic ultraviolence that involve minority bodies. Yet when a film like *Martyrs* does, it makes visible the violence that operates when bodies must erase or ignore difference to move in a supposedly neutral public sphere. Horror films that deal with questions of national identity, suburban marginalization, and French colonial history are arguably not as legible outside France as those that deal with issues of gender or sexual identity. Yet the codes of horror cinema offer one way to make a national geography of difference intelligible, even if the films examined in this chapter do not always do so without the excesses of confusion or caricature. The next chapter will continue to analyze the kinds of genre-based cinematic images that are created through the bodies of minority actors by taking up the case of France's arguably best-known minority star, Omar Sy. While Sy is known for comedy rather than horror, his career offers an important way to understand how film genres and minority actors interact in France and how genre codes represent and misrepresent the French banlieues when these films circulate internationally.

NOTES

1. For an overview of this corpus and its reception by scholars, see Austin 2015.

2. For a discussion of how the pressures of auteurism in France impact French horror filmmakers and their relationships with public funding structures, see Bey-Rozet 2021, 191–195.

3. For the former, see Beugnet 2007; Palmer 2011; West 2016. For the latter, see Lübecker 2015; Horeck and Kendall 2013; Frey 2016. For a good overview of extreme cinema studies as a subfield, see Bordun 2017.

4. The school's website can be found at https://cinema.ecolekourtrajme.com/.

FIVE

OMAR SY

Black Superstardom in Contemporary France

OMAR SY IS ONE OF French cinema's few domestically and internationally well-known Black stars. Sy was born and grew up in the western suburbs of Paris and was propelled to stardom by his stunning performance in Éric Tolédano and Olivier Nakache's 2011 *Intouchables*, the second most successful French film domestically and the most profitable French film in international release (*Libération* 2012). While *Intouchables* is a mainstream comedy film that primarily takes place in the city center, it is also a banlieue film, as Sy's character, Driss, lives in the suburbs and viewers see his family life there, however briefly. Sy's performance won him a César for Best Actor in 2012, the first time a Black man has won that honor. His popularity has only grown, and since 2012, the French public has repeatedly voted him their number one or number two preferred personality, according to IFOP/*Le Journal du dimanche*'s semiannual survey, despite his decision to relocate to Los Angeles in 2012.[1] He now has a sizable body of work in France and in Hollywood, and the transnational coordinates of his stardom and the ways in which his Blackness signifies within and beyond France make him an especially interesting case to examine. Furthermore, his status as France's first homegrown Black superstar whose star persona depends in part on roles connected to the French suburbs offers an important counterpoint to the use of nonprofessional minority actors in suburban films like Abdellatif Kechiche's *Games of Love and Chance* (*L'Esquive*, 2003), Jacques Audiard's *Dheepan* (2015), and Céline Sciamma's *Girlhood* (*Bande de filles*, 2014).

While his stardom is just over a decade old, Sy nevertheless represents an important data point for a long-standing debate within French film studies: Does a star system like that of Hollywood exist in France? Guy Austin notes how star studies as a field in the Anglo-American academy has tended to focus on Hollywood as the quintessential example of a star system (2003, 3–4). In reflecting on whether a star system could be said to exist in France, Austin references Colin Crisp's industrial history of the classical period (1930–1960), in which the latter suggests that there is a close relationship between stardom and a genre system. For Crisp, stars and genres represent two powerful techniques that Hollywood developed for creating and maintaining mass audiences (1997, 215–216). He ultimately concludes that France did not have a star system during the classical period because it lacked Hollywood's industrial studio infrastructure. The implication that a star system necessarily depends on an industrial base is debatable, and Ginette Vincendeau makes the opposite case: "France has a star system by virtue of the number of major film stars in activity, the length of their filmographies and the discursive production that exists around them" (2000, 1). A full consideration of this issue would take us too far afield, but I want to suggest that the debate about the existence of a star system in France is analogous to the one I referenced in the introduction in which, for some critics, a French genre system requires an industrial studio model akin to that of Hollywood.

The important point for my purposes here is the close relationship between stardom and genre cinemas. Both stars and genres emphasize reproducibility and predictability on the production side in terms of profits and on the reception side in terms of fandom. To examine the rise of minority stars in France is thus also to consider the genre(s) through which they emerged. These genres are simultaneously that which make them possible in France and that which they make possible for France. As Richard Dyer puts it, "all performers use their bodies and have their bodies used" (2003, 124–125). I am suggesting that local and transnational genres are one of the cinematic tools that stars use and that these same genres also use stars in a self-reinforcing feedback loop. For Dyer, star vehicles—that is, the particular type or types of films that come to define a star—are roughly equivalent to film genres (1998, 62). Andrew Britton, by contrast, argues that genres in fact precede stars and condition star vehicles. In his view, the meanings that stars and genres embody are always in relation to each other: "The star in his/her films must always be read as a dramatic presence which is predicated by, and which intervenes in, enormously complex and elaborate themes and motifs, and thereby refers us to a particular state of the social reality of genre, and of the relation between genres" (1991, 198, 205). For example, Charlie Michael analyzes genre instability in the opening sequence of *Intouchables*, during which Driss drives Philippe around in the latter's Maserati. The sequence is shot like an action or car heist film in which Driss could be a criminal, and it is only once the police finally pull them over that the sequence switches from creating tension to evoking the laughter of comedy (Michael 2014, 124–125). Even this brief example indicates just how important genre is to understanding Sy's stardom.

The choice in a film like *Intouchables* to adapt 1980s Hollywood interracial buddy comedies to France is thus *also* an attempt to reproduce the kinds of Black stardom and the narratives about Blackness found in those films through Sy. The genre cannot entirely work without the star and vice versa. It is for this reason that I will focus primarily on genre in connection to Sy's stardom in this chapter, rather than on other elements of star studies, such as fandom, promotional materials, or lifestyle. While I will offer my most sustained analysis of the link between genre and minority stardom here in this chapter through Sy, the relationship between genre and performance informs the other chapters in which French genre films involve the banlieues and the creative labor of minority actors.

In her essay on ethnic stardom in France, Vincendeau positions Sy as part of a new generation of minority, mostly male comedians who have gone on to become legitimate stars in France. The majority are French Maghrebi or French Jewish, and Sy is the only French Black actor included in this new generation. Vincendeau's account raises a central difficulty in studying the relationship between race, ethnicity, and stardom, especially in France. On the one hand, actors everywhere want to be recognized as artists, independent of their personal biographies, including racial or ethnic backgrounds (Vincendeau 2015, 550). This is especially true in a country like France that prizes color-blind forms of universalism. On the other, as Dyer argues, "stars are also embodiments of the social categories in which people are placed and through which they have to make sense of their lives," including race and ethnicity (2003, 16). In the same way that axes of difference signify in the social sphere whether one wants them to or not, race and ethnicity help construct the meanings and pleasures of a star's celebrity, especially when they achieve crossover success with different kinds of audiences.

Vincendeau and Austin in their analyses of French minority stardom have both noted that the ways the faces and skin color of Maghrebi and Jewish actors signify are malleable (Austin 2003, 135–137; Vincendeau 2015, 550). In some films, the narrative or actors' specific roles position them as Maghrebi or Jewish, and in others, they are marked as white. While these two categories can pass as white or at least off-white, Black skin is not malleable in quite the same way. Lighter shades of Black skin can be made to suggest other racial or ethnic identities, such as the case of France's other significant Black star, American expat Josephine Baker, who sometimes played North African characters, as in *Princess Tam-Tam* (1935).[2] However, while darker shades of Black skin can be made to suggest a generic foreign otherness, they cannot disappear into whiteness in the same way that the skin of Maghrebi and Jewish stars can at certain times in certain films. However, Black skin can disappear into the universal or the unmarked. This desire for skin color not to signify is what many French minority actors mean when they say they would like to be thought of as actors or artists first and foremost, rather than as members of this or that regional or racial category (Vincendeau 2015, 550). Indeed, when *Intouchables* directors Nakache and Tolédano defended their decision to cast Sy when the real-life inspiration for his character was a French man of Algerian descent, they explained that the "limited options" of people living in the banlieues transcend racial and ethnic differences (quoted in Kealhofer-Kemp 2017, 163–164). The fact that Sy grew up in the banlieues thus made him eligible for the role. Such statements reveal that even France's suburban poor are imagined through the universalist cast of French republicanism in which the citizen is a public individual abstracted from particularities like race, ethnicity, and religion, if not always geography.

What categories of Blackness—French, global, or American—should be brought to bear on some of Sy's films has been a matter of debate. Emine Fişek has argued that despite the transnational appeal of a film like *Intouchables*, Sy's casting and performance must be understood through the lens of French colonial history and the sense of foreignness through which French Blacks, and colonial subjects generally, have long been viewed in France (2018, 192). This is certainly true; however, in the case of Sy, we cannot limit our examination of Blackness to the categories found in France, for it is not the case that local audiences experience Blackness only through local categories, though these are no doubt important. As I will argue in this chapter, Sy's entry into superstardom also took place in connection with the racialized tropes of the Hollywood interracial buddy comedy and the history of blackface and minstrelsy that impact that tradition and Black comedians generally in the United States.[3] This transatlantic entanglement is all the more surprising because, unlike in the case of horror considered in the last chapter, if there is a genre with which French cinema is well associated, it would be comedy. French comedies accounted for 66.5 percent of receipts at the domestic box office between 1995 and 2014, and 71.5 percent of the 1,647 comedy films made during this period were exported abroad (Deleau 2016, 22). What is more, France has a tradition of mismatched buddy films that turn around social class and geographic and regional differences, such as *Welcome to the Sticks* (*Bienvenue chez les Ch'tis*,

2008) and *Dinner for Schmucks* (*Le Dîner de cons*, 1998), to name just two of the best-known examples.[4] Why, then, would French filmmakers look to Hollywood for inspiration in this arena?

The answer, I suggest, has to do with the fact that Blackness can be deployed in comedy in ways that are simultaneously culturally specific and globally generic, allowing films with minority stars to travel as transnational texts about social marginalization and mobility that can be understood by international audiences. We see this most powerfully, I will argue, in the case of *Intouchables*, but it has become a part of Sy's star persona across his body of films. In my view, it is not a question of having to choose local French categories of Blackness over transnational ones in making sense of Sy's career. Rather, it is the transnational framing of Blackness in a film like *Intouchables* that allows both local and transnational references to coexist and interact with the reception contexts in which the film is viewed. This transnational framing of Sy's Blackness in comedy is also a strategy that other producers are seeking to replicate with other Black comedians, such as Ahmed Sylla in the 2017 film *The Climb* (*L'Ascension*).[5]

There are several potential explanations for Sy's achievement of stardom with *Intouchables*. Régis Dubois notes that Sy's explosive rise to fame was in part because it was time for a major French star who happened to be Black (2016, 79). Most of the roles in popular cinema previously available to Black actors were secondary, minor, and/or heavily stereotyped. Russell Meeuf and Raphael Raphael note that new stars often arise at moments of acute social change and serve to mediate and even assuage cultural tensions and crises, including issues of national identity, race, gender, sexuality, and globalization (2013, 4). In terms of cultural tensions, one could point to the aftermath of the 2005 suburban protests and the positive and negative visibility it brought to racialized forms of discrimination in France. One could also point to the presidency of Nicolas Sarkozy, who promised to be tough on immigrants and launched national debates about French identity, which, for critics, stigmatized France's minority communities. It is no accident, then, that many of the films Sy stars in contain narratives of social mobility and integration.

Looking beyond the borders of France, I would add that part of the sense that France needed a Black star was due to the election of Barack Obama in the United States and the images of him that circulated in the media. While the election of Obama was hardly a crisis for France, it did, as I will explain later in this chapter, cause several French commentators at the time to ask themselves about the relative lack of positive images of Black men in the media. It is no accident that some of the white French characters in *Intouchables* compare Sy's character to Obama, especially once he has replaced his initial hoodie and jeans with a fitted suit. Sy's meteoric rise is part of a reassessment in France of images of Blackness circulating throughout the world.

Not everyone in France viewed the success of *Intouchables* favorably. As Leslie Kealhofer-Kemp has shown, some saw the film as heralding a new age in which Black actors can be bankable stars. Others saw it as rehearsing the worst kind of race- or class-based stereotypes (Kealhofer-Kemp 2017, 162–163). All minority stars face the dilemma of agency with respect to stereotypes and comedy, and it is arguably nowhere better analyzed than in Spike Lee's 2000 film *Bamboozled*. Lee's film tells the story of a Black television writer who, in a bid to change the fortunes of an ailing television channel, creates a neo-minstrelsy series that he intends as satire. Lee powerfully analyzes the pressures Black stars face in mainstream media, especially the way they are often forced to play into long-standing stereotypes for laughs and financial success at the expense of their own souls.

Bamboozled self-reflexively stages the iconographic and material presence of the blackface and minstrelsy tradition in the form of posters, statues, and audiovisual clips that crowd the production design and image track. Sy's films make a bid for the mainstream, and consequently we do not find the same degree of reflexivity in Sy's work as in Lee's film. Nevertheless, this does not mean that Sy or the filmmakers he works with are not self-aware about how his Blackness operates within a film and across his star career. A careful consideration of genre and intertextuality across his work, especially as these relate to French and Hollywood cinematic contexts, reveals much about the possibilities and limits of Black stardom in France. Sy's career offers a powerful example of how producers, filmmakers, and minority actors have used American comedy traditions to create mainstream career paths in France at the same time that it reveals the multiple glass ceilings French minority actors still face at home and abroad.

THE SUCCESS OF *INTOUCHABLES*

Tolédano and Nakache's 2011 film *Intouchables* is an interracial buddy comedy that tells the story of Driss, a young Black Senegalese man from the Parisian banlieues who befriends Philippe, the older quadriplegic upper-class Frenchman who employs him as a caretaker. As of January 2013, *Intouchables* was the most financially successful non-English language film of all time, earning profits of just over $425 million (*Libération* 2012).[6] Harvey Weinstein's company distributed *Intouchables* in the United States, where it grossed over ten million dollars, thus breaking the "subtitle barrier" that often limits the popular appeal of French films exhibited on US screens. Within France, *Intouchables* was the second most successful French film of all time at the French box office, selling nearly twenty million tickets over twenty-eight weeks in theatrical release. It did not, however, surpass Danny Boon's *Welcome to the Sticks*, another film about marginalized identity in contemporary French society, albeit one focused on regional stereotypes about white people in Northern France.

The astounding domestic and international success of *Intouchables* owes much to the visibility of debates about immigration, cultural diversity, and the neocolonial space of the banlieues in contemporary France, but directors Tolédano and Nakache also took advantage of long-standing transatlantic codes for the representation of these concerns that have circulated from the United States to the rest of the world via Hollywood cinema. In an interview, Tolédano and Nakache admit that they, like Michel Hazanavicius with *The Artist* (2011), were nourished (*nourris*) by American films, particularly American buddy films (*Direct Matin* 2012). Hollywood interracial buddy comedies featuring Eddie Murphy, such as *48 Hrs.* (1982), *Trading Places* (1983), and *Beverly Hills Cop* (1984), are an important component of this genre category, in part because they succeeded in attracting mainstream audiences during the 1980s (Donalson 2006, 98–99).

American popular cinema has a long tradition of casting Black comedians, including Stepin Fetchit, Mantan Moreland, and Willie Best, though they were often relegated to servile roles. Donald Bogle notes that Hollywood has also long featured interracial buddy pairs in popular cinema: "Bing Crosby and Louis Armstrong, Will Rogers and Stepin Fetchit, Jack Benny and Eddie 'Rochester' Anderson, and Frank Sinatra and Sammy Davis, Jr.... Such movie friendships have usually held to one dictum: namely, that interracial buddies can be such only when the white buddy is in charge" (2001, 271–272). It is this power dichotomy that 1980s interracial buddy comedies begin to challenge. In addition to the three Murphy films mentioned above, there are other important interracial buddy pairs in the 1980s, including Danny Glover and Mel Gibson in the *Lethal Weapon* franchise (an *Intouchables* deleted scene explicitly references Glover's iconic moment in the bathtub) and Richard Pryor in a series of early 1980s films opposite different white actors. However, *48 Hrs.*, *Trading Places*, and *Beverly Hills Cop* are essential reference points, in part because they helped establish recurring character types that Black actors would occupy in subsequent interracial buddy films—cop, criminal, con man, or some combination of the three. They are also important because Murphy was among the most visible and ambivalent Black comedians and actors in the 1980s. As Bogle points out, Murphy's comedy, while certainly angry at times, lacked the unrestrained edge and thoroughgoing critique of race relations found in the stand-up work of other Black comedians like Pryor. This meant that Murphy's stand-up, sketch comedy, and films were popular with white audiences from the beginning of his career, which sometimes led critics to call into question just how progressive they were (Bogle 2001, 281).

In the case of *Intouchables*, the performance of French Black actor and comedian Sy anchors the film's connections to African American male archetypes in Hollywood cinema. Sy's mannerisms and energy channel the wisecracking urban troublemaker archetype that Murphy pioneered in the early 1980s. Murphy's films locate vitality and authenticity on the side of Blackness, and they have a pedagogical dimension in which the Black character teaches the white characters about Black culture as a means of helping them loosen up. These are, of course, long-standing stereotypes about Black culture, but Murphy's films reactivated them during a conservative moment in American history (Donalson 2006, 67–68). Murphy's corpus gave rise to an interracial comic buddy film formula that Hollywood would reproduce during the 1990s and 2000s with other African American actors, including Chris Tucker, Chris Rock, Will Smith, and Jamie Foxx. As if to confirm the transatlantic links between Sy's Driss and the Murphy-inspired American version of Blackness, African American stand-up comedian and actor Kevin Hart stars in the Weinstein Company's American remake of *Intouchables*, entitled *The Upside* (2019), alongside Bryan Cranston as Philippe.

French and American critics noted these transatlantic influences upon the film's release. For example, *Le Figaro*'s film critic Eric Neuhoff commented that an "overdressed" Sy "explodes" in *Intouchables*' birthday party scene "in the style of [*façon*] Eddie Murphy" (2011), and Guillaume Loison, writing in *Le Nouvel Observateur*, observed that Sy "affirms here the authority and fantasy of a French Eddie Murphy" (2012a). In their reviews of Tolédano and Nakache's film for the *New York Times*, film critics A. O. Scott and Stephen Holden both expand on the connections between Sy and African American comedian-actors. Scott tells his readers that they "can easily imagine this movie—you probably have already seen it—with Richard Pryor or Eddie Murphy in Mr. Sy's role" (2012), and Holden characterizes the film as a "crass escapist comedy that feels like a Gallic throwback to an '80s Eddie Murphy movie" (2012).

I would add that along with following Hollywood's interracial buddy film formula, *Intouchables* also draws on the legacy of American racial caricature and stereotype found in the nineteenth- and twentieth-century traditions of blackface and minstrelsy. In talking about Sy's performance alongside 1980s

Murphy films, I do not mean to suggest that either are examples of literal blackface or neo-minstrelsy. However, Ed Guerrero offers a reminder that Black comedians, in seeking mainstream success, often veer close to the stereotypes and clichés of the minstrelsy tradition: "Not so surprisingly, as Spike Lee argues [in *Bamboozled*], the same vexed issues and devalued images of African Americans can arise as the creations of ambitious blacks themselves, squirming for a break, and perhaps success, in the same mainstream movie business. ... What once was literalized in the comedic, vulgar racism of the nineteenth-century 'white-blackface' minstrel show, is now suggested and/or literalized, in many themes and genres from neorealist ghetto-gangster drama, to low 'black-blackface' comedy or an endless string of bourgeois wedding melodramas, with much of this work produced and performed by blacks themselves" (Guerrero 2012, 109–110). Guerrero is pessimistic that the tropes of blackface and minstrelsy will ever disappear from American media, and he concludes that Black comedians and actors will always have to position themselves with respect to this tradition (2012, 124). In Bambi Haggins's analysis of Murphy's comic persona, she reproaches Murphy for his lack of critical distance from Black stereotypes. She writes that Murphy often parodied them without offering any kind of ideological critique. His work on *Saturday Night Live* from 1980 to 1984 involved recurring characters such as a grown-up Buckwheat (a character from *The Little Rascals*, 1922–1944) and a Mister Rogers of the hood named Mr. Robinson (Haggins 2007, 70–71).

While Guerrero's and Haggins's comments concern Black comedians in America, Sy's rise to stardom that culminated in his winning a French César for his performance in the role of Driss demonstrates a similar trajectory and ambivalence, suggesting unsurprisingly that French Black comedians and actors must also contend with stereotypes in seeking mainstream recognition. Like Murphy, Sy became known through television comedy. He and his comedy partner, Fred Testot, had a successful comedy sketch show on Canal+ entitled *After Sales Service* (*Service après vente*) from 2005 to 2012.[7] One of them dressed in a red sports jacket and answered a bank of customer service telephones while the other called in with a crazy story that included such things as exaggerated accents and gestures, cross-dressing, and a lack of political correctness. Each skit would last fifteen to twenty seconds and generally ended when one made the other laugh and break character. Sy's recurring characters included Captain Chocolate (an airline pilot); a filthy young person (*sale jeune*, a play on words of the racist epithets *sale nègre* or *sale arabe*); a magus in African dress marked ambivalently female who predicts the future by intoning a series of metaphors in an affectedly low and gravelly male voice (a possible reference to Dave Chappelle's Negrodamus skit or American television psychic Miss Cleo); Black and Maghrebi men and women with exaggerated accents; a Black person who always misunderstands what he hears or reads, resulting in malapropisms when he repeats it back or asks questions; Malleus Maleficarum, a voodoo sorcerer; and his most famous character, Doudou, who parodies celebrity singers. It should be clear from this nonexhaustive list of Sy's characters on *After Sales Service* that the show plays with and parodies racist stereotypes in a way that walks the difficult line between critiquing and reinforcing them. I suggest that it shares this ambivalence with the American blackface and minstrelsy tradition.

Race is less a feature of Testot's characters on *After Sales Service* than of Sy's, though it sometimes plays a significant role. For example, Fred occasionally performs a literal blackface version of Omar's Doudou, called Doudou Galak, and one of Fred's more famous characters is a white French man—François le Français—who dresses in blue, white, and red and is excessively proud of his (white) Frenchness. Another of Fred's recurring characters is an Arab man wearing a fez who calls Abdallah (played by Omar) to fight with him about their relationship. The sketch ends when Fred's character tells Abdallah that he will go cheat on him with another man named Ahmed. While this chapter focuses on Sy and the question of Blackness, I would add in passing that French Maghrebi comedians and actors often negotiate similar terrain in France. To mention just one example, Gad Elmaleh, a French Moroccan Jew, walks a fine line between perpetuating and critiquing French stereotypes about Arabs as his various characters (such as Chouchou) move among his stand-up shows, his television sketch comedy work, and his film performances (Higbee 2013, 38–47).

Racial stereotypes are as much in play in *Intouchables* as in *After Sales Service*. Jay Weissberg alluded to American blackface and minstrelsy in his vitriolic review of *Intouchables* in *Variety* when he called the film "offensive" because it "flings about the kind of Uncle Tom racism one hopes has permanently exited American screens" (2011). By "Uncle Tom racism," he means the ways Driss evokes the American Black archetype that Eric Lott describes as "the gentle, childlike, self-sacrificing, essentially *aesthetic* slave" found in Harriet Beecher Stowe's novel *Uncle Tom's Cabin* (1852) (2013, 34, original emphasis). Discussing cinematic versions of the "Tom" in Edwin S. Porter's early twentieth-century films, Bogle writes that even though characters corresponding to this archetype are always "chased, harassed, hounded, flogged, enslaved, and insulted, they keep the faith, n'er turn against their white masses, and remain hearty, submissive, stoic, generous, selfless, and oh-so-very kind. Thus they endear themselves to white audience and emerge as heroes of sorts" (2001, 4–5). Despite Driss's discontent with his own lack of opportunities, he never calls into question the racial or class hierarchies of French society and remains Philippe's devoted friend to the end, a fact that caused some reviewers to refer to *Intouchables* as "Driving Monsieur Daisy" (O'Hehir 2012). These accusations of racism irked French reviewers and journalists, who tended to view it as the imposition of American political correctness. Michael has shown that French reviewers were initially divided in their response to *Intouchables*. Some celebrated its populist social conscience and even saw Driss as an "'authentic' representative of the French urban underclass," while others panned it for its mass cultural taste and its unselfconscious fairy-tale moral. After American accusations of racism began to emerge, however, they "closed national ranks" and defended Tolédano and Nakache's film (Michael 2014, 133–135).

In *Intouchables*, American images and tropes drawn from 1980s Hollywood films and the American blackface and minstrelsy tradition both align and do not align with debates about contemporary France's multiculture and banlieues. In this chapter, I neither want to confirm accusations of the film's racism nor recuperate Driss as an exemplar of France's social underclass. Rather, I want to understand how these various readings can coexist on both sides of the Atlantic and to account for how and why American tropes of Blackness, blackface, and neo-minstrelsy circulate in the film. I suggest that the ambivalent critical reception of the film's representation of race and class relations correlates to the contradictory politics of the blackface and minstrelsy tradition, both in and of itself and as it is represented in Tolédano and Nakache's film. The universalist cast of France's republican traditions has rendered it difficult to make race visible in French politics and policy, and it is significant that Tolédano and Nakache look outside France to the legacy of American racial representations to craft a popular social fable about class inequality and "multiculturalism." In fact, the very term *multiculturalism* is polemical in France, as intellectuals and policy makers often view it as an imported concept inadequate to Gallic traditions. Alec Hargreaves notes that such commonly used terms in the Anglo-American world as *minority, ethnicity, race relations,* and *multiculturalism* are taboo in France except among a small circle of French academics who look to the United States and the United Kingdom for ways to openly discuss matters of race. In the case of France's ethnic minorities, policy makers prefer to speak of integration rather than multiculturalism and cultural diversity (Hargreaves 2007, 9–10).

TRANSNATIONAL BLACKFACE

Tolédano and Nakache's most important and controversial choice in representing race relations and multiculture in contemporary France was the modification they made to the film's source material to cast Sy in the role of Driss. In the real-life story that inspired the film, Driss was a Frenchman of North African descent. Tolédano and Nakache justified their choice to cast Sy in the role in terms of their long-standing working relationship with him on two of their previous films (Norman 2012). Furthermore, they argued that race does not matter in the French banlieues, thus drawing on France's republican tradition of conceiving the citizen in universalist terms that abstract from "particularisms" like race and gender (Tolédano and Nakache 2012). Raphaëlle Moine has claimed that the casting choice in the French context served to downplay "threatening" features of the original source material because racism and Islamophobia target French North Africans more than they do French Blacks (2018, 43). However, their choice of a Black actor had an important strategic function in visualizing multiculture for international audiences. It effectively reduces matters of racial discrimination in contemporary France to a simplified, quasi-abstract Black-white binary that viewers can attach to long-standing visualizations of racial hierarchy found in Hollywood cinema. Even though Tolédano and Nakche do mention Driss's Senegalese and Mauritian background and briefly show his life in the banlieues, the film's Black-white binary allows audiences—especially non-French audiences—to intuit the cultural differences at play, even if they lack specific knowledge about contemporary France. Michael has argued that the film's production design and cinematography reinforce the differences between Philippe and Driss at the level of the image: the sequences in Philippe's house are well-lit and spacious, whereas the scenes in Driss's apartment are gray and cramped (2014, 132). While images of cramped apartments, single mothers, and large numbers of children are common to French representations of the suburban poor, as Fişek has argued (2018, 197), this knowledge is not necessary for international audiences to understand the race and class differences at play in the film.

Intouchables' use of American tropes for representing Blackness can be considered an example of what Catherine M. Cole has called *transnational blackface*. For Cole, the central element necessary for the existence and circulation of blackface tropes outside the United States is colonialism (2012, 225–226). Not only does France have a history of colonialism, political philosopher Étienne Balibar has written about the "recolonization" of social relations with respect to immigrants and foreigners living in contemporary France (2004, 38–42).

According to Cole, "the masquerade of minstrelsy flourishes in worlds that are at once destabilized and highly stratified; worlds where aspirations for upward mobility are intense but their realization remains elusive; worlds in which the very act of impersonation seems to hold promise as a means of performative self-actualization, perhaps as important as the attainment of an actual degree or school certificate" (2012, 249–250). This narrative of upward mobility is precisely what Driss comes to embody toward the end of the film, when he convinces a human resources worker at a shipping company to give him a job because of his knowledge of and ability to embody the values of dominant French culture.

By emphasizing the importance of neo-minstrelsy tropes and Hollywood cinema for *Intouchables*, I do not mean to say that French cinema does not have its own stereotypes for Black characters. In an article about Tolédano and Nakache's film, Dubois writes that French cinematic stereotypes of Blackness tend to stress the exoticism of Black characters and their bodies. Black actresses tend to be cast as nannies, while young Black men are cast as the "funny, wily, and chatty young Black man" (*jeune black rigolo, débrouillard et tchatcheur*) (Dubois 2013, 369–370). Dubois does not object to the presence of these stereotypes per se, especially in comedy, but rather to the fact that these are the dominant images of Blacks in French cinema. Interestingly, the stereotypes that Dubois mentions overlap with American traditions for representing Blackness and enable genre formulae and character types to travel. In Bogle's typology of Black character types in Hollywood cinema, Dubois's nanny and funny young Black man correspond to the "mammy" and the "comic coon," respectively (Bogle 2001, 7–9).

The intersections of such stereotypes allow French and American popular films to be adapted across borders. As Toby Miller argues with respect to Hollywood films distributed abroad, the most successful ones in international markets are those that can be made to signify differently according to the local markets in which they appear (1998, 377–378). In a related vein, Isabelle Vanderschelden contends that the most successful transnational French films are those that "through a combination of national, international and post-national elements, at both a production and a textual level, deliberately blend nations and cultures, rather than simply erasing cultural specificity" (2007, 38). One important function of Tolédano and Nakache's shift to a Black-white binary in *Intouchables* is that it enables domestic and international audiences to situate the film's story in light of forms of racial discrimination found in local markets. I suggest that the significant financial success of the film and the hostility of some American critics to the film's racial stereotyping prove that the directors' choice paid off.

Tolédano and Nakache sought to make the film accessible both in France and abroad, and their primary challenge was to find a way to represent the French banlieues for international audiences.[8] Their third film, *So Close* (*Tellement proches*, 2009), deals with the question of the banlieues; however, it was not exported outside France. In *Intouchables*, their fourth film, they sought to calibrate the narrative in such a way that it touched on what they call the "wars in the projects" in France while representing a "ghetto" generic enough to be comprehensible abroad (Weil and Amarou 2011). Driss's banlieue origins are visually and narratively marked in the film; however, they also remain vague enough to evoke the impoverished urban areas attached to all major metropolises throughout the world. For audiences familiar with the French context, the film's depiction of rent-controlled project housing (the HLMs or habitations à loyer modéré), the Parisian regional train system, the RER (Réseau express régional), and the racially and ethnically diverse population that employs it to reach the city center are banal tropes from French banlieue cinema. The film's soundtrack relies on soul, funk, and disco music, a reference to popular Black culture in the United States and elsewhere. However, its images of Black people and culture are not always celebratory. The gang members and drug dealers operating out of expensive Mercedes SUVs come as much from sensationalized American representations of gangsters in rap videos as they do from the French context. Tolédano and Nakache's mix of imagery representing the banlieues gestures to the Frenchness of the space but also seeks to align it with global peripheral zones through imagery that circulates in part through American films and television shows.

DRISS AND/IN BLACKFACE

While the film does not feature literal blackface, the comedy behind Sy's performance depends on other elements of the minstrelsy performance tradition. Cole defines blackface as "blackened face makeup, whitened lips, exaggerated gestures, malapropisms, derogatory accents, and cartoonish dress" (2012, 223), and Stephen Johnson adds to this list a woolly wig and certain musical tunes, lyrics, and dance styles (2012, 5). Johnson is likely thinking of the American, African, and European folk rhythms and dance styles that historian W. T. Lhamon Jr. has argued entered into contact in thriving market spaces on rivers during the early nineteenth century and eventually coalesced into the minstrel show (1998, 1–18). Furthermore, Lhamon has argued elsewhere that blackface has given rise to many modern "gestural surrogates" that have coexisted alongside the dress and makeup. For Lhamon, phenomena ranging "from standup comedy to the parade of black musics, on to rag trade attire and end-zone dancing" represent the modern surrogates of blackface and minstrelsy (2012, 35, 40). Sy's performance as Driss in *Intouchables* draws on various elements of the minstrelsy tradition and its surrogates, including exaggerated gesture and costume, soft-shoe dancing, soul, funk, and disco music, and even the ghostly apparition of blackface makeup itself.

Driss does not speak with a racially marked accent or use frequent malapropisms, though his banlieue accent and vocabulary do contrast with the more refined French spoken in Philippe's milieu. In creating Driss's language, the directors draw on the way Black speech is used in 1980s Hollywood interracial buddy films. As B. Lee Artz explains, "Black culture appears as stereotypically 'jive'" in these films (1998, 73). However, in two deleted scenes from *Intouchables*, derogatory accents and malapropisms can in fact be found. The first occurs during a moment cut from the nighttime café scene in which Philippe and Driss talk about sex after Philippe has his first panic attack. Tolédano and Nakache explain that they wanted a shot of Philippe laughing and instructed Sy to do something. Harking back to his characters from *After Sales Service*, Driss performs an exaggerated African immigrant persona talking about how the presidency of Sarkozy is not going to end well. The humor in another deleted scene depends on malapropism. It follows up on the scene in which Philippe buys a painting of a giant red streak over a white background. As Driss and Philippe discuss the possible purchase, Philippe is unsatisfied with Driss's explanation that people like art because it is a business, so he offers his own account: "It's the only trace of our passage on Earth" (*C'est la seule trace de notre passage sur terre*). In the deleted scene, Driss attempts to seduce Philippe's secretary, Magalie. His tactic is to discuss art in front of the painting Philippe purchased; however, he confuses and inverts Philippe's description of art: "It's the only, the only passage of the trace, when the Earth passes, for example, there's a trace ... and that trace is art" (*C'est la seule, c'est le seul passage de la trace, quand la terre elle passe par exemple, il y a une trace ... cette trace-là c'est de l'art*). Unlike the later scene in which Driss convinces the shipping clerk to give him a job by discussing Dalí, here he has not yet mastered the phrasing needed to demonstrate an understanding of high culture.

Many components of blackface, however, do remain in the theatrical cut of the film. The physicality of Sy's performance as Driss often strays into exaggerated gesture. Sy alternates between banlieue tough-guy swagger and comic trickster moments designed to make white people laugh. When he plays the tough guy, he hunches his shoulders forward, walks by lumbering exaggeratedly in a slightly bent-leg stance, and keeps his face taut and his lips pursed.

When Driss jokes with Philippe, he often first plays the situation seriously and then exaggerates his laugh and gestures to telegraph the joke. For example, in the art gallery scene, Driss refuses to give Philippe an M&M when he asks for one, telling him "no arm, no chocolate" (*pas de bras, pas de chocolat*), which became one of the film's most well-known jokes. When Driss lets him in on the joke and defuses the tension, he draws out his laugh, distorts his facial features, and raises his arm over his head, laughing with his whole body.

Driss's costumes are just as exaggerated and as reminiscent of blackface as his gestures. In preparation for the birthday party, Philippe takes Driss to be fitted for a suit. The scene pokes fun at respectable clothing, but also at Driss's discomfort in the milieu where such dress is appropriate. Driss keeps his tennis shoes on, a stark contrast to the smart black suit. Visually, Tolédano and Nakache mark the suit as ill fitting. Driss does not tuck in the white collared shirt, and its cuffs extend well below his suit sleeves. The salesperson tugs on the bottom as if hoping to make the jacket longer, while Driss looks back at Philippe and bursts out laughing.

Music serves in the film to mark class, and through it, race. Johnson notes that minstrel shows often parodied classical opera music and dance (2012, 8), and much of the humor in *Intouchables* turns around the opposition between Driss's lowbrow tastes and Philippe's refinement. In a scene that takes place just before the birthday party, Driss accompanies Philippe to the opera. The curtain rises on a musical number from the first act of Carl Maria von Weber's opera *The Freeshooter* (*Der Freischütz*, 1821), featuring the Max Kuno assistant forester character dressed up as a tree, complete with green facial makeup. Driss bursts out laughing as soon as he belts out the first notes of "O This Sun" ("O diese Sonne"), telling Driss that this tree singing in German might have mental problems. The birthday party scene continues to lampoon Driss's lack of knowledge about high culture. Philippe has hired a small orchestral ensemble to entertain his guests, and he asks them to play a series of pieces that could be called the greatest hits of classical music. While Philippe's guests seem bored, Driss amuses himself by naming all the TV commercials in which the pieces appear. He even recognizes one as the hold music for the ASSEDIC (L'Association pour l'emploi dans l'industrie et le commerce), the French agency that disburses unemployment benefits. When the musicians play Bach's Badinerie, Driss bounces up and down on his chair as if riding a horse and says mockingly, "Hear ye, hear ye, by decree, I am expected at the castle of Vaux-le-Vicomte. I must guide some minstrels there.... Yes, I am a goodly knight" (*Oyez, oyez, par mandat, on m'attend au château de Vaux-le-Vicomte. Je dois y conduire des ménestrels.... Oui, je suis bon chevalier*). Driss's antiquated diction, with his use

Figure 5.1 Driss dances to "Boogie Wonderland" in *Intouchables*, 2011.

of the older verb *ouïr* for *entendre* (to hear), and his citation of chivalric motifs shows that he knows enough about high culture to parody it, but even so, at this moment he risks coming across to audiences as a buffoon.

After several minutes of listening to Philippe's music, Driss plugs in his iPod and blasts what he calls "his" music, encouraging the uptight white people to cut loose and dance. Ironically, what counts as "his" music is not twenty-first century rap or hip-hop music of either the French or American variety, but rather Earth, Wind, and Fire's 1979 disco number "Boogie Wonderland." Driss's choice echoes the Rodney Dangerfield character's use of the same song in *Caddyshack* (1980) to enliven an otherwise straitlaced party.[9] Driss could perhaps be forgiven for naming such a popular, accessible, and even generic song as *his*, if not for the cultural significance of the dance steps he goes on to use. Driss's dance moves recall those of Earth, Wind, and Fire's frontman, Maurice White, but also, strangely, the choreography from the 2006 Hollywood film *Happy Feet*'s "Boogie Wonderland" sequence, in which a differently colored penguin breaks with penguin cultural tradition and soft-shoes for his mate instead of singing. Whether this is a case of influence or coincidence remains unclear, but both films use the same song and the soft-shoe dance style to deal with questions of difference, whether concrete as in *Intouchables* or abstract as with the misfit penguin of *Happy Feet*.

The dance style used in *Happy Feet* is not unique to the film; rather, it echoes the soft-shoe tap steps that descend from the minstrel show. Dance historian

Constance Hill explains that "the soft-shoe is the oldest and most revered dance form in the tap repertory. A fusion of Irish jig, English clog, and African shuffle, it was developed as a stage dance in eighteenth- and nineteenth-century America" (2010, 161). She further notes that all of the form's innovators concur that the best soft-shoe dancer was George Delaney Primrose, an Irishman who became famous in nineteenth-century America by performing minstrel shows in blackface (2010, 61). Black and white performers alike soft-shoed well into the twentieth century, and the style still has cultural currency today. In the birthday party scene of *Intouchables*, Tolédano and Nakache seek to portray French and European high culture as stifling and in need of new energy, and they indicate that this dynamism can come from below—that is, from Driss and the banlieues—but their suburbs are a periphery that is not linked to any authentic culture or space. Rather, the banlieues function as a placeholder for a detour through the global reach of American mass culture, including echoes of the blackface and minstrelsy tradition that continue to surface in it.

The most literal example of Driss in/as blackface takes place toward the end of the film, after Driss has stopped working for Philippe. In a narrative moment that is never fully explained, Philippe decides that Driss can no longer work for him after the gang violence associated with Driss's life and family in the banlieues arrives on the doorstep of Philippe's mansion. Adama, Driss's younger cousin, comes to the heart of Paris, the Île de la Cité, to hide out from the gang leaders for whom he has been dealing drugs. The unexplained termination of Driss's employment, I suggest, has to do with the ways Driss's home and family life call into question Philippe's image of Driss as the happy, funny Black man who helps white people loosen up. After Driss's departure, his successors have not pleased Philippe, and he is becoming increasingly discontent. Once Philippe's crisis has escalated to a breaking point, Philippe's aide, Yvonne, calls on Driss to help, and Tolédano and Nakache suggest that Driss is coming to Philippe's mansion to spend the weekend. The scene of Driss's return takes place at night, and Tolédano and Nakache shoot it in near darkness. Philippe is in his room, lit by his beside lamp, the sole warm light source in the scene. The only illumination in the courtyard outside is a nondirectional diffuse blue light that suggests nighttime. Tolédano and Nakache locate the camera in the courtyard and shoot Driss's return through a shot and reverse shot construction. Driss emerges from the darkness of the house, separated from the background only by the ambient light. Wearing a black puffer coat and dark pants, Driss is barely visible, and nowhere else in the film is Driss filmed with such obscurity. Tolédano and Nakache cut to an over-the-shoulder shot from Driss's perspective looking in on an unhappy Philippe. They cut back to a medium-long shot of a static Driss, who smiles and begins to laugh as he moves toward the camera, revealing brilliant white teeth that stand out against the darkness of the image. Tolédano and Nakache cut away before Driss's features become fully visible. The resultant image, deliberately or not, suggests the iconic look of blackface. Driss and Philippe look at each other for a moment through the window as if staring through the accretion of clichés and stereotypes that separate them. Rather than call these clichés about Blackness into question, Driss chooses to reenter them to help Philippe. When Tolédano and Nakache cut back to a medium shot of Driss, he is bouncing up and down and laughing as he asks Philippe what he is playing at with his unkempt new look—French socialist Jean Jaurès or Al Pacino's character from the 1973 Sidney Lumet film *Serpico*. Again, Tolédano and Nakache barely light Driss's face, suggesting the look of the blackface minstrel. While it is possible to read these images as merely underlit shots of a Black actor's face, the fact that Driss references several historical and pop culture images evoked by Philippe's face suggests that media images of Blackness are also present in the way Philippe looks at Driss. The film's self-consciousness about images continues in a later scene at the beach. When Driss progressively shaves Philippe's shaggy beard, he compares Philippe's different looks to José Bové, the Village People, and even Hitler. Once Driss comes inside after the scene in which they are first reunited, he tells Philippe that his disheveled look confirms that it was time for a visit. Philippe has forgotten all the ways to have fun that Driss brought to him during his employment. Whereas Philippe fired Driss when his family problems spilled out of their proper space into his rich Parisian home, he welcomes back into his life a stereotyped Driss. As much as Tolédano and Nakache anchor Driss in the cultural space of the banlieues, it is this comic vision of Blackness that Philippe really desires.

    I do not mean to suggest that Tolédano and Nakache consciously draw on the tradition of blackface and neo-minstrelsy. Rather, as Johnson suggests, the images and tropes of blackface and minstrelsy remain a visceral and latent element of a North American and even global collective unconscious, one whose literal and figurative echoes continue to surface in films, on television, and on the internet (2012, 2–5). Lott proposes that Obama's ascension to the American presidency has led to a return of blackface comedy in the years since his election (2013, 250), and it is thus no accident that Magalie compares Driss to Obama when he appears in a tailored suit at Philippe's birthday party. Driss jokes that the stuffy old white man sitting next to him looks more like Jean-Pierre Raffarain, one of former president Jacques Chirac's prime ministers, or Georges Marchais, who headed the French Communist Party for over two decades, from the 1970s to the early 1990s. Driss's references to decades past suggest the belatedness and outmodedness of French approaches to race. The joke also suggests that a hip Black man will be the new figure for an inclusive democratic politics.

Obama's election as US president in 2008 represented a moment that forced French readers, viewers, and journalists to assess the state of France's own progress in matters of cultural diversity and multiculturalism, though they did so through their own racial categories. In her analysis of how French journalists translated Obama's race, Valérie Loichot notes that they preferred the colonial term *métis* (mixed-race) to other adjectives, like Black or African American, that cannot be reconciled with French universalism (2012, 77–82). France is still legally unable to track racial statistics in its public policy documents, and the enactment of affirmative action policies (called "discrimination positive" in France) has proved difficult except with respect to gender parity. For many disaffected youth in the banlieues, Obama's election represented the possibility for a different kind of world in which race could be publicly celebrated. Journalist Luc Bronner described how "the shock wave of Barack Obama's election on Tuesday, November 4th hit the banlieues hard. Emotion. Joy. Pride in being Black or Maghrebi. And among the projects' thirty-somethings, an increased will to give birth to French Obamas in fifteen or twenty years. Whether the French elites want it or not" (Bronner 2008b).

Obama's popularity with different French demographics caused journalists and researchers to give thought to racial representation in French public media. One study released right around the 2008 election concludes that French television was "too pale" (Girard 2008), and another article laments that French school textbooks are "too white" and ridden with stereotypes (Eeckhout 2008). In the case of cinema, Olivier Barlet argues that France's assimilationist colonial and now immigration policies have made it difficult for a Black cinema to come into being in France the way that it did in the United States and the United Kingdom (2013, 346). Véronique Maurus went so far as to write that after Obama's election, French journalists could finally write the word *noir* "without being accused of racism" (2008). Sy's performance as Driss reflects France's anxieties about race and identity and channels these through recognizable tropes drawn from American visualizations of race. In this case, American representations of race in public media served as the catalyst for staging such discussions in France.

OMAR SY: THE FRENCH EDDIE MURPHY?

As the journalists cited earlier have noted, Sy's character and performance in *Intouchables* also evoke Murphy's 1980s persona, which Melvin Donalson characterizes as that of "a con artist and self-serving manipulator" whose antics gradually convert the stuffy white people around him to more easygoing, fun-loving modes of living and even criminal activity (2006, 78). The first meeting between Philippe and Driss is a con, though Tolédano and Nakache anchor it in the realities of French social services. Philippe is interviewing for a new caretaker, and there is a long line of applicants in his home. Driss sits in the long row of chairs, his tennis shoes and jeans a stark contrast to the dress pants and shoes of the white candidates. Tolédano and Nakache insert a montage of interviews with the other applicants to contrast their dullness with Driss's energy. Driss eventually loses his patience and barges in for an interview in place of another applicant. Driss lumbers up to the desk and slams down a piece of paper for the interviewers to sign. It is a document that proves he is actively looking for work so that he can continue receiving unemployment benefits. Driss seems to take it as a foregone conclusion that they will not hire him, so he would rather not go through the charade of the interview. When Philippe's secretary, Magalie, pushes him for references, he names the iconic 1970s soul and funk groups Kool and the Gang as well as Earth, Wind, and Fire. Philippe asks him if Driss knows Berlioz or Chopin, and Driss responds that he doubts Philippe knows anyone in Berlioz. The joke turns on a homophone malapropism in which Driss believes Philippe to be referring to a suburban neighborhood, rather than the nineteenth-century French composer.

Driss's first meeting with Philippe echoes similar scenes from Murphy's early 1980s films, either those in which viewers first encounter the Murphy character or those in which the interracial buddies first meet. The opening scene of *Trading Places* features a fast-talking Murphy pretending to be a homeless, legless Vietnam War veteran, a ruse that the local beat cops eventually expose. The meeting between the Murphy and Nick Nolte characters in *48 Hrs.* takes place in prison, where Murphy's character, Reggie Hammond, lives like a king. Murphy sits in a leather recliner chair in sunglasses while belting Sting's "Roxanne," which is pouring out of his Walkman headphones. In *Beverly Hills Cop*'s first scene, Murphy's character, Axel Foley, pretends to be a drug dealer in order to catch two criminals in a sting. In each case, the con artist ends up exposing the films' various ne'er-do-wells and helping out those on the side of the law. Driss's character in *Intouchables* follows a similar trajectory. He begins with welfare fraud, becomes Philippe's employee and friend, and eventually transforms into an upstanding French citizen.

Sy and Murphy's physicality and gestures also have important similarities. Murphy's wide grin and infectious laugh find correlates in Sy's rendition of Driss. Moreover, Murphy's characters often transition abruptly between comic laughter and an intense, rage-filled gaze as a means of defusing tension or exerting control over others. For example, in a scene in *Beverly Hills Cop* in which a security guard catches Axel in a warehouse where he should not be, Axel first waves his hand in greeting with a wide grin before shifting to a commanding tone as he orders the unwitting guard to get his supervisor. Sy's character employs similar tactics in *Intouchables*. Philippe has been having problems with his neighbors, who often park their cars in front of his driveway. As Driss prepares to drive Philippe, one of the neighbors is parked out front talking on his cell phone. Driss jumps out of Philippe's car and walks toward the neighbor's car. Driss bangs on the car hood, opens the door, and then smiles and jokes with the man, saying "Hi, how are you? Am I bothering you? ... You want a coffee?" (*Bonjour, ça va? Je te dérange pas? ... Tu veux un café?*) before forcibly ripping him out of the car and pressing his face against the no parking sign. Tolédano and Nakache cut back to Philippe, who comments sarcastically, "That's the way to do things" (*c'est la bonne méthode*).

Despite these similarities, there are also important differences between the two actors and the ways they translate their comedy into film work. In an Associated Press article published around the release of *Jurassic World* (2015), in which he played a supporting role, Sy talks about *Intouchables* as the project during which he began to think of himself as an actor as opposed to a comedian (*humoriste*) (Bahr 2015). Sy's performance in *Intouchables* reflects this point of transition in Sy's career, and his post-*Intouchables* work can be understood as a series of attempts to move into drama. His performance in *Intouchables* contains moments that could be seen as sketch comedy in miniature, like the scenes I discussed earlier of Philippe in the art gallery, Driss's job interview, or the classical music discussion during Philippe's birthday party. Driss's witty references to popular culture in *Intouchables* are reflective of his style of sketch comedy in *After Sales Service*, and Tolédano and Nakache sometimes asked Sy to improvise on set; as I argued earlier, improvisation in this context produced impersonation and caricature.

The Murphy films that I have discussed here could similarly be seen in terms of Murphy's *Saturday Night Live* sketch comedy. The opening scene from *Trading Places* and the first meeting between Nolte and Murphy in *48 Hrs.* could both be seen in this light. However, some of the self-contained moments in Murphy's films possess a harder, angrier edge than the previous examples and Sy's work. Consider the scene in *Beverly Hills Cop* when Murphy's character accuses the Beverly Hills hotel desk clerk of discrimination to get a room or the racist Country Western bar scene in *48 Hrs.*, when Murphy impersonates a police officer and roughs up the crowd after they refuse to give information to a Black man. The edge to Murphy's stand-up comedy and certain scenes in his films, though arguably less biting than Pryor's comedy from the same period, is a key difference between Murphy and Sy. While Sy's work in *After Sales Service* and *Intouchables* does at times critique race relations in France, it lacks the tone of anger and derision sometimes found in Murphy's work.

Murphy's various personae in his early 1980s movies are self-sufficient in their masculinity; they are comfortable in their own skin and seek to call attention to racial injustice and teach the white characters about Black culture. The white characters initially display aggression and rivalry, contesting the Black character's model of masculinity. However, as they realize the effectiveness of Murphy's characters' willingness to bend the law in search of justice, they gradually adopt elements of the con-artist spirit. Tolédano and Nakache preserve the basic narrative pattern of these films in *Intouchables*. Driss shares his energy, humor, and joie de vivre with the white French characters who work in Philippe's mansion. Yvonne begins dating the gardener, and Philippe starts using Driss's popular slang, as in the scene where he admits that he really "digs" his pen pal, Eléanor (*j'ai kiffé grave*); he even smokes marijuana.

However, *Intouchables* differs from its 1980s American predecessors in one important respect. Tolédano and Nakache modify the pattern of cultural exchange at work in those films to move in both directions. Though Driss is a positive disruptive force in white milieus, he is not as self-sufficient or self-assured as Murphy's characters. As Tolédano and Nakache fill in Driss's background, viewers learn that he has failed in his roles as an adopted son to his aunt and as a stand-in parent for his stepbrother, Adama. Driss resolves these plot issues by the end of the film in large part because Philippe teaches Driss how to pass as an educated, white-acting French citizen. Murphy teaches white characters how to bring a bit of Blackness into their white world, but he does not need to learn anything in return; he is always just visiting and will return, as in the *Beverly Hills Cop* franchise, to his familiar Black milieu. Driss, however, is not just visiting—he must continue to negotiate the demands of white, bourgeois French culture, especially when his employment with Philippe ends. This difference may have to do with the assimilationist cast of French immigration policies.

Over the course of his job interview with a shipping company, Driss successfully challenges the interviewer's perceptions that he is an uneducated hustler or con artist from the projects. The scene begins with a medium-long shot that locates Driss between framed copies of the company's logo and Salvador Dalí's *The Persistence of Memory*. The interview does not seem to be going well, and the interviewer forces Driss to undergo a reading test. She tells him, "Take the time to read our slogan" (*Prenez le temps peut-être de lire notre slogan*).

Driss quickly outdoes her, saying that her question is an alexandrine verse, the twelve-syllable meter of classical French poetry. She smiles shyly, affirming that it was unintentional. Driss then reads her the slogan "All in good time" (*En temps et en heure*) and links it to the melting clocks in the Dalí painting. He flips their roles and asks her what painters she likes. When she replies that she enjoys Goya, Driss jokes with her that Goya has not done anything since "Pandi Panda." Driss conflates Spanish painter Francisco Goya with singer Chantal Goya and her 1984 children's song about a panda bear. However, unlike in earlier scenes in the film, when Driss mistakenly confused high culture for mass culture, resulting in malapropisms, his knowing laugh in the interview scene suggests that he intentionally conflated the two to show his mastery of both cultural codes and to put his interviewer at ease through humor. Driss has synthesized the spirit of the Murphy-style outsider con artist with the educated insider who can switch between cultural registers when he needs to. In the end, he gets the job.

Driss has even assimilated the values of the French republic, such as a respect for law and bureaucratic procedure. As Driss takes his leave of Philippe following the termination of his employment, another neighbor parks in front of Philippe's courtyard. This time, he knocks on the hood and calmly interrupts another man talking on his cell phone. Driss explains with the patience of a teacher that he cannot park his car there because of the signs and asks him politely to move his vehicle. In the first neighbor scene, Driss employed the informal *tu* with someone he did not know, intentionally refusing the man social respect. However, in the second scene, he uses the formal *vous*, and the man agrees to move his car. As Adama and Driss head for the metro following this incident, Adama belittles Driss for "breaking the guy's balls" (*tu lui casses les couilles*). Adama's comment points to the relationship to the law that characterized Driss earlier in the film, but Driss's second method indicates another. Driss defends his choice, saying that the respect of no parking signs is a "question of principles." Driss's affirmation of principle here suggests that he has accepted the French republic's rule of law, which displays a significant change from his con-artist attitude.

Even though *Intouchables* represents a departure from the politics of racial integration in the early 1980s Murphy corpus, it paradoxically preserves the social containment at work in these films and adapts it to the French context. Writing about 1980s Hollywood interracial buddy films, Artz argues that they "invite" white audiences to "approve of existing race relations" by demonstrating that "White authorities are ultimately in charge," by separating the "lone Black hero ... from his community," and by presenting "the fantasy of

Black-White cooperation [that] appears possible within the context of the status quo" (1998, 73). The status quo in the American context inhibits a questioning of white authority and maintains a separate but theoretically equal model of race relations that French commentators often deride as "communitarianism" or as a "ghettoization" of public life. To be fair, Tolédano and Nakache do represent their Black protagonist as a part of a banlieue community and even return him to it. However, they ultimately reify the French status quo with respect to race relations by forcing Driss to accept the rules of French society prior to securing employment. Guerrero's conclusion about Murphy's 1980s corpus could apply equally well to Tolédano and Nakache's film: "While Murphy gets the upper hand in almost all filmic encounters and confrontations, the ultimate result of such a challenge is integration and acceptance on White terms in these film's [sic] plots and resolutions" (1993, 244). Race and discrimination are no longer problems in *Intouchables* for Driss because he accepts dominant French values and culture.

French critics defended *Intouchables* not simply as a reaction against American political correctness; rather, their support bears witness to a complex relationship between French cinema and the history of racial representation in mainstream Hollywood films. In response to Weissberg's excoriating *Variety* review, François Dupaire, a French historian, writer, and professor, argued that *Intouchables* was no more racist than *Beverly Hills Cop* and would not have given rise to the same outcry had it been released during the 1980s. Dupaire concedes that Murphy's 1980s persona is a stereotype; however, he counters that Black audiences of the time preferred to see a caricatured Black person rather than to find no Black characters at all represented in the cinema. Whereas times in the United States have changed in the twenty years since, Dupaire claims that France is not as far along in dealing with questions of diversity and multiculturalism (2011). In a similar vein, Dubois writes in an essay about *Intouchables* that France is thirty years behind the United States with respect to "the Black question" (*la question noire*) (2013, 368).

I contend that the casting of Sy as opposed to a Frenchman of North African descent in the role of Driss is not a casual choice enabled by the theoretical interchangeability of France's ethnic minorities. Rather, it represents an explicit attempt to insert the character and the film into the transatlantic lineage of Murphy and other American Black actors and comedians. The French response to race is not necessarily belated; Tolédano and Nakache's choice to evoke a particular moment in the history of Hollywood cinema's representation of race has less to do with French society and more to do with presenting a film that would appeal to international and domestic audiences equally well.

Undeniably, the "Americanness" of casting Sy helped the film export profitably. It also allowed the filmmakers to make questions of race and cultural diversity visible to mainstream French audiences by drawing on popular Hollywood cinematic traditions that broach questions of race directly, if problematically. Dupaire ultimately concludes that despite the film's flaws, *Intouchables* does succeed in bringing issues of multiculturalism and discrimination into public conversation through a popular medium. In the French public sphere, American culture has long functioned as a model for the exploration of such issues because, as Pap Ndiaye has argued, French politics and social sciences have long relied on a universalist conception of the citizen that elides the question of race (2009, 37–40).

The film *Intouchables* demonstrates that the tropes and gestural surrogates of American blackface performance traditions also have currency in neocolonial contexts like the French banlieues, where minority citizens and immigrants are living side by side with a dominant culture they must both imitate and resist. The film's ambivalent representation of racial stereotypes and its divided reception on both sides of the Atlantic correspond to the contradictory readings of the American minstrelsy tradition itself. Lott has shown that commentators in the nineteenth and early twentieth centuries saw in it an authentically American "people's culture," whereas others, especially those writing during and after the civil rights era, viewed it as an unequivocal form of racial domination. Lott's history of blackface and minstrelsy attempts to account for both readings, affirming the tradition's inherent racism while analyzing the reasons for its popularity among disaffected working-class audiences, Black and white (2013, 7–8). Lhamon goes farther than Lott and suggests that there is a certain social utility to blackface and minstrelsy tropes. In his analysis of the pervasiveness of the Jim Crow figure from the 1830s up to Obama's election in 2008, Lhamon argues that before it became a synecdoche for racism, oppression, and segregation in the early 1840s, it represented a trickster that "figured white and black relations, particularly their overlapping problems within a country that promised self-evident equality but withheld it from poor people, whether or not they were or had ever been enslaved" (2012, 25). For Lhamon, the Jim Crow character gave nineteenth-century Americans a way to "tr[y] out their racial attitudes" in order to imagine and eventually desire changes in laws about race and social exclusion (2012, 19). In my view, *Intouchables* is situated in the same uncomfortable territory as the blackface and neo-minstrelsy tradition itself, namely in the volatile mixture of racism, discomfiting laughter, and populist rebellion that seeks to visualize the links between race and inequality in contemporary France as a provisional step in generating a desire for change.

POST-*INTOUCHABLES* SY: BETWEEN FRANCE AND HOLLYWOOD

Sy's career in France after *Intouchables* has continued to focus on narratives of social mobility and characters that circulate among different cultures, classes, and geographic spaces. His French films repeatedly position the characters he plays with respect to white characters and whiteness generally. Sy often plays one half of a comic duo, the other half of which is a white man. In his films and television series that move toward drama, Sy's love interests are white women (*Samba*, 2014; *Two Is a Family* [*Demain tout commence*, 2016]; *Chocolat*, 2016; *Knock*, 2017; *Lupin*, 2021). The two patterns are not mutually exclusive and often mix within an individual film. This dramatic structure of framing Sy within a Black-white binary, which crosses the different genres that Sy's post-*Intoucahbles* films invoke—family comedy, social drama, crime film, heritage film, and so on—indicates the extent to which reflecting on the relationship between white dominant cultures and minority cultures remains essential to his star persona. In each case, his films seek to validate the goodness of his character, which confirms his integration in society.

In the context of *Intoucahbles*, Fişek suggests, drawing on the work of Linda Williams, that melodrama has been the essential mode of racial politics in the United States because it creates a sense of shared values through its emotional appeals in a post-sacred age. As Fişek puts it, "Melodrama . . . makes a particularly robust claim on viewers' moral repertoires, often by reference to the absolute truth of victimhood, innocence and virtue" (2018, 194). As I discussed in chapter 1 in connection to *La Haine*, melodrama's appeal to Manichean values of good and evil is something that Williams sees across genres and media, especially those forms of American popular culture that deal with questions of race and class (2001, 16–22).

By enabling an emotional appeal to shared values, the melodramatic mode employed in many of Sy's French films is what enables his characters to affirm their inclusion within the universal. This inclusion may be doubted by other characters in the films, but it is not doubted by Sy's characters. In *On the Other Side of the Tracks* (*De l'autre côté du périph*, 2012), Sy plays a wisecracking suburban cop who must team up with a supposedly refined and brilliant cop from the city center. Sy gradually convinces the other Parisian cop of his competence and earns a transfer to Paris at the end of the film. Here, virtue takes the form of competency. In *Samba*, Sy plays an undocumented worker from Senegal who, over the course of the film, gets papers and falls in love with a white French woman played by Charlotte Gainsbourg. *Samba* was made by the same directors as *Intouchables*, and it mixes scenes that foreground Sy's comic persona with a dramatic portrayal of the everyday difficulties that undocumented immigrants face. This film employs the most classic melodramatic structure, and Gainsbourg's character falling in love with Sy's character (and thus recognizing his virtue) delineates a potential path for the audience to follow in their own viewing. In *Two Is a Family*, a former one-night stand leaves Sy's character to raise their three-month-old daughter by himself, and the former playboy moves to London, becomes a successful stuntman, and learns to be a devoted father. These are classic melodramatic tropes of redemption. *Knock* tells the story of a former petty criminal turned legitimate doctor who sets up shop in a small town in the south of France during the 1950s. When the townspeople learn about his past, his new life is threatened, but they eventually rally to keep him with them. Finally, in the 2016 heritage film/biopic *Chocolat*, Sy plays Rafael Padilla, a former Cuban slave who came to Paris and, with French clown Georges Footit, became one of the most famous circus performers around the turn of the twentieth century. Here, melodrama takes the form of the biopic's rise-and-fall narrative, with virtue affirmed even though the film ends by showing just how far Chocolat has fallen. The vast majority, then, of Sy's French output after *Intouchables* offers narratives of cultural integration and social mobility through an appeal to goodness.

The sense of Sy being a French Murphy has proved a durable shorthand in some of Sy's subsequent films. *On the Other Side of the Tracks* (2012) is a movie that explicitly, from beginning to end, seeks to imitate Hollywood interracial buddy comedies, including *Beverly Hills Cop*, *48 Hrs.*, and *Lethal Weapon*. In the making-of portion, the director talks about making an "old-time buddy film" (*buddy film à l'ancienne*) and respecting the rhythms of Hollywood cinema, and the two screenwriters discuss imitating the codes of Hollywood cinema and bringing them to France. The film itself is self-consciously littered with references to these early 1980s buddy films. Sy's partner in the film finds all the Hollywood films I just mentioned in Sy's DVD collection. Sy's character's cell phone ringtone is the famous "Axel F" electronic theme from *Beverly Hills Cop*, and he makes several references to Axel Foley over the course of the film. The only French film Sy's character mentions with approbation is *The Professional* (*Le Professionnel*, 1981), starring Jean-Paul Belmondo, but Sy is careful to tell his son that the value of Belmondo's film does not equal that of a Murphy picture. *Two Is a Family*, from 2016, a father-daughter dramedy in a very different register, also winks at the Murphy connection. Sy's character in that film has concocted a series of outrageous stories about where his daughter's mother is to hide the fact that she abandoned her. When daughter and mother finally meet, the daughter asks the mother a series of questions to verify these tall tales, including whether she has visited Madagascar. The mother plays along hesitantly and says that she met none other than Murphy while visiting there.

While many of Sy's post-*Intouchables* French films do wink at Hollywood films, as I have shown, *Chocolat* (2016) represents a departure from this pattern. Directed by Roschdy Zem, a well-known French Maghrebi actor turned director, *Chocolat* tells the story of Padilla, France's first Black clown and arguably first Black superstar. The screenwriters drew on the historical reconstruction of Padilla's life and career by Gérard Noiriel, a well-known French historian of immigration (2016). However, they modified some of the material to make his life fit the rags-to-riches myth of the star biopic, including conspicuous consumption, sexual conquests, drug and gambling problems, and the eventual fall from grace. While the historical Chocolat was somewhat known outside France thanks to a famous Toulouse-Lautrec poster, the 2016 film anchors his Blackness firmly within a French historical context. Like Lee's *Bamboozled*, the film takes viewers through the racialized forms of iconography and spectacle common to France, including the distorted Black faces used in advertising and the "zoos" where colonial subjects who were brought to France to "act" in pseudo-ethnographic scenes of everyday life in the colonies were put. Chocolat's rise to stardom mediates the film's exploration of French Blackness as he offers his face to sell products and takes a trip through the colonial zoo with his white lover.

The film is at once historical in its attempt to document turn-of-the-twentieth-century Blackness through production design and contemporary in how it departs from what we know of Padilla's biography to reflect on minority stardom in general. Noiriel explains that Padilla, through Chocolat, innovated a form of Black clowning specific to France. While traveling American minstrel shows were popular in London, they did not do well in Paris in the latter half of the nineteenth century because elite audiences found the "epileptic" movements of the Black performers in poor taste. It would not be until the cakewalk craze of the 1910s that urban French audiences would be taken by a form of African American culture recognized as such. This did not mean that minstrel shows were not performing in Paris, nor does it mean that a performer like Padilla was unaware of them. Noiriel shows that Padilla and his producers knew about minstrel shows and that they were able to synthesize the gestures and movements of American minstrels with the European tradition of the Pierrot clown, helping to create a new clown type in France called the *auguste* (2016, 120–123, 210).

Zem and Sy talk about the film *Chocolat* as an attempt to recreate traces of what Footit and Chocolat's acts might have looked like through collaboration

Figure 5.2 Footit and Chocolat perform together at the height of their fame. *Chocolat*, 2016.

with a contemporary actor and circus artist, James Thierrée, grandson of Charlie Chaplin. The duo's acts involve both words and gesture and tend to end in some form of physical abuse for Chocolat, famously a slap or a swift kick in the hindquarters. Chocolat becomes extremely famous by any criteria we might use for stardom: his performances are well attended; the duo gets significant newspaper coverage; people, especially children, seek him out for autographs; the "Footit et Chocolat" name increasingly dominates marquees and posters; and his name and likeness are used to advertise commercial products, a first for a circus performer, according to the circus's owner. As Chocolat's fame grows and Padilla's desire for artistic autonomy intensifies, he becomes increasingly uncomfortable with the stereotypes and servile roles that he plays, and he wants to turn his attention to what he considers serious art—that is, "legitimate" theater. He convinces the owner of the elite Théâtre Antoine to let him play the role of Othello, the first time a Black man will have played that role in France. The Othello sequence offers, I argue, the most sustained reflection on minority stardom in the film.

William Shakespeare's *Othello* has functioned through its performance history as a bellwether for assessing the current state of race relations within a given society. It also serves as a vehicle through which Black stars can test what they can and cannot do on stage and with respect to white characters and audiences. In his analysis of Hollywood's first Black superstar, Paul Robeson, who played Othello three times in the early twentieth century, Dyer explains that performance and reception of a Black actor in the role of Othello turns on how much violence and jealousy is deemed appropriate or necessary for the staging. To track the divergences between white and Black notions of Blackness, Dyer reads Robeson's performances in the context of the critical responses to them (2003, 74–75). The film *Chocolat* self-reflexively enacts this analytic dyad of performance and reception by showing both Padilla's performance as Othello and a white bourgeois audience's reaction to it in the theater.

Returning to Robeson, in the critical reviews of his performances in the United Kingdom and New York, Dyer shows how some saw Othello's violence as a descent into primeval savagery, whereas others saw the restraint of defending one's racial honor. The savagery deemed necessary for the role can be understood in individual terms (Othello's personal jealousy) or in racial terms (the supposed savagery of the Black race that cannot be fully contained by civilization). Drawing on the scholarship into the history of how directors and audiences have understood Othello, Dyer notes that the more common interpretation has been the latter—that the Black man is a primitive barbarian that civilization has only somewhat tamed. However, the savagery of his passions is always latent, and the right circumstances can cause him to fall back into it with devastating consequences. Robeson did not hide the racial dimensions of the role, but Dyer shows that in his performances he sought to portray the dignity of Othello as a social outsider. Dyer's analysis reveals, however, that many critics at the time wanted to see Blackness through the lens of essentialized racial difference—that is, "the blackness of emotionality, unreason and sensuality"—and were thus unsatisfied with Robeson's performance (2003, 74–75).

In *Chocolat*, the storyline in the film about Othello does not fully track with what we know of Padilla's biography. He was the first Black performer to play Othello in France, but he did so in a burlesque sequence that ended one of his regular circus performances in 1894. It was the first time Padilla played a role traditionally associated with "serious" theater, and he would go on to play others in his career, but typically with a tone of parody. The French press recognized Footit and Padilla as actors (*comédiens*), but this was due to their cross-dressing and playing roles associated with women. Late in his career, Padilla did attempt to cross over to the legitimate stage at the Théâtre Antoine, but the play was *Moïse*, a short vaudeville by Edmond Guiraud, and not *Othello*. What is more, this play was just an opener, meant to precede the Antoine's adaptation of Fyodor Dostoyevsky's *The Eternal Husband* in 1911. While the Antoine's director at the time, Firmin Gémier, was a well-meaning leftist who was sensitive to class differences among whites, he was not so with Blacks. He cast Padilla in a role that required a bourgeois French delivery from a Black man, and Padilla could not shed his foreign, popularly accented French.

The play's author eventually removed many of Padilla's lines, replacing them with laughter to give him less to say. However, *Moïse* was a failure with critics, one that Noiriel attributes to a French relationship to language, rather than race. Gémier expressed regret ten years after the failure of *Moïse* at not having thought to cast Padilla in *Othello*, but with Footit as Desdemona, again suggesting that the point of this would have been parody, rather than serious art (Noiriel 2016, 233–234, 478, 383, 484–495).

While *Chocolat*'s filmmakers do not mention Robeson or other famous Black actors who played Othello outside France, their choice to reorient Padilla's biographical material around Shakespeare's play signals, I argue, an attempt to reflect on the possibilities and constraints of Black stardom in France. The film repeatedly stages the negotiation between Black star and audience about what kinds of Black performance are acceptable. In an early scene, when Footit and Chocolat seek to prove their new clown act for a regional circus, the audience remains impassive until Footit has the idea to kick Chocolat in the hindquarters. Spectators begin to laugh, cementing the duo's most iconic bit. A Black man is acceptable in comedy as the butt (literally) of the joke. During the later rehearsals for *Othello* at the Théâtre Antoine, it is clear that even if Padilla has the authenticity of being Black that will enable him to bring realism to the role, he lacks performance training in the theater, as he repeatedly turns his back to the audience. Nothing about circus performance has prepared him to act on the legitimate stage, for it is not enough to be Black; he needs to play a different kind of Black character within a different set of conventions and expectations. After an extended sequence in which Padilla doubts his ability to play Othello, he premieres the role. Sy, as Padilla, opts for a restrained and dignified performance, letting the violence of jealousy show but without making a spectacle of his rage. The film shows the final monologue in which Othello pleads with the audience to view him as just a man who was uncharacteristically overcome by the excitement of jealousy, thus leading him to commit a horrible act of violence. This scene asks the audiences of and in the film to see Othello/Padilla/Sy in the position of the universal. The reaction of the audience in the film to Sy/Padilla's performance is an initial round of applause, followed by booing from several bourgeois men. They call him an impostor and say his presence on stage is a scandal. They alternately tell him to go home (i.e., back to wherever he came from outside the Hexagon) or to go back to the circus. The film ends with Padilla dying of tuberculosis while working as a janitor for a regional circus. In his final conversation with Footit on his deathbed, Padilla explains that he could not shed his Black skin, and audiences were not ready for a Black man in a dramatic role in the legitimate theater.

The film thus repeatedly thematizes the calibration required between racially marked minority star and mainstream, dominant audience, both in terms of what roles are acceptable (stereotypes vs. "realism") and what genres are appropriate (comedy vs. drama). Many of France's recent minority media stars have emerged through comedy but do not want to remain trapped by always playing stereotypes for laughs.[10] Furthermore, art and auteurist cinemas continue to be more prestigious than popular genre cinemas like comedy.

The way that Sy's French star persona post-*Intouchables* has seemingly resolved the issue of genre, tone, stereotype, and prestige is by embracing these contradictions and mixing tones within each individual film. *Chocolat, On the Other Side of the Tracks, Samba, Two Is a Family,* and *Knock* alter the dosage between comedy and drama, with an increasing portion of the film leaning toward dramatic material. What remains to be seen is if, like the fictional Chocolat, Sy will ever try to do the equivalent of *Othello*—that is, an exclusively realist, serious drama about racial tensions in France or a serious drama about a universal human story. In his post-*Chocolat* French films, Sy has returned to police comedy in *Belleville Cop* (*Le Flic de Belleville*, 2018), and he has made a French costume drama, *Knock*, that mixes comedy and melodrama. The former was directed by none other than Franco-Algerian filmmaker Rachid Bouchareb, who is one of the focuses of chapter 3. In the second, Sy's character, Dr. Knock, falls in love, is very successful at his job, and brings new vitality into a town's social life. When his place in the town is questioned by the village priest at the end, all the residents come together to prevent him from leaving in an excessive spectacle of integration as virtue recognized. Like *Chocolat*, *Yao* (2018) offers another showcase for Black stardom, but in this film, Sy plays a fictional Senegalese actor in Dakar. For the moment, Sy seems content in his French career to give audiences the comedic pleasures that launched his stardom while slowly expanding the roles and emotions they expect from him. This has meant that his racial and class backgrounds have remained significant vectors of meaning in most, but not all, of his French films.

TO HOLLYWOOD

How, then, do the racially marked aspects of Sy's star persona translate across national borders into Hollywood? It was more than a little surprising that Sy signed with Creative Artists Agency, one of Hollywood's most powerful talent agencies, and moved to Los Angeles with his wife in 2012, despite the fact that at the time of *Intouchables*, he could not speak more than ten words of English (Bonnefoy 2015; Loison 2012b; Bahr 2015). Vincendeau explains that a star's decision or refusal to learn English is a key element of a French star's ability to move to Hollywood, though she is also careful to point out that the French language does not inhibit French stars to the same extent that other "minority" languages do. It is still possible to have a French star speaking in French and accented English in an English-language film because of the prestige of both the French language and French cinema (Vincendeau 2000, 38–39).

One of the reasons for the speed of Sy's move to Hollywood likely had to do with the fact that English-speaking audiences around the world saw and enjoyed *Intouchables*. Seeing a star's films made abroad is often an important way that a star generates popularity with US audiences, but it is also one that does not easily happen, because popular foreign films do not regularly succeed in the mainstream US market.[11] Instead, they tend to be distributed as art films for a much smaller audience. Sy's choice to pursue a Hollywood career is also surprising because so much of his star persona in France depends on perceptions of him as a French Murphy on screen, if not in his personal life. Over the nearly four decades since Murphy's own rise to stardom, Hollywood has positioned a whole collection of Black comedians/actors in leading roles of the kind Murphy pioneered, including Rock, Tucker, and the ubiquitous Hart, who played Sy's role in the Hollywood remake of *Intouchables*. Given that Sy initially lacked English-language fluency or the cultural authenticity of US Black culture, what kinds of leading roles could Hollywood imagine for him?

Up until the time of writing, the five films Sy has made in Hollywood have mostly seen him in secondary roles, not always the Black sidekick, but hardly the equal partner in a comic duo either. He has also done voice-over work for animated films. Sy's roles in live-action films have alternated between marking him as a generic, foreign Black *other* or as French. In *X-Men: Days of Future Past* (2014), he played the role of Bishop, who, in the comic books, was the child of Australian Aboriginal mutant refugees, so here Sy is standing in for generic foreign Blackness. However, his next four films in Hollywood have marked him as French. Following *X-Men*, he played a French gangster living in the East End that James Franco and Kate Hudson rob in *Good People* (2014). Sy is also marked as French in *Burnt* (2015), the picture with Bradley Cooper and Sienna Miller that centers on the competitive world of high-end London restaurateurs. Sy plays one of the cooks Cooper worked with in a Parisian restaurant when they were all young and learning the ropes. In *Inferno* (2016), Sy plays opposite Tom Hanks and Felicity Jones as part of a survey and response team for the World Health Organization that is working to contain the next big plague. In *Jurassic World* (2016), the Francophile director, Colin Trevorrow, wrote a role especially for Sy, whose work he admires. Sy plays the assistant to Chris Pratt and helps care for velociraptors. At least this film did not kill him off in the end, but the same cannot be said for *X-Men* or *Inferno*. Overall, Sy's roles have earned him good visibility in terms of the scale and budget of the Hollywood films, if not in terms of quality. They have tended to stress his Frenchness, rather than his Blackness, and some roles even celebrate his Frenchness by allowing him to speak French at certain moments.

CONCLUSION

Sy's French films have emphasized his Blackness as a meaningful character trait more than they have let it disappear into the territory of the unmarked, and they always represent his characters as fully integrated members of society, even if it takes some characters in the films time to recognize this. The narratives of social mobility and integration that define Sy's star persona thus represent a universalizing impulse that crosses the many different genres that mix in his French films. This push to universalism can at times have perverse effects, such as in *Knock*, in which he is the only Black character in the film. While characters in the film refer elliptically to his Black skin in the beginning, his Blackness seems to disappear into invisibility for the characters by the end. In this, the film stages a color-blind version of universalism.

Sy's Hollywood films have emphasized his cosmopolitan Frenchness more than they have his Blackness, though of course his Blackness helps make his star image signify as cool. Hollywood still marks him as an *other*, but this otherness is hardly negative, and it has more to do with national borders than racial categories. If there is a malleability in Sy's star persona, it is arguably more of a transnational malleability than a trans-ethnic one. In France, Sy manages to embody and update the values of classic Hollywood interracial buddy comedies, while in Hollywood, Sy's relaxed and fun-loving star persona also helps project an image of a modern, nonracist, and diverse France. His presence offers a very different tone from that of a white French man in a Hollywood film. On the French side of the Atlantic, it will be significant to see if and how much Sy moves away from comedy in his films over the next five years. On the Hollywood side, Sy has still not overcome the obstacle that many transnational stars face: breaking into a leading role in an English-language film. Sy's biggest international success to date after *Intouchables* has been the Netflix French-language series *Lupin* (2021), which I will discuss in this book's conclusion. The series represents a creative blend of his domestic and international star persona. Finally, it will be interesting to see whether Sy's trajectory creates new pathways and new kinds of roles for minority French actors, in France or in Hollywood. In Jean-Pascal Zadi's *Simply Black* (*Tout simplement noir*, 2020), a fictional docucomedy that features several well-known Black French celebrities and takes aim at stereotypes about Black people in French movies, Sy makes an appearance as himself. The main character, JP, played by Zadi, is a struggling Black actor who organizes a protest march to commemorate the abolition of slavery. During a conversation with comedian Fary Lopes B, Fary suggests involving Omar Sy to bring international visibility to JP's march. JP demurs, saying that Sy does not fit his "charter" of the "new Black man." When pressed as to why, JP explains that when someone like Sy is the country's "preferred citizen," something is wrong because "when you are Black, you are supposed to be unsettling [*déranges*]." JP's ambivalence about Sy in the film suggests that the latter's status as France's Black international superstar has not necessarily opened as much space for other minority actors and nonstereotyped roles as many had hoped. The next and final chapter will take up some of this concern in the context of nonprofessional casting practices for minority actors in French films about multiculture and the suburbs. Sy's stardom is still young, relatively speaking, and it will be important to see how durable it is, what shape it will take in the 2020s, and how many other minority French actors can achieve the same level of recognition with mainstream audiences in France and internationally.

NOTES

1. Sy first broke into the top fifty at the number three spot in December 2011, when *Intouchables* was in theaters. He moved to the number two spot in July 2012 and then displaced Yannick Noah from the number one spot in December 2012. Every year since, he has been at the number two spot behind singer Jean-Jacques Goldman, except for July and December 2016, when he was again voted number one. Search results are published on IFOP's site, https://www.ifop.com/publication/le-top-50-des-personnalites-decembre-2018/ (accessed March 19, 2022). Search for "Le top 50 des personnalités" to view previous years' results.

2. Dyer suggests that in the Anglo-American context, the fairer tones of Black women stars was directly connected to their sex appeal, whereas the same was not true for Black men stars (2003, 110).

3. Lisa Serero reads the rise of French minority stars through comedy in general as neo-minstrelsy (2011, 61), but Vincendeau notes that others valued it more positively (2015, 556–557).

4. For a longer list of films in what Vincendeau calls the French "comedy of ethnic integration," see Vincendeau 2015, 557–558. Mireille Rosello analyzes a similar corpus, which French bloggers and internet users term "communitarian

comedies" (*comédies communautaires*) (2018). See also Moine, who traces this tendency back to Louis de Funès (2018, 41).

5. Like *Intouchables*, *The Climb* is based on a true story, and producers decided to switch the racial and ethnic identity of the main character from Maghrebi to Black. In this case, it is a young man from the banlieues with no climbing experience who decides to ascend Mt. Everest to impress a girl.

6. Box Office Mojo lists *Intouchables*' worldwide gross profits at $426,588,510. See https://www.boxofficemojo.com/title/tt1675434/ (accessed May 20, 2022).

7. The pairing of a Black and white comedian is not new in France. Comedians Élie Semoun and Dieudonné formed the comic duo Élie et Dieudonné that was active during the 1990s.

8. Michael suggests that these two filmmakers are best understood in terms of what he calls the category of the "professionalist" (2014, 128, 130). See chapter 2 for a discussion of these categories.

9. Thank you to John Taylor for this *Caddyshack* connection.

10. For a history of minority stars achieving mainstream success through television sketch comedy, see Quemener 2012.

11. In a roundtable on transnational stardom, Corey Creekmur explains that in Indian cinema, where many of the stars are fluent in English, they do not often cross over into Western films because they do not want to go from superstar to "brown sidekick" (Beltran et al. 2013, 20–22). This is one of the reasons why Sy's case is particularly interesting for star studies: his superstardom with *Intouchables* hit in France and around the world at the same time.

SIX

BEYOND THE ART/GENRE DIVIDE

Céline Sciamma's *Girlhood*

CÉLINE SCIAMMA'S 2014 FILM GIRLHOOD (*Bande de filles*), which is about a group of four young French Black girls who live a series of adventures in and around the suburbs of Paris, begins with one of the most seemingly incongruous prologues in a banlieue film: an American football game. The opening shots present bodies in uniforms, the line of scrimmage, the hike, and three different plays, finishing with a long pass and run to the end zone. The scene is heavily stylized, unfolding almost entirely in slow motion. Light Asylum's song "Dark Allies" from 2010 plays over the scene, though its sound feels like a throwback to 1980s electronic music (F. Smith 2020, 48). Viewers might ask why American football is being played instead of soccer in France, and they might also wonder who exactly is playing. The helmets and framing initially hide who the players are, and it is only when they remove their helmets after the game for the traditional high five that viewers learn it is in fact young French Black women who are playing football. So the scene is unusual not only for how it highlights American football but also for how it features women playing a sport that is typically marked as masculine. The prologue thus signals how the film will go on to explore how young Black women negotiate gender identity and roles in the banlieues, especially after the main character, Marième/Vic, drops out of the group of friends and works for a local drug dealer while experimenting with different gender presentations.

Explanations of the meaning of this scene vary widely. Frances Smith reads it as a way of flagging how important ritualized competition and violence are for the film's exploration of girlhood (2020, 46). Isabelle McNeill interprets it as an introduction to the film's project of "queer disorientation" (2018, 331), and Alice Pember argues that Sciamma's use of a Light Asylum song sung by a Black lesbian singer sets up the film's criticisms of resilience for minority communities (2020, 3–4, 7). Ouma Amadou is the only commentator to notice how important American culture is for the first third of the film (2016), and the extent to which the opening scene also announces the film's engagement with Hollywood genre traditions has been underappreciated. Sciamma is an avowed fan of the US television series *Friday Night Lights* (2006–2011) (Dozol 2015), and in addition to the opening sequence being a wink at this intertext, it also signals *Girlhood*'s desire to represent the banlieues as a kind of universal French "heartland," a potentially startling comparison of France's suburbs to the middle America of Texas that the US series brought to the small screen. The prologue signals, in other words, the extent to which US mass culture and media will play an important role in the film.

While *Girlhood*'s viewers might understandably prepare themselves for the genre pleasures of the Hollywood teen movie or the American music soundtrack choices that are sometimes used in French banlieue films, it is important to stress that Sciamma is a quintessential French auteur, and the film's narrative, stylistic choices, and production history locate the film firmly in the context of French art cinema. We can see this in how the French press covers Sciamma, the production processes she uses to make films, and even the ways she was trained to think about film production. As journalists often note as a means of categorizing her, Sciamma attended France's state film school, La Fémis, an institution that film scholar Tim Palmer argues is distinctive for the ways its curriculum and pedagogy have historically emphasized auteurism and cinephilia (2011, 202–208). Sciamma's œuvre thus far seemingly confirms central tenants of auteurism: a personal vision, voice, and style and shared thematic concerns across her body of films. *Girlhood*, Sciamma's third film, closes out a trilogy about young girls' adolescence from a queer perspective that includes *Water Lilies* (*Naissance des pievures*, 2007) and *Tomboy* (2011). Her film after *Girlhood*, *Portrait of a Lady on Fire* (*Portrait de la jeune fille en feu*, 2019), continues her focus on young women and the role of romance and sexuality in their lives. Sciamma is a consummate stylist, bringing careful attention to the pictorial beauty of her films, especially how she uses camera, framing, and mise-en-scène. Her films are budgeted, produced, and distributed at the scale of auteur films; this means modest budgets, usually drawing on the French National Center for Cinema and the Moving Image's (CNC) juried selective aid. Her films are initially released on the festival circuit, usually Cannes, before distribution to domestic and international art house or mainstream theaters. Sciamma's education as a filmmaker and the production histories of her films should thus place her at the antipodes of the mainstream and genre-oriented films I have been analyzing in this book.

However, this claim assumes that we view genre as the antithesis of art cinema, something that many film scholars have challenged. As I will show in this chapter, Sciamma's own interests and film practice challenge this binary, bringing art and genre together.[1] The film *Girlhood* and Sciamma's career defy simple oppositions between art films and genre cinemas in ways that raise important questions about how contemporary filmmakers, especially women filmmakers, are questioning ideas about what genres are appropriate to represent the French banlieues at the same time that they are challenging the production, education, and casting practices that can include or exclude women and other minority filmmakers from the industry.

Sciamma's free mixing of the codes of the art film and genre cinemas in her work is not something unique to her; it is part of a longer and more complicated history that is shared by women filmmakers in general as they have sought to enter a male-dominated industry. The notion of the auteur—and the investment in art cinema that subtends it—has been a mixed blessing for women filmmakers in that it has excluded just as often as it has included them. Carrie Tarr suggests that the auteur is often conceptualized as a gender-neutral category (2001, 9), though the extent to which supposedly neutral categories are in fact marked by unacknowledged forms of (white male) privilege should give us pause. Angela Martin argues that the historical emergence of the auteur in France reveals it to be anything but a neutral category. In her view, the original *Cahiers du cinéma* critics in the 1960s articulated a heavily gendered conception of the auteur that was based on virility and in which creativity is a violent act of self-expression, one that breaks with the conventions of the society in which the male artist lives. Consequently, the lists of recommended films to see in this period rarely included women filmmakers (Martin 2008, 128–129). Many feminist critics did not want to jettison the category of the auteur, even as scholars across the humanities were calling into question the notion of authorship altogether in the 1960s and 1970s because women filmmakers still had yet to be recognized as auteurs.

Writing in 2001, Tarr argues that auteurism, despite its problems, remains the best way to bring attention to the contributions of French women filmmakers since the 1980s. First, she contends that auteurism is a key component of French cinema's self-identity because it allowed French cinema to distinguish itself from commercial mainstream cinema, whether local or transatlantic (i.e., Hollywood) (2001, 9). The fact that auteurism organizes much of the French industry means that public funding structures support filmmakers who present themselves as auteurs. What is more, the CNC's juried selective aid that give funds to first-time filmmakers has launched the careers of many women. Second, Tarr notes that from an industrial perspective, women filmmakers, like filmmakers who affiliate with other minority racial, ethnic, or sexual communities, often downplay their identity as women in a bid for cultural legitimacy in France (2001, 9). This tendency is part of the problematic legacy of French universalism that extends to how critics and industry professionals understand creative labor. The unfortunate irony is that many filmmakers present themselves in this way even though a blindness to difference in fact prevents minority communities from making demands for better representations on screen and for better access to the means of representation.

Despite the importance of auteurism for French women filmmakers since the 1980s, Tarr does admit that there is a clear shift away from women making small-scale, independent, and theoretically oriented feminist films in the 1970s toward directing mainstream films, including the appropriation of popular genres (2001, 5). For Brigitte Rollet, writing in 2015, women filmmakers' move into the mainstream is surprising given that they have historically distrusted popular genres such as comedy, the crime film, and the road movie because these often espouse a conservative view of gender and sexual identity. When French women directors such as Coline Serreau, Josiane Balasko, and Tonie Marshall used genres, their point was to subvert, rather than celebrate them. However, Rollet admits that contemporary women filmmakers increasingly work between auteurist and popular modes, as comedy and television series have become the preferred genres and media for these filmmakers to reach large audiences (2015, 964, 961–962, 967–968).

Auteurism is not simply about how a film is made or how a filmmaker understands their work; it is also about how scholars and journalists make sense of an individual film or a filmmaker's career. Martin explains that historically, reading for women's authorship has involved attributing "a film's autobiographical reference," "a filmmaker's actual presence in the film," and "the evidence of a female voice within the narrative (however located)" (2008, 131). However, this mode of reading for the author does not always work in practice, especially in cases like that of American filmmaker Kathryn Bigelow, who works primarily in genres coded as "masculine" and does not typically subvert the pleasures of genre or reorient them toward women's experience. An example like Bigelow suggests that traditional modes of reading for authorship are not always adequate to understand the work of women filmmakers today. By way of an alternative, Martin recommends a contextual approach for analyzing films by women filmmakers that considers the film itself, the director's intentions, and the production and reception histories surrounding a film. Martin writes of "the sense of a film being produced in a context of dialogue within which the filmmaker, the context, and the reader/spectator all participate and from which they all produce meanings that will at least overlap if not actually agree. We need to find a way of recognizing the kind of conceptual and aesthetic work around the production of a film. We particularly need to do this for women filmmakers, and we need to do it for exactly the same reasons as we need to claim women filmmakers as auteurs or to define and defend notions of female authorship" (Martin 2008, 132). Martin's call to examine the multiple articulations of meaning between filmmakers, context, and audience offers the best way to approach a filmmaker like Sciamma, who takes varying positions herself in interviews with respect to the art film and genre cinema and is placed in various locations on the auteur/mainstream or art/genre spectrums. This chapter will thus attend to Sciamma's career, the production histories of her films, the ways *Girlhood* employs the codes of art cinema, and finally the role of Hollywood genres and American music in the film.

Production history, promotional materials, and reception contexts matter for *Girlhood* precisely because of the film's disproportionate impact relative to other banlieue films from the same period. Sciamma's *Girlhood* is arguably to the 2010s what Mathieu Kassovitz's *La Haine* was to the 1990s: the defining banlieue film of its decade in terms of its national and international visibility, including being seen in French-language classrooms all around the world, and in terms of the amount of scholarly debate that it has generated. Whereas *La Haine* was confrontational for the ways it sought to introduce the French suburbs on screen through American cultural references and film genres in the context of a national film tradition that prized art and auteurism, *Girlhood* scrambles the simplistic opposition between art and genre in ways that have important consequences for how it represents the banlieues on mainstream screens. Sciamma's film is typical of a new generation of filmmakers that no longer takes the opposition between art film and genre cinema as seriously as previous generations, even as the French film industry remains very much structured by notions of art cinema and auteurism in terms of how producers and distributors fund and package films.

Whether scholars and critics position *Girlhood* in terms of genre or art cinemas, the film's use of both sets of codes has important consequences for how the film universalizes Black adolescence. Mame-Fatou Niang has carefully scrutinized Sciamma's interviews and concluded that the director did indeed seek, in Niang's words, to "create a work in which the universal would be Black" (2019, 207). Niang does not take issue with the goal of the universal becoming

Black, but she does object to the way Sciamma went about it in her third film. For Niang, *Girlhood* attempts to treat its young Black women as if they were "blank pages" somehow divorced from the legacy of French colonial history and the historical weight of stereotypical images of Blackness and the banlieues over the course of the nineteenth and twentieth centuries. In Niang's view, Sciamma does not give much psychological depth to the individual characters or shared history for the families or communities living in the banlieue neighborhood depicted in the film. The effect of this, Niang argues, is that viewers must rely on stereotypes to fill in *Girlhood*'s gaps, whether this concerns why the girls are loud and confrontational or why the protagonist's brother acts as a violent enforcer of patriarchy in a family that mysteriously lacks a father figure. Niang reads the film's intense stylization and the many social roles and gender identities Marième/Vic tries on over the course of the film as mere surface, lacking any psychological or historical depth (2019, 210–211, 225, 228–232).

Niang's objections to how Sciamma's film embodies the universal through style rather than psychology or history are well taken. However, I think Niang neglects the way *Girlhood* operates with respect to the context of art cinema and auteurism that structure the French film industry, especially around auteurist films that seek national and international prestige. The aesthetic charges Niang levels at the film point to well-recognized features of French art cinema that extend back to David Bordwell's influential definition of its style: lack of psychological depth, lack of a goal-oriented narrative structure, and an overarching sense of ambivalence that requires readers to seek intensely for meaning (2002). While these are not the only stylistic features that lead to a film becoming an art film, they are among the most traditional or conventional features.

The problem, then, is not so much the stylistic choices Sciamma makes in the film, but the genre frameworks in which she and the film operate. Niang begins from the assumption that films about the banlieues should in some sense be realistic, be directed by members of banlieue communities, or preferably both. These are laudable goals, and there are important reasons to advocate for them that I discussed in the introduction to this book. However, charging *Girlhood* for not being sufficiently realist in its use of history and psychology actually inhibits us from understanding the industrial and critical structures through which the film was taken to be verisimilar, even when, as I will argue, it manifestly is not.

Ultimately, I contend that the ways *Girlhood* universalizes Black adolescence are best understood by thinking of Sciamma as a filmmaker who operates beyond the traditional divide between French art and auteurist cinema on the one hand and popular film genres on the other, including Hollywood genres like the teen movie, the romantic comedy, the musical, and the female friendship film. However, despite Sciamma's engagement with mainstream popular genres, one of the merits of *Girlhood* is the film's insistence that the style of a certain kind of art cinema is appropriate for a film about the banlieues and young Black women. If we understand art cinema as a universalist mode through the ways it critically recognizes and canonizes films, then the decisions of journalists, critics, and scholars to affiliate *Girlhood* with art cinema is a significant part of how it universalizes Black experience. However, we need to attend carefully to the implications of *Girlhood*'s relationship to art cinema. Seeing *Girlhood* through the stylistic and contextual codes of art cinema frames the film's relationship to the banlieues in a way that reinforces the blindness to local issues of French colonial history that Niang discussed. *Girlhood* is ultimately more about how Black women's bodies and the French banlieues interface with genres that circulate internationally, including French art cinema, in ways that sometimes occlude local histories. While there is undoubtedly a universalizing aspect to *Girlhood*, it also comes with limitations when its viewers assume a direct correspondence to the social reality of the banlieues, when in fact, as I will argue, there is none.

THE EDUCATION OF A YOUNG AUTEUR

Interviews and scholarly articles about Sciamma repeatedly situate her career with respect to French conceptions of art cinema and auteurism, and *Girlhood*'s production and distribution history aligns with the French industrial structures that favor conceptualizing film projects in auteurist terms. Sciamma attended France's state film school La Fémis, though it is far from clear that the school is the bastion of auteurism and art cinema that it was perceived to be in the past. In support of how La Fémis potentially fosters a conception of filmmaking anchored in auteurism and art cinema, it is important to note that the school's entrance exam is extremely competitive, and it requires, among other tests, that candidates conduct an analysis of a film sequence orally in front of a jury. A knowledge of film history and an ability to perform the stylistic analysis of mise-en-scène are thus part of the sorting process by which a very small number of students gain entry. Tim Palmer explains that a focus on cinephilia has historically structured the school's curriculum, notably through Alain Bergala, a former editor of *Cahiers du cinéma* and filmmaker in his own right, who teaches classes at La Fémis and who established a list of 156 films that students must see during their years in the school. Palmer views these curricular choices as evidence of an ideology that seeks to steep students in forms of cinephilia and cineliteracy. Coursework and curricula supposedly help students understand themselves as artists and the filmmaking process as, in the words of alumna Marina de Van, "intensive artistic research" (Palmer 2011, 202, 206–207). The step from artist to auteur is a small one, and Palmer's fieldwork and research suggest that La Fémis encourages an auteurist and art cinema orientation to filmmaking. In this, it represents the opposite cultural politics of the film school Luc Besson helped found that I discussed in chapter 2.

However, what form this investment in auteurism and art cinema takes among contemporary directors, including La Fémis alumni, is a more open question, one that film scholar Alistair Fox nuances by noting that the styles of contemporary auteurs can vary widely, from minimalist introspective films like Noémie Lvovsky's *Forget Me* (*Oublie-moi*, 1994) to films that rely on cinematic spectacle and intense stylization, such as Léos Carax's *Holy Motors* (2012) or François Ozon's *Eight Women* (*8 Femmes*, 2002). Ultimately, Fox argues that auteur cinema bears witness to "the almost ubiquitous presence of cinephilic practices and references, in a distinctive outlook on the world, and, above all, in the omnipresence of a personal dimension informing the whole, both stylistically and thematically" (2015, 514–516, 517). In this reading, evidence of a personal voice, whatever a director's stylistic choices, counts above all else in assessing the presence or absence of auteurism.

However, even a filmmaker like Sciamma, who is largely understood as an auteur for her cineliteracy, her attention to mise-en-scène, and her focus on young women, romance, and queer sexualities, does not fit into a neat opposition between art and auteur cinema on the one hand and genre or popular cinema on the other. Indeed, one of the things that makes many French women filmmakers, including Sciamma, distinct is their refusal to see genre, entertainment, and art as antithetical categories. Unlike cinephile critics who seek to police these borders or male auteurs like Olivier Assayas who have repeatedly staged the relationship between art and genre cinemas as torturous in films like *Irma Vep* (1996) or *Something in the Air* (*Après mai*, 2012), Sciamma is seemingly unphased by this distinction, despite how journalists and critics position her career.

In a 2011 interview with French producers in *L'Express* around the time of the success of films like *Intouchables* (2011) and *The Artist* (2011), Alain Attal, who produced *Polisse* (2011), a film by another emerging woman director, Maïwenn, wrote, "We're currently dealing with a generation of filmmakers who have shed all cinephilic complexes. They know the classics, they stuff themselves with films, but keep their references in a corner of their head like one remembers a Michael Jackson or Earth, Wind, and Fire hit" (Carrière 2011). Attal implicitly contrasts this new commercial trend with the highly self-conscious and self-referential mode of engagement with cinephilia one finds in the French New Wave and its imitators. In a related vein, Laurent Zeitoun, one of *Intouchables'* producers, explained, "There is no longer any shame in writing personal films with the desire to have them seen by the largest number of people" (Carrière 2011). These remarks from producers suggest a shift in the auteurist narratives that have long structured the French film industry.

In an article dating from the release of *Portrait of a Lady on Fire*, one of her fellow students from La Fémis, Rebecca Zlotowski, confirms Sciamma's position at the intersection of auteurist and popular modes: "One of the successful wagers of her cinema and personality is to invest politics with something fun and fresh" (Dryef 2019). The journalist notes that Zlotowski and Sciamma are just as likely to spend their evenings playing video or board games as reading Marcel Proust. For the students now coming out of La Fémis, this is arguably more of a rule than an exception. In a *Les Inrocks* article from 2006 that surveyed several current La Fémis students, one explains, "The school is open to genre. Now one can say that *Die Hard* is a great film without being insulted." What is more, pragmatism has replaced fixed ideas about what cinema is or should be: "The pedagogy is to make films, see what works. It's not to discuss what cinema is" (Barnett 2006). *Positif* critics Franck Garbarz and Dominique Martinez asked Sciamma if she "was not scared of being formatted into a vein of French auteurist cinema" during her time at La Fémis. She replied that she was not because she had "no idea what that meant." Instead, she saw fellow students interested in a diversity of types of films. However, where the effects of formatting are felt, she argues, is in the industry when one must finance and make a film (Garbarz and Martinez 2014, 26). In other words, funding and production structures are more responsible for the maintenance of auteurism than the desires, affinities, or education of filmmakers. This is why it is crucial to attend to how a film like *Girlhood* was made and how it was framed by producers, distributors, and journalists for domestic and international release in terms that largely reproduce traditional conceptions of art cinema and the filmmaker as auteur.

BANDE DE CINÉASTES: ART CINEMA AS A NETWORK EFFECT IN THE FRENCH INDUSTRY

In the realm of making auteurist art cinema, the influence of an elite school like La Fémis is arguably felt less at the level of ideology than in terms of networking effects among the school's students. It is important to note that Sciamma graduated from La Fémis's screenwriting track, not its directing/production track (La Fémis n.d.). In an interview, when asked how so many screenwriting graduates went on to successful careers as directors in the late 2000s and early 2010s, Sciamma shared her hypothesis that it costs nothing for producers to submit a completed feature-length screenplay by a Fémis graduate for the CNC's juried selective aid. A directing graduate might have four or five short films in their portfolio, but the French public system for funding films is set up to allocate funds based on written screenplays, not oral pitches or short films. Directing graduates, in Sciamma's view, have less experience with the solitary work of writing, and they must learn to do this after graduation when they seek to fund their first films, whereas screenwriting graduates have already had to write during their four years of school (Pu 2014).

Regardless of one's track at La Fémis and even of which film school or apprenticeship one does, Sciamma argues for the importance of "meeting one's generation" (Pu 2014). The networking effects of elite schools are well known in many kinds of fields, and in the case of Sciamma and her generation of La Fémis graduates, it appears particularly pronounced. In a *Le Monde* article dating from the time of the 2014 Cannes festival where *Girlhood* premiered, journalist Clarisse Fabre noted just how many Fémis graduates' works were featured in the festival, and not just in the directing or screenwriting position. In terms of nontechnical, above-the-line positions, Fémis alumni produce and distribute each other's films, and in terms of below-the-line technical crew positions, they work as directors of photography, sound recording artists, and sound engineers. Even Para One, the pseudonymous composer of Sciamma's film scores, is a La Fémis production track alumnus. Fabre jokingly calls all these Fémis graduates a "mafia," which Marc Nicolas, a former director of La Fémis, reframes as an "artistic pack or gang" (*bande artistique*) in a wink at Sciamma's then just released film (Fabre 2014).

In the case of *Girlhood*, Bénédicte Couvreur, a Fémis alumna in production, has produced all four of Sciamma's films, including *Portrait of a Lady on Fire*, through her companies Hold-up Films and Lilies Films. Another Fémis alumna, Roxane Arnold, works for Pyramide Films, the company that handled the French release of *Girlhood*, as director of distribution. The Fémis networking effects are particularly powerful because of how challenging it is to secure funding or distribution, as an interview with Eric Lagesse, one of Pyramide Films' sales representatives, makes clear. Film has always been a high-risk industry because it is difficult to predict reliably in advance which films will sell well and generate audiences and which will not. In a discussion of Pyramide's recent acquisitions, Lagesse talks about the importance of Arnold's personal connections to other young women filmmakers, such as Marie Amachoukeli and Claire Burger (Lemercier 2014). Personal connections can minimize perceptions of risk among funding sources and distributors and thus remove barriers to entry for young, unproven filmmakers.

This is not to say that attending La Fémis is an automatic ticket to entry into the industry or a successful career in it—far from it. In fact, Couvreur's discussions in interviews about her work with Sciamma reveal the extent to which making and distributing auteur cinema remain a precarious enterprise in France. In a collective interview in *Libération* with several French producers who focus on auteur cinema, Couvreur described how Sciamma's second film, *Tomboy*, initially began production with below-the-line technical crew members being paid 50 percent of the wages stipulated in a 1950 collective labor agreement (Péron et al. 2014). This charter was unsuccessfully renegotiated in 2012, and it does not have the force of law, because the labor minister does not enforce the 1950 charter. While many technicians' unions signed the 2012 charter, not a single producers' organization signed. Wages for below-the-line labor can thus be negotiated by producers, something that those working on low-budget auteur films regularly take advantage of. In effect, the principal challenge of negotiating a new labor convention is that budgets vary so widely between auteur and commercial films. In the early 2010s, it was very common to reduce below-the-line wages to make the budgets for auteur films work (Fabre 2013).

In the case of *Tomboy*, Sciamma wrote the script with a rough idea of the budget and how many weeks they could shoot (Fabre 2013). Contracts generally stipulate that technical crew will be paid the rest of their wages if additional funding sources are secured or when a film becomes profitable upon its release. Couvreur did secure additional funding from Canal+ and Arte after the shooting of *Tomboy* ended, thus allowing everyone to be paid at their full wages (Péron et al. 2014). *Girlhood* emerged from this same precarious terrain, and Couvreur was able to fully finance its budget when it was selected by two different juries to receive the CNC's selective aid funding and a coproduction agreement with Arte (Père 2013). The film also benefited from support from the Ile-de-France regional government and Cofinova, a SOFICA (*société pour le financement de l'industrie cinématographique et audiovisuelle*) or private media investment firm, a form of private corporate financing that emerged after 1985. Television distribution rights for *Girlhood* were prepurchased by the private premium channels Canal+ and Cine+ (Lemercier 2013). As we saw in chapter 2's discussion of how EuropaCorp funds its films, the advance acquisition of television rights by public and private channels even before shooting begins has become a key financing mechanism for film production at all scales.

The precarity of funding I have described here does not end once shooting begins. The distribution and exhibition of *Girlhood* were equally precarious. Sciamma has worked with Arnold on all her projects with Pyramide Films. Arnold handles the acquisition of films for distribution, and then Pyramide takes care of all the stages of distribution, from marketing and trailers to media campaigns. She describes the company as having an exclusive focus on auteurist films, which for her means films "carried by a true discourse" (*portés par un vrai discours*) (Pons Belnoue 2016). The challenge for auteurist films is to generate visibility among the press, exhibitors, and international distributors, and this generally requires a festival release, preferably with a prize. If festivals accord all films that screen at them what David Andrews has called "artfilmness," this does not imply automatic entry into the national or international canons of art cinema. Such canonization still requires critical recognition, whether institutionally through festival prizes or individually through journalists and scholars writing about a film in the mainstream press or in magazines and blogs that straddle the lines between cinephile and scholarly audiences (Andrews 2014, 29). While Arnold targets all festivals, in her view, Cannes is the determining factor for French cinema: "Everything is decided at Cannes, the press only deals with films that have been to Cannes, and yearlong partnerships with [the radio station] *France Inter* are decided at Cannes" (Pons Belnoue 2016). Ultimately, Arnold suggests that Cannes does not determine whether audiences will like a film, but it does affect if and how films are distributed in theaters and promoted in the press. *Girlhood* benefited from a Cannes premiere in the prestigious Quinzaine des réalisateurs, or Directors' Fortnight. Given the financial stakes of an individual film being perceived as an instance of auteurist art cinema, it should come as no surprise that French producers and distributors carefully signal a film's affiliation with the aesthetic notions of what auteurist art cinema is. The vehicle for such signaling is often paratextual materials, including official press packets, marketing materials, and the many interviews filmmakers must endure on promotional tours, which include festivals, radio and television talk show appearances, and interviews with film magazines and blogs.

THE IMPORTANCE OF CASTING PRACTICES IN FRAMING FRENCH ART CINEMA

Even as I will argue later that Sciamma in fact represents the kind of auteurist filmmaker who sees no issue with a mode of address that combines genre and entertainment with more serious concerns of personal voice and cinematic style, it is important to appreciate how such a blending must be able to move successfully through a French industrial landscape that continues to be structured by art cinema and auteurism. This framing of a film like *Girlhood* as an instance of auteurist art cinema has, in turn, important effects on how viewers perceived the film's four main characters as emblematic of Black suburban adolescence. The extent to which Pyramide films sought to position the film as an example of French auteurist and art cinema is clear from its official press packet. However, it is not the case that the distributor simply reformatted *Girlhood* as an art film. Sciamma made important choices during preproduction in terms of the screenwriting process—and, most crucially, the casting—that enabled the film to be easily framed as an instance of art cinema.

It is common for French press packets to include interviews with the director and other key above-the-line personnel (actors, producers, or screenwriters). The choice of questions and the answers given signal to journalists how the distributor would like to position the film, and then of course they are free to take up this framing or not. *Girlhood*'s press packet is sparse, and the centerpiece is an interview with Sciamma. The questions include what the genesis of the project was and how Sciamma "informed herself" (*se documenter*) when writing about the experience of Black women as a white filmmaker (Pyramide Films 2014, 4). They asked about how the casting of nonprofessional actors took place and what their role was in the filmmaking process. They also asked about the use of on-set improvisation. Finally, they inquired about how the film departs from the codes of banlieue cinema and what the role of music is in the film, both Para One's remarkable electronic score and of course the Rihanna "Diamonds" scene. The choice of questions establishes a framing discourse of auteurism by inviting Sciamma to respond in terms that rhetorically construct her personal authenticity and voice. Sciamma's construction of her personal voice as authentic is especially complicated in the case of *Girlhood*, because the film is about young Black girls from poor neighborhoods, a life experience that Sciamma does not share on multiple levels. At times, Sciamma makes references to genres like the coming-of-age film to shore up her claim to a personal voice as director, but it is clear that the way she worked with her nonprofessional cast is the most important signal of her auteurist stamp. Unsurprisingly, *Girlhood*'s press packet discusses the casting and the role of nonprofessional actors in the making of the film at some length (Pyramide Films 2014, 4–5), and this question recurred in several interviews with Sciamma around the film. To understand why nonprofessional actors are so important to *Girlhood*'s status as an art film, we need first to trace the links between nonprofessional actors and historical conceptions of art cinema that emerged in France in the mid-twentieth century. Then we must reconstruct from interviews how Sciamma worked with her actors and how viewers related to their performances as nonprofessionals.

Unlike stardom, casting does not have much purchase as a critical concept in the discipline of film and media studies. Instead, I have had to turn to theater and performance studies, where there is a rich set of reflections regarding what are now called nontraditional casting practices that emerged in Anglo-American contexts after the 1960s. While casting used to be a background element of the theater, Angela Pao has argued that in the age of nontraditional casting, it has become a fundamental means of expression, because it is no longer about "convention" or "mimetic correspondence" between character and actor or character and social world. Rather, nontraditional casting asks its spectators to "exercise new modes of perception and learn new protocols of reception," as in the casting of a Black King Lear (Pao 2010, 27).

Pao's phrase *protocol of reception* is especially important for understanding what minority actors signify and how they are ultimately cast in French films about the banlieues. Many French films about the banlieues encode some kind of discourse on the real. In connection, Brandi Catanese has suggested that debates around nontraditional casting practices in the theater have tended to take place in terms of realism (2011, 13). In French art cinema, and indeed in world art cinemas generally that circulate on the festival circuit, I suggest that neorealism remains one of the most powerful ideological frames on the real that continues to perform this work of mapping bodies and cultures for directors and audiences alike.

The French response to mid-twentieth-century Italian neorealism plays an outsize role in the history of how French filmmakers have understood cinema and, by consequence, how the French industry assumed the structure it did. In a 2010 manifesto, Dudley Andrew offers a history and defense of the notion of cinema that emerged in France in the mid-twentieth century through André Bazin, who was part of the initial generation of *Cahiers du cinéma* critics, and those who followed in the 1980s and 1990s. His book is tellingly titled *What Cinema Is*, reanimating the central question these French critics and filmmakers were asking in their day, questions that the Fémis students in the 2006 *Les Inrocks* interview I discussed earlier admit they are no longer asking. Andrew defines what he alternately terms the *Cahiers* "axiom" or "line" as the idea that cinema, in the words of Serge Daney, has a "fundamental rapport with reality and that the real is not what is represented" (quoted in Andrew 2010, 5). Andrew elaborates this as a notion of cinema as discovery, encounter, confrontation, and revelation, as opposed to the manipulations of special effects, computers, animation, and digital modes of cinema. For Bazin, this meant primarily a use of long takes and deep-focus photography, though Andrew is careful to remind readers that many other stylistic techniques can achieve the same effect. Ultimately, for Bazin, a filmmakers' choice of shots and camera angles allows viewers to see and participate in an event that unfolded before and around a camera at a moment in time, even simultaneously in the case of certain forms of live television (Andrew 2010, xviii, xxv, 17, 43).

This definition of cinema emerged through an intense engagement on the part of Bazin with Italian neorealism. Neorealism is important because it came, through Bazin's writings, to symbolize for many the true vocation of cinema: the revelation of reality in as unadorned a way as possible. For Bazin, the neorealist film is an authentic social document that captures reality through what film scholar Karl Schoonover has called *the contingency of the image*, or the accidental, spontaneous, unintended aspects of a film, which neorealist filmmakers amplified through shooting practices, including the use of nonprofessional actors (2012, xxviii–xxix). These stylistic features serve to amplify rhetorically the authenticity of film as a social document. Neorealism has been tendentious to specify as a historical movement in Italy and as a transnational or transhistorical style. For me, it is most helpful to think about neorealism as a protocol of reception, one that operates especially well when viewers do not share the same world as the characters in the film. While we often think of a protocol as a set of rules for behavior, in the realm of information technology, it refers to formatting conventions for headers and footers appended to data that enable them to circulate through distributed computer networks around the world. Thinking about neorealism as a protocol in this sense implies both the formatting and packaging of films for international markets and the interpretative frameworks viewers activate to make sense of such films, like the kind we find in press packets and interviews.

Paratextual materials, stylistic features, and knowledge of production history can activate this protocol of reception, emphasizing some of the features that Bazin believed central to the neorealist style, including "natural settings," "out-of-doors scenes," "natural lighting," and "non-professional actors" (2009, 231). The architectural space of suburban courtyards and project housing on screen is one powerful type of image that activates this protocol of reception in films about the banlieues, and I argue that the use of nonprofessional actors is another. We find both in Sciamma's *Girlhood*.

Bazin is suspicious of professional actors for some of the same reasons that he is suspicious of Soviet montage and German Expressionism. His notion of realism in cinema distrusts the way a film or director makes reality conform to the expressive effects of, say, melodrama, with moody lighting or conspicuous editing. It is not that realism is not stylized; it is that style for Bazin is discovered through the camera's contact with reality before or beyond any kind of aesthetic conventions. In effect Bazin mainly objects to professional actors and stars because so many preconceived ideas come into play, both for themselves as they craft their performance and for audiences in the moment of watching the film.

The notion of nonprofessionals "playing themselves" recurs again and again in Bazin's writings on Italian neorealism: "In these films the very concept of actor, performance, character has no longer any meaning. . . . We should talk today of a cinema without acting, of a cinema of which we no longer ask whether the character gives a good performance or not, since here man and the character he portrays are so completely one" (1971, 2:56). This is not the absence of the actor or performance, but the realization of the ideal of Western drama since the Renaissance: near total fusion between actor and role.

For Bazin, an actor's training produces artifice, not skill, and the actor's body or life story must correspond to the *director's* idea of the character. Schoonover argues that Bazin's focus on nonprofessionals is not about the lived history of an actor, but rather about "physiognomic peculiarities . . . as if the lives of these amateurs can be read on their bodies and in their movements" (2012, 45). Bazin's conception of the actor fragments both body and subjectivity, and Schoonover suggests that "Bazin continually encourages his reader to think of the onscreen actor less as a performer and more as a filmed body" as a means of bringing film acting closer to documentary and thus challenging the star system (2012, 40). Casting nonprofessional actors in films about the banlieues and promoting them as such in paratexts like interviews and promotional materials brings the context of the films' reception closer to that of documentary or ethnographic cinema.

On the one hand, *Girlhood*'s exemplary embodiment of French art and auteurist cinema, with its careful focus on the expressivity of mise-en-scène, seemingly places it at the antipodes of neorealism. On the other, Sciamma has justified her choice of subject matter by explaining that she wanted to make a film to flesh out the lives of all the stylish young Black women she encountered around Paris in the metro and in public spaces surrounding Les Halles and Gare du Nord, two metro and regional train stations that connect the Parisian banlieues to the heart of the city. Importantly, she says that she wanted to portray these women "in groups, lively and dancing" (Pyramide Films 2014, 4). Sciamma envisioned this eminently neorealist subject as a coming-of-age story. Sciamma grew up in the suburb of Cergy Pontoise to the northwest of Paris, but when they ask about how she "researched" the film, interviewers are asking her to justify her position as a white filmmaker representing Black experience.

For Sciamma, the moment of "documentation" was the casting (Lalanne 2014), which took four months total (Grassin 2014). Much like Abdellatif Kechiche did with *Games of Love and Chance* (*L'Esquive*, 2003) and Jacques Audiard did with *Dheepan* (2015), Sciamma highlights her choice to cast nonprofessional actors as a means of establishing the film's authenticity. Sciamma speaks about being struck by the "presence" and "energy" of the young women they met during the "casting sauvage" (Pyramide Films 2014, 4). The French expression for open casting could be translated as wild casting, but the word *sauvage* is charged, to say the least, something that Sciamma's use of primitivist clichés like *presence* and *energy* only reinforces. Niang has analyzed a comprehensive corpus of *Girlhood*'s reviews in the French-language press, and she finds significant evidence of similar primitivist stereotypes of Blackness in the emotionally charged, embodied, and eroticized vocabulary that many reviewers used to describe the film and the actors' "energetic" performances (2019, 234–239). In the interview about casting, Sciamma says the women also had intelligence, humor, invention, and style, and the casting process bolstered her sense that these women needed to be on screen as bodies and characters, not as a "diversity film" that stages "the gesture of representation" (Pyramide Films 2014, 4). Sciamma's answers to these questions about casting signal a desire on the part of distributors to frame the film through a neorealist protocol of reception.

An article in *Les Inrocks* written during the film's promotional tour shows how this protocol of reception was used by journalists to frame the film for audiences. It talks about the infectious energy of the four young women when they are together. It describes how they befriended Sciamma and helped annotate the script as they rehearsed it. It also stresses how they know the film's coming-of-age story because they all come from Paris's "working-class neighborhoods" or its "near suburbs" and how they "have all more or less gone through the same doubts and ordeals of their characters" (Blondeau 2014). Niang notes that Karidja Touré (Marième) is from the fifteenth arrondissement of Paris and Assa Sylla (Lady) is from the eighteenth, so they could hardly be said to have grown up in the impoverished suburban neighborhood that Sciamma depicts in *Girlhood* (2019, 239–240). Nevertheless, the *Inrocks* article indexes how journalists and the actors themselves frame the film in neorealist terms by viewing the nonprofessional actors as coming from banlieue neighborhoods like the one in the film.

Despite Sciamma's signals about possible convergences between the film and the realities of young Black women in the banlieues, too obvious a social agenda would undercut the complexity and ambivalence needed for an auteurist art film. Consequently, Sciamma is also careful to distinguish herself from neorealist filming practices in interviews. When talking about *Girlhood*'s relationship to other films about the banlieues, Sciamma emphasizes how important stylization was. Here, she means the use of fixed tripod and Steadicam shots rather than shaky handheld camerawork, a use of widescreen CinemaScope, long-take sequence shots, and a careful use of color, especially blue, which Sciamma admits to liking, but also orange. Sciamma notes that the outdoor sequences were shot in Bagnolet and Bobigny but that interior apartment scenes were shot in studios so that colors could be controlled (Pyramide Films 2014, 5). However, even the outdoor scenes are highly stylized. *Girlhood* was filmed in the same neighborhood as Houda Benyamina's *Divines* (2016), though the sense of place in each could not look and feel more different on screen, suggesting that location shooting is not a guarantor of realism in any simple sense. Sciamma talks about a "desire not to succumb to verismo [*vérisme*], a camera . . . involved in a documentary quest." Rather, she wanted to "dream this world [of the banlieues] as well" (Gava 2014). The film's intense stylization was thus meant to signal a break with previous films about the banlieues, or more properly with the sense that only a documentary-style camera is appropriate for filming France's suburbs. However, as I argued earlier, intense stylization is not completely opposed to neorealism in Bazin's sense; if anything, it can heighten it.

Sciamma also tries to distance *Girlhood* from neorealism by saying she is not obsessed with nonprofessional casting as a guarantor of authenticity. She simply wanted her actors to be the age of the characters in the film. She further suggests that she is not trying to create "bridges" between their lives and the film, "even if we obviously talked about it. They have an expertise and are empowered to tell me when I'm going down the wrong path" (Gallot 2014). In an even more direct interview in *Positif*, she tells the story of "submitting" the script to the actors and awaiting their "verdict." If they had requested changes, she would have made them, but they accepted it as is, thus "validating" the script (Garbarz and Martinez 2014, 28). Through adverbs like *obviously* or the phrase *more or less gone through*, both the *Inrocks* article and the Sciamma interview simultaneously avow and disavow the extent to which the nonprofessional minority actors were expected to use the expertise of their social, racial, or ethnic backgrounds to authenticate the film. In interviews, what seems to compensate for such "exploitation" is futurity—that is, the possibility that these young nonprofessional actors might wish to go on to careers in the movies. This exact question commonly ends interviews with nonprofessional actors. In the *Inrocks* interview, the writer explains that Sylla has already worked on two French TV shows (*Falco* [2013–2016] and *Spiral* [*Engrenages*, 2005–2020]), but the article paints Karidja and Mariétou Touré as wanting to wait, even though they "dream of being like Omar Sy," which is another way of signaling that they hope to be widely acclaimed Black stars (Blondeau 2014). In an *Elle* interview with Karidja Touré, the last question is also whether she wants to continue with the cinema, and she responds yes, she will see what happens after the film's release (Delbecq 2014).

HOLLYWOOD GENRES AND THE USE OF MUSIC IN *GIRLHOOD*

The casting of nonprofessionals, with the authenticity that it supposedly signals, might seem to break with the codes of the Hollywood teen movie and other proximate genres such as the female friendship film, the film musical, or the romantic comedy. And yet, the film's representations of female adolescence and friendship have much in common with how these other genres operate, especially in terms of how young women relate to consumerism. The codes of these genres are most visible in the lead-up to *Girlhood*'s most famous sequence, the four girls singing Rihanna's "Diamonds" in a hotel room after having extorted money from weaker girls and stolen fancy clothes from a department store to spend a night on the town together. Sciamma is steeped in Hollywood genres, admitting in an interview that Hollywood teen movies "are her culture."[2] Film scholar Frances Smith, however, reads Sciamma's engagement with genre through the common auteurist approach of specifying how a filmmaker subverts genre codes in the name of individual expression. Smith locates this subversion in how Sciamma's first three films deemphasize the stereotypical teen movie quest for sex and mark certain forms of desire as abject and monstrous (2020, 17–18). However, placing *Girlhood* alongside other banlieue female friendship films and musicals that came out a few years before it reveals that mainstream French films are also capable of engaging critically, rather than slavishly, with genre tropes. This suggests that the true subversive gesture may have less to do with the auteur's presence and more to do with the decision to relocate genres to the banlieues. In fact, Sciamma's *Girlhood* has much in common with other films directed by women, such as Géraldine Nakache and Hervé Mimram's *All That Glitters* (*Tout ce qui brille*, 2010), Audrey Estrougo's *Leila* (*Toi, moi, les autres*, 2010), and Houda Benyamina's *Divines* (2016), that rework Hollywood genres in the spaces of the banlieues.

The crucial element to appreciate about these films is the importance of fashion and shopping as a means of addressing how women relate to consumerism. Mary Harrod notes that there are no French equivalents to Hollywood "'shopping' rom-coms" like *Pretty Woman* (1990), arguably one of the urtexts for how women can experience a makeover and social transformation through shopping and consumption (2015b, 94). Nevertheless, scenes of shopping and consumer desire in female friendship films explore the same terrain, especially in the encounter between banlieue women and mainstream French communities. It is not that other banlieue films do not explore the interactions between banlieue youth and the city center. Such encounters have been staples of the genre, usually involving an RER (Réseau express régional) ride to the city center and a series of humorous or violent interactions with those living in the city, as in *La Haine*. It is also not that shopping and consumption are uniquely features of the city center either. Banlieue-typical sartorial choices regarding sneakers, jeans, track pants, and T-shirts can serve as markers of taste hierarchies in the same way that a choice of shirt or skirt might in the city center. Rather, scenes of shopping in female friendship films set in the banlieues typically mediate the relationship between models of women's identity in the banlieues and those in mainstream society.

Moreover, such shopping scenes in female friendship films represent the promise of social transformation through consumption even as they occlude how questions of labor and access to money necessarily frame consumerism, especially for women from working-class suburban backgrounds. One of the problems that Harrod identifies with most post-2000 French "chick flicks" is their embeddedness in "bourgeois, white settings" that reflect the backgrounds of the women who directed them (2016, 40). By resituating the codes of female friendship films into the space of the banlieues, *Girlhood* foregrounds inequalities of labor, education, and money while still offering viewers some of the genre pleasures associated with such films. Ultimately, the ambivalence of *Girlhood*'s relationship to consumerism is not unique to Sciamma's personal voice as auteur or the film's status as an art film. Rather, it is shared across mainstream popular films and art films by and about women from the banlieues, such as *All That Glitters*, which was codirected by Géraldine Nakache, brother of Olivier Nakache, who codirected *Intouchables*.

All That Glitters focuses on two young suburban French women, Ely (played by Nakache) and Lila (Leïla Behkti), who grew up reading about nightclubs, global fashion trends, dance styles, and glamorous city-center life in women's magazines. The film tracks their attempts to pass as sophisticated, well-to-do urban socialites. Much of the humor in the film arises from their spectacular failures; it seems that the rich Parisians mark them immediately and push them toward more traditional roles for banlieue women, like the nanny or the exotic seductress.[3] Rather than reinforce the utopic dimensions of shopping on screen through easy access to money and things, *All That Glitters* reveals how Lila and Ely must hustle for enough money to buy fancy clothes or nice shoes. The two sit near Paris's financial district, La Défense, the same space where the four young girls in Sciamma's *Girlhood* participate in a hip-hop dance off. La Défense is a large public space in the heart of Paris's financial district. It houses a mall and serves as a liminal space between some of Paris's wealthiest neighborhoods and the much less well-off suburban neighborhoods just next to them. As Lila and Ely contemplate their relative poverty, two boys come up in yellow T-shirts collecting donations for a Haitian aid campaign entitled "Say No to Poverty." After listening to their detailed presentation, Lila grabs the T-shirts and tells the kids scram, rhetorically asking why she and Ely should care about the poor. They then begin to solicit money from the well-to-do passersby, mounting a personal campaign against their own poverty that ends with a new pair of shoes.

The shopping scene in *All That Glitters* begins at the end, as it were, after Lila and Ely have selected the shoes, and it does not contain the pounding of a pop soundtrack or the elliptical montage editing typically found in such scenes. It is important to stress that they intend to purchase *one* pair of shoes to share and are preparing to buy them. The clerk tells them that she will wait for them at the checkout counter, as if to defer the moment of purchase and thus foreground the question of whether they will in fact be able to pay for the shoes that do not even have a price tag. Lila and Ely take their time making their way to the front of the store, as if they want to linger in the pleasurable state of being able to purchase the shoes. The clerk takes her time wrapping the box, again waiting for the moment she expects when they will reveal that they cannot purchase the shoes. Her disdainful gaze suggests that she sees them for what they are, even if they do not. After a pause, Lila produces a wad of crinkled bills as the two discuss plans for how they will share the shoes. Rather than presenting consumerism as the ticket to riding the elevator to a higher social class, this scene highlights the structural inequalities that define the city center even for women from the banlieues who relocate there. Consumption on screen seems to offer the ability to change social classes or pass as wealthy, but *All That Glitters* suggests that it is not so easy to do.

Girlhood shares with *All That Glitters* a desire to foreground the economic difficulties of enacting social mobility through consumerism. Sciamma shows that Marième must extort money from other girls at her school and that the four girls steal clothes in order to organize the utopic party scene in the hotel room set to Rihanna's "Diamonds." This well-known scene uses music, song, and dance to create an aspirational image of universal Black girlhood that was intensely pleasurable for many viewers. For this reason, it has also been the

Figure 6.1 Ely and Lila purchase a pair of expensive shoes. *All That Glitters*, 2010.

subject of intense debate about how the film progressively or regressively represents Black girls' adolescence. To understand how the film universalizes Black girlhood through Rihanna's song, we first need to consider the role of music in banlieue cinema generally.

Popular song in cinema is another key vector for creating feelings of utopia, solidarity, and class mobility, although the sense of passing or belonging afforded by music is arguably less tangible and durable than the purchase of clothes or shoes. In addition to vectors of utopic feeling and solidarity, the selection of popular songs in films about the banlieues also serves as a key marker of cultural distinctions. In his analysis of how popular songs function in French cinema generally, Phil Powrie notes that when directors turn to songs in French by French groups, they tend to select from songs from the 1930s and from the period that stretches from the 1960s to the 1980s. He argues that French songs from "historical periods" evoke nostalgia "for a lost way of life under the pressure of Americanization, nostalgia for the family that fragile 'tribal' communities are replacing" (2015, 542). When directors choose songs in English by anglophone groups, Powrie suggests that they "tend to indicate the fracture of community or family without the appeal to the past and its ideals, but with a much more future-facing attitude" (2015, 541). While American songs certainly can evoke the centrifugal pressures of globalization on French society, this is not their only function, especially when one looks at how they are used in films about the banlieues. Far from evoking the inescapable fragmentation of community and solidarity, the deployment of American songs in certain film soundtracks offers filmmakers the opportunity to question France's color-blind conception of republican universalism. At its most radical, American popular music allows minority groups in France to assume the place of the universal.

This use of American popular music, especially rap and hip hop, in films about the banlieues and issues of cultural difference stretches back to the earliest examples of *beur* and banlieue cinema from the 1980s, such as Medhi Charef's *Tea in the Harem* (*Le Thé au harem d'Archimède*, 1985) or Rachid Bouchareb's *Bâton rouge* (1987). Will Higbee argues that what counts in those two films is not how music indicates ethnic belonging, but rather how the young characters collectively identify with youth culture that is at once French, American, and generically Western (2009, 233). The question of hip hop took on a particular international visibility with Kassovitz's *La Haine*, whose use of hip-hop aesthetics I analyzed in chapter 1. As Felicia McCarren has argued, French hip hop evolved into distinctly Gallic forms in the late twentieth and early twenty-first centuries, even if many in France still perceive its origins and cultural affinities as rooted in US culture (2013, xxxvii–xxxviii). French banlieue and rap musicals such as Malik Chibane's *Voisins, voisines* (2005) or Pascal Tessaud's *Brooklyn* (2014) harness the authenticity of French rap, often by casting real-life rappers in starring roles, to create soundscapes that visually and aurally bring the suburbs to the screen. Both these films motivate their musical numbers diegetically, opting for realism over the more imaginative possibilities offered by the musical film genre. Both films show explicitly how rap music functions as an outlet for individual feelings of outrage, a shared language of social critique, an alternate model of community for the marginalized, and a means of earning a living. Introducing hyper-contemporary French rap songs from the banlieues to a wider moviegoing public that might not otherwise hear them expresses a commitment to local authenticity.

While rap and hip-hop songs can function as markers of cultural authenticity in nonmainstream banlieue films, in the realm of mainstream French comedy, especially comedy that deals with issues of multiculture, the sounds of hip hop and rap often function as a sonic shorthand to mark which side of the proverbial tracks a character comes from. For example, the popular comedy *Neuilly Yo Mama!* (*Neuilly sa mère!*, 2009) tells the story of Sami, a young boy from the banlieues whose mother sends him to live with her richer sister's family and attend school in the Neuilly-sur-Seine, the same well-to-do neighborhood adjacent to Puteaux and La Défense that appears in *All That Glitters*. There Sami finds young white boys who love rap and tell him that their songs about Picasso are better than those from the banlieues. He also meets a young white girl with whom he falls in love and who plays violin in the school orchestra. Lacking the significant funds and many years of musical training required to play classical music, he sits in the back of the orchestra attempting to strike a triangle on cue. Over the course of the film, evolving musical tastes among characters and the selection of songs in the soundtrack mark the changing level of cultural integration between the boy from the banlieues and the upperclass community of Neuilly. The sonic shorthand of opposed musical tastes in *Neuilly Yo Mama!* also structures the use of popular song in *Intouchables* that I analyzed in chapter 5.

It is important to stress that there is also nothing a priori utopic or progressive about American popular music as opposed to French popular music, as the example of the banlieue musical *Leila* will make clear. *Leila* was made by Estrougo, a young filmmaker who grew up partially in the banlieues and first came to prominence when she made *Ain't Scared (Regarde-moi)* in 2007 at the age of twenty-three. Following the release of *Ain't Scared*, producers Olivier Delbosc and Marc Missonnie of Fidelité Films approached her about doing a musical. Estrougo had already been working on a script about undocumented workers in Paris and only agreed to make the film if it could combine the two. She was specifically interested in using the genre because she thought it would allow her to talk about a serious topic with a lighter tone accessible to a wide audience (Dailymotion 2011). The film is set in the Goutte d'or neighborhood in the eighteenth arrondissement of Paris, which is not technically a suburb but is one of the city's last culturally diverse, working-class neighborhoods. Consequently, Estrougo's film engages with many of the same issues of identity and belonging as banlieue films set in the suburbs. *Leila* faithfully reproduces the narrative structures of the classical Hollywood musical instead of experimenting with the relationship between sound and image like many other French musicals.[4] In the case of Estrougo's film, the character Leila comes from a close-knit yet fragmented French Maghrebi family. Whereas Leila is working many odd jobs to become a lawyer to advocate for her friends, family, and surrounding community, Gabriel, by contrast, comes from a wealthy and traditional French family that Estrougo represents as stifling. His father is a police prefect responsible for locating and deporting undocumented workers.

Leila's approach to its pop soundtrack is an exception to the trend Powrie noted in which French classic popular song is used to express nostalgia, and *Leila* is also exceptional among other banlieue musicals, like *Geronimo* (2014), *Voisins, voisines, 100% Arabica* (1997), or *Brooklyn*. Estrougo does not represent culturally diverse communities through an appeal to ethnically, racially, or spatially marked forms of music; that is, she does not use raï, zouk, Gallic or American forms of rap and hip hop, or folk music, nor does she use American popular music as a more inclusive alternative to classical music or French popular music, as in *Intouchables*. Instead, she opts for rearranged covers of a series of French popular songs from the mid-1950s to the 1990s and early 2000s, including an

Figure 6.2 Singing and dancing in the streets in *Leila*, 2010.

American-style gospel setting of Daniel Balavoine's 1985 song "Sauver l'amour" and Téléphone's 1984 song "Un autre monde" transformed from a Pat Benatar–esque rock ballad into a mournful lamentation. In this resetting of a French popular song, *Leila* participates in the cover song aesthetic made famous by the American TV musical series *Glee* (2009–2015). The Fox channel's hit series is responsible for not only rehabilitating the genre of television musical but also reinvigorating the use of cover songs as a soundtrack strategy in films and television series alike. Estrougo shares with *Glee* a focus on the preexisting recognizability of certain songs. In an interview, she explains that she wanted "to say something to everyone through the songs, and I thought to myself that using already recognizable songs was surely the most effective means [of doing this]" (Dailymotion 2011). She then focused on what the lyrics said regardless of the song's historical period or style and replaced dialogue with song.

SHINE BRIGHT LIKE A DIAMOND

Sciamma's use of Rihanna's "Diamonds" in *Girlhood* represents a fusion of two of these strategies; she employed one of the most recognizable songs to come out of the United States in the 2010s but had her four main characters sing along in an intimate cover. The scene thus combines Estrougo's choice to restage classic recognizable songs in the manner of *Glee* and *Intouchables*'s use of "Boogie Wonderland" to bring minority and dominant audiences together through music, dance, and live performance. While Sciamma's use of Rihanna's song certainly seeks to universalize Black experience through feeling in the manner of these other films, I contend that how Sciamma shoots the hotel scene is ultimately more significant than the song itself. Sciamma's film positions its characters in the place of the universal through the long-take style with which she shot the sequence, an aesthetic choice that highlights the importance of performance and encounter between characters and viewers. This style has long been associated with a certain strain of French art cinema, and here it serves to universalize Black women's experience through the recognizability of these stylistic codes.

The "Diamonds" scene takes place a third of the way into the film, when the four girls rent a hotel room in Paris and spend a night on the town partying. After drinking and smoking, they dance and sing karaoke to the sounds of Barbados-born singer Rihanna's song "Diamonds" in a scene that interrupts the narrative and transports viewers to a different plane of cinematic experience. The song's inclusion was far from an editing room accident; it was very difficult and expensive to acquire the rights to use Rihanna's song. Sciamma shot the scene to the song even before she had secured rights, and the finished scene had to be screened for the rights holders, including Rihanna herself, before Sciamma was allowed to use it in the final film (Péron and Franck-Dumas 2014). Unlike the self-authored or contemporary rap songs from the French banlieue musicals I mentioned earlier, "Diamonds" was an international hit in many different countries among many different audience groups. Its function in Sciamma's film is thus radically different from the music in *Voisins, voisines* or *Brooklyn*. "Diamonds" is a key moment in the film's project of making Black bodies, especially women's bodies, aspirational and universal. It is also the moment that achieves the fusion between local aesthetic codes of art cinema and global, especially American, forms of mass culture, including Hollywood genres and popular music.[5]

The "Diamonds" scene has generated significant critical commentary—positive, negative, and ambivalent—among scholars from a diverse set of perspectives. The effect of the scene is undeniable, yet there is much debate about what the powerful embodied responses can mean and whether the scene in its universalizing gesture in fact betrays some of the cultural specificities of France's Black communities. Frances Smith read the scene as a powerful statement of utopic togetherness (2020, 68–69). McNeill views the scene as a moment of queer, nonnormative potential in which a moment of liberation also reveals how the girls are recuperated into the commodified logic of neoliberalism (2018, 338). Pember offers an overview of feminist readings of the scene as one of embodied empowerment and then challenges how these readings view the scene as one of resistance. Instead, Pember views such readings as falling into the trap of neoliberal discourses of resilience, something that the film challenges through its appeal to a counter-resilient melancholy also found in Rihanna's music (2020, 1–2, 9).

The debate about the film's feminist politics turns around the ways Rihanna's music creates exuberance or melancholy, depending on how the viewer perceives it. However, the debate thus far does not fully consider the importance of mise-en-scène, especially Sciamma's use of long-take aesthetics in the scene and in the whole film. While much of the pleasure the scene elicits has been tied to Rihanna's song and the direct-address style of music videos, I want to suggest that a significant source of exuberance has to do with how Sciamma employs the stylistic features of the French art cinema, especially those that echo Bazin's take on Italian neorealism. As much as promotional paratexts might seek to activate neorealism as a protocol of reception, such a viewing orientation must also be grounded in the aesthetic choices of the film. We see this strongly in the "Diamonds" scene's use of long takes and the ways Sciamma frames the scene as one of encounter and discovery. These stylistic features of French art cinema mix seamlessly with American popular music and the direct address of music video aesthetics to create the film's powerful fusion of the genre cinema and art film codes.

Girlhood's "Diamonds" scene is remarkable for how slow and seemingly continuous it is, a move that seems to depart from the spatial fragmentation and fast-paced editing of music videos that originated on the American channel MTV in the 1980s and 1990s. Comparing Rihanna's "Diamonds" video to the "Diamonds" scene in Sciamma's film, McNeill notes that the average shot length is 1.8 seconds in the former and 14.7 seconds in the latter (2018, 336). Calculating average shot length involves noting the duration of every shot in a film (or sequence) and averaging them. While it is an imperfect metric because shot length can vary within a film, it offers a helpful way to approximately quantify changes in editing rhythm among types of films or films from different historical periods. To offer another metric, the "Diamonds" sequence, which lasts three minutes and forty-four seconds, contains only thirteen edits. Thus, the scene does not qualify as a sequence shot or a single long take. The classical continuous sequence shot in the film is when Marième delivers drugs to a party; a single two-minute shot using a mobile Steadicam camera follows hers up the stairs, into the apartment, and back out again. However, *Girlhood* in general espouses a long-take aesthetic by holding individual shots for twenty to thirty seconds or more and by using camera movement to create the sense of continuous flow around an action even when there is editing. The best example of this is the sequence that follows the film's football prologue, when the girls return to their neighborhood. The camera follows the girls as they return and gradually peel off to go home or talk to the boys hanging out in the courtyard. There is editing and there are even insert shots that suggest the point of view of

Figure 6.3 Rihanna's "Diamonds" in *Girlhood*, 2014.

girls as they look at the boys, but the movements of the camera mimic the pace and direction of the girls' walking, thus creating the feeling of a continuous sequence shot, even if it is not.

The ostensible goal of long-take aesthetics is to create the sense of an event unfolding on screen—one that the camera, filmmakers, and viewers encounter and discover, albeit at different moments in the production process. While there is not movement in the sense of characters walking through space that the camera follows, there is continuous movement within the shots in the form of their dancing and singing. The girls' moving bodies create a sense of an event unfolding because Sciamma plays Rihanna's song uninterrupted and does not leave the hotel room during the scene.

Despite the relatively continuous sense of space and time created by the hotel room and the song respectively, McNeill argues that the scene is still defined by the dynamism of a music video aesthetics through "framing, camera movement and variable selective focus" (2018, 336). Emma Wilson writes about the camera's "levity" as it moves with the girls while they dance (2017, 16). While these techniques are indeed used in the scene, their effects are subtle. There is not much camera movement except for when the camera slowly pulls back from Lady as she begins to lip-synch and pushes in slowly on Marième as she watches from the bed. The camera moves slightly at times to keep the girls in frame, especially given the wide aspect ratio of CinemaScope. The "Diamonds" scene is notable for its use of relatively close shots, especially given that the whole film was shot in CinemaScope. The longer lens used in these close shots does mean there are changes in selective focus to keep characters sharp, but these slight adjustments are not the conspicuous shifts of a rack focus shot. If anything, Sciamma's camera emphasizes keeping the girls in view so that we can watch

Figure 6.4 Neorealist style in *Girlhood*, 2014.

them dance, rather than having us pay attention to what the camera is doing. From this perspective, I agree with McNeill that the "synergy" of a music video style takes place between music, dancing, and singing (2018, 336). The event may feel continuous; however, it is not. Sciamma repeatedly cuts between different close-ups at the same shot scale, a "violation" of continuity editing style, but used here it serves to draw attention to the dancing. The uninterrupted music gives the scene the continuous flow of an event that viewers discover.

Smith takes a different tack and argues that we can see the influence of music video aesthetics in the use of direct address. She draws on Richard Dyer's writings about utopia in the film musical to argue that Sciamma's decision to have Lady look at the camera as she begins to lip-synch intensifies "the affective pull of the utopia" (2020, 63–64). While some of the other critics already discussed have read the scene as a melancholic commentary about feelings of utopia and solidarity, Smith notes that Sciamma's interviews do not reveal her to have such a critique in mind, nor have many critics interpreted the scene in this manner. What is more, Smith points out that Sciamma breaks with the conventions of the music video and allows viewers to hear the diegetic voices of the girls at the end of the song. For Smith, this choice intensifies the utopic promise of the scene, something that continues through the rest of the film (2020, 68–69). I would add that letting viewers hear the girls sing along in accented English further highlights the scene as an event that viewers witness, rather than just a popular song they hear and enjoy in the soundtrack.

Pember's point about counter-resilient melancholy is that viewers need not choose between the utopic and the melancholy readings of the "Diamonds" scene (2020, 16). Both are part of the scene's intense power to affect viewers. Dyer's analysis of the politics of pastiche in cinema, I argue, accounts for the complex mixture of feeling in the "Diamonds" scene: "Pastiche articulates this sense of living permanently, ruefully but without distress, within the limits and potentialities of the cultural construction of thought and feeling" (2006, 180). Dyer's diction in "ruefully but without distress" and "limits and potentialities" captures the extent to which human beings cannot go beyond the social construction of their world, and this fact can alternately be experienced as imprisonment or freedom. The "Diamonds" scene is a contingent moment in the film, made possible by activities of dubious legal status and taking place in a space far removed from the suburban neighborhood. Yet, it is also the moment in which the girls are the freest and most in tune with each other. Dyer goes on to explain that pastiche "imitates formal means that are themselves ways of evoking, moulding, and eliciting feeling, and thus in the process is able to mobilise feelings even while signalling that it is doing so. Thereby it can, at its best, allow us to feel our connection to the affective frameworks, the structures of feeling, past and present, that we inherit and pass on. That is to say, it can enable us to know ourselves affectively as historical beings" (Dyer 2006, 180). By lip-synching Rihanna's "Diamonds," the four girls, and by extension viewers, come to know their own positions as historical beings affectively bound to a shared world of culture that is at once local and global, with all the limitations and possibilities that such bonds bring. It reveals the girls to have occupied the position of the universal, however contingent, fleeting, or complicit their hold on this moment might be.

The scene's use of music, the direct camera address, and a long-take aesthetics of duration embody the mixing of commercial, popular genres and the intense stylization of art cinema that define the whole film. Much has been made of the film's conspicuous use of popular Hollywood genres like the teen movie and US cultural references like American football or popular music. The use of American mass cultural forms definitely qualifies as pastiche in Dyer's sense of signaled close imitation rather than parody. However, the presence of stylistic features of European art cinema has been less remarked and theorized, though I contend that it is no less imitative than *Girlhood*'s use of American culture. The scene's use of long-take aesthetics invokes the memories and pleasures of the stylistic choices early New Wave films like *Breathless* (*À bout de souffle*, 1960) or *400 Blows* (*Les Quatre cents coups*, 1959) made when Jean-Luc Godard and François Truffaut wished to capture the exuberance of youth on screen. That this notion of style, of what cinema is, is simply one more choice among many does not detract from its utopian potential. If anything, it reveals the possibilities that this style still has to affect viewers in the early twenty-first century. The fact that this aspect of the film's address to viewers has been less appreciated in the scholarly commentary on Sciamma's film likely has to do with the stylistic aspects of French films that are taken for granted.

When Dyer discusses how cinematic pastiche operates, he takes up the example of Truffaut's film *Shoot the Piano Player* (*Tirez sur le pianiste*, 1960), which he reads as an instance of neo-noir in that it knowingly signals how it is reproducing (and departing from) tropes drawn from American B pictures like *Detour* (1945) or *Gun Crazy* (1950). However, Dyer argues that we must think about pastiche with respect to the local production context for film. While Truffaut's film knowingly winks at its use of American film culture, the ways it reproduces the sense of "everyday life and unmarried domesticity" characteristic of French cinema, including Jean Gabin's poetic realist films, among others, are not signaled as imitation despite being no less conventional than the American imports. For Dyer, this means that pastiche relates to the American works, but it is not operative with respect to the French production context (2006, 127–128).

It is tempting to view stylistic features that are typical of auteurist films, such as the presence of a director's personal discourse, or formal qualities that are reflective of art cinema, such as long-take aesthetics or stylized mise-en-scène, as simply part of the taken-for-granted furniture of many contemporary French films. However, in my view, *Girlhood*'s relationship to the codes of French auteur and art cinema is no less imitative than its approach to American cinema and mass culture. Sciamma's intense stylization at the level of image (color and Widescreen cinematography), setting (the stylized interiors), and shot selection (long-take and mobile shots) represents a departure from the stylistic codes and expectations of films about the banlieues to such an extent that it signals itself as an imitation, one that has been transplanted from the typical subjects of French art cinema into banlieue cinema. This recontextualization defamiliarizes how viewers have previously seen those spaces on screen. The point of *Girlhood* is not to offer a more "realistic" picture of the banlieues, whatever that might mean, but rather to signal that the stylization of art cinema is *also* appropriate to mediate the banlieues. Furthermore, this style can engage without contradiction with the global youth culture, including Hollywood genres and American music, that is so important to the communities that live there. Finally, Sciamma's blend of space and style can create the sense of fun and exhilaration that popular genres regularly produce.

CONCLUSION

Within the context of France, art cinema is arguably a universal mode in terms of the cultural prestige it holds for domestic audiences and its international reach in terms of how the French industry represents itself abroad at film festivals and through film exports. It is possible to argue that while the codes of art cinema may well function as a universal in France, they are in fact a particularistic position defined by historically white, male filmmakers from the New Wave on. However, part of my argument here has been that through *Girlhood*, Sciamma rearticulates the codes of art cinema as universal from her own positionality as a queer woman filmmaker through a film about Black adolescence in the suburbs. Substantiating the point about queerness would require an examination of Sciamma's other films and make an already long chapter even longer, so I leave this work to others. My claim here is that to represent the banlieues in part through the codes of auteurist art cinema and to promote *Girlhood* as an art film on the elite festival circuit is to characterize the film's Black women characters as universal. By bringing this kind of stylization—and the cultural reputation that surrounds it—to cinematic representations of the banlieues, *Girlhood* rearticulates the universal in relation to Blackness, gender, and sexuality.

However, this rearticulation of the universal with respect to Blackness comes with a price. As I discussed earlier, Niang has taken *Girlhood* to task for the ways a white filmmaker is presenting her own exoticizing relationship to Black women. Niang also notes that *Girldhood*'s reception in the Franco-African community was negative, both for the film's reproduction of stereotypes and for the way it once again gives the camera to a white person, rather than allowing Black people to represent their own experience (2019, 251). In a related vein, Frances Smith has argued that the violence in the film activates moral panic discourses in viewers who do not live in the banlieues. Smith contends that the price to pay for a move toward the universal is paradoxically a move away from Frenchness. She points to the fact that the generic, non-French aspects of many spaces in the film—the architecturally modern La Défense, the nondescript hotel room, or the mall—serve to downplay the girls' Frenchness, a move that also downplays their Blackness (2020, 51–52, 74).

These accusations of inauthenticity carry some weight, and indeed, some specificity is lost when visibility is sought through external cultural traditions, though it is equally important to ask what is gained. In my view, these critics misrecognize the extent to which *Girlhood* participates in the general phenomenon I have been analyzing in this book, namely how American cinema and mass culture have offered ways for French minorities to become visible in a color-blind universalist culture. *Girlhood* entered production not long after Barack Obama began his second term, and rightly or wrongly, this was a moment when American conceptions of Blackness could still potentially serve to bring visibility to France's Black communities. There are limits to this strategy that I will take up in the book's conclusion, and these limits are signaled by the uneasy reception *Girlhood* found among some critics and especially members of France's Black communities. However, I contend that far from reflecting a break with *La Haine*'s use of American mass culture to make the multiculture of France's suburbs visible, *Girlhood* is better understood as an update of it nearly twenty years later, one appropriate to Obama's America, in which images of a postracial society, false though they were, had significant global appeal. Whereas *La Haine* sought to break with the conventions of French art cinema, at least in terms of how Kassovitz promoted the film, Sciamma embraces the conventions of art cinema. *Girlhood* suggests that different images of France's banlieues can be brought to the screen and that not all of these images are antithetical to genre codes. American mass culture and Hollywood film genres are essential to both Kassovitz's and Sciamma's undertakings. What differs is how the films' production histories and promotional paratexts positioned them with respect to the auteurist and art cinema framework that still structures the French film industry. The embrace of art cinema in the case of *Girlhood* created among some viewers expectations of realism that the film could not ultimately pay off, at least in part because Sciamma did not wish to do so. Furthermore, *Girlhood*'s engagement with American genres and mass culture enabled international circulation at the same time that it partially occluded local histories of race and colonialism, as we saw was also the case with *La Haine*. However, it is fair to say that the high degree of visibility and discussion the film generated within and beyond the Hexagon about France's multiculture means that Sciamma's strategy to universalize Black adolescence was in part successful.

Sciamma is not exceptional for how her filmmaking career and a film like *Girlhood* scramble a rigid opposition between genre cinema and art film even as they reveal the enduring influence of art film and auteurism on the education, production, distribution, and reception structures that continue to condition the French media industry. Women filmmakers in France have long refused to accept a rigid opposition between genre and art or between mainstream success and auteurist authenticity. I briefly mentioned the examples of *All That Glitters* and *Leila*, suggesting that *Girlhood* is not the only example of a banlieue film by a woman filmmaker that mixes genres to bring the thematic concerns of women-oriented genres to the suburbs on screen, thus challenging the masculine orientation that has characterized so many films about the banlieues. *Girlhood* also makes the case for one of the main claims I have been making throughout this book, namely that the politics of style cannot be separated from the politics of production in films about the banlieues. As new generations of young filmmakers emerge from France's official state film school and from the other alternative education institutions and initiatives I have discussed throughout this book, this trend of not accepting a rigid opposition between genre and art seems likely to continue and expand beyond just women filmmakers, especially in films by and about France's suburban communities. In the conclusion, I will take up the question of genre and multiculture in the French media industry in the context of French television and streaming platforms, another disruptive force in the French industry with important consequences for how French mainstream media can seek to rearticulate the universal.

NOTES

1. For the purposes of this chapter, I will use the terms *art cinema* and *auteur* and *auteurism* somewhat interchangeably while recognizing that they are not equivalent. The ideology of the auteur and auteurism, particularly salient in a country such as France, is one way films are granted membership in the category of art cinema, though it is by no means the only way.

2. Cited in F. Smith 2020, 8.

3. Harrod argues that an important aspect of Lila and Ely's failure to pass as cosmopolitan, upper-middle-class women is their inability to understand and speak English (2015a, 153).

4. For more information about the musical tradition in France, see Conway 2013, 37.

5. McNeill theorizes how the song "Diamonds" does this through Anna Everett's notion of digitextuality, whose resonance "opens out into the global space of social, digital media, a space inhabited by both the fictional characters and the viewers of the film" (McNeill 2018, 328).

CONCLUSION

Genre, Inclusive Casting, and the
Suburbs in the Age of SVoD

I BEGAN WRITING THIS BOOK during the Barack Obama years in the United States, and the corpus of films it examines largely dates from 2000 to 2016. As I write this conclusion on the other side of the Donald Trump administration and the Black Lives Matter protests against police violence that took place during the COVID-19 pandemic, it is clear to me that any lessons about multiculture that the United States might have had to offer the rest of the world have profoundly changed. The heady sense of a post-racial United States that circulated in France, Europe, and other parts of the world during the years of the Obama presidency came crashing down with Trump's election and the racially motivated violence in Charlottesville, Virginia, in 2017. I want to be clear here, in the conclusion, that this book never set out to argue that the United States' race-conscious, differentialist model of multiculture should be adopted by other countries, if indeed any book could ever hope to prove such a claim. I began this project from the more modest belief shared by many Anglo-American scholars working in French studies that openly discussing questions of race, ethnicity, and multiculture in the realms of French culture, art, and public policy allows for systemic racism to be addressed. Not mentioning them under the French model of color-blind universalism makes resolving the problems of systemic racism more difficult—of that at least I am still convinced.

The tenor of the transatlantic conversations around race and multiculture have certainly changed as President Emmanuel Macron and others in France have grown bolder in criticizing the United States' differentialist understanding of identity following two instances of domestic terrorism in France in late 2020. These include the beheading of Samuel Paty, a schoolteacher in Paris's suburbs, on October 16, 2020, after he showed the Charlie Hebdo caricatures of Mohammed to his students, and the murder of three churchgoers two weeks later, on October 29, by a Tunisian man. In the wake of the beheading, Macron took on a securitarian tone as he argued in a key speech that France had to fight against what he termed "Islamic separatism," anathema in a country whose values emphasize unity and universalism. The suburbs figured in Macron's speech as one of the main symptoms of the problem: "We have ourselves constructed our own kind of separatism. It's those of our [suburban] neighborhoods [*nos quartiers*]. It's the ghettoization that our Republic, initially with the best intentions in the world, allowed to happen. In other words, we've had a policy. It has sometimes been called a policy of immigration [*politique du peuplement*], but we have constructed a concentration of misery and difficulties, and we know this full well. We have often concentrated populations as a function of their origins and social milieus" (*Le Monde* 2020).

Interestingly, the problem Macron diagnoses is not systematic racism in French society, but rather that suburban neighborhoods have developed relatively homogenous populations around a single racial or ethnic identity category. His use of the word *ghettoization* channels the polemical connotations that I have discussed throughout this book and that index French fears of suburban unrest like the kind that takes place in the US urban neighborhoods defined around racial identity. In this rhetorical move, Macron suggests that the problem is not French universalism itself, but rather that France has knowingly allowed its suburbs to move over time toward the racial and ethnic identity models of American differentialism. In terms of solutions, he proposed better education, increased social services, and more mixing of social classes and identity groups to diminish racial, ethnic, or religious identity as meaningful social categories (*Le Monde* 2020). In other words, Macron doubles down on French universalism.

Perhaps unsurprisingly, the French government's circling of the wagons around secularism and universalism led journalists in the United States and the United Kingdom to suggest that France's universalist policies might only be making social divisions worse by failing to address the root causes of what *Washington Post* journalist James McAuley termed "the alienation of French Muslims," which include the social inequalities that many French Muslims face in the suburbs (*New York Times* 2020; McAuley 2020). Macron then went on the offensive, accusing international journalists of legitimizing the violence of domestic terrorism. *New York Times* journalist Ben Smith received a personal call from Macron, who accused American media of "bias," an "obsession with racism," and an inability to understand what *laïcité* (secularism) means for France (2020). From this position, anyone who brings attention to issues of race inequality or Islamophobia in France risks being written off as complicit with spectacular instances of domestic terrorism. Scholars and researchers have also found themselves targeted by this kind of thinking. Professors in France, especially those in the social sciences, have been alternately accused of Islamophobia and Islamophilia, and Jean-Michel Blanquer, the French minister of education, went so far as to characterize universities as spaces where radical "Islamic-leftism" takes root in France's youth (Le Nevé 2020; *Le Monde* 2021). These debates would take much more space to unpack, but they do prove that the issues raised in this book around French universalism and suburban spaces continue to be vitally important. Hopefully some time will allow for rational conversation again, but I am aware that this book risks being seen as yet another instance of a racism-obsessed American academic blaming France for not taking an American view of things.[1]

Such charges would, in my opinion at least, be unfair, but they point to a potential problem with using American cultural references and theoretical frameworks to advocate for French minority communities within the country's universalist political culture. Mame Fatou-Niang explains that employing American cultural references to bring visibility to racial inequality in France poses the significant risk of what she calls "foreignization" (*étrangéisation*). Niang notes the extent to which Black communities in France often use English-language concepts or refer to African American intellectuals such as bell hooks or Kimberlé Crenshaw on social media. Such references, Niang argues, "can be detrimental to understanding Black lives in France or even participate in the marginalization of experiences and voices perceived to belong to a foreign cultural sphere" (2019, 299). The risk is especially great, in Niang's view, because the Black community does not exist politically in France in the way that it does in the United States.

Niang's point is well-taken, but the argument of this book has not concerned the adoption of US critical race theory or US analyses of systemic racism to the French context. The argument here has been that attempts to create a popular, genre-based cinema in France has significantly depended on the increased visibility of suburban characters and spaces in mainstream cinema during the early decades of the twenty-first century. That the films considered in this book reworked American genres is in part because the French film industry does not have the same history of genre filmmaking and industrial structures to support it. It may well be that the social agendas of the mainstream B movies and perhaps TV series of the future might more powerfully reach domestic audiences by looking to French cultural references, rather than American, as a means of bringing visibility to contemporary multiculture in France. The turn to Hollywood genres in the films considered in this book is best understood as a strategic yet provisional development that partially enabled the emergence of racially and culturally diverse mainstream French genre films about the suburbs. The Hollywood connections are not necessary for its continuation. Indeed, the most widely mediatized and financially successful banlieue film as of this book's writing, Ladj Ly's *Les Misérables* (2019), is a crime film that employs the codes of cinematic genre in conjunction with a French literary reference, Victor Hugo's well-known nineteenth-century novel. Ly should be a familiar figure after my discussion in chapter 4 of the Kourtrajmé collective that he helped found with Kim Chapiron, Romain Gavras, and others.

Les Misérables tells the story of three police officers working in an anti-crime unit in the suburban neighborhood of Montfermeil in the eastern suburbs of Paris, the place where Hugo wrote the novel that frames the film. A young boy, Issa, steals a lion cub from a traveling circus, and police efforts to locate the boy and the cub escalate into a *bavure*, an instance of police misconduct in which one of the officers shoots Issa in the face with a nonlethal riot gun. The police officers try to cover it up with some help from local leaders, and in the film's final ten minutes, the neighborhood's youth, led by Issa, band together to attack the leaders and the police officers in vengeance. The influence of Mathieu Kassovitz's *La Haine* (1995) on Ly's film should be clear even from this short summary; it mixes police misconduct, confrontation with suburban youth, and crime film tropes with the codes of banlieue cinema. The film echoes *La Haine*'s emphasis on toxic masculinity among police officers, and it also mimics Kassovitz's use of lyrical aerial shots of project housing by having one young character film the bavure in Montfermeil using his drone.

However, there are also important differences, most significantly in terms of how *Les Misérables* relates to US cultural references. Like Kassovitz, Ly begins his film with a credits sequence intercut with a sequence that mixes history and fiction. Unlike in *La Haine*, the focus is not on street protests against police violence, but on street celebrations following France's win of the 2018 World Cup. Ly begins in the suburban neighborhood of Montfermeil as young Issa walks to the bus station with a French tricolor flag strapped to his back. He meets friends, and they all head into the city to watch the match and then celebrate. As Issa and his friends move through the crowds gathered in the streets of Paris and in bars, French flags are everywhere. There is one Algerian flag at a prominent moment in the opening sequence, but overall, French flags overwhelm the mise-en-scène through sheer quantity, and contemporary French multiculture is emphasized by scenes of Black, Brown, and white people celebrating together and even singing the French national anthem, "La Marseillaise." Once the

CONCLUSION 279

Figure 7.1 French flags and World Cup celebrations in the streets in *Les Misérables*, 2019.

French team's victory is assured, Issa and his friends celebrate in the streets with everyone else, creating images not of street protests or violence, but jubilant revelry. Even though the rest of the film will explore police discrimination and local responses to it, *Les Misérables* sets a very different tone in the beginning from *La Haine*: the suburban youth are French, and they do not need US culture to mark their identity or belonging.

In contrast to *La Haine*'s incessant references to US culture in its visual design, dialogue, soundtrack choices, and genre codes, such references in *Les Misérables* are almost nonexistent. There is one moment when viewers see a Mohammed Ali tracing on the wall of Salah's kebab restaurant, and there are some T-shirts with English phrases, but that is the extent of it. What is more, Ly's film looks not to the urban cinema and gangster films of Spike Lee or Martin Scorsese for its crime tropes, but rather it loosely adapts one of France's best-known novels. It thus rejects the "strangeification" Niang identifies as a risk of US references in works that engage with the banlieues. By eschewing US references in favor of a novel that could not be more French, *Les Misérables* the film calls attention to the existence of a popular literary tradition in France that can be activated in a mainstream French genre film that examines questions of class and multiculture together. The popular appeal of genre does not recede, as the film is a crime film, but it changes how Hugo's novel has been adapted in the past. Instead of being a highbrow heritage film, *Les Misérables* is an intense, present-day suburban crime film. Ly's *Les Misérables* is thus distinct from the project of Abdellatif Kechiche's *Games of Love and Chance* (*L'Esquive*, 2003), which sought to elevate suburban youth by having them perform French classical theater. By contrast, Ly's *Les Misérables* brings Hugo's novel down, as it were, to the French suburbs and to French crime cinema. Many of the films analyzed in this book looked to the US genre traditions for ways to make mainstream films about suburban communities, thus challenging the dominance of art cinema and the sociological and documentary traditions that have historically represented these communities. Ly's *Les Misérables* preserves the mainstream, genre-oriented appeal of the films discussed in this book, but it does so with French cultural references. Though it is impossible to predict the future, I think Ly's film may represent a new direction in the phenomenon I have analyzed in this book, and it remains to be seen if the next decade's French B movies—that is, mainstream banlieue genre films—will continue in this vein.

Les Misérables is also significant for the ways that it brings attention to the importance of genre and inclusive casting for international distribution, especially through streaming platforms. *Les Misérables* was released theatrically in France, but Amazon Prime purchased the international distribution rights for its subscription-based video-on-demand (SVoD) streaming service. This release strategy is not a new development, but rather an attempt on Amazon Prime's part to imitate what Netflix has been doing in France with respect to casting diversity, genre-oriented media, and suburban multiculture since its first French film acquisition at the Cannes Film Festival in 2016, Houda Benyamina's *Divines* (Goodfellow 2016).

Netflix was the first among the US-based streaming platforms, which also include Amazon, Hulu, or Apple, to move into localized media production as way of expanding its subscriber base globally (Scarlata et al. 2021, 2–3). Netflix and other SVoD services are unique in that they want the media they acquire or commission to be simultaneously successful at the local level but also to work in the many global markets in which the service operates. They do not see a disconnect between the embeddedness of media in a local culture and the global circulation of media. While not every local reference makes it into the final cut of a series or film, Kelly Luegenbiehl, Netflix's vice president of international originals, has said that "the more local that we are and the more specific we are, the more universal we actually are" (quoted in Scarlata et al. 2021, 4). Local embeddedness that later supports global circulation can take many forms, including famous directors, adaptations or remakes of well-known local series or novels, recognizable locations, use of genre codes, and inclusive casting.

Netflix is known for its desire to curate a racially, culturally, and linguistically diverse catalog. In a 2016 event in Seoul, Ted Sarandos, the co-CEO and chief content officer of Netflix, explained the reason for this commitment by noting that half of Netflix's subscriber base is outside the United States and that international subscribers are essential for the company's growth. In his view, being a global SVoD service requires a different approach to casting, one that favors inclusivity and diversity. Sarandos suggested that while traditional Hollywood studios have experienced ongoing difficulties moving toward more inclusive representation in front of and behind the cameras, Netflix has an edge in this regard, and the company will only seek to become more diverse and inclusive in the casting of its series and films (Hyo-won 2016). While Netflix's casting practices support the fight against systemic racism in the United States, they also make economic sense for a streaming company that releases content simultaneously in many markets around the world, not all of which are countries in which white communities are the dominant social group. This had led many of Netflix's original series to the practice of what media scholars Alexa Scarlata, Ramon Lobato, and Stuart Cunningham call "circulation-based casting"—that is, a diverse and international cast of actors who are well-known in different local markets and who often speak in accented English or another language (2021, 9).

Netflix also demonstrates its commitment to local markets by opening offices in other countries and investing in local filmmakers. In the case of France, Netflix opened an office in Paris in January 2020, after several years of tense relations with the French media industry and its protectionist policies. The relationship between Netflix and the French industry got off to a bad start in 2017, when the Cannes Film Festival refused to screen Netflix-produced films in competition because they had never been released in theaters (Cousin 2018, 1–5). Netflix chose not to release those films in French theaters because that would have locked them into France's strict media chronology, which regulates the timeline when a film can be commercialized in secondary media markets, such as disc rentals, private pay-channel broadcast, public television broadcast, and, of course, video-on-demand (VOD) release. The media chronology was changed in 2018, and for SVoD companies that choose not to give some portion of their subscriber fees back to local French media production and state aid structures, VOD release cannot take place until nearly three years after a film has been released in French theaters. For those "virtuous" platforms that do give back, the delay is only fifteen months (Piquard and Bougon 2018).[2] For some, even this somewhat reformed media chronology is an antiquated leftover from a different media ecology. For others, it is a way to protect the theatrical experience and encourage television producers to invest in domestic film production.[3] While these debates have not entirely been resolved as of the time of this writing, Netflix's opening of a French office at least bodes well for the company's desire to work within the local media ecosystem.

Netflix's worldwide hit French-language series, *Lupin* (2021), starring Omar Sy, reflects a commitment to local production in terms of casting and language. The series adapts one of the most famous early twentieth-century series of popular novels about a Parisian gentleman thief named Arsène Lupin. Like Ly's choice of source material in *Les Misérables*, *Lupin* also suggests that French popular culture can represent contemporary multiculture and reach international audiences. The Netflix series was made in French, rather than English, and the casting choices reflect a diverse blend of talent: the actors in this series include two familiar French actresses, Clotilde Hesme and Nicole Garcia, known for their roles in several mainstream and auteurist films; Vincent Londez, who is best known for his television work in French crime series; Fargass Assandé, an Ivorian actor and director known for his theatrical work; and Sy, whose star persona I analyzed in chapter 5. These casting choices represent at attempt to appeal to different types of domestic and international viewers who watch the kinds of media the actors are known for. The series itself also mixes many different genres from one episode to the next, cycling freely among drama, action, and comedy. Netflix's adaptation has Sy's character, Assane Diop, move between disguises drawn from high and low culture and from different social classes. In the first episode, he poses as a janitor who works at the Louvre. Later in the same episode, the character re-disguises himself as a tech millionaire, closer in his class markers to the high-society gentleman thief of Maurice Leblanc's original novels. Diop's real social class is unclear; his talent for theft has given him access to wealth, and his education makes it possible for him to imitate members of the upper class. Yet the character never forgets his roots as the son of a Senegalese immigrant, and his main desire is to get justice (or perhaps revenge) for his father, who was wronged by his upper-class employers. The use of Sy as an everyman who belongs to every social class (and therefore none of them) not only tracks with Netflix's commitment to diverse casting that I discussed earlier but it also aligns the series with Sy's international star persona—a persona that largely rests on the film *Intouchables* (2011), also viewable on Netflix, in which he played a Senegalese immigrant character who successfully learned the social codes of the upper classes. By Netflix's own account, *Lupin* was widely successful, with seventy million subscribers from all different markets watching the series in the twenty-eight days that followed its drop. In an interview, Sy reports receiving fan messages from as far away as Brazil and Colombia (Roxborough 2021).

The push to casting diversity we find in the commissioned series of Netflix and other SVoD services is felt differently when an SVoD platform acquires locally produced films. When commissioning a series, Netflix or Amazon

Figure 7.2 *Lupin*'s (2021) first episode contains an early sequence set in the French suburbs.

has direct control over casting, talent, and the production of the series. Yet we nevertheless see a similar commitment to diversity in terms of the kinds of local films or media that an SVoD platform acquires for its catalog. In the case of Netflix, the first film that it acquired at the Cannes Film Festival was Benyamina's *Divines*, which I analyzed in chapter 3. This was simply the first in a series of acquisitions that focused on youth, multiculture, and genre-oriented media. Netflix later acquired another banlieue film, *Street Flow* (*Banlieusards*, 2019), by Leïla Sy and Kery James, and subsequent acquisitions and commissions have favored stories about diverse young characters growing up in France, including *Brother* (*Mon frère*, 2019) and *Shéhérazade* (2018). This strategy backfired somewhat with the release of *Cuties* (*Mignonnes*, 2020), a film that purported to criticize the hypersexualization of young girls through the story of a French-Senegalese girl who grew up in a Muslim family and joined a hip hop dance troupe. However, some US critics accused Maïmouna Doucouré's film of doing exactly what it set out to criticize, namely sexualizing its young actresses.[4] Netflix has also sought to bring suburban stand-up comedian Fary and French Moroccan comedian and actor Gad Elmaleh into the US stand-up comedy special format to mixed results in *Gad Gone Wild* (2017), *Gad Elmaleh: American Dream* (2018), and *Fary: Hexagone* (2020). Finally, Netflix has invested heavily in genre-oriented media in its French series commissions, including no fewer than three French horror series: *Marianne* (2019), *Mortel* (2019, set in the suburbs), and *Vampires* (2020, starring Oulaya Amamra from *Divines*). Taken together, these commissioned series and acquired films reflect a different image of France's contemporary multiculture back to the country's own domestic subscriber as well as to Netflix's international viewers.

This commitment to representing a diverse contemporary France extends beyond casting and commissioning to include investments in film education. Netflix has partnered with French film schools and other film education programs to assure that an increasingly diverse set of young filmmakers have access to training and production facilities. These efforts include establishing an eleven-month residency for young students from disadvantaged backgrounds at France's state film school La Fémis and partnering with Houda Benyamina's 1000 Visages Association, which seeks to democratize the French industry through training and production support for filmmakers from the suburbs (Goodfellow 2020). These and other efforts to expand who can make films in France confirm that in the case of films about the French suburbs, questions of representation must be considered alongside industrial considerations of media production and education. In the context of Netflix's efforts on the ground in France, Amazon Prime's acquisition of the rights to distribute Ly's *Les Misérables* internationally seems to be an attempt to catch up to what Netflix has already begun to build in France. It is possible to read Netflix and Amazon's casting and commissioning practices as simply part of the contemporary logic of neoliberalism applied to the media industry—that is, that globally recognizable genres and inclusive casting practices are required to capture new markets and accrue capital. Yet, I would not be so quick to reject out of hand all these new films, series, and distribution deals as somehow complicit or inauthentic. Rather, I suggest we need to examine each instance closely, as I have endeavored to do with the films and filmmakers considered in this book.

This book has shown that the French suburbs and their attendant multiculture are often easily able to be received as universal on international screens, even if this is not always true in the domestic marketplace. Genre codes that are familiar internationally, like those of the genres examined in this book, function in popular French banlieue films like media interfaces that enable local contextual situations to translate to viewers outside France. The pairing of genre codes and the French suburbs is simultaneously part of an ongoing process to rearticulate the universal within the borders of a color-blind universalist republic and an element in a strategy on the part of French filmmakers and now SVoD services to "universalize" local French media exports in global markets. The globalized codes of Hollywood genres and the visibility of casting diversity are two key interfaces through which local French media circulate in global markets. This book's analysis of the imbrication of genre filmmaking and the suburbs in French films from the 1990s on—what I have been calling French B movies—indicates that the content acquisition and commissioning trends of the SVoD era is not a new phenomenon. Rather, it is merely the latest development in a media production trend that began with Kassovitz's *La Haine* and continues into the present in a film like Ly's *Les Misérables*. Most importantly, it is not a foreign import or an American imposition; it is an inclusive production strategy that French filmmakers from many different backgrounds and at many different production scales have already been exploring themselves for the past several decades.

NOTES

1. Smith discusses this issue with respect to American journalists (2020).

2. For a discussion of the limits of the previous media chronology, which was put into place in 2009, see Harari Baulieu 2018, 87. See also the presentation on the French Ministry of Culture's website, https://www.culture.gouv.fr/Actualites/Chronologie-des-medias-un-nouvel-equilibre (accessed March 23, 2022).

3. For a discussion of the different points of view on the question of SVoD platforms and media chronology, see Cousin 2018, 116–124; Harari Baulieu 2018, 86–92.

4. For an overview of the controversy and an account of the film's divergent reception in France and the United States, see Tillet 2020.

BIBLIOGRAPHY

Adi, Yasmina, Didier Daeninckx, François Gèze, Guy Seligman, Pascal Blanchard, Mohammed Harbi, Gilles Manceron, Gilbert Meynier, Gérard Noiriel, Jean-Pierre Peyroulou, Benjamin Stora, and Sylvie Thénault. 2010. "Le film *Hors-la-loi* de Rachid Bouchareb: les guerres de mémoires sont de retour." *Le Monde*, May 5, 2010. https://www.lemonde.fr/festival-de-cannes/article/2010/05/05/le-film-hors-la-loi-de-rachid-bouchareb-les-guerres-de-memoires-sont-de-retour-par-yasmina-adi-didier-daeninckx_1346714_766360.html.

Aftab, Kaleem. 2010. "Dangerous Liaisons: Why Jacques Audiard Is the French Scorsese." *The Independent*, January 21, 2010. http://www.independent.co.uk/arts-entertainment/films/features/dangerous-liaisons-why-jacques-audiard-is-the-french-scorsese-1874047.html.

Alexander, Karen. 1995. "*La Haine*." *Vertigo* 1 (5): 42–47.

Allucineazioni. 2009. "*Martyrs*. Pascal Laugier: amo giocare con lo spettatore. E dedico il mio film a Dario Argento." *Allucineazioninterviste* (blog), June 12, 2009. https://allucineazioninterviste.wordpress.com/2009/06/12/martyrs-pascal-laugier-amo-giocare-con-lo-spettatore-e-dedico-il-mio-film-a-dario-argento/.

Altman, Rick. 1999. *Film/Genre*. London: British Film Institute.

Amadou, Ouma. 2016. "Constructing (Black) Girlhood: Americanization, Assimilation, and Ambivalence." *Film Matters* 7 (3): 5–11.

Andrew, Dudley. 1995. *Mists of Regret: Culture and Sensibility in Classic French Film*. Princeton, NJ: Princeton University Press.

———. 2010. *What Cinema Is!* Malden, MA: John Wiley and Sons.

Andrews, David. 2014. *Theorizing Art Cinemas: Foreign, Cult, Avant-Garde, and Beyond*. Austin: University of Texas Press.

Appadurai, Arjun. 1996. *Modernity at Large: Cultural Dimensions of Globalization*. Minneapolis: University of Minnesota Press.

Arbrun, Clément. 2016. "'T'as du clitoris!': la bande annonce euphorisante de *Divines*." *Les Inrockuptibles*, July 8, 2016. https://www.lesinrocks.com/inrocks.tv/bande-annonce-euphorisante-de-divines/.

Archer, Neil. 2010. "Virtual Poaching and Altered Space: Reading Parkour in French Visual Culture." *Modern & Contemporary France* 18 (1): 93–107.

Artz, B. Lee. 1998. "Hegemony in Black and White: Interracial Buddy Films and the New Racism." In *Cultural Diversity and the US Media*, edited by Yahya R. Kamalipour and Theresa Carilli, 67–78. Albany: State University of New York Press.

Austin, Guy. 2003. *Stars in Modern French Film*. New York: Bloomsbury.

———. 2015. "Contemporary French Horror Cinema: From Absence to Embodied Presence." In *A Companion to Contemporary French Cinema*, edited by Alistair Fox, Michel Marie, Raphaëlle Moine, and Hilary Radner, 275–288. Malden, MA: Wiley-Blackwell.

Badiou, Alain. 2009. *Saint Paul: The Foundation of Universalism*. Translated by Ray Brassier. Stanford, CA: Stanford University Press.

Baecque, Antoine de. 2002. "Messier, mots à maux." *Libération*, January 2, 2002. https://www.liberation.fr/culture/2002/01/02/messier-mots-a-maux_389168/.

Bahr, Lindsey. 2015. "International Star Omar Sy Learns the Language of Hollywood." *Associated Press*, July 24, 2015. https://apnews.com/article/4bc4fobf92ff48cba28927505682d2c3.

Balibar, Étienne. 2004. *We, the People of Europe?: Reflections on Transnational Citizenship*. Translated by James Swenson. Princeton, NJ: Princeton University Press.

———. 2014. *Equaliberty: Political Essays*. Translated by James Ingram. Durham, NC: Duke University Press.

———. 2016. *Des universels: essais et conférences*. Paris: Galilée.

Barlet, Olivier. 2010. "Hors-la-loi." *Africultures* (blog), May 25, 2010. http://africultures.com/hors-la-loi-9500/.

———. 2013. "Y a-t-il un cinéma noir français?" *Africultures* 92–93 (2): 342–353.

Barnett, Emily. 2006. "L'esprit Fémis." *Les Inrockuptibles*, January 1, 2006. https://www.lesinrocks.com/cinema/films-a-l-affiche/lesprit-femis/.

Bataille, Georges. 1989. *The Tears of Eros*. Translated by Peter Connor. San Francisco: City Lights Books.

Bazin, André. 1971. *What Is Cinema?* Translated by Hugh Gray. Vol. 2. Berkeley: University of California Press.

———. 1998. *Le Cinéma français de la Libération à la Nouvelle Vague (1945–1958)*. Paris: Cahiers du cinéma.

———. 2009. *What Is Cinema?* Translated by Timothy Barnard. Montreal: Caboose.

Becattini, Edoardo. 2009. "*Martyrs*: per una metafisica della sofferenza." MYmovies.it, June 10, 2009. https://www.mymovies.it/cinemanews/2009/10098/.

Beier, Lars-Olav. 2010. "The Pariah from Paris: Luc Besson's Cité du cinéma to be France's Largest Studio." *Der Spiegel Online*, October 5, 2010. http://www

.spiegel.de/international/zeitgeist/the-pariah-from-paris-luc-besson-s-cite-du
-cinema-to-be-france-s-largest-studio-a-720244.html.

Belhaj Kacem, Mehdi. 2006. *La psychose française: les banlieues, le ban de la république*. Paris: Gallimard.

Belpêche, Stéphanie. 2006. "Ce diable de Vincent Cassel." *Le Journal du Dimanche*, January 29, 2006.

Belting, Hans. 2014. *An Anthropology of Images: Picture, Medium, Body*. Translated by Thomas Dunlap. Princeton, NJ: Princeton University Press.

Beltran, Mary, Corey Creekmur, Sangita Gopal, and Raphael Raphael. 2013. "A Panel Discussion on Transnational Stardom." In *Transnational Stardom: International Celebrity in Film and Popular Culture*, edited by Russell Meeuf and Raphael Raphael, 19–28. New York: Palgrave Macmillan.

Bergfelder, Tim. 2005. "National, Transnational or Supranational Cinema? Rethinking European Film Studies." *Media, Culture & Society* 27 (3): 315–331.

Besson, Luc. 2015. "Aidez cette jeunesse qui ne demande qu'à faire partie de la société." *Le Monde*, January 10, 2015. https://www.lemonde.fr/police-justice/article/2015/01/10/reparons-ensemble-l-injustice-faite-a-la-jeunesse_4553440_1653578.html.

Beugnet, Martine. 2007. *Cinema and Sensation: French Film and the Art of Transgression*. Edinburgh: Edinburgh University Press.

Bey-Rozet, Maxime. 2020. "Irredeemable: Céline, Extreme Cinemas, and the Opacity of Trauma." PhD diss., University of Pittsburgh.

———. 2021. "Cycles of Death and Rebirth in Twenty-First Century French Horror." *French Screen Studies* 21 (3): 191–203.

Binet, Stéphanie. 2006a. "Les premiers films ont une énergie vitale qui se perd ensuite." *Libération*, February 1, 2006.

———. 2006b. "'Sheitan,' le diable par la queue." *Libération*, February 1, 2006.

Blanchard, Pascal, and Gilles Boëtsch. 2016. "Le retour de la 'race' dans les discours publics et scientifiques." In *Vers la guerre des identités? de la fracture coloniale à la révolution ultranationale*, edited by Pascal Blanchard, Nicolas Bancel, and Dominic Richard David Thomas, 47–58. Paris: La Découverte.

Blanchard, Sandrine. 2018. "A Saint-Denis, l'école de cinéma de Luc Besson en difficulté." *Le Monde*, July 11, 2018. https://www.lemonde.fr/cinema/article/2018/07/11/l-ecole-de-cinema-de-luc-besson-en-difficulte_5329669_3476.html.

Blatt, Ari J. 2008. "The Play's the Thing: Marivaux and the Banlieue in Abdellatif Kechiche's *L'Esquive*." *French Review: Journal of the American Association of Teachers of French* 81 (3): 516–527.

Blondeau, Romain. 2014. "T'en vois beaucoup, des films avec des Noirs?" *Les Inrockuptibles*, October 22, 2014. https://www.lesinrocks.com/cinema/ten-vois-beaucoup-films-noirs-100824-22-10-2014/.

Bloom, Peter J. 2008. *French Colonial Documentary: Mythologies of Humanitarianism*. Minneapolis: University of Minnesota Press.

Bogle, Donald. 2001. *Toms, Coons, Mulattoes, Mammies, and Bucks: An Interpretive History of Blacks in American Films*. 4th ed. New York: Bloomsbury.

Bonnefoy, Nawal. 2015. "Omar Sy à la conquête d'Hollywood." *BFMTV*, November 4, 2015. http://people.bfmtv.com/cinema/omar-sy-a-la-conquete-d-hollywood-927680.html.

Bordun, Troy Michael. 2017. "The End of Extreme Cinema Studies." *Canadian Review of Comparative Literature* 44 (1): 122–136.

Bordwell, David. 2002. "The Art Cinema as a Mode of Film Practice." In *The European Cinema Reader*, edited by Catherine Fowler, 94–102. New York: Routledge.

———. 2006. *The Way Hollywood Tells It: Story and Style in Modern Movies*. Berkeley: University of California Press.

Bouchareb, Rachid. 2010a. *Outside the Law*. Blu-ray Disc. London: Optimum Home Entertainment.

———. 2010b. "Rachid Bouchareb: 'Tous des hors-la-loi.'" *L'Humanité*, September 22, 2010. https://www.humanite.fr/rachid-bouchareb-tous-des-hors-la-loi.

Bourdieu, Pierre. 1984. *Distinction: A Social Critique of the Judgement of Taste*. Translated by Richard Nice. Cambridge, MA: Harvard University Press.

Bourdon, Gwenael. 2018. "Saint-Denis: rentrée partielle à l'école de la Cité du cinéma." *Le Parisien*, October 8, 2018. http://www.leparisien.fr/seine-saint-denis-93/saint-denis-rentree-partielle-a-l-ecole-de-la-cite-du-cinema-08-10-2018-7914054.php.

Bret, David. 1988. *The Piaf Legend*. London: Robson.

Brick, Emily. 2012. "*Baise-Moi* and the French Rape-Revenge Films." In *European Nightmares: Horror Cinema in Europe Since 1945*, edited by Patricia Allmer, Emily Brick, and David Huxley, 93–102. New York: Columbia University Press.

Britton, Andrew. 1991. "Stars and Genre." In *Stardom: Industry of Desire*, edited by Christine Gledhill, 198–206. New York: Routledge.

Bronner, Luc. 2008a. "Luc Besson: La banlieue est un trésor." *Le Monde*, September 29, 2008. https://www.lemonde.fr/societe/article/2008/09/29/luc-besson-la-banlieue-est-un-tresor_1100740_3224.html.

———. 2008b. "En banlieue, la volonté est forte de 'taper à la porte de la République.'" *Le Monde*, November 6, 2008. http://www.lemonde.fr/politique/article/2008/11/06/en-banlieue-la-volonte-est-forte-de-taper-a-la-porte-de-la-republique_1115644_823448.html.

Brook, Timothy, Jérôme Bourgon, and Gregory Blue. 2008. *Death by a Thousand Cuts*. Cambridge, MA: Harvard University Press.

Buchsbaum, Jonathan. 2017. *Exception Taken: How France Has Defied Hollywood's New World Order*. New York: Columbia University Press.

Burgoyne, Robert. 2010. "Bare Life and Sovereignty in *Gladiator*." In *The Epic Film in World Culture*, edited by Robert Burgoyne, 82–97. New York: Routledge.

Burke, Carolyn. 2011. *No Regrets: The Life of Edith Piaf*. New York: Knopf.

Butler, Judith. 1999. *Gender Trouble: Feminism and the Subversion of Identity*. New York: Routledge.
Canal+ Cinéma. 2016. *Houda Benyamina, Caméra d'Or, Divines, Cannes 2016*. YouTube video, May 24, 2016. https://www.youtube.com/watch?v=6IYm9AcVDhw.
Carpentier, Laurent. 2016. "Houda Benyamina: 'Quand on ouvre sa gueule, on change le monde.'" *Le Monde*, August 30, 2016. https://www.lemonde.fr/festival/article/2016/08/30/houda-benyamina-quand-on-ouvre-sa-gueule-on-change-le-monde_4989704_3476.html.
Carrière, Christophe. 2003. "Europa Corp. sur tous les fronts." *L'Express*, April 3, 2003. http://www.lexpress.fr/culture/cinema/europa-corp-sur-tous-les-fronts_651127.html.
———. 2011. "Mais qu'arrive-t-il au cinéma français?" *L'Express*, November 30, 2011. http://www.lexpress.fr/culture/cinema/the-artist-intouchables-polisse-le-cinema-francais-en-pleine-forme-enquete_1056697.html.
Catanese, Brandi Wilkins. 2011. *The Problem of the Color[blind]: Racial Transgression and the Politics of Black Performance*. Ann Arbor: University of Michigan Press.
Catroux, Sébastien. 2004. "Le cinéma caricature notre génération." *Le Parisien*, November 10, 2004. http://www.leparisien.fr/loisirs-et-spectacles/le-cinema-caricature-notre-generation-10-11-2004-2005443765.php.
Certeau, Michel de. 1984. *The Practice of Everyday Life*. Translated by Steven Rendall. Berkeley: University of California Press.
———. 1990. *L'invention du quotidien, tome 1: Arts de faire*. Paris: Gallimard.
Chabrol, Dominique. 2001. *Michel Audiard: "c'est du brutal."* Paris: Flammarion.
Charles, Bénédicte. 2009. "Banlieues: Luc Besson fait tout à partir de lien." *Marianne*, June 26, 2009. http://www.marianne2.fr/Banlieues-Luc-Besson-fait-tout-a-partir-de-lien_a181164.html.
Chebil, Mehdi. 2012. "Luc Besson inaugure Hollywood-sur-Seine." *France 24*, September 22, 2012. http://www.france24.com/fr/20120921-images-luc-besson-inaugure-hollywood-seine-cite-du-cinema-seine-saint-denis-photo-diaporama-studios.
Cho, Michelle. 2015. "Genre, Translation, and Transnational Cinema: Kim Jee-Woon's *The Good, the Bad, the Weird*." *Cinema Journal* 54 (3): 44–68.
Chombart de Lauwe, Paul-Henry. 2008. "Périphérie des villes et crise de civilisation." In *Banlieues: une anthologie*, edited by Thierry Paquot, 107–119. Lausanne, CH: Presses polytechniques et universitaires romandes.
Christensen, Jerome. 2008. "Studio Authorship, Corporate Art." In *Auteurs and Authorship: A Film Reader*, edited by Barry Keith Grant, 167–179. Malden, MA: Blackwell.
Clover, Carol J. 1993. *Men, Women, and Chain Saws: Gender in the Modern Horror Film*. Princeton, NJ: Princeton University Press.

CNC (Centre national du cinéma et de l'image animée). 2018. "Le CNC crée un soutien pour les films de genre." May 2, 2018. https://www.cnc.fr/cinema/communiques-de-presse/le-cnc-cree-un-soutien-pour-les-films-de-genre_571601.

———. 2019. "Appel à projets de films de genre." December 13, 2019. https://www.cnc.fr/professionnels/aides-et-financements/cinema/production/appel-a-projets-de-films-de-genre_563143.

Cohen, Jeffrey Jerome. 1996. *Monster Theory: Reading Culture*. Minneapolis: University of Minnesota Press.

Cole, Catherine M. 2012. "American Ghetto Parties and Ghanaian Concert Parties: A Transnational Perspective on Blackface." In *Burnt Cork: Traditions and Legacies of Blackface Minstrelsy*, edited by Stephen Johnson, 223–257. Boston: University of Massachusetts Press.

Conley, Tom, and Jenny Lefcourt. 1998. "*La Haine* and the Caméra-Graffito." *Contemporary French Civilization* 22 (2): 227–239.

Conway, Kelley. 2004. *Chanteuse in the City: The Realist Singer in French Film*. Berkeley: University of California Press.

———. 2013. "France." In *The International Film Musical*, edited by Corey K. Creekmur and Linda Y. Mokdad, 29–44. Edinburgh: Edinburgh University Press.

Coquery-Vidrovitch, Catherine. 2010. "Le tropisme de l'université française face aux *postcolonial studies*." In *Ruptures postcoloniales: les nouveaux visages de la société française*, edited by Nicolas Bancel, Florence Bernault, Pascal Blanchard, and Valérie Amiraux, 317–327. Paris: Découverte.

Cousin, Capucine. 2018. *NETFLIX & Cie: Les coulisses d'une (r)évolution*. Paris: Armand Colin.

Crisp, Colin. 1997. *The Classic French Cinema: 1930–1960*. Bloomington: Indiana University Press.

Crofts, Stephen. 2006. "Reconceptualising National Cinema/s." In *Theorising National Cinema*, edited by Valentina Vitali and Paul Willemen, 44–58. London: BFI.

Crosland, Margaret. 2002. *A Cry from the Heart: The Life of Edith Piaf*. London: Arcadia.

Cupers, Kenny. 2014. *The Social Project: Housing Postwar France*. Minneapolis: University of Minnesota Press.

Cusset, François. 2006. *French theory: Foucault, Derrida, Deleuze & Cie et les mutations de la vie intellectuelle aux États-Unis*. Paris: Découverte.

Dailymotion. 2011. "'Toi, moi, les autres': Interview d'Audrey Estrougo." https://www.dailymotion.com/video/xh5zpo.

Danan, Martine. 2006. "National and Postnational French Cinema." In *Theorising National Cinema*, edited by Valentina Vitali and Paul Willemen, 172–185. London: BFI.

Delbecq, Françoise. 2014. "Karidja Touré dans *Bande de filles*: elle a tout d'une grande!" *Elle*, October 21, 2014. http://www.elle.fr/Loisirs/Cinema/News/Karidja-Toure-dans-Bande-de-filles-elle-a-tout-d-une-grande-2851740.

Deleau, Quentin. 2016. "Quels sont les genres du cinéma français qui s'exportent le mieux?" Paris: Unifrance. https://medias.unifrance.org/medias/125/97/156029/piece_jointe/the-top-selling-french-film-genres-in-foreign-markets.pdf.

Delorme, Stéphane. 2015. "La loi de la jungle: Audiard & co." *Cahiers du cinéma*, September 2015.

Deplasse, Hervé. 2003. "Besson m'a tué mon cinéma." *Brazil* 4 (January 2003).

Diao, Claire. 2014. "Pour une reconnaissance des métiers artistiques: Entretien avec Isabelle Agid et Catherine Jean-Joseph." *Africultures* (blog), September 22, 2014. http://africultures.com/pour-une-reconnaissance-des-metiers-artistiques-12435/.

———. 2017. *Double Vague: Le nouveau souffle du cinéma français*. Vauvert: Au Diable Vauvert.

Direct Matin. 2012. "Intouchables: Canal+ prépare le terrain pour les Oscars." December 24, 2012. http://www.directmatin.fr/culture/2012-12-20/intouchables-canal-prepare-le-terrain-pour-les-oscars-296736.

Djament-Tran, Géraldine. 2015. "L'actualisation du patrimoine face à la métropolisation. Le cas de Saint-Denis." *L'Information géographique* 79 (2): 41–54.

Dobson, Julia. 2016a. "Audiard A–Z." *Studies in French Cinema* 16 (3): 262–268.

———. 2016b. "Jacques Audiard: Twenty-First Century Auteur." *Studies in French Cinema* 16 (3): 187–189.

———. 2017. "Dis-Locations: Mapping the Banlieue." In *Filmurbia: Screening the Suburbs*, edited by David Forrest, Graeme Harper, and Jonathan Rayner, 29–48. London: Palgrave Macmillan.

Donadey, Anne. 2014. "'Wars of Memory': On Rachid Bouchareb's *Hors la loi*." *Esprit Createur* 54 (4): 15–26.

Donalson, Melvin Burke. 2006. *Masculinity in the Interracial Buddy Film*. Jefferson, NC: McFarland.

Doughty, Ruth, and Kate Griffiths. 2006. "Racial Reflection: *La Haine* and the Art of Borrowing." *Studies in European Cinema* 3 (2): 117–127.

Dozol, Vincent. 2015. "Céline Sciamma: 'Dans *Bande de filles*, la banlieue est vue comme un lieu de fiction.'" France-Amérique, January 30, 2015. https://france-amerique.com/en/celine-sciamma-dans-bande-de-filles-la-banlieue-est-vue-comme-un-lieu-de-fiction/.

Dryef, Zineb. 2019. "Céline Sciamma, la femme qui filmait les femmes." *Le Monde*, August 30, 2019. https://www.lemonde.fr/m-le-mag/article/2019/08/30/celine-sciamma-la-femme-qui-filmait-les-femmes_5504326_4500055.html.

Dubois, Régis. 2013. "Ce que le succès d'*Intouchables* révèle sur la situation des acteurs Noirs en France." *Africultures* 92–93 (2): 366–371.

———. 2016. *Les Noirs dans le cinéma français*. La Madeleine: LettMotif.
Dunlop, Jérôme. 2019. *Les 100 mots de la géographie*. Paris: Presses Universitaires de France.
Dupaire, François. 2011. "*Intouchables* n'est pas plus raciste que le *Flic de Beverly Hills*." Atlantico, December 11, 2011. http://www.atlantico.fr/decryptage/intouchables-racisme-noirs-cinema-variety-francois-durpaire-242817.html.
Ďurovičová, Nataša. 2010. "Preface." In *World Cinemas, Transnational Perspectives*, edited by Nataša Ďurovičová and Kathleen E. Newman, ix–xv. New York: Routledge.
Dyer, Richard. 1998. *Stars*. New ed. London: BFI.
———. 2003. *Heavenly Bodies: Film Stars and Society*. London: Routledge.
———. 2006. *Pastiche*. New York: Routledge.
Eeckhout, Laetitia van. 2008. "Des manuels encore un peu trop blancs." *Le Monde*, November 16, 2008. http://www.lemonde.fr/societe/article/2008/11/06/des-manuels-encore-un-peu-trop-blancs_1115559_3224.html.
Etchegoin, Marie-France. 2017. "Les démons de Mathieu Kassovitz." *Le Monde*, September 15, 2017. https://www.lemonde.fr/m-actu/article/2017/09/15/les-demons-de-mathieu-kassovitz_5186279_4497186.html.
EuropaCorp and Magnolia Pictures. 2004. "*District B13* Press Kit." http://www.magpictures.com/films/District13/db13notesfinal.doc.
Ezra, Elizabeth, and Terry Rowden. 2006. "What Is Transnational Cinema?" In *Transnational Cinema: The Film Reader*, edited by Elizabeth Ezra and Terry Rowden, 1–12. New York: Routledge.
Fabre, Clarisse. 2013. "Convention collective du cinéma: 'ça tourne!' (mal)." *Le Monde*, February 4, 2013. https://www.lemonde.fr/culture/article/2013/02/04/convention-collective-du-cinema-ca-tourne-mal_1826780_3246.html.
———. 2014. "A Cannes, une bande de filles et de garçons sortis de la Fémis." *Le Monde*, May 22, 2014. https://www.lemonde.fr/festival-de-cannes/article/2014/05/22/a-cannes-une-bande-de-filles-et-de-garcons-sortis-de-la-femis_4423402_766360.html.
Fevret, Christian, and Jean-Marc Lalanne. 2007. "*La Graine et le Mulet*: entretien avec Abdellatif Kechiche." *Les Inrockuptibles*, December 11, 2007. https://www.lesinrocks.com/cinema/entretien-abdellatif-kechiche-la-graine-et-le-mulet-1207-7827-11-12-2007/.
Fiddler, Michael. 2013. "Playing *Funny Games* in *The Last House on the Left*: The Uncanny and the 'Home Invasion' Genre." *Crime, Media, Culture* 9 (3): 281–299.
Finkielkraut, Alain. 1987. *La défaite de la pensée*. Paris: Gallimard.
———. 2015. *L'identité malheureuse*. Paris: Gallimard.
Fişek, Emine. 2018. "Rethinking *Intouchables*: Race and Performance in Contemporary France." *French Cultural Studies* 29 (2): 190–205.
Fourcaut, Annie. 2000. "Aux origines du film de banlieue: Les banlieusards au cinéma (1930–1980)." *Sociétés & Représentations* 8 (1): 113.

———. 2008. "Pour en finir avec la banlieue." In *Banlieues: une anthologie*, edited by Thierry Paquot, 121–131. Lausanne, CH: Presses polytechniques et universitaires romandes.

Fox, Alistair. 2015. "Auteurism, Personal Cinema, and the Fémis Generation: The Case of François Ozon." In *A Companion to Contemporary French Cinema*, edited by Alistair Fox, Michel Marie, Raphaëlle Moine, and Hilary Radner, 508–565. Malden, MA: Wiley-Blackwell.

Fredman, Sandra. 2016. "Substantive Equality Revisited." *International Journal of Constitutional Law* 14 (3): 712–738.

French Embassy US. 2018. "On @TheDailyShow, @Trevornoah Called the @FrenchTeam's World Cup Win an 'African Victory.' Read Ambassador @GerardAraud's Response." Tweet. *@franceintheus* (blog), July 18, 2018. https://twitter.com/franceintheus/status/1019691552384352257.

Frey, Mattias. 2016. *Extreme Cinema: The Transgressive Rhetoric of Today's Art Film Culture*. New Brunswick, NJ: Rutgers University Press.

Fumaroli, Marc. 1992. *L'Etat culturel: une religion moderne*. Paris: Fallois.

Gaertner, Julien. 2012. "Une nouvelle 'Nouvelle Vague'?. Comment l'immigration maghrébine régénère le cinéma français (1970–2012)." *Hommes & migrations. Revue française de référence sur les dynamiques migratoires* 1297 (May): 6–19.

Gallot, Clémentine. 2014. "Où sont les jeunes comédiennes noires aujourd'hui en France?" *ChEEk Magazine*, October 20, 2014. https://www.lesinrocks.com/cheek/les-jeunes-comediennes-noires-aujourdhui-en-france-315346-20-10-2014/.

Garbarz, Franck, and Dominique Martinez. 2014. "Entretien avec Céline Sciamma." *Positif*, October 2014.

Gava, Annie. 2014. "Like Diamonds in the Sky: Entretien avec Céline Sciamma." *Zibeline*, June 2, 2014. https://www.journalzibeline.fr/programme/like-diamonds-in-the-sky/.

Genty, Jean-René. 2011. "Images, lettres et sons." *Vingtième Siecle. Revue d'histoire* 110 (2): 161–170.

Germain, Félix, and Silyane Larcher, eds. 2018. *Black French Women and the Struggle for Equality, 1848–2016*. Lincoln: University of Nebraska Press.

Gimello-Mesplomb, Frédéric. 2012. "Produire un film de genre fantastique en France, entre hétérotopie artistique et quête de légitimité: Analyse d'une tension identitaire dans le champ de la création." In *Les cinéastes français à l'épreuve du genre fantastique: socioanalyse d'une production artistique*, edited by Frédéric Gimello-Mesplomb, 9–69. Paris: L'Harmattan.

Girard, Laurence. 2008. "Une télévision française toujours trop pâle." *Le Monde*, November 12, 2008. http://www.lemonde.fr/actualite-medias/article/2008/11/12/une-television-francaise-toujours-trop-pale_1117564_3236.html.

Girard, René. 2011. *Mensonge romantique et vérité romanesque*. Paris: Fayard.

Gleich, Joshua. 2012. "Auteur, Mogul, Transporter: Luc Besson as Twenty-First-Century Zanuck." *New Review of Film and Television Studies* 10 (2): 246–268.

Goldszal, Clémentine. 2019. "Kourtrajmé, la petite famille du cinéma." *Le Monde*, November 8, 2019. https://www.lemonde.fr/m-le-mag/article/2019/11/08/kourtrajme-la-petite-famille-du-cinema_6018507_4500055.html.

Gonzalès, Paule. 2013. "EuropaCorp mise sur la télé et les salles de cinéma." *Le Figaro Bourse*, January 13, 2013. http://bourse.lefigaro.fr/indices-actions/actu-conseils/europacorp-mise-sur-la-tele-et-les-salles-de-cinema-342426.

Goodfellow, Melanie. 2016. "Is Netflix's *Divines* Acquisition a Game-Changer for Indie Film?" *Screen Daily*, November 8, 2016. https://www.screendaily.com/is-netflixs-divines-acquisition-a-game-changer-for-indie-film/5110974.article.

———. 2020. "Netflix Woos France with New Shows and Investment as Paris Office Opens." *Screen International*, January 17, 2020.

Goreau-Ponceaud, Anthony. 2011. "L'immigration sri lankaise en France: Trajectoires, contours et perspectives." *Hommes & Migrations* 1291 (May): 26–39.

Grant, Barry Keith. 2012. "Experience and Meaning in Genre Films." In *Film Genre Reader IV*, edited by Barry Keith Grant, 133–147. Austin: University of Texas Press.

Grassin, Sophie. 2014. "*Bande de filles* montre des Blacks à l'écran et ça nous rend fières." *L'Obs*, May 16, 2014. https://www.nouvelobs.com/cinema/festival-de-cannes/20140516.OBS7394/bande-de-filles-montre-des-blacks-a-l-ecran-et-ca-nous-rend-fieres.html.

Green, Amy M. 2011. "The French Horror Film Martyrs and the Destruction, Defilement, and Neutering of the Female Form." *Journal of Popular Film & Television* 39 (1): 20–28.

Greenhouse, Emily. 2013. "Did a Director Push Too Far?" *New Yorker*, October 24, 2013. https://www.newyorker.com/culture/culture-desk/did-a-director-push-too-far.

Grossberg, Lawrence. 2010. "Affect's Future: Rediscovering the Virtual in the Actual." In *The Affect Theory Reader*, edited by Melissa Gregg and Gregory J. Seigworth, 309–338. Durham, NC: Duke University Press.

Guerrero, Ed. 1993. "The Black Image in Protective Custody: Hollywood's Biracial Buddy Films of the Eighties." In *Black American Cinema*, edited by Manthia Diawara, 237–246. New York: Routledge.

———. 2012. "*Bamboozled*: In the Mirror of Abjection." In *Contemporary Black American Cinema: Race, Gender and Sexuality at the Movies*, edited by Mia Mask, 109–127. New York: Routledge.

Guerrin, Michel. 2016. "Luc Besson made in France." *Le Monde*, February 19, 2016. https://www.lemonde.fr/idees/article/2016/02/19/luc-besson-made-in-france_4868410_3232.html.

Guyonnet, Paul. 2018. "Victoire de 'l'Afrique' au Mondial: Trevor Noah répond aux critiques et joue l'apaisement." *Huffington Post* (blog), July 19, 2018. https://www.huffingtonpost.fr/2018/07/18/victoire-de-lafrique-au-mondial-trevor-noah-repond-aux-critiques-et-joue-lapaisement_a_23485087/.

Hacker, Violaine. 2011. "Cultiver la créativité, corollaire de la diversité culturelle européenne." *Géoéconomie* 58 (3): 31–44.

Haddad, Léonard. 2015. "Jacques Audiard: 'Je n'ai pas envie de me défendre de la fin de *Dheepan*.'" *Première*, September 14, 2015. http://www.premiere.fr/Cinema/News-Cinema/Jacques-Audiard-Je-nai-pas-envie-de-me-defendre-de-la-fin-de-Dheepan.

Haggins, Bambi. 2007. *Laughing Mad: The Black Comic Persona in Post-Soul America*. New Brunswick, NJ: Rutgers University Press.

Halle, Randall. 2014. *The Europeanization of Cinema: Interzones and Imaginative Communities*. Urbana-Champaign: University of Illinois Press.

Harari Baulieu, Simone. 2018. *La chaîne et le réseau: pourquoi Internet ne va pas tuer la télévision*. Paris: L'Observatoire.

Hargreaves, Alec G. 2007. *Multi-Ethnic France: Immigration, Politics, Culture and Society*. 2nd ed. London: Routledge.

Harrod, Mary. 2015a. "Franglais, Anglais and Contemporary French Comedy." In *The Europeanness of European Cinema: Identity, Meaning, Globalization*, edited by Mary Harrod, Mariana Liz, and Alissa Timoshkina, 145–158. London: I. B. Tauris.

———. 2015b. *From France with Love: Gender and Identity in French Romantic Comedy*. London: Bloomsbury.

———. 2016. "Girlfriends, Postfeminism, and the European Chick-Flick in France." In *International Cinema and the Girl: Local Issues, Transnational Contexts*, edited by Fiona Handyside and Kate Taylor-Jones, 35–47. New York: Palgrave Macmillan.

Hay, Jean-Christian. 2013. "Léa Seydoux assume ses propos sur Abdellatif Kechiche." *Gala*, October 7, 2013. https://www.gala.fr/l_actu/news_de_stars/lea_seydoux_assume_ses_propos_sur_abdellatif_kechiche_299309.

Haylett Bryan, Alice. 2021. "Inhospitable Landscapes: Contemporary French Horror Cinema, Immigration and Identity." *French Screen Studies* 21 (3): 224–238.

Hayward, Susan. 1993. *French National Cinema*. New York: Routledge.

Hayward, Susan, and Phil Powrie, eds. 2006. *Essays on Luc Besson: Master of Spectacle*. Manchester: Manchester University Press.

Heinich, Nathalie. 2008. "Malaises dans la culture: quand rien ne va plus de soi." *Le Débat* 152 (5): 58–74.

Henley, Paul. 2009. *The Adventure of the Real: Jean Rouch and the Craft of Ethnographic Cinema*. Chicago: University of Chicago Press.

Henni, Jamal. 2020. "La Caisse des dépôts renonce à réclamer 45 millions d'euros à Luc Besson." *Capital*, July 29, 2020. https://www.capital.fr/entreprises-marches/la-caisse-des-depots-fait-une-croix-sur-une-grosse-dette-due-par-luc-besson-1376589.

Higbee, Will. 2006. *Mathieu Kassovitz*. Manchester: Manchester University Press.

———. 2009. "Displaced Audio: Exploring Soundscapes in Maghrebi-French Film-Making." *Studies in French Cinema* 9 (3): 225–241.

———. 2013. *Post-Beur Cinema: North African Émigré and Maghrebi-French Filmmaking in France since 2000*. Edinburgh: Edinburgh University Press.

Higbee, Will, and Song Hwee Lim. 2010. "Concepts of Transnational Cinema: Towards a Critical Transnationalism in Film Studies." *Transnational Cinemas* 1 (1): 7–21.

Higgins, Dalton. 2009. *Hip Hop World*. Berkeley: Groundwood Books.

Higson, Andrew. 2006. "The Limiting Imagination of National Cinema." In *Transnational Cinema: The Film Reader*, edited by Elizabeth Ezra and Terry Rowden, 15–25. New York: Routledge.

Hill Collins, Patricia, and Sirma Bilge. 2020. *Intersectionality*. 2nd ed. Medford, MA: Polity Press.

Hill, Constance. 2010. *Tap Dancing America: A Cultural History*. New York: Oxford University Press.

Hill, John. 1992. "The Issue of National Cinema and British Film Production." In *New Questions of British Cinema*, edited by Duncan J. Petrie, 10–21. London: BFI.

Hills, Matt. 2005. *The Pleasures of Horror*. New York: Continuum.

Hjort, Mette. 2010. "On the Plurality of Cinematic Transnationalism." In *World Cinemas, Transnational Perspectives*, edited by Nataša Ďurovičová and Kathleen E. Newman, 12–33. New York: Routledge.

Holden, Stephen. 2012. "*Intouchables* in Rendez-Vous With French Cinema Festival." *New York Times*, February 29, 2012. http://www.nytimes.com/2012/03/01/movies/intouchables-in-rendez-vous-with-french-cinema-festival.html.

Horeck, Tanya, and Tina Kendall, eds. 2013. *The New Extremism in Cinema: From France to Europe*. Edinburgh: Edinburgh University Press.

Hunt, Leon. 2008. "Asiaphilia, Asianisation and the Gatekeeper Auteur: Quentin Tarantino and Luc Besson." In *East Asian Cinemas: Exploring Transnational Connections on Film*, edited by Leon Hunt and Leung Wing-Fai, 220–236. New York: I. B. Tauris.

Hyo-won, Lee. 2016. "Ted Sarandos: Netflix's Global Platform Will Bring Diversity to Hollywood." *Hollywood Reporter*, June 30, 2016. https://www.hollywoodreporter.com/news/ted-%20sarandos-netflixs-global-platform-907558.

Iordanova, Dina. 2010. "'Rise of the Rest:' Globalizing Epic Cinema." In *The Epic Film in World Culture*, edited by Robert Burgoyne, 101–123. New York: Routledge.

Irbah, Djamel Eddine. 2010. *Algérie—Hors La Loi—Conférence de Presse (4 sur 4)*. YouTube video, May 21, 2010. https://www.youtube.com/watch?v=zMT7cJd9bOE.

Jaafar, Ali. 2011. "Algeria Rising." *Sight and Sound*, June 2011.

Jeamart, Audrey. 2007. "Mater Tenebrarum." *Critikat*, June 12, 2007. https://www.critikat.com/panorama/entretien/julien-maury-et-alexandre-bustillo/.

Jein, Gillian. 2016. "Suburbia, Interrupted: Street Art and the Politics of Place in the Paris *Banlieues*." In *Cities Interrupted: Visual Culture and Urban Space*, edited by Shirley Jordan and Christoph Lindner, 87–104. New York: Bloomsbury.

Johnson, Stephen. 2012. "Introduction: The Persistence of Blackface and the Minstrel Tradition." In *Burnt Cork: Traditions and Legacies of Blackface Minstrelsy*, edited by Stephen Johnson, 1–17. Boston: University of Massachusetts Press.

Jørholt, Eva. 2016. "To Remember in Order to Be Able to Forget: Rachid Bouchareb's *Outside the Law* and the Construction of a New, Inclusive French National Identity." *Studies in European Cinema* 13 (1): 50–63.

Kaganski, Serge. 2004. "*L'Esquive*, un film subtil et électrisant." *Les Inrockuptibles*, January 7, 2004. https://www.lesinrocks.com/cinema/lesquive-2-24020-07-01-2004/.

———. 2009. "Jacques Audiard: 'Je n'ai pas fait un film sur la politique carcérale.'" *Les Inrockuptibles*, August 26, 2009. http://www.lesinrocks.com/2009/08/26/cinema/actualite-cinema/jacques-audiard-je-nai-pas-fait-un-film-sur-la-politique-carcerale-1138044/.

Kaganski, Serge, Samuel Blumenfeld, and Mathieu Kassovitz. 1995. "Le Clash: Matthieu Kassovitz." *Les Inrockuptibles*, May 31, 1995. http://www.lesinrocks.com/1995/05/31/cinema/actualite-cinema/le-clash-matthieu-kassovitz-11222121/.

Kealhofer-Kemp, Leslie. 2017. "Unpacking the Success and Criticisms of *Intouchables* (2011)." In *French Cultural Studies for the Twenty-First Century*, edited by Masha Belenky, Kathryn Kleppinger, and Anne O'Neil-Henry, 155–170. Newark: University of Delaware Press.

Kerner, Aaron Michael, and Jonathan L. Knapp. 2016. *Extreme Cinema: Affective Strategies in Transnational Media*. Edinburgh: Edinburgh University Press.

Kilani, Mondher. 2014. *Pour un universalisme critique: essai d'anthropologie du contemporain*. Paris: La Découverte.

King, Gemma. 2014. "The Power of the Treacherous Interpreter: Multilingualism in Jacques Audiard's *Un Prophète*." *Linguistica Antverpiensia, New Series—Themes in Translation Studies* 13:78–92.

Kirszbaum, Thomas, ed. 2015. *En finir avec les banlieues? Le désenchantement de la politique de la ville*. La Tour d'Aigues: L'Aube.

Köksal, Özlem, and Ipek A. Çelik Rappas. 2019. "A Hand That Holds a Machete." *Third Text* 33 (2): 256–267.

Konstantarakos, Myrto. 1999. "Which Mapping of the City? *La Haine* (Kassovitz, 1995) and the Cinéma de Banlieue." In *French Cinema in the 1990s: Continuity and Difference: Essays*, edited by Phil Powrie, 160–171. New York: Oxford University Press.

Krämer, Peter. 2005. *The New Hollywood: From Bonnie and Clyde to Star Wars*. London: Wallflower.

Laclau, Ernesto. 2007. *Emancipation(s)*. London: Verso.

La Fémis. n.d. "Céline Sciamma." Lafemis.fr. Accessed October 8, 2020. https://www.femis.fr/index.php?page=fiche_ancien&id_ancien=4984.

Lagrange, Hugues. 2013. *Le déni des cultures*. Paris: Seuil.

Lalanne, Jean-Marc. 2004. "*L'Esquive*: entretien avec Abdellatif Kechiche." *Les Inrockuptibles*, January 7, 2004. https://www.lesinrocks.com/cinema/entretien-abdellatif-kechiche-lesquive-0104-7820-07-01-2004/.

———. 2014. "Céline Sciamma: 'Je vois les personnages de *Bande de filles* comme des activistes.'" *Les Inrockuptibles*, October 22, 2014. https://www.lesinrocks.com/cinema/celine-sciamma-107153-22-10-2014/.

Lalanne, Jean-Marc, and Olivier Joyard. 2018. "Spielberg, le cinéma français et son projet de série: la grande interview de Mathieu Kassovitz." *Les Inrockuptibles*, October 16, 2018. https://www.lesinrocks.com/series/mathieu-kassovitz-dans-la-legende-va-tous-mourir-cest-genial-178633-16-10-2018/.

Lapeyronnie, Didier, and Laurent Courtois. 2008. *Ghetto urbain: ségrégation, violence, pauvreté en France aujourd'hui*. Paris: Laffont.

Lauro, Sarah Juliet. 2015. *The Transatlantic Zombie: Slavery, Rebellion, and Living Death*. New Brunswick, NJ: Rutgers University Press.

Lebovics, Herman. 1995. *Mona Lisa's Escort: Andre Malraux and the Reinvention of French Culture*. Ithaca, NY: Cornell University Press.

———. 2011. "Cultural Policy." In *The French Republic: History, Values, Debates*, edited by Edward Berenson, Vincent Duclert, and Christophe Prochasson, 344–354. Ithaca, NY: Cornell University Press.

Le Figaro. 2008. "Des voitures brûlées privent Montfermeil de Travolta et de Besson." October 14, 2008. http://www.lefigaro.fr/actualite-france/2008/10/14/01016-20081014ARTFIG00534-des-voitures-brulees-privent-montfermeil-de-travolta-et-de-besson-.php.

Le Guilcher, Geoffrey. 2016. *Luc Besson, l'homme qui voulait être aimé: la biographie non autorisée*. Paris: Flammarion.

Lemercier, Fabien. 2013. "*Bande de filles*: Céline Sciamma boucle sa trilogie." Cineuropa, July 16, 2013. https://cineuropa.org/fr/newsdetail/241774/.

———. 2014. "Entretien: Eric Lagesse, Vendeur, Pyramide International." Cineuropa, May 7, 2014. https://cineuropa.org/fr/interview/256749/.

Le Monde. 2005. "Nicolas Sarkozy continue de vilipender 'racailles et voyous.'" November 11, 2005. https://www.lemonde.fr/societe/article/2005/11/11/nicolas-sarkozy-persiste-et-signe-contre-les-racailles_709112_3224.html.

———. 2013. "Des techniciens racontent le tournage difficile de *La Vie d'Adèle*." May 24, 2013. https://www.lemonde.fr/festival-de-cannes/article/2013/05/24/des-techniciens-racontent-le-tournage-de-la-vie-d-adele_3417150_766360.html.

———. 2018a. "L'enquête sur la Cité du cinéma de Luc Besson classée sans suite." May 11, 2018.

———. 2018b. "Le réalisateur Luc Besson visé par une plainte pour viol." May 19, 2018. https://www.lemonde.fr/police-justice/article/2018/05/19/le-realisateur-luc-besson-vise-par-une-plainte-pour-viol_5301800_1653578.html.

———. 2018c. "Une école de cinéma gratuite lancée en Seine-Saint-Denis par le collectif Kourtrajmé." October 4, 2018. https://www.lemonde.fr/campus/article/2018/10/04/une-ecole-de-cinema-gratuite-lancee-en-seine-saint-denis-par-le-collectif-kourtrajme_5364720_4401467.html.

———. 2019. "L'enquête pour viol visant Luc Besson classée sans suite." February 25, 2019. https://www.lemonde.fr/societe/article/2019/02/25/l-enquete-pour-viol-visant-luc-besson-classee-sans-suite_5428081_3224.html.

———. 2020. "'Notre République a laissé faire la ghettoïsation'; extraits du discours de Macron." October 2, 2020. https://www.lemonde.fr/politique/article/2020/10/02/notre-republique-a-laisse-faire-la-ghettoisation-extraits-du-discours-de-macron_6054575_823448.html.

———. 2021. "Tribune: L'affaire des professeurs accusés d'islamophobie 'est une illustration des pressions politiques et économiques qui s'exercent sur l'université.'" March 17, 2021. https://www.lemonde.fr/idees/article/2021/03/17/professeurs-accuses-d-islamophobie-cette-affaire-est-une-illustration-des-pressions-politiques-et-economiques-qui-s-exercent-sur-l-universite_6073388_3232.html.

Le Nevé, Soazig. 2020. "Polémique après les propos de Jean-Michel Blanquer sur 'l'islamo-gauchisme' à l'université." *Le Monde*, October 23, 2020. https://www.lemonde.fr/societe/article/2020/10/23/polemique-apres-les-propos-de-jean-michel-blanquer-sur-l-islamo-gauchisme-a-l-universite_6057164_3224.html.

Lentin, Alana, and Gavan Titley. 2011. *The Crises of Multiculturalism: Racism in a Neoliberal Age*. New York: Zed Books.

L'Express. 2008. "Montfermeil privé de Besson et Travolta?" October 14, 2008. http://www.lexpress.fr/actualite/societe/montfermeil-prive-de-besson-et-travolta_590436.html.

Lhamon, W. T., Jr. 1998. *Raising Cain: Blackface Performance from Jim Crow to Hip Hop*. Cambridge, MA: Harvard University Press.

———. 2012. "Turning around Jim Crow." In *Burnt Cork: Traditions and Legacies of Blackface Minstrelsy*, edited by Stephen Johnson, 18–50. Boston: University of Massachusetts Press.

Lherm, Sophie. 2010. "Rachid Bouchareb affronte le tabou sur la guerre d'Algérie." *Télérama*, May 9, 2010. https://www.telerama.fr/cinema/rachid-bouchareb-affronte-le-tabou-sur-la-guerre-d-algerie,55718.php.

Libération. 2012. "*Intouchables*, film non-anglophone le plus rentable au monde." March 23, 2012. https://www.liberation.fr/cinema/2012/03/23/intouchables-film-non-anglophone-le-plus-rentable-au-monde_805296/.

Libiot, Éric. 2015. "Jacques Audiard: 'Je ne sais plus à quoi sert le cinéma.'" *L'Express*, August 25, 2015. http://www.lexpress.fr/culture/cinema/videos-jacques-audiard-je-ne-sais-plus-a-quoi-sert-le-cinema_1708195.html.

Loichot, Valérie. 2012. "Creolizing Barack Obama." In *American Creoles: The Francophone Caribbean and the American South*, edited by Martin Munro and Celia Britton, 77–94. Liverpool: Liverpool University Press.

Loison, Guillaume. 2012a. "*Intouchables*, d'Eric Toledano et Olivier Nakache." *L'Obs*, January 13, 2012. http://tempsreel.nouvelobs.com/cinema/20120113.CIN0375/intouchables-d-eric-toledano-et-olivier-nakache.html.

———. 2012b. "Omar Sy rejoint l'agence d'acteurs la plus prestigieuse de Hollywood." *L'Obs*, December 5, 2012. http://tempsreel.nouvelobs.com/cinema/20121205.CIN6094/omar-sy-rejoint-l-agence-d-acteurs-la-plus-prestigieuse-de-hollywood.html.

Looseley, David. 1995. *The Politics of Fun: Cultural Policy and Debate in Contemporary France*. Washington, DC: Berg.

———. 2003. *Popular Music in Contemporary France: Authenticity, Politics, Debate*. New York: Berg.

Lott, Eric. 2013. *Love and Theft: Blackface Minstrelsy and the American Working Class*. New York: Oxford University Press.

Loustalot, Ghislain. 2006. "A l'occasion de la sortie d'*Angèle A*, les confessions de Luc B." *Première*, January 2006.

Lowenstein, Adam. 2015. "Feminine Horror: The Embodied Surrealism of *In My Skin*." In *The Dread of Difference: Gender and the Horror Film*, edited by Barry Keith Grant, 2nd ed., 470–487. Austin: University of Texas Press.

Lübecker, Nikolaj. 2015. *The Feel-Bad Film*. Edinburgh: Edinburgh University Press.

Mack, Mehammed Amadeus. 2017. *Sexagon: Muslims, France, and the Sexualization of National Culture*. New York: Fordham University Press.

Mandelbaum, Jacques. 2009. "Jacques Audiard: 'Le cinéma sert à certifier le réel.'" *Le Monde*, July 30, 2009. http://www.lemonde.fr/cinema/article/2009/07/30/jacques-audiard-le-cinema-sert-a-certifier-le-reel_1224207_3476.html.

Maniglier, Patrice. 2016. "L'universel contrarié." *Critique* 833 (October): 772–788.

Marshall, Bill. 2010. "Running across the Rooves of Empire: Parkour and the Postcolonial City." *Modern & Contemporary France* 18 (2): 157–173.

Martin, Angela. 2008. "Refocusing Authorship in Women's Filmmaking." In *Auteurs and Authorship: A Film Reader*, edited by Barry Keith Grant, 127–134. Malden, MA: Blackwell.

Mauger, Gérard. 2006. *L'émeute de novembre 2005: une révolte protopolitique.* Bellecombe-en-Bauges: Croquant.

Maule, Rosanna. 2006. "Du Côté d'Europa, via Asia: The 'post-Hollywood' Besson." In *The Films of Luc Besson: Master of Spectacle*, 23–41. Manchester: Manchester University Press.

Maurus, Véronique. 2008. "Appeler un Noir un Noir." *Le Monde*, November 15, 2008. http://www.lemonde.fr/idees/article/2008/11/15/appeler-un-noir-un-noir-par-veronique-maurus_1119102_3232.html.

Mazdon, Lucy. 2001. *France on Film: Reflections on Popular French Cinema.* London: Wallflower.

Mbembe, Achille. 2010. "Faut-il provincialiser la France ?" *Politique africaine* 119:159–88.

———. 2011. "Provincializing France?" *Public Culture* 23 (1): 85–119.

McAuley, James. 2020. "Instead of Fighting Systemic Racism, France Wants to 'Reform Islam.'" *Washington Post*, October 23, 2020. https://www.washingtonpost.com/outlook/macron-france-reform-islam-paty/2020/10/23/f1a0232c-148b-11eb-bc10-40b25382f1be_story.html.

McCarren, Felicia. 2013. *French Moves: The Cultural Politics of Le Hip Hop.* New York: Oxford University Press.

McNeill, Isabelle. 2018. "'Shine Bright Like a Diamond': Music, Performance and Digitextuality in Céline Sciamma's *Bande de Filles* (2014)." *Studies in French Cinema* 18 (4): 326–340.

McPhee, Ruth. 2016. *Female Masochism in Film: Sexuality, Ethics and Aesthetics.* New York: Routledge.

Meeuf, Russell, and Raphael Raphael, eds. 2013. *Transnational Stardom: International Celebrity in Film and Popular Culture.* New York: Palgrave Macmillan.

Mellier, Denis. 2010. "Sur la dépouille des genres: Néohorreur dans le cinéma français (2003–2009)." *Cinémas: Revue d'études cinématographiques* 20 (2–3): 143–164.

Merkel, Ian. 2013. "Rachid Bouchareb's *Outside the Law*: Aesthetics and Reception in France." *Nka Journal of Contemporary African Art* 2013 (32): 62–69.

Met, Philippe. 2012. "Fantastique et horreur à la française: une (re)naissance ?" In *L'Invention d'un genre: le cinéma fantastique français ou les constructions sociales d'un objet de la cinéphilie ordinaire*, edited by Frédéric Gimello-Mesplomb, 25–46. Paris: L'Harmattan.

———. 2018. "The Banlieue Wore Black: Post-War French *Polar*, from Becker to Corneau." In *Screening the Paris Suburbs: From the Silent Era to The 1990s*, edited by Derek Schilling and Philippe Met, 10–22. Manchester: Manchester University Press.

Michael, Charlie. 2014. "Interpreting *Intouchables*: Competing Transnationalisms in Contemporary French Cinema." *SubStance* 43 (1): 123–137.

———. 2015. "Historicizing Contemporary French Blockbusters." In *A Companion to Contemporary French Cinema*, edited by Alistair Fox, Michel Marie, Raphaëlle Moine, and Hilary Radner. Malden, MA: Wiley-Blackwell.

———. 2019. *French Blockbusters: Cultural Politics of a Transnational Cinema*. Edinburgh: Edinburgh University Press.

Milleliri, Carole. 2011. "Le cinéma de banlieue: un genre instable." *Mise au point* 3 (January). http://journals.openedition.org/map/1003.

———. 2012. "La France Black-Blanc-Beur en quête d'identité: l'américanité du cinéma de banlieue." *CinémAction* 143 (June): 189–197.

Miller, Toby. 1998. "Hollywood and the World." In *The Oxford Guide to Film Studies*, edited by John Hill and Pamela Church Gibson, 371–381. New York: Oxford University Press.

Mingant, Nolwenn. 2013. "Hollywood au 21e siècle: les défis d'une industrie culturelle mondialisée." *Histoire@Politique: Politique, culture, société* 20 (2): 1–11.

Mittell, Jason. 2013. *Genre and Television: From Cop Shows to Cartoons in American Culture*. New York: Routledge.

Moine, Raphaëlle. 2015. *Les genres du cinéma*. 2nd ed. Paris: Armand Colin.

———. 2018. "Stereotypes of Class, Ethnicity and Gender in Contemporary French Popular Comedy: From *Bienvenue chez les Ch'tis* (2008) and *Intouchables* (2011) to *Qu'est-ce qu'on a fait au Bon Dieu?* (2014)." *Studies in French Cinema* 18 (1): 35–51.

Moinereau, Laurence. 1994. "Paysages de cinéma: Les figures emblématiques d'une banlieue imaginaire." *Les Cahiers de la cinémathèque* 59/60 (February): 35–46.

Momcilovic, Jérôme. 2015. "Cannes 2015 #12: les bigorneaux (bilan)." *Chronic'art* (blog), May 25, 2015. https://www.chronicart.com/cinema/cannes-201512-les-bigorneaux-bilan/.

Morales, Ed. 2018. *Latinx: The New Force in American Politics and Culture*. London: Verso.

Morel, Pierre. 2006. *District B13*. DVD. Magnolia.

Morgan, Daniel. 2016. "Where Are We?: Camera Movements and the Problem of Point of View." *New Review of Film and Television Studies* 14 (2): 222–248.

Morson, Gary Saul, and Caryl Emerson. 1990. *Mikhail Bakhtin: Creation of a Prosaics*. Stanford, CA: Stanford University Press.

Moulier Boutang, Yann. 2005. *La révolte des banlieues, ou, les habits nus de la République*. Paris: Éditions Amsterdam.

Moussa, Nedjib Sidi. 2012. "L'Histoire et la politique hors-la-loi? Reflexions autour d'un film sur des indépendantistes algériens." *French Politics, Culture & Society* 30 (3): 119–129.

Mrabet, Emna. 2016. *Le cinéma d'Abdellatif Kechiche: prémisses et devenir*. Paris: Riveneuve.

Mucchielli, Laurent, and Abderrahim Aït-Omar. 2006. "Introduction générale: Les émeutes de novembre 2005, les raisons de la colère." In *Quand les banlieues brûlent: retour sur les émeutes de novembre 2005*, edited by Véronique Le Goaziou and Laurent Mucchielli, 5–30. Paris: Découverte.

Murphy, David, and Charles Forsdick. 2010. "Réactions françaises à une perspective postcoloniale: 'retour au pays natal' ou invention anglo-saxonne ?" In *Ruptures postcoloniales: les nouveaux visages de la société française*, edited by Nicolas Bancel, Florence Bernault, Pascal Blanchard, and Valérie Amiraux, 139–148. Paris: Découverte.

Ndiaye, Pap. 2009. *La Condition noire: Essai sur une minorité française*. Paris: Gallimard.

Nelson, Rob. 2010. "*A Prophet*: The 'French Scorsese' Jacques Audiard Arrives with His '70s-Style Gangster Epic." *Miami New Times*, March 18, 2010. https://www.miaminewtimes.com/film/a-prophet-the-french-scorsese-jacques-audiard-arrives-with-his-70s-style-gangster-epic-6366777.

Nettelbeck, Colin. 2007. "Kechiche and the French Classics: Cinema as Subversion and Renewal of Tradition." *French Cultural Studies* 18 (3): 307–319.

Neuhoff, Eric. 2011. "Chaise tordante." *Le Figaro*, November 1, 2011. http://www.lefigaro.fr/cinema/2011/11/01/03002-20111101ARTFIG00519-chaise-tordante.php.

New York Times. 2020. "Responding to Terrorism in France." Editorial, December 5, 2020. https://www.nytimes.com/2020/12/04/opinion/macron-terrorism-france.html.

Niang, Mame-Fatou. 2019. *Identités françaises: Banlieues, féminités et universalisme*. Boston: Brill.

Nicolet, Vincent. 2020. "Entretien avec Xavier Gens: Hallucinations Collectives." Culturopoing, September 25, 2020. https://www.culturopoing.com/cinema/entretiens-cinema/entretien-avec-xavier-gens-hallucinations-collectives/20200925.

Noiriel, Gérard. 2016. *Chocolat: la véritable histoire d'un homme sans nom*. Paris: Bayard.

Norman, Alex. 2012. "Interview with Eric Toledano and Olivier Nakache, the Directors of Untouchable." The Digital Fix, September 21, 2012. https://www.thedigitalfix.com/film/interview-with-eric-toledano-and-olivier-nakache-the-directors-of-untouchable/.

O'Hehir, Andrew. 2012. "*The Intouchables*: Racial Comedy, French Style." Salon.com, May 22, 2012. http://www.salon.com/2012/05/22/the_intouchables_racial_comedy_french_style/.

Oliete-Aldea, Elena, Beatriz Oria, and Juan A. Tarancón. 2015. "Introduction: Questions of Transnationalism and Genre." In *Global Genres, Local Films: The Transnational Dimension of Spanish Cinema*, edited by Elena Oliete-Aldea, Beatriz Oria, and Juan A. Tarancón, 1–15. New York: Bloomsbury.

Olney, Ian. 2013. *Euro Horror: Classic European Horror Cinema in Contemporary American Culture*. Bloomington: Indiana University Press.

Oscherwitz, Dayna. 2010. *Past Forward: French Cinema and the Post-Colonial Heritage*. Carbondale: Southern Illinois University Press.

———. 2015. "Monnet Changes Everything? Capitalism, Currency and Crisis in Jacques Becker's *Touchez pas au grisbi* (1954) and Jacques Audiard's *Un prophète* (2009)." *Studies in French Cinema* 15 (3): 258–274.

O'Shaughnessy, Martin. 2007. *The New Face of Political Cinema: Commitment in French Film since 1995*. New York: Berghahn Books.

Oui, Mathieu. 2007. "L'École de la cité: un nouveau cursus cinéma pour les bacheliers." *L'Étudiant*, May 21, 2007. https://www.letudiant.fr/etudes/ecoles-specialisees/etudier-a-la-cite-du-cinema-deux-ecoles-sur-un-grand-plateau-16255/lecole-de-la-cite-un-nouveau-cursus-cinema-pour-les-bacheliers-18113.html.

Palmer, Tim. 2011. *Brutal Intimacy: Analyzing Contemporary French Cinema*. Middletown, CT: Wesleyan University Press.

Pao, Angela Chia-yi. 2010. *No Safe Spaces: Re-Casting Race, Ethnicity, and Nationality in American Theater*. Ann Arbor: University of Michigan Press.

Paquot, Thierry. 2008. "Banlieues, un singulier pluriel." In *Banlieues: une anthologie*, edited by Thierry Paquot, 1–20. Lausanne, CH: Presses polytechniques et universitaires romandes.

Pasquier, Dominique. 2007. "Les lycéens et la culture. Entretien." *Le Débat* 145 (3): 142–151.

Pember, Alice. 2020. "'Visions of Ecstasy': Resilience and Melancholy in the Musical Moments of *Bande de filles* (Céline Sciamma, 2014)." *French Screen Studies* 20 (3–4): 298–316.

Père, Olivier. 2013. "ARTE France Cinéma coproduit les prochains films de Naomi Kawase, Céline Sciamma, Benoit Jacquot et Miguel Gomes." *Olivier Père* (blog), June 14, 2013. https://www.arte.tv/sites/olivierpere/2013/06/14/arte-france-cinema-coproduit-les-prochains-films-de-naomi-kawase-celine-sciamma-benoit-jacquot-et-miguel-gomes/.

Pérez, Claude-Pierre. 2014. "'L'imaginaire': naissance, diffusion et métamorphoses d'un concept critique." *Littérature* 173 (May): 102–116.

Péron, Didier. 2001. "Yamakasi, les Robin des banlieues." *Libération*, April 5, 2001. https://www.liberation.fr/culture/2001/04/05/yamakasi-les-robin-des-banlieues_360350/.

Péron, Didier, and Elisabeth Franck-Dumas. 2014. "Céline Sciamma: 'Les grands films libèrent des territoires plutôt qu'ils ne les occupent.'" *Libération*, October

17, 2014. https://next.liberation.fr/cinema/2014/10/17/celine-sciamma-les-grands-films-liberent-des-territoires-plutot-qu-ils-ne-les-occupent_1124324.
Péron, Didier, Bruno Icher, and Julien Gester. 2014. "Entretien: 'Il faut beaucoup de films pour découvrir beaucoup de talents.'" *Libération*, May 13, 2014. http://next.liberation.fr/cinema/2014/05/13/il-faut-beaucoup-de-films-pour-decouvrir-beaucoup-de-talents_1016600.
Pettersen, David. 2015. "Echoes of Poetic Realism in Matthieu Kassovitz's *La Haine*." *Cincinnati Romance Review* 39 (Fall): 27–57.
———. 2016. *Americanism, Media and the Politics of Culture in 1930s France*. Cardiff: University of Wales Press.
———. 2021. "*Les Revenants*: Horror in France and the Tradition of the Fantastic." *French Screen Studies* 21 (3): 239–257.
Piquard, Alexandre, and François Bougon. 2018. "Chronologie des médias: bientôt des films plus récents sur tous les écrans?" *Le Monde*, March 9, 2018. https://www.lemonde.fr/economie/article/2018/03/09/chronologie-des-medias-bientot-des-films-plus-recents-sur-tous-les-ecrans_5268095_3234.html.
Pogam, Pierre-Ange Le. 2007. "EuropaCorp." *Le journal de l'ecole de Paris du management* 67 (5): 31–37.
Poirrier, Philippe. 2008. "Une éphémère (re)politisation du champ culturel. Politique culturelle et débat public en France lors des élections de 2002." *Territoires contemporains* 1 (June). http://tristan.u-bourgogne.fr/UMR5605/publications/autreslieux/P_Poirrier.htm.
Pons Belnoue, Hervé. 2016. "Tout se joue à Cannes ?" ALCA Nouvelle-Aquitaine, November 1, 2016. https://prologue-alca.fr/fr/actualites/tout-se-joue-cannes.
Porton, Richard. 2005. "Marivaux in the 'Hood': An Interview with Abdellatif Kechiche." *Cineaste* 31 (1): 46–49.
Powrie, Phil. 1997. *French Cinema in the 1980s: Nostalgia and the Crisis of Masculinity*. New York: Clarendon Press.
———, ed. 1999. *French Cinema in the 1990s: Continuity and Difference, Essays*. New York: Oxford University Press.
———. 2015. "Soundscapes of Loss: Songs in Contemporary French Cinema." In *A Companion to Contemporary French Cinema*, edited by Alistair Fox, Michel Marie, Raphaëlle Moine, and Hilary Radner, 527–546. Malden, MA: Wiley-Blackwell.
Pratt, Mary Louise. 2008. *Imperial Eyes: Travel Writing and Transculturation*. 2nd ed. New York: Routledge.
Prédal, René. 2002. *Le Jeune Cinéma français*. Paris: Nathan.
Prince, Stephen. 2000a. "Graphic Violence in the Cinema: Origins, Aesthetic Design, and Social Effects." In *Screening Violence*, edited by Stephen Prince, 1–44. New Brunswick, NJ: Rutgers University Press.

———. 2000b. "The Aesthetic of Slow-Motion Violence in the Films of Sam Peckinpah." In *Screening Violence*, edited by Stephen Prince, 174–201. New Brunswick, NJ: Rutgers University Press.

Pu, Lisha. 2014. "Rencontre avec Céline Sciamma." *Maze*, October 4, 2014. https://maze.fr/2014/10/rencontre-avec-celine-sciamma/.

Pulver, Andrew. 2012. "Jacques Audiard: 'My Work Is like Rolling Thunder.'" *The Guardian*, October 24, 2012. https://www.theguardian.com/film/2012/oct/24/jacques-audiard-interview-rust-bone.

Pyramide Films. 2014. "*Bande de filles*: Dossier de presse." Pyramidefilms.com. 2014. http://distrib.pyramidefilms.com/pyramide-distribution-catalogue.html?task=download&collection=telechargements&xi=0&file=fichiers&id=661.

Quandt, James. 2013. "Flesh and Blood: Sex and Violence in Recent French Cinema." In *The New Extremism in Cinema: From France to Europe*, edited by Tanya Horeck and Tina Kendall, 18–25. Edinburgh: Edinburgh University Press.

Quemener, Nelly. 2012. "Disarticulated Laughers: Backlash in Broadcasted Comedy in France." *Derecho a Comunicar* 4 (April): 213–231.

Raengo, Alessandra. 2016. *Critical Race Theory and* Bamboozled. New York: Bloomsbury.

Rancière, Jacques. 1995. *La Mésentente: politique et philosophie*. Paris: Galilée.

———. 1999. *Disagreement: Politics and Philosophy*. Translated by Julie Rose. Minneapolis: University of Minnesota Press.

Raphaël, Garrigos. 2001. "Quel sublime faux procès!" *Libération*, December 20, 2001. http://www.liberation.fr/medias/2001/12/20/quel-sublime-faux-proces_387987.

Rassial, Jean-Jacques. 2002. "Les villes à la campagne." In *Y a-t-il une psychopathologie des banlieues?*, 9–15. Toulouse: Erès. http://www.cairn.info/y-a-t-il-une-psychopathologie-des-banlieues--9782865865871-page-9.htm.

Rauger, Jean-François. 2008. "*Martyrs*: rude expression d'un cinéaste en colère." *Le Monde*, September 2, 2008. http://www.lemonde.fr/cinema/article/2008/09/02/martyrs-rude-expression-d-un-cineaste-en-colere_1090590_3476.html.

Ray, Robert B. 1985. *A Certain Tendency of the Hollywood Cinema, 1930–1980*. Princeton, NJ: Princeton University Press.

Reader, Keith. 1995. "After the Riot." *Sight and Sound* 5 (11): 12–14.

———. 2003. "Flaubert's Sparrow, or the Bovary of Belleville: Édith Piaf as Cultural Icon." In *Popular Music in France from Chanson to Techno: Culture, Identity, and Society*, edited by Steve Cannon and Hugh Dauncey, 205–223. Burlington, VT: Ashgate.

Reeser, Todd W. 2010. *Masculinities in Theory: An Introduction*. Malden, MA: Wiley-Blackwell.

Renan, Ernest. 1945. "Qu'est-ce qu'une nation?" In *Ernest Renan et l'Allemagne*, 165–98. New York: Brentano's.

Reyes, Xavier Aldana. 2016. *Horror Film and Affect: Towards a Corporeal Model of Viewership.* New York: Routledge.
Ricœur, Paul. 1981. "Mimesis and Representation." *Annals of Scholarship* 2:16–32.
Riding, Alan. 2001. "Remark by Vivendi Chief Unnerves French Film Industry." *New York Times,* December 24, 2001. http://www.nytimes.com/2001/12/24/movies/remark-by-vivendi-chief-unnerves-french-film-industry.html.
Rochant, Éric. 2017. "Naissance d'un showrunner français ou l'art de produire des séries TV." *Le journal de l'ecole de Paris du management* 127 (5): 21–27.
Rocher, Benjamin, and Yannick Dahan. 2010. *The Horde.* DVD. IFC Independent Film.
Rollet, Brigitte. 2015. "French Women Directors Since the 1990s." In *A Companion to Contemporary French Cinema,* edited by Alistair Fox, Michel Marie, Raphaëlle Moine, and Hilary Radner, 941–86. Malden, MA: Wiley-Blackwell.
Romney, Jonathan. 1995. "Suburban Blues: French Style." *New Statesman & Society* 8 (379): 34.
———. 2016. "Jacques Audiard: 'I Wanted to Give Migrants a Name, a Shape, a Violence of Their Own.'" *The Guardian,* April 3, 2016. http://www.theguardian.com/film/2016/apr/03/jacques-audiard-interview-dheepan-prophet-rust-done-director.
Rose, Steve. 2016. "*Divines* Director Houda Benyamina: 'It's Better to Make a Film than a Bomb.'" *The Guardian,* November 10, 2016. https://www.theguardian.com/film/2016/nov/10/divines-director-houda-benyamina-its-better-to-make-a-film-than-a-bomb.
Rose, Sven-Erik. 2007. "Mathieu Kassovitz's *La Haine* and the Ambivalence of French-Jewish Identity." *French Studies* 61 (4): 476–491.
Rosello, Mireille. 1998. *Declining the Stereotype: Ethnicity and Representation in French Cultures.* Hanover, NH: University Press of New England.
———. 2018. "L'émergence des comédies communautaires dans le cinéma français: ambiguïtés et paradoxes." *Studies in French Cinema* 18 (1): 18–34.
Rouyer, Philippe, and Yann Tobin. 2015. "Entretien avec Jacques Audiard: 'A la hauteur des personnages, pas plus haut.'" *Positif,* September 2015.
Roxborough, Scott. 2021. "Omar Sy on Making Netflix Hit *Lupin* Under COVID Lockdown." *Hollywood Reporter,* March 15, 2021. https://www.hollywoodreporter.com/news/omar-sy-netflix-lupin.
Sachs, Leon. 2014. *The Pedagogical Imagination: The Republican Legacy in Twenty-First Century French Literature.* Lincoln: University of Nebraska Press.
Sallé, Caroline. 2018. "Les exportations de films français dépendent trop de Luc Besson." *Le Figaro,* January 19, 2018. http://www.lefigaro.fr/medias/2018/01/19/20004-20180119ARTFIG00356-les-exportations-de-films-francais-dependent-trop-de-luc-besson.php.
Samuels, Maurice. 2016. *The Right to Difference: French Universalism and the Jews.* Chicago: University of Chicago Press.

Sauvion, Marie. 2004. "*Banlieue 13*: pas de." *Le Parisien*, November 10, 2004. http://www.leparisien.fr/loisirs-et-spectacles/banlieue-13-pas-de-10 -11-2004-2005443754.php.
Sayanoff, Xavier, and Tristan Schulmann. 2009. *Viande d'origine française*. Aired November 14, 2009, on Canal+.
Scarlata, Alexa, Ramon Lobato, and Stuart Cunningham. 2021. "Producing Local Content in International Waters: The Case of Netflix's *Tidelands*." *Continuum* 35 (1): 137–150.
Schoonover, Karl. 2012. *Brutal Vision: The Neorealist Body in Postwar Italian Cinema*. Minneapolis: University of Minnesota Press.
Schor, Naomi. 2001. "The Crisis of French Universalism." *Yale French Studies* 100: 43–64.
Schur, Richard L. 2009. *Parodies of Ownership: Hip-Hop Aesthetics and Intellectual Property Law*. Ann Arbor: University of Michigan Press.
Scott, A. O. 2012. "*The Intouchables* Arrives From France." *New York Times*, May 24, 2012. http://www.nytimes.com/2012/05/25/movies/the-intouchables-arrives -from-france.html.
Scott, Joan W. 2005. *Parité! Sexual Equality and the Crisis of French Universalism*. Chicago: University of Chicago Press.
Sedel, Julie. 2009. *Les médias & la banlieue*. Latresne: Le Bord de l'eau.
Serero, Lisa. 2011. "Retours sur *La Case départ*." *Respect Mag* 31 (December): 61.
Sharma, Sanjay, and Ashwani Sharma. 2000. "'So Far So Good . . .' La Haine and the Poetics of the Everyday." *Theory, Culture & Society* 17 (3): 103–116.
Silverstein, Paul A. 2004. *Algeria in France: Transpolitics, Race, and Nation*. Bloomington: Indiana University Press.
Smith, Ben. 2020. "The President vs. the American Media." *New York Times*, November 16, 2020. https://www.nytimes.com/2020/11/15/business/media /macron-france-terrorism-american-islam.html.
Smith, Frances. 2020. Bande de filles: *Girlhood Identities in Contemporary France*. New York: Routledge.
Smouts, Marie-Claude. 2010. "Les études postcoloniales en France: émergences et résistances." In *Ruptures postcoloniales: les nouveaux visages de la société française*, edited by Nicolas Bancel, Florence Bernault, Pascal Blanchard, and Valérie Amiraux, 309–316. Paris: Découverte.
Sobchack, Vivian. 1990. "'Surge and Splendor': A Phenomenology of the Hollywood Historical Epic." *Representations* 29 (January): 24–49.
Sojcher, Frédéric. 2002. "Luc Besson, ou les contradictions du cinéma français: Face à Hollywood." In *Quelle diversité face à Hollywood?*, edited by Jérôme Clément, Lord David Puttnam, and Thomas Paris, 142–156. Condé-sur-Noireau: Corlet.

Solomons, Jason. 2009. "Interview: Jacques Audiard." *The Guardian*, December 6, 2009. https://www.theguardian.com/film/2009/dec/06/jacques-audiard-interview-a-prophet.

Sorman, Guy. 2002. "La culture française, ni exceptionnelle ni menacée." *Le Figaro*, January 2, 2002.

Strand, Dana. 2009. "Etre et parler: Being and Speaking French in Abdellatif Kechiche's *L'Esquive* (2004) and Laurent Cantet's *Entre les murs* (2008)." *Studies in French Cinema* 9 (3): 259–272.

Studio Canal. 2010. "*Hors la loi*: Dossier de presse." https://medias.unifrance.org/medias/35/177/45347/presse/hors-la-loi-dossier-de-presse-francais.pdf.

Swamy, Vinay. 2007. "Marivaux in the Suburbs: Reframing Language in Kechiche's *L'Esquive* (2003)." *Studies in French Cinema* 7 (1): 57–68. https://doi.org/10.1386/sfci.7.1.57_1.

Tarr, Carrie. 1997. "Ethnicity and Identity in *Métisse* and *La Haine* by Mathieu Kassovitz." In *Multicultural France*, edited by Tony Chafer, 40–47. Portsmouth: School of Language and Area Studies.

———. 2001. *Cinema and the Second Sex: Women's Filmmaking in France in the 1980s and 1990s*. New York: Continuum.

———. 2005. *Reframing Difference: Beur and Banlieue Filmmaking in France*. Manchester: Manchester University Press.

———. 2007. "*L'Esquive* (Kechiche 2004): Reassessing French Popular Culture." In *France at the Flicks: Trends in Contemporary French Popular Cinema*, edited by Darren Waldron and Isabelle Vanderschelden, 130–141. Newcastle: Cambridge Scholars.

Tessé, Jean-Philippe. 2013. "Tomber le masque: Entretien avec Abdellatif Kechiche." *Cahiers du cinéma*, October 2013.

———. 2015. "Audiard, la Palme c'est son genre." *Cahiers du cinéma*, June 2015.

Tetreault, Chantal. 2015. *Transcultural Teens: Performing Youth Identities in French Cités*. West Sussex: Wiley Blackwell.

Thomas, Dominic. 2013. *Africa and France: Postcolonial Cultures, Migration, and Racism*. Bloomington: Indiana University Press.

Tillet, Salamishah. 2020. "What the *Cuties* Critics Can't See: The Complexities of Black Girlhood." *New York Times*, October 2, 2020. https://www.nytimes.com/2020/10/02/movies/cuties-netflix.html.

Tissot, Sylvie. 2007. *L'État et les quartiers: Genèse d'une catégorie de l'action publique*. Paris: Seuil.

Todd, Emmanuel. 2015. *Qui est Charlie? sociologie d'une crise religieuse*. Paris: Seuil.

Tolédano, Éric, and Olivier Nakache. 2012. "An Intouchable World?" *Huffington Post* (blog), May 7, 2012. http://www.huffingtonpost.com/eric-toledano-and-olivier-nakache/an-intouchable-world_b_1497787.html.

Toussay, Jade, and Hortense de Montalivet. 2018. "'Bravo l'Afrique': la colère de Nicolas Batum après les commentaires du 'Daily Show' sur la victoire des Bleus." *Huffington Post* (blog), July 18, 2018. https://www.huffingtonpost.fr/2018/07/18/nicolas-batum-en-colere-apres-les-commentaires-du-daily-show-sur-la-victoire-des-bleus-a-la-coupe-du-monde_a_23484314/.

Truffaut, François. 2009. "A Certain Tendency in French Cinema." In *The French New Wave: Critical Landmarks*, edited by Peter Graham and Ginette Vincendeau, 39–63. London: Palgrave Macmillan.

Turk, Edward Baron. 1989. *Child of Paradise: Marcel Carné and the Golden Age of French Cinema*. Cambridge, MA: Harvard University Press.

Vadjoux, Thibaud. 2007. "Luc Besson (EuropaCorp): 'Nous ne voulons pas américaniser le cinéma français mais l'internationaliser.'" *Boursorama*, June 27, 2007.

Valo, Martine. 2006. "Les Sauvageons font leur cinéma." *Le Monde*, January 21, 2006.

Vanderschelden, Isabelle. 2007. "Strategies for a 'Transnational'/French Popular Cinema." *Modern & Contemporary France* 15 (1): 37–50.

———. 2008. "Luc Besson's Ambition: EuropaCorp as a European Major for the 21st Century." *Studies in European Cinema* 5 (2): 91–104.

Vieillard-Baron, Hervé. 2001. *Les banlieues: Des singularités françaises aux réalités mondiales*. Paris: Hachette.

———. 2008. "La banlieue: question de définition." In *Banlieues: une anthologie*, edited by Thierry Paquot, 21–33. Lausanne: Presses polytechniques et universitaires romandes.

Vincendeau, Ginette. 1987. "The Mise-en-scène of Suffering: French Chanteuses Réalistes." *New Formations* 3 (Winter): 107–128.

———. 2000. *Stars and Stardom in French Cinema*. New York: Continuum.

———. 2005. *La Haine*. Urbana-Champaign: University of Illinois Press.

———. 2015. "From the Margins to the Center: French Stardom and Ethnicity." In *A Companion to Contemporary French Cinema*, edited by Alistair Fox, Michel Marie, Raphaëlle Moine, and Hilary Radner, 547–569. Malden, MA: Wiley-Blackwell.

Vitali, Valentina, and Paul Willemen. 2006. "Introduction." In *Theorising National Cinema*, edited by Valentina Vitali and Paul Willemen, 1–14. London: BFI.

Vulser, Nicole. 2017. "Une grande zone de turbulences pour EuropaCorp." *Le Monde*, September 6, 2017. https://www.lemonde.fr/economie/article/2017/09/06/une-grande-zone-de-turbulences-pour-europacorp_5181707_3234.html.

———. 2018. "*Valérian* fait le beau temps sur le cinéma français à l'international." *Le Monde*, January 19, 2018. https://www.lemonde.fr/economie/article

/2018/01/19/valerian-fait-le-beau-temps-sur-le-cinema-francais-a-l-international_5244339_3234.html.

———. 2020a. "EuropaCorp: Le groupe de Luc Besson passe sous pavillon américain." *Le Monde*, February 29, 2020. https://www.lemonde.fr/economie/article/2020/02/29/europacorp-le-groupe-de-luc-besson-passe-sous-pavillon-americain_6031334_3234.html.

———. 2020b. "EuropaCorp doit renoncer aux aides à la production." *Le Monde*, August 26, 2020. https://www.lemonde.fr/economie/article/2020/08/26/europacorp-doit-renoncer-aux-aides-a-la-production_6049958_3234.html.

Wacquant, Loïc. 2007. *Parias urbains: ghetto, banlieues, État*. Translated by Sébastien Chauvin. Paris: La Découverte.

Weil, Laurent, and Valérie Amarou. 2011. "*Intouchables*: Interview with Olivier Nakache and Eric Toledano." *La Quotidienne du cinéma*. Aired October 31, 2011, on TPS Star.

Weissberg, Jay. 2011. "Untouchable." *Variety*, September 29, 2011. http://variety.com/2011/film/reviews/untouchable-1117946269/.

West, Alexandra. 2016. *Films of the New French Extremity: Visceral Horror and National Identity*. Jefferson, NC: McFarland.

Willemen, Paul. 2006. "The Nation Revisited." In *Theorising National Cinema*, edited by Valentina Vitali and Paul Willemen, 29–43. London: BFI.

Williams, James S. 2013. *Space and Being in Contemporary French Cinema*. Manchester: Manchester University Press.

Williams, Linda. 2001. *Playing the Race Card: Melodramas of Black and White from Uncle Tom to O.J. Simpson*. Princeton, NJ: Princeton University Press.

Williams, Raymond. 2006. "The Analysis of Culture." In *Cultural Theory and Popular Culture: A Reader*, edited by John Storey, 3rd ed., 32–40. New York: Pearson.

Wilson, Emma. 2017. "Scenes of Hurt and Rapture: Céline Sciamma's *Girlhood*." *Film Quarterly* 70 (3): 10–22.

Yee, Jennifer. 2003. "Métissage in France: A Postmodern Fantasy and Its Forgotten Precedents." *Modern & Contemporary France* 11 (4): 411–425.

Zadi, Jean-Pascal, and Stéphanie Binet. 2011. "Des histoires qu'on ne voit jamais au cinéma." *Libération*, June 8, 2011. https://www.liberation.fr/cinema/2011/06/08/des-histoires-qu-on-ne-voit-jamais-au-cinema_741163/.

Zolberg, Vera L. 2007. "The Happy Few—En Masse: Franco-American Comparisons in Cultural Democratization." In *The Arts of Democracy: Art, Public Culture, and the State*, edited by Casey Nelson Blake, 97–122. Philadelphia: University of Pennsylvania Press.

INDEX

Figures are noted in italics

2015 terrorist attacks, 120
2018 World Cup, 15–16, 278–79

actors, nonprofessional, 36, 53, 58, 148, 164, 204, 239; and authenticity, 144–46, 256–59; and codes of art cinema, 37, 42, 253–55
affirmative action (positive discrimination), 24, 223
al-din Attar, Farid, 55
Alessandrin, Patrick, 111–12; *District 13: Ultimatum (Banlieue 13: Ultimatum)*, 33, 91, *104*, 111–13, 120
Alexander, Karen, 40–41
Algeria, 9, 130, 132, 174, 183, 207, 236, 278; 1945 Sétif massacre, 34, 131, 136–38; Franco-Algerian coproduction, 134; War of Independence, 34, 76–77, 129, 139–43
Algerian National Liberation Front (FLN), 34, 131–33, 135–43, 164
Algerian National Movement (MNA), 132, 137, 140
Altman, Rick, 11
Amachoukeli, Marie, 251
Amadou, Ouma, 242
Amamra, Oulaya, 283
Amazon Prime, 37, 280, 284
Americanization, 69, 77, 96–97, 114, 120, 148, 262

Andrew, Dudley, 72–73, 254–55
Andrews, David, 252
Appadurai, Arjun, 29–31, 103
Apple, 280
Araud, Gérard, 16
Argento, Dario, 168
Arnold, Roxane, 250, 252
Arte, 251
Artz, B. Lee, 218, 227
Assandé, Fargass, 282
Assayas, Olivier: *Irma Vep*, 248; *Something in the Air (Après mai)*, 248
ASSEDIC (L'Association pour l'emploi dans l'industrie et le commerce), 219
Astruc, Alexandre, 48
Attal, Alain, 248–49
Audiard, Jacques, 1, 127, 130, 150–55, 157, 162, 164; and auteurism, 2–4, 7, 27, 144–45, 148; Cannes Film Festival Palme d'Or, 2, 145, 148; casting nonprofessional actors, 144–46, 204, 257; *A Prophet (Un prophète)*, 34, 144, 147–49, 156. See also *Dheepan* (Audiard)
Audiard, Michel, 144
Austin, Guy, 168, 204–6
auteurism, 11, 27, 35, 101, 155, 166, 168–69, 236, 274n1, 282; in approaches to film history, 93, 96–97; and Audiard, 2, 4, 144–45; and

auteurism (*Cont.*)
    gender, 243–45; and industrial models, 3, 110, 116–17, 124n3; and Kassovitz, 44, 85, 89; and Kechiche, 39, 56, 58–60, 87; *la politique des auteurs*, 48; and Sciamma, 242–49, 251–53, 256–60, 271–73; and self-branding, 8, 144–45, 148, 244; and small-scale production, 6–7, 33, 90–91, 131
automatic aid (*avances sur recettes*), 6, 8, 110, 114
average shot length (ASL), 66–67, 267

Baartman, Saartjie, 55
Bach, Johann Sebastian, 219
Badiou, Alain, 21–22, 45
Baker, Josephine, 207
Bakhtin, Mikhail, 128, 133, 149
Balasko, Josiane, 244
Balavoine, Daniel: "Sauver l'amour," 265
Balibar, Étienne, 17, 21–22, 31, 104, 159, 186, 215
Barlet, Olivier, 132, 223
Bataille, Georges, 197–201
Bazin, André, 42, 73–74, 254–56, 258, 267
Becker, Jacques, 11
Béghin, Cyril, 57
Bekhti, Leïla, 174
Belle, David, 93, 102, 108, 124n2
Belle Époque, 11
Belmondo, Jean-Paul, 81, 231
below-the-line labor, 250–51
Belpêche, Stéphanie, 176
Belting, Hans, 196–97
Ben Ammar, Tarak, 134
Ben Arous, 134
Benyamina, Houda, 34, 157, 258–59, 280, 283; and 1000 (Mille) Visages Association, 155, 284; and Cannes Film Festival Golden Camera Award, 155, 163; critique of violent genres, 35, 127, 130–31, 154–56, 159–64. *See also Divines* (Benyamina)
Bergala, Alain, 247
Bergfelder, Tim, 96, 111
Berlant, Lauren, 83
Berlioz, Hector, 224
Besson, Luc, 2, 4, 7, 34, 90, 116, 118–19, 248; *Arthur and the Minimoys* trilogy, 115; *Brick Mansions*, 122; and *District 13: Ultimatum* (Alessandrin), 33, 91, 111–13, 120; and *District B13* (Morel), 33, 91, 101–3, 105, 107, 109–12, 120, 122–23; and École de la Cité, 117, 125n14; *The Fifth Element (Le cinquième élément)*, 89, 113–14; *The Last Battle (Le dernier combat)*, 111; *Léon: The Professional (Léon)*, 89; *Lucy*, 115; *Nikita (La femme Nikita)*, 89; and parkour, 91–95, 98–99, 103, 110–12, 121–23; press caricatures of, 96–98; *The Professional (Le Professionnel)*, 231; *Subway*, 89; *Taken* franchise, 115; *Taxi*, 99, 101, 109, 113, 115; *Transporter* franchise, 102, 115; *Valerian and the City of a Thousand Planets (Valérian et la Cité des mille planets)*, 91, 115; and *Yamakasi, the Samurai of Modern Times (Yamakasi, les samouraïs des temps modernes)*, 33, 91, 98–99, 101, 109, 113, 124n6. *See also* EuropaCorp
Best, Willie, 210
beur cinema, 12, 60, 70, 98–99 131, 263
Bey-Rozet, Maxime, 172
Bigelow, Kathryn, 244
Binet, Stéphanie, 176
black-blanc-beur (Black-white-Arab), 61
Black comedians, 36, 206–13, 224–28, 237, 239, 240n7, 240n10
blackface minstrelsy, 36, 209, 211–14, 216–23, 241n3; and colonialism, 207, 215, 229
Black girlhood, 241–42, 246, 253, 259, 272; and dance, 256, 260–62, 265–66, 268–69
Black Lives Matter protests, 275
Black sidekick trope, 237
Black stardom, 36, 204–12, 230–39, 240nn10–11, 259
Black urban cinema, 61, 65, 79
Blanquer, Jean-Michel, 277
Blatt, Ari, 45, 50, 53
Blue, Gregory, 198
body horror, 2, 191–201
Bogle, Donald, 210, 213, 216
Boon, Danny: *Bienvenue chez les ch'tis (Welcome to the Sticks)*, 124n6, 207–8, 210
Bordwell, David, 65–68, 246
Bouchareb, Rachid, 7, 58, 124, 136, 149; *Bâton rouge*, 263; *Belleville Cop (Le Flic de Belleville)*, 131, 236; *Days of Glory*

(*Indigènes*), 101, 131; and epic mode, 134–35; and gangster genre, 34, 127, 130–33, 137–44, 148, 154–55, 162–63; *London River*, 131. *See also Outside the Law (Hors la loi)* (Bouchareb)
Bourdieu, Pierre, 43, 46–50, 56, 58, 79
Bourgon, Jérôme, 198
Boutang, Yann Moulier, 24
Bresson, Robert: *Diary of a Country Priest (Journal d'un curé de campagne)*, 199
Brick, Emily, 172–73
British cinema, 100–101
Britton, Andrew, 205
Bronner, Luc, 120, 122, 223
Brook, Timothy, 198
brown sidekick trope, 240n11
Brown, Wendy, 21
Bryan, Alice Haylett, 168, 185
Buchsbaum, Jonathan, 7, 96
buddy genre, 2, 44, 103, 131; interracial, 36, 206–7, 209–11, 218, 227, 231, 238
Burger, Claire, 151
Burgoyne, Robert, 135
Bush, George W., 181
Bustillo, Alexandre: *Inside (À l'intérieur)*, 35, 167–68, 177, 190–95, 201–2
Butler, Judith, 80

Cahiers du cinéma, 3–4, 27, 42, 48, 57–58, 144–45, 243, 247, 254
Caisse des dépôts et consignation, 116
camerawork, handheld, 63, 181, 258. *See also* cinematography; Steadicam
Campion, Jane, 101
Canal+, 89, 118–19, 212, 251
Cannes Film Festival, 120, 132, 142, 177, 242, 250, 252, 280–81, 283; Best Director Prize, 40, 85; Director's Fortnight series (Quinzaine des réalisateurs), 155; Golden Camera, 155, 163; Palme d'Or, 2, 56, 145, 148
Carax, Léos: *Holy Motors*, 248
Carné, Marcel, 73; *Daybreak (Le jour se lève)*, 72, 74, 77, 126, 143; *Port of Shadows (Quai des brumes)*, 72, 126; *Wasteland (Terrain vague)*, 11
Carpenter, John, 105; *Assault on Precinct 13*, 34, 102; *Escape* films, 34, 102–3, 106

Cassel, Vincent, 61, 174, 176, 179
casting practices, 44, 53, 58, 66, 243, 263–64; and art cinema conventions, 37, 42, 253–54, 256–59; and Black comedians, 210, 216, 234–35; inclusive, 11, 36, 144–45, 163, 175, 280–81; at Netflix, 281–84; nontraditional, 59, 239, 254; and Omar Sy, 207, 215, 228–29. *See also* actors, nonprofessional
casting sauvage, 257
Catanese, Brandi, 59, 254
Catholicism, 6, 17, 38n7, 199
Céline, Louis-Ferdinand, 10
Césars, 40, 204, 212
chanson réaliste, 61, 76–78, 88n3
Chapiron, Christian (Kiki Picasso), 175
Chapiron, Kim: *Sheitan*, 35, 167–68, 174–80, 183–84, 187, 195, 201–2
Chaplin, Charlie, 47, 233
Chappelle, Dave, 213
Charef, Mehdi, 131; *Tea in the Harem (Le Thé au harem d'Archimède)*, 263
Charlie Hebdo, 120, 275–76
Chibane, Malik: *Voisins, voisines*, 263–64, 266
Chirac, Jacques, 222
Chopin, Frédéric, 224
Christensen, Jerome, 94, 124n3
chronology of French media, 281, 285nn2–3
Cine+, 251
Cinecittà, 90
cinéma de papa, 7–8
CinemaScope, 148, 156, 268
cinematography, 63–67, 98, 102, 134, 149, 215, 251–52, 255, 271
cinéma vérité, 33, 42, 58, 295
cinephilia, 4, 47, 58, 86, 102, 176, 242, 247–49, 252
cité (project), 10, 61, 63, 70, 121, 145, 189
Cité du cinéma, 34, 90, 93–94, 97, 113, 116–19, 122
city-revenge genre. *See* urbanoia genre
class, 72, 74, 84, 87, 144–45, 169, 176, 236; and casting at Netflix, 282; and decolonization, 64, 142–43; economic resentment, 170–74, 179, 186, 190, 193, 202; and interracial buddy comedies, 36, 207, 214–15, 219; and intersectionality,

class (*Cont.*)
26; marked by music, 88n3, 219; and mobility, 43, 46–49, 52–53, 230, 257, 260–62, 264; and parkour films, 98–100, 103, 105, 113, 116–17; and passing, 41, 274n3; prioritized over racial awareness, 24, 79, 234; and social mixing, 276; and stereotyping, 11, 98–99, 175, 202, 209, 229; and universalism, 18, 35, 62; and urban planning, 9–10, 20–24; and working-class iconography, 76–77
Clover, Carol, 169–71, 179–80, 186, 190, 193, 201–2
Cohen, Jeffrey Jerome, 202
Cole, Catherine M., 215–17
colonialism, 14, 34, 190, 215, 223; French colonies, 2, 8–9, 18, 28, 173, 184, 186–88, 202–3, 207, 232; Hollywood as colonizer, 6, 95, 170, 215; and public memory, 3, 16, 26, 72, 101, 130–31, 137–39, 142–43, 189; suburban colonial subjects, 30, 77, 104, 246–47, 273. *See also* decolonization; neocolonialism; postcolonial studies
color-blind universalism, 16–18, 22, 26–28, 172, 238, 262, 275, 284; and *Frontier(s)* (Gens), 184; and *Games of Love and Chance* (Kechiche), 59; and *Girlhood* (Sciamma), 272; and *La Haine* (Kassovitz), 79; and *The Horde* (Dahan and Rocher), 190; and *Intouchables* (Tolédano and Nakache), 206; and *Martyrs* (Laugier), 195; and *Sheitan* (Chapiron), 167
Comédie française, 51
Conley, Tom, 82–83
Conway, Kelley, 88n3
Coppola, Francis Ford, 39, 71; *The Godfather*, 34, 132, 139–41
coproductions, international, 6, 114–15, 119, 134, 251
cosmic zooms, 199–200
Costa-Gavras, 175
countryside, 8, 167–69, 174–75; and city-country resentment, 170–72, 177–82, 184–90, 193, 202
Court, Jean-François, 6
Couvreur, Bénédicte, 250–51

COVID-19 pandemic, 275
Creative Artists Agency, 236
Creekmur, Corey, 240n11
Crenshaw, Kimberlé, 277
creolization, 26, 31, 119, 187
crime film (*film policier*) genre, 4, 41, 126, 132, 176, 230, 244, 278–80
Crisp, Colin, 205
Critikat, 193
Crofts, Stephen, 110–11, 119
cultural racism, 19–20
cultural state (*état culturel*), 45–46
cultural studies, 24–25, 100
Cunningham, Stuart, 281
Cupers, Kenny, 9, 10–11, 14

Dahan, Yannick: *The Horde* (*La Horde*), 35, 167–68, 186–90, 195, 202
Dalí, Salvador, 218, 226–27
Dalle, Béatrice, 173, 194
D'Amario, Tony, 106, 108
Danan, Martine, 96, 110
dance, 41, 65, 75–76, 129, 155, 161–62, 283; and blackface, 217–21; and Black girlhood, 256, 260–62, 265–66, 268–69
Daney, Serge, 254
de Baecque, Antoine, 97
Debbouze, Jamel, 131
de Certeau, Michel, 29–31, 92
decolonization, 64, 76, 130–31, 142–43, 184, 188–89
de Gaulle, Charles, 76
Delbosc, Olivier, 264
Delorme, Stéphane, 3–4, 27, 148
De Niro, Robert, 65, 155
Denis, Claire: *35 Shots of Rum* (*35 rhums*), 173; *Trouble Every Day*, 35, 166–67, 172–73
De Palma, Brian, 39, 126; *Scarface*, 102, 106, 124n9, 156
Deplasse, Hervé, 97
Derrida, Jacques, 168
Descas, Alex, 173
Despentes, Virginie: *Baise-moi*, 35, 167, 172–73
de Van, Marina, 248
Dheepan (Audiard), 3, 34–35, 130, 155, 163, 165n4; and Cinemascope, 156; inescapable

mediation in, 146, 157; nonprofessional actors in, 144–45, 164, 204, 257; Steadicam in, 146, 151; Tamil identity in, 1–2, 130, 144–45, 147, 149–50, 152, 154; ultraviolence in, 127, 150–54; winning 2015 Palme d'Or, 2, 145, 148

dialogue, 63, 67–68, 105, 117, 265, 279; in Arabic, 59, 143, 178; slang, 144, 174–75, 181, 192, 226; in Tamil, 1, 145, 149, 152; vernacular, 33, 40–41, 50–51, 58. *See also* screenwriting

Diao, Claire, 121

Digital Factory, 118

Divines (Benyamina), 157–58, 177, 258–59; at Cannes Film Festival, 155, 163, 280, 283; critique of violent genres, 35, 127, 130–31, 154–56, 159–63, 195

DJ Cut Killer, 76

Dobson, Julia, 12, 146

documentary genre, 120, 129, 166, 189, 256, 280; and *Dheepan* (Audiard), 144; and *Games of Love and Chance* (Kechiche), 33, 42–43; and *Girlhood* (Sciamma), 258; and *La Haine* (Kassovitz), 40, 61, 63, 70; and *Outside the Law* (Bouchareb), 133; and parkour films, 98–99, 108

Dogma 95, 95

Donadey, Anne, 136–37

Donalson, Melvin, 223–24

Dostoyevsky, Fyodor, 234

Doucouré, Maïmouna: *Cuties (Mignonnes)*, 283

Dubois, Régis, 208, 216, 228

Ducournau, Julie: *Raw (Grave)*, 38n3, 166, 169

Dunlop, Jérôme, 171

Dupaire, François, 228–29

Ďurovičová, Nataša, 92

Duvivier, Julien: *Pépé le Moko*, 78, 143

Dyer, Richard, 205–6, 233–34, 239n2, 269–71

Earth, Wind, and Fire, 224, 248; "Boogie Wonderland," 220, 265

École de la Cité, 117, 125n14

École nationale supérieure Louis Lumière, 90, 117

editing, 42–43, 98, 181, 261; of German Expressionism, 255–56; and *Girlhood* (Sciamma), 266–67, 269; and *La Haine* (Kassovitz), 65–68, 71, 126; and *Outside the Law* (Bouchareb), 127, 136

Eisenstein, Sergei, 31

Élie et Dieudonné, 240n7

Elmaleh, Gad, 213, 283; *Gad Elmaleh: American Dream*, 283; *Gad Gone Wild*, 283

Emerson, Caryl, 129

epic genre, 129, 132–36, 138, 143

Estrougo, Audrey: *Ain't Scared (Regarde-moi)*, 264; *Leila (Toi, moi, les autres)*, 37, 259, 264–65, 273

ethnicity, 147, 244, 258; and French concepts of difference, 18–20, 24, 56, 214, 275; and French Maghrebi *(beur)* cinema, 98; and interchangeability, 228, 239n4, 240n5; marked by music, 75, 217, 263–65; multiethnic characters, 12, 14, 61, 99, 112, 175, 180; and revenge films, 170–71; and stardom, 206–7, 238; U.S. concepts of, 15–16, 22–23, 26–28, 32, 79, 87

ethnoparodic comedy, 99

Euro horror, 168

EuropaCorp, 4, 7, 113, 118, 124n10; and financing, 7, 114–17, 123, 251; and international coproductions, 114–15, 119; as misunderstood, 122–23; and parkour films, 33, 92, 95, 98–99, 101, 110–11, 113, 120–21; seeking cultural shift, 90–91, 93–94, 96–97

Everett, Anna, 274n5

Exarchopoulos, Adèle, 58

Expressionism, German, 255

Ezra, Elizabeth, 95–96

Fabre, Clarisse, 250

Falco, Hubert, 132

Fanon, Frantz, 30

Fary (Fary Lopes B), 239; *Fary: Hexagone*, 283

fascism, 21, 180–81, 183–84, 202

female friendship genre, 37, 129, 162, 247, 259–60

La Fémis, 117, 155, 176, 242, 247–51, 254, 284

Ferran, Pascale, 7
Fetchit, Stepin, 210
Fiddler, Michael, 190
Fidelité Films, 264
film and media studies, 73, 92, 95, 100, 203n3, 204, 254
film noir, 34, 126, 271
film schools, 33–34, 47, 58, 116, 274; 1000 (Mille) Visages Association, 155, 284; École de la Cité, 117, 125n14; École nationale supérieure Louis Lumière, 90, 117; La Fémis, 117, 155, 176, 242, 247–51, 254, 284
films du milieu (middle-scale films), 7
films policiers (crime films). *See* crime film (*film policier*) genre
final girl trope, 170, 181, 185–86
Finkielkraut, Alain, 20, 32, 46
Fişek, Emine, 207, 215, 230
Floyd, George, 62
Footit, Georges, 231–35
Ford, John, 4
foreignization (*étrangéisation*), 277
Forestier, Sara, 40, 53
Forsdick, Charles, 25
Fourcaut, Annie, 11, 128
Fox, Alistair, 248
France Inter, 252
la France profonde, 182, 189
Franco-Arab cinema. *See* beur cinema
Franju, Georges, 35, 168; *Eyes Without a Face (Les Yeux sans visage)*, 166, 198–99
French Communist Party, 222
French Defense Ministry, 132
French-Indochina War, 188–89
French Ministry of Culture, 15
French Musée de l'Homme, 198
French New Wave, 7, 47, 96, 117, 144, 175, 249, 272; and Hollywood genre cinema, 4, 27, 34–35, 39, 42, 48, 72, 85, 126; and long-take aesthetics, 57, 71, 270
Fumaroli, Marc, 45

Gabin, Jean, 78, 271
Gainsbourg, Charlotte, 230–31
Games of Love and Chance (L'Esquive) (Kechiche), 35, 39, 61–63, 69, 80, 86–87,

148; function of theatre in, 40–41, 44–45, 48, 50–56, 59, 279; nonprofessional actors in, 42, 58, 144–45, 204, 257; as political cinema, 42–43, 49–51, 54–56, 60, 70, 85; significance of language in, 33, 40–42, 50–51, 56–59
Garbarz, Franck, 249
Garcia, Nicole, 282
Gaumont, 98, 113–14
Gavras, Alexandre, 175
Gavras, Romain, 175–76, 278
gender, 24, 55, 88n3, 212–13, 215, 223, 230, 234; in *All That Glitters* (Nakache and Mimram), 260–61, 274n3; and anxieties about motherhood, 167, 190–93; critique of hypermasculine genres, 11, 35, 130–31, 154–56, 162–64; in *Girlhood* (Sciamma), 241–42, 246–47, 253, 256–57, 266–67; in horror genre, 169–70, 174, 178, 180, 182, 195–97, 199–203; and male privilege, 20, 23, 162, 243, 272–73; and masculinity, 79–82, 183, 226, 241, 244, 278; and stardom, 208, 239n2; and women's authorship, 243–45, 248, 251, 259
General Agreement on Tariffs and Trades (GATT) treaty, 96
genre memory, 129, 133, 142–44, 147, 164
Gens, Xavier, 2; *Frontier(s) (Frontière(s))*, 35, 166–68, 177, 180–87, 195, 201–2
ghettoization, 24, 228, 276
ghettos, 10, 22–24, 30, 105, 212, 217
Gimello-Mesplomb, Frédéric, 166
Girlhood (Bande de filles) (Sciamma), 87, 248, 251; and art cinema conventions, 37, 241–47, 256, 258, 267–73; Cannes Film Festival premiere, 250, 252; critics' framing of, 249–50, 253, 257, 272; music in, 259–62, 265–69; nonprofessional actors in, 42, 145, 204, 253–55
Gleich, Joshua, 93
Glissant, Edouard, 54
Godard, Jean-Luc, 42, 48, 71; *Alphaville*, 4; *Breathless (A Bout de souffle)*, 4, 34, 65, 81, 105, 126, 270
Goldman, Jean-Jacques, 239n1
Grant, Barry Keith, 81
Green, Amy, 196

INDEX

Grossberg, Lawrence, 73–74
Grossman, Walter, 112–13
Guerrero, Ed, 212, 228
Guerrin, Michel, 119
Guiraud, Edmond: *Moïse*, 234–35

habitation à loyer modéré (HLM), 8, 47, 63, 182, 188–89, 217
Hacker, Violaine, 118
Haggins, Bambi, 212
La Haine (Kassovitz), 1, 35, 87n1, 124n6, 230, 285; and abstraction, 61–65, 69, 74, 82, 84; and average shot length (ASL), 66–67; at Cannes Film Festival, 40, 85; at Césars, 40; and cultural politics, 33, 48–49, 60, 245, 273, 279; and Hollywood intertextuality, 39, 41, 65, 68, 71, 80–84, 107, 124n9, 126; influence on other films, 89, 99, 103, 174–76, 178, 181, 278; and realism, 33, 40–44, 61, 70–74, 77–79, 88n2, 109, 144; use of music, 48, 65, 75–78, 263; violence in, 62, 69, 80–86, 99, 112, 126–28, 181, 260
Hallyday, Johnny, 78
Handel, George Frideric, 161
Hargreaves, Alec, 214
harkis, 132, 137
Harrod, Mary, 259–60, 274n3
Hart, Kevin, 211, 237
Hate. See *La Haine* (Kassovitz)
Hawks, Howard: *Scarface*, 83–84
Hayward, Susan, 93, 115
Hazanavicius, Michel: *The Artist*, 210
Heinich, Nathalie, 114
Hesme, Clotilde, 282
Hexagon, 10, 22, 28, 188, 190, 235, 273
Higbee, Will, 12, 95–96, 99–101, 263
Higson, Andrew, 100–101
Hill, Constance, 221
Hill, John, 100
Hills, Matt, 169
hip hop, 6, 11, 15, 38n9, 46, 59, 112, 120, 176, 263–64; dance, 261, 283; and *La Haine* (Kassovitz), 33, 39, 41, 48, 61, 65, 74–76, 78–79, 81. See also rap
Hitchcock, Alfred, 4; *Vertigo*, 40
Hjort, Mette, 95–96

Holden, Stephen, 211
Hold-up Films, 250
home-invasion subgenre, 190–93
hooks, bell, 277
Hooper, Tobe: *The Texas Chainsaw Massacre*, 174, 180, 182–83, 185
Hugo, Victor: *Les Misérables*, 56, 176, 278–79
Hulu, 280
Hunt, Leon, 103
hybridity, 10, 14–15, 20, 65, 70, 76, 98, 100, 102; and creolization, 26, 119, 187
Hyper Cacher, 120

immigration, 8, 14, 25–26, 28, 210, 232; and assimilationism, 168, 183, 223, 226; and documentation, 230–31, 264; global migratory flows, 2–3, 14, 18–19, 29, 64, 186, 188–89; *issus de l'immigration* (from an immigrant background), 19, 191; policy of immigration (*politique du peuplement*), 276; and politics, 208, 218; and social relations, 9–10, 23, 34, 51, 99, 130–31, 142–43, 215, 229, 282
Les Indigènes de la République (The Republic's Indigenous Peoples), 24
Intouchables (Tolédano and Nakache), 162, 205–6, 213–22, 223–29, 264–65; and Black stardom, 207–8, 211, 239n1, 240n11; financial success of, 36, 124n6, 204, 209–10, 216, 240n6, 248–49; Omar Sy's career after, 230–32, 236, 238, 282; remake of, 237

Jackson, Michael: "Thriller," 187
James, Kery: *Street Flow (Banlieusards)*, 283
Jaurès, Jean, 222
Jeamart, Audrey, 193–94
Jein, Gillian, 116
Johnson, Stephen, 217, 219, 222
Jones, Felicity, 237
Juppé, Alain, 61

Kacem, Mehdi Belhaj, 156, 187
Kaganski, Serge, 53
Kassovitz, Mathieu, 1, 50, 61, 70, 72, 86, 87n1, 174, 245; *Assassin(s)*, 86; *Babylon A.D.*, 43, 86; and *The Bureau (Le Bureau des légendes)*, 89, 118; Cannes Film Festival

Kassovitz, Mathieu (Cont.)
  Best Director Prize, 40; *Crimson Rivers (Les Rivières pourpres)*, 43, 86; economic background of, 48–49, 74, 175–76; and film violence, 62, 69, 81–85, 181; *Gothika*, 43, 86; and hip-hop aesthetics, 65, 75–78, 263; and image composition, 63–68, 71, 144, 181; influence on other filmmakers, 99, 103; and production strategy, 40, 89–90, 278, 285; *Rebellion (L'ordre et la morale)*, 43, 86; significance of Hollywood films to, 33, 39, 41–44, 58, 79–80, 85, 124n9, 126, 273. See also *La Haine* (Kassovitz)
Kassovitz, Peter, 175
Kealhofer-Kemp, Leslie, 209
Kechiche, Abdellatif, 33, 39–40, 44, 57–58, 61, 69–70, 144; background of, 47, 131; *Black Venus (Vénus noire)*, 55; *Blue Is the Warmest Color (La vie d'Adèle)*, 50, 55–58; Cannes Film Festival Palme d'Or, 56; casting nonprofessional actors, 42, 53, 58, 145, 148, 204, 257; cultural mediation in films of, 41, 45, 48–55, 279; and importance of minority representation, 59–60; as industry outsider, 58, 85, 87, 89; *Poetical Refugee (La Faute à Voltaire)*, 40; *The Secret Life of Grain (La Graine et le mulet)*, 55. See also *Games of Love and Chance (L'Esquive)* (Kechiche)
Kerner, Michael, 196, 197–8
King, Gemma, 164n3
Kirzbaum, Thomas, 17
Knapp, Jonathan, 196, 197–8
Köksal, Özlem, 151, 165n4
Konstanarakos, Myrto, 80–81
Kool and the Gang, 224
Kourtrajmé collective, 2, 174–77, 278
Kristeva, Julia, 196
KRS-One: "Sound of Da Police," 76
Kurosawa, Akira: *Seven Samurai*, 98

Lagesse, Eric, 250–51
Lagrange, Hughes, 20
laïcité (secularism), 17, 276
Lalevée, Fabrice, 114
Lang, Jack, 6–7, 46, 96
Lapeyronnie, Didier, 24, 30, 80

Laugier, Pascal: *Martyrs*, 35, 166, 195–203
Lauro, Sarah, 187
Leblanc, Maurice, 282
Lee, Spike, 33, 39, 101, 279; *Bamboozled*, 209, 212, 232; *Do the Right Thing*, 65, 78
Lefcourt, Jenny, 82–83
Le Guilcher, Geoffrey, 114
Lentin, Alana, 19, 37n1
Leone, Sergio, 126, 133–34, 137; *Once upon a Time in America*, 132, 135–36
Le Pen, Jean-Marie, 181
Le Pen, Marine, 181
Lethal Weapon films, 131, 210, 231
Lévy-Hartmann, Florence, 114
Lhamon, W. T., Jr., 217–18, 229
Light Asylum: "Dark Allies," 241
Lilies Films, 250
Lim, Song Hwee, 95–96, 100–101
Loach, Ken, 86
Lobato, Ramon, 281
localization, 37, 74, 84, 169, 189–190, 202–3, 280
Loichot, Valérie, 223
Loison, Guillaume, 211
Londez, Vincent, 282
Looseley, David, 78
Lott, Eric, 213, 222, 229
Louis the XIV, King, 17
Lowenstein, Adam, 191
Luca, Lionnel, 132
Lucas, George, 86; *Star Wars*, 5, 97, 135
Luegenbiehl, Kelly, 280
Lumet, Sidney: *Serpico*, 209
Lvovsky, Noémie: *Forget Me (Oublie-moi)*, 248
Ly, Ladj, 174–75, 178, 180; *Les Misérables*, 37, 176, 278–80, 282, 284–85

Mack, Mehammed, 163
Macron, Emmanuel, 275–76
Magnolia Pictures, 109, 111
Maïwenn: *Polisse*, 248
Malraux, André, 96
Marchais, Georges, 222
Marivaux, Pierre: *The Game of Love and Chance*, 40–41, 44–45, 48, 50–56, 59
Marker, Chris, 175

Marley, Bob: "Burnin' and Lootin'," 64
"La Marseillaise," 76, 278
Marshall, Bill, 108, 123n2, 244
Marshall, Tonie, 244
martial arts genre, 69, 98, 102–3, 127
Martin, Angela, 243–45
Martinez, Dominique, 249
Mauger, Gérard, 24
Maule, Rosanna, 102, 118
Maurus, Véronique, 223
Maury, Julien: *Inside (A l'intérieur)*, 35, 167–68, 177, 190–95, 201–2
Mbembe, Achille, 18, 28
McAuley, James, 276
McCarren, Felicia, 38n9, 263
MC Jean Gab'1, 108
McNeill, Isabelle, 241, 266–69, 274n5
McPhee, Ruth, 196
Meeuf, Russell, 208
Mellier, Denis, 168
melodrama, 78–79, 81, 83, 85–87, 134, 230–31, 236, 255
Melville, Jean-Pierre: *Army of Shadows (L'Armée des ombres)*, 132, 137
Memmi, Albert, 30
Messier, Jean-Marie, 97
métissé (mixed form of cinema), 11–12
#MeToo, 91
Met, Philippe, 168, 185, 189
Michael, Charlie, 5–7, 110, 118, 205, 214–15, 240n8
Milleliri, Carole, 11–12
Miller, Toby, 216
Mimram, Hervé: *All that Glitters (Tout ce qui brille)*, 37, 177, 259–63, 273
Mingant, Nolwenn, 119
mise en abyme, 30
mission civilisatrice, 106–7
Missonnie, Marc, 264
Mittell, Jason, 14–15
Mitterrand, François, 113
Moine, Raphaëlle, 4, 215
Morales, Ed, 25–26
Moreland, Mantan, 210
Morel, Pierre: *District B13 (Banlieue 13)*, 33, 91, 93, 101–13, 120, 122–23; *From Paris with Love*, 120

Morgan, Daniel, 158–59
Morson, Gary Saul, 129
Motion Picture Association of America Production Code, 127
Moussa, Nedjib Sidi, 132–33
Mrabet, Emna, 54, 56–57, 59
multiculturalism, 17, 142, 147, 175–76, 182, 184, 195, 239; banlieues as symbols of, 1, 10, 70, 76, 85, 87, 122, 171; and function of Hollywood genres, 2–3, 31, 34, 85, 100–101, 135, 155, 202, 215, 229; and international audiences, 186, 215, 223, 229, 273–75, 282–84; intersecting with class, 214, 277–80; as linguistic void, 20; lived multiculture, 19, 37n1; marked by music, 263; and the United States, 22, 25–26
Murphy, David, 25
Murphy, Eddie, 211–12, 223, 227, 232, 237; and *48 Hrs.*, 36, 210, 224–25, 231; and *Beverly Hills Cop*, 36, 131, 210, 224–26, 228, 231; and *Trading Places*, 210, 224–25
musicals, 79, 259, 263–66
music videos, 37, 59, 65, 175–77, 217, 267–69
Muslim identity, French, 174, 183, 200–1, 215, 276–77, 283

Naceri, Bibi, 101, 106–8, 111, 222
Nakache, Géraldine: *All that Glitters (Tout ce qui brille)*, 37, 177, 259–63, 273
Nakache, Olivier, 204, 223–26, 228, 260; casting Omar Sy, 207, 211, 215; and minstrelsy tropes, 36, 209–10, 214, 216–19, 221–22; *So Close (Tellement proches)*, 217. *See also Intouchables* (Tolédano and Nakache)
Nanterre, 130–31, 139, 142–43, 154
National Assembly (2013), 19
National Center for Cinema and the Moving Image (CNC), 38n3, 114, 116, 169, 176; juried selective aid, 110, 155, 242, 244, 250
National Liberation Front, 34, 131, 181
Nazism, 62, 105, 167, 180–84
Ndiaye, Pap, 28, 229
neo-colonialism, 13, 21, 34, 101, 107, 189–90, 210, 229
neoliberal capitalism, 13, 116, 156–57, 266, 284

neo-minstrelsy, 36, 209, 212, 214, 216, 222, 229, 239n3. *See also* blackface minstrelsy
neorealism, 33, 37, 42–43, 109, 145, 147, 212, 254–58, 267, 269
Netflix, 37, 122, 238, 280–84
Nettelbeck, Colin, 54
Neuhoff, Eric, 211
Neuilly Yo Mama! (Neuilly sa mère!), 263–64
Nevé, Éric, 174
New French Extremity (NFE), 35, 167–68, 171–74
New Hollywood period, 34, 39, 127, 130, 133, 135, 194; films of, 61, 65, 71–72, 79, 126, 137
Newman, Kathleen, 92
news footage, 10–11, 39–40, 62–66, 128, 159, 177, 181–82, 187, 191–95
Niang, Mame-Fatou, 20, 38n10, 155, 245–47, 257, 272, 277, 279
Nice Conservatory, 47
Nicolas, Marc, 250
Noah, Trevor, 15–16
Noah, Yannick, 239n1
Noé, Gaspard: *Irreversible*, 35, 167, 172–73
Noiriel, Gérard, 232, 235
Nordic Film initiatives, 95
Nouvel, Jean, 113
NWA: "Fuck tha Police," 76

Obama, Barack, 208–9, 222–23, 229, 272–73, 275
Oliete-Aldea, Elena, 91
Olney, Ian, 167–68
Organisation de l'armée secrète (Organization of the Secret Army [OAS]), 76
Oria, Beatriz, 91
Oscherwitz, Dayna, 45, 72, 164n3, 171
O'Shaugnessey, Martin, 42, 70
Outside the Law (Hors la loi) (Bouchareb), 34, 154–55, 163; controversy about, 130–33; and epic mode, 134–135; and gangster genre, 139–43; and restrained violence, 127, 136–38, 144, 149
Ozon, François: *Eight Women (8 Femmes)*, 248

Pacino, Al, 106, 140, 222
Padilla, Rafael, 231–35
Pagnol, Marcel, 42, 56–57
Palmer, Tim, 173, 242, 247–48
Pao, Angela, 254
Paquot, Thierry, 10
Paradis, Allyson, 194
Para One, 250, 253
parité law (2000), 23–24
parkour, 92–94, 123; films about, 33, 95, 98–99, 101–3, 110–13, 121–22
le partage du sensible (the distribution of the sensible), 27
particularism, 17, 21–24, 215
Pasquier, Dominique, 49
pastiche, 4, 72, 269–71
Pathé, 114
Paty, Samuel, 275
Peckinpah, Samuel, 127, 137, 151–53, 194; *Straw Dogs*, 130, 144, 150, 190; *The Wild Bunch*, 136
Peirce, Charles Sanders, 73
Pember, Alice, 241
Péron, Didier, 99
Piaf, Édith, 88n3; "Non, je ne regrette rien," 76–78
Pialat, Maurice, 42, 56; *Graduate First (Passe ton bac d'abord)*, 57
Picasso, Kiki (Christian Chapiron), 175
pieds noirs (French settlers in Algeria), 9, 132, 142
Pignon, Yves, 188
Pinewood Studios, 90
poetic realism, 61, 72–74, 76–77, 79, 83, 126, 143–44, 271
Pogam, Pierre-Ange Le, 98, 101
Polanski, Roman, 168
police violence, 11, 141, 164, 202, 275, 278; and *Frontier(s)* (Gens), 181, 183; and *La Haine* (Kassovitz), 39, 61–64, 68–71, 78, 82–84, 86; as metaphor, 3, 27; and *Outside the Law* (Bouchareb), 136–38. *See also* ultraviolence; violence
Popular Front, 72, 77, 83
Porter, Edwin S., 213
Porton, Richard, 41
postcolonial studies, 24–26, 100

Powrie, Phil, 61, 77, 93, 262, 264
Prédal, René, 61
Prévert, Jacques, 144
Primrose, George Delaney, 221
Prince, Stephen, 127, 136, 149, 152–53, 164, 194–95, 201
production scale, 6–8, 33, 116, 134–35, 238, 242, 251, 285
protests, 11, 64, 128, 202, 239; of 2005, 24, 35, 90, 105, 120, 143, 167, 176, 178, 187–89, 191–94, 208; Black Lives Matter, 275; in *Divines* (Benyamina), 155–56, 159–61; in *Frontier(s)* (Gens), 181–82; in *La Haine* (Kassovitz), 61, 63, 67–68, 74, 77, 82; in *Les Misérables* (Ly), 278–79; Sétif, 136, 138, 141
Proust, Marcel, 249
Pryor, Richard, 210–11, 226
Pyramide Films, 250, 252–53

Quandt, James, 35, 168, 172
queerness, 163, 241–42, 248, 266, 272

racism, 25, 69, 81, 189, 225, 238; accusations against *Intouchables* (Tolédano and Nakache), 36, 213–215, 228; antisemitism, 17–18, 21, 62, 105, 183–84; and blackface, 36, 211–15, 223, 229; and Black Lives Matter protests, 275; cultural, 19–20; Islamophobia, 215, 277. See also blackface minstrelsy
Raffaelli, Cyril, 102–3
Raffarain, Jean-Pierre, 222
Rancière, Jacques, 3, 21, 27–28
rap, 6, 15, 46, 59, 108, 121, 217, 263–64; in *Frontier(s)* (Gens), 182; in *La Haine* (Kassovitz), 33, 39, 65, 74–78, 81; videos in *Sheitan* (Chapiron), 175, 177–78, 180. See also hip hop
rape-revenge genre, 35, 169–73, 186, 190
Raphael, Raphael, 208
Rappas, Ipak, 151, 165n4
Rassial, Jena-Jacques, 171
Rauger, Jean-François, 197
Ray, Robert, 71
Reader, Keith, 77

realism, 2, 12–13, 40–41, 44, 135, 246, 263, 273; aestheticized, 70–71, 85; Audiard's use of, 144–47, 152–53; and Black performers, 235–36; displaced by abstraction, 62–64, 69, 78, 84; in horror genre, 168–69, 182–83, 193–94, 201; Kechiche's use of, 56–58; neorealist genre, 33, 37, 42–43, 109, 145, 147, 212, 254–58, 267, 269; and parkour films, 92, 101–2, 108–9; poetic, 61, 72–74, 76–77, 79, 83, 126, 143–44, 271; and popular taste, 48–49
reception studies, 29, 254
Reeser, Todd, 80
Renan, Ernest, 46
Renoir, Jean, 42, 56, 66; *La vie est à nous (The World is Ours)*, 83
RER (Réseau express regional), 217, 260
resentment, economic, 170–71, 179–80, 186, 190, 193
Resnais, Alain: *Night and Fog (Nuit et brouillard)*, 184
Returned, The (Les Revenants), 170
Reyes, Xavier Aldana, 196
Richet, Jean-François: *The Emperor of Paris (L'Empereur de Paris)*, 41; *Mesrine*, 41; *My City's Gonna Crack (Ma 6-T va craquer)*, 41
Ricœur, Paul, 29–30
Rihanna: "Diamonds," 253, 259, 261–62, 265–70, 274n5
Rivette, Jacques, 48
Robeson, Paul, 233–35
Rochant, Eric, 118
Rocher, Benjamin: *The Horde (La Horde)*, 35, 167–68, 186–90, 195, 202
Rock, Chris, 211, 237
Rohmer, Éric, 48
Rollet, Brigitte, 244
Rollin, Jean, 35, 166
romanesque mode, 133–34
romantic comedy genre, 1, 129–30, 146–47, 152, 154, 247, 259
Romero, George, 189
Romney, Jonathan, 69
Rosello, Mireille, 2, 239n4
Rose, Steve, 155
Rose, Sven-Erik, 70
Roth, Eli: *Hostel*, 173, 182, 185, 194

Rouch, Jean, 42, 58
Rowden, Terry, 95–96

Sachs, Leon, 52–55
Samuels, Maurice, 17, 21, 32
Sarandos, Ted, 280–81
Sarkozy, Nicolas, 35, 105, 113, 116, 132, 156, 178, 181, 191, 208, 218
Saturday Night Live, 212, 225
Saw films, 173, 185
Scarlata, Alexa, 281
school system, French, 51, 59, 123, 147, 155. *See also* film schools
Schoonover, Karl, 255–56
Schur, Richard, 15, 75
Schwarzenegger, Arnold, 80–81
Sciamma, Céline, 87, 243, 252, 259–61, 271–73; casting nonprofessional actors, 37, 42, 145–46, 204, 253–58; and exoticization of Blackness, 245–46; and La Fémis, 242, 247–51; *Portrait of a Lady on Fire (Portrait de la jeune fille en feu)*, 242, 249–50; *Tomboy*, 242, 251; use of music, 241, 265–69; *Water Lilies (Naissance des pievures)*, 242. *See also Girlhood (Bande de filles)* (Sciamma)
science fiction, 4, 13, 41, 47, 79, 86, 103
Scorsese, Martin, 33, 39, 126, 155, 279; *Mean Streets*, 67; *Raging Bull*, 132; *Taxi Driver*, 65, 71, 74, 148, 151–53
Scott, A. O., 211
Scott, Joan W., 21
screenwriting, 47, 56, 93, 144, 209, 249, 264; at Cité du cinéma, 116, 118; and *District B13* (Morel), 101, 106–7, 111; at La Fémis, 250; and *Games of Love and Chance* (Kechiche), 40, 58; and *Girlhood* (Sciamma), 253, 257–58; and *La Haine* (Kassovitz), 62, 80–81, 83, 107; and *Intouchables* (Tolédano and Nakache), 231–32; and *Outside the Law* (Bouchareb), 132; role in auteurism, 7, 60; and *Tomboy* (Sciamma), 251
segregation, 9, 22–24, 112, 229
Seine-Saint-Denis, 90, 113, 121; Saint-Denis, 94, 108, 117, 119–20, 175–76, 178, 278. *See also* protests: of 2005

self-reflexivity, 4, 36, 60, 78, 127, 146, 159, 209
Serero, Lisa, 239n3
Serreau, Coline, 244
sexual violence, 91, 150, 161, 163, 170, 173, 182. *See also* ultraviolence; rape-revenge film; violence
Seydoux, Léa, 58
Shakespeare, William: *Othello*, 233–36
Sharma, Ashwani, 64–65, 70, 78
Sharma, Sanjay, 64–65, 70, 78
Silverstein, Paul, 9, 142
Singleton, John, 33, 39; *Boyz 'n the Hood*, 65
slasher genre, 35, 127, 166, 177, 185–86, 194
slavery, 23–26, 28, 187, 213, 229, 231; abolition of, 239
Smith, Ben, 276, 285n1
Smith, Frances, 241, 259, 266, 269, 272
Sobchack, Vivian, 134–35
SOFICA *(société pour le financement de l'industrie cinématographique et audiovisuelle)*, 251
Sojcher, Frédéric, 90
Soviet montage, 255
Spielberg, Steven, 86; *Jaws*, 5; *Raiders of the Lost Ark*, 135
squibs, 126–27, 136–38, 149, 151
Stallone, Sylvester, 80–81
Steadicam, 63, 67–68, 136, 146, 258, 267
Sting: "Roxanne," 224
Stora, Benjamin, 142
Stowe, Harriet Beecher, 213
subscription-based video-on-demand (SVoD), 280–85
suburbanoia genre, 172, 179–80, 186, 192, 201–2
Suprême NTM: "Nique la police," 76
Swamy, Vinay, 50–51
Sy, Leïla: *Street Flow (Banlieusards)*, 283
Sylla, Ahmed: *The Climb (L'Ascension)*, 208, 240n5
Sylla, Assa, 257–58
Sy, Omar, 203, 215–17, 219–23, 229; and *After Sales Service (Service après vente)*, 212–13, 218, 225–26; compared to Eddie Murphy, 211–12, 224–28, 231, 237; and *Knock*, 231, 236, 238; and *Lupin*, 37, 238, 282–83; and *On the Other Side of the Tracks (De l'autre*

côté du périph), 230, 236; and *Samba*, 230–31, 236; and stardom, 36, 204–12, 230–39, 240n11, 259; and *Two Is a Family* (Demain tout commence), 231, 236; and *X-Men: Days of Future Past*, 237–38

Tamil Tigers, 1, 145, 152
Tarancón, Juan, 91
Tarantino, Quentin, 4–5, 39, 72
Tarr, Carrie, 12, 50, 70, 243–44
teen movie genre, 37, 155, 162, 242, 247, 259, 270
Téléphone: "Un autre monde," 265
television, 74, 79, 81, 170, 201, 217, 222, 255, 274, 281; Canal+ series, 89, 118, 212; and deregulation, 7; and distribution rights, 115, 251; and genre mixing, 14–15, 29, 230, 282; and globalization, 41; and intertextual references, 209, 219, 242, 244, 265, 267, 277; and news coverage, 10–11, 39–40, 62–66, 128, 159, 177, 181–82, 187, 191–95; sketch comedy, 212–13, 240n10
Tessaud, Pascal: *Brooklyn*, 263–64, 266
Tessé, Jean-Philippe, 57, 146
Testot, Fred, 212–13
Tetreault, Chantal, 30
Théâtre Antoine, 233–35
Thierrée, James, 233
Thomas, Dominic, 19
Titley, Gavan, 19, 37n1
Todd, Emmanuel, 38n7
Tolédano, Éric, 204, 223–26, 228; casting Omar Sy, 207, 211, 215; and minstrelsy tropes, 36, 209–10, 214, 216–19, 221–22; *So Close (Tellement proches)*, 217. *See also* *Intouchables* (Tolédano and Nakache)
Touré, Karidja, 257, 259
Touré, Mariétou, 259
traceurs, 92, 94–95, 98–99, 111–12, 122–23. *See also* parkour
Trevorrow, Colin: *Jurassic World*, 36, 225, 237
Trinh Thi, Coralie: *Baise-moi*, 35, 167, 172–73
Truffaut, François, 7–8, 48, 71; *400 Blows (Les Quatre cents coups)*, 270; *Shoot the Piano Player (Tirez sur le pianiste)*, 4, 271
Trump, Donald, 37, 275
Tucker, Chris, 211, 237

ultraviolence, 34, 130, 164, 181, 201, 203; conceptualization of, 127, 194–95; and *Dheepan* (Audiard), 144, 149–54; and *Outside the Law* (Bouchareb), 133, 135–38. *See also* police violence; sexual violence; violence
urbanoia genre, 169–71, 179–80, 190, 193, 201–2

Vanderschelden, Isabelle, 93, 102, 114, 216
Verissimo, Dany, 103
vertical integration, 7, 90, 97, 115, 117, 122
Vichy Government, 18, 184
Vieillard-Baron, Hervé, 9–11, 20
Vietnam War, 127, 194, 224
vigilante genre, 1, 130, 144, 146–47, 149, 152, 190
Vincendeau, Ginette, 42, 64, 128, 205–6, 236–37, 239nn3–4; on *La Haine* (Kassovitz), 66, 70, 72, 75–76, 82, 124n9
Vine Alternative Investments, 115
violence, 1–2, 11–12, 21, 36, 121, 129–30, 166–68, 174; and *Chocolat* (Zem), 234–35; and *Dheepan* (Audiard), 144–46, 148–53, 165n4; and *District B13* (Morel), 105–7; and *Divines* (Benyamina), 35, 131, 154–56, 159–64; and *Frontier(s)* (Gens), 180–81, 184–86; in *Games of Love and Chance* (Kechiche), 44, 53, 57; and *Girlhood* (Sciamma), 241, 243, 246, 260, 272; in *La Haine* (Kassovitz), 39, 61–62, 64, 69–70, 77–84, 86, 126, 128; and *The Horde* (Dahan and Rocher), 187, 189; and *Inside* (Bustillo and Maury), 191–93; and *Intouchables* (Tolédano and Nakache), 221; and *Martyrs* (Laugier), 195–203; in *Outside the Law* (Bouchareb), 132–43; and rape-revenge genre, 170, 172–73, 186, 190; and rap lyrics, 75, 177–78, 180; in *Yamakasi*, 98–99. *See also* police violence; sexual violence; ultraviolence
Vitali, Valentina, 91
Vivendi-Universal, 97
von Weber, Carl Maria: *The Freeshooter (Der Freischütz)*, 219

Wacquant, Loïc, 23
Warner Brothers, 68, 93

Weinstein Company, 209, 211
Weinstein, Harvey, 209
Weissberg, Jay, 213, 228
Western genre, 1, 11, 34, 127, 130, 132, 134, 147, 170, 198, 240n11
White, Maurice, 220
whiteness, 2, 9, 16, 19–20, 142–43, 167, 243; and blackface minstrelsy, 212–13, 217; and casting practices, 281; and *Chocolat* (Zem), 232–34; in *Dheepan* (Audiard), 147; and *Frontier(s)* (Gens), 185; in *The Horde* (Dahan and Rocher), 188; and interracial buddy comedy genre, 210–11, 226–28, 240n6; and *Intouchables* (Tolédano and Nakache), 206–8, 214, 220–24, 229–30; in Kassovitz's films, 61–62, 71; in Kechiche's films, 41, 44, 53, 55–56, 59–60; in *Neuilly Yo Mama!*, 263; and racial binary, 22, 25–26, 36, 215–16, 230; in rape-revenge horror, 170; and Sciamma, 253, 256, 260, 272–73; in *Sheitan* (Chapiron), 174, 180

Willemen, Paul, 91, 100
Williams, James, 50–51, 54–55, 59–60
Williams, Linda, 78–79, 83, 86–87, 230
Williams, Raymond, 73
Wilson, Emma, 268
Wollheim, Richard, 158
World War II, 6, 38n8, 96, 199; Jewish deportation during, 18, 62, 183–84

Yee, Jennifer, 15
YouTube, 92, 176, 201

Zadi, Jean-Pascal, 112; *Simply Black (Tout simplement noir)*, 239
Zanuck, Darryl, 93
Zeitoun, Laurent, 249
Zem, Roschdy, 131; *Chocolat*, 36, 230–36
Zlotowski, Rebecca, 249
zombie genre, 35, 173, 187–89

DAVID PETTERSEN is Director of the Film and Media Studies Program and Associate Professor of French and Film and Media Studies at the University of Pittsburgh. He is author of *Americanism, Media and the Politics of Culture in 1930s France*.

www.ingramcontent.com/pod-product-compliance
Lightning Source LLC
Chambersburg PA
CBHW021342300426
44114CB00012B/1043